CAMBRIDGE TEXTS IN THE
HISTORY OF POLITICAL THOUGHT

—

NICHOLAS OF CUSA
The Catholic Concordance

CAMBRIDGE TEXTS IN THE HISTORY OF POLITICAL THOUGHT

Series editors
RAYMOND GUESS *Columbia University*
QUENTIN SKINNER *Christ's College, Cambridge*

The series is intended to make available for students the most important texts required for an understanding of the history of political thought. The scholarship of the present generation has greatly expanded our sense of the range of authors indispensable for such an understanding, and the series will reflect those developments. It will also include a number of less well-known works, in particular those needed to establish the intellectual contexts that in turn help to make sense of the major texts. The principal aim, however, will be to produce new versions of the major texts themselves, based on the most up-to-date scholarship. The preference will always be for complete texts, and a special feature of the series will be to complement individual texts, within the compass of a single volume, with subsidiary contextual material. Each volume will contain an introduction on the historical identity and contemporary significance of the work or works concerned, as well as a chronology, notes on further reading and (where appropriate) brief biographical sketches of significant individuals mentioned in each text.

For a list of titles published in the series, please see end of book.

NICHOLAS OF CUSA

The
Catholic Concordance

EDITED AND TRANSLATED BY

PAUL E. SIGMUND
Department of Politics, Princeton University

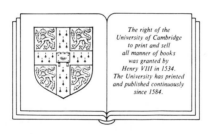

The right of the
University of Cambridge
to print and sell
all manner of books
was granted by
Henry VIII in 1534.
The University has printed
and published continuously
since 1584.

CAMBRIDGE UNIVERSITY PRESS
CAMBRIDGE
NEW YORK   PORT CHESTER
MELBOURNE   SYDNEY

Published by the Press Syndicate of the University of Cambridge
The Pitt Building, Trumpington Street, Cambridge CB2 1RP
40 West 20th Street, New York, NY 10011-4211, USA
10 Stamford Road, Oakleigh, Melbourne 3166, Australia

© Cambridge University Press 1991

First published 1991

Printed in Great Britain by The Bath Press, Avon

British Library cataloguing in publication data
Nicholas, Cardinal 1401–1464
The Catholic concordance. – (Cambridge texts in the
history of political thought).
1. Politics – Christian viewpoints
I. Title   II. Sigmund, Paul E. (Paul Eugene)
261.7

Library of Congress cataloguing in publication data
Nicholas, of Cusa, Cardinal, 1401–1464.
[De concordantia Catholica. English]
The Catholic concordance / Nicholas of Cusa: edited and
translated by Paul E. Sigmund.
p.   cm. – (Cambridge texts in the history of political
thought)
Translation of: De concordantia Catholica.
Includes bibliographical references (p.   ) and index.
ISBN 0–521–40207–7
1. Church and state – Catholic Church – Early works to 1800.
2. Conciliar theory – Early works to 1800.   3. Catholic Church –
Government – Early works to 1800.   I. Sigmund, Paul E.   II. Title.
III. Series.
BX1790.N5C613   1991
262'.02–dc20   90–22085   CIP

ISBN 0521 40207 7 hardback

Contents

Translator's preface

Some years ago, the late Ewart Lewis observed that it was likely to be a long time before the "average professor of political theory will turn to his well-underlined copy of Nicholas of Cusa's *De concordantia catholica* with the same facility with which he turned to Aristotle's *Politics*."[1] This first complete translation of the *Concordantia* into English is an effort to make this major work of political and eccelesiological theory available to contemporary scholars. Before its publication the only English translation was a sometimes inaccurate excerpt containing the sections dealing with the theory of consent and Nicholas' proposals for a system of representative councils in the medieval empire.[2] The lack of a definitive Latin text, the length of the work, and the considerable linguistic problems arising from Cusanus' awkward style and defective knowledge of Latin[3] have long deterred scholars from undertaking the formidable task of translation.

The problem of establishing the Latin text has been resolved, thanks to the work of dedicated German scholars. In 1928, Professor Gerhard Kallen agreed to prepare a critical Latin edition under the auspices of the Heidelberg Academy of Sciences. Books I and II were published in 1939 but the publication of Book III was delayed by

[1] Ewart Lewis, *Medieval Political Ideas*, vol. I, New York, 1954, p. vii.
[2] Francis W. Coker, *Readings in Political Philosophy*, 2nd edn, New York, 1938, pp. 257–76. An Italian translation has been published by Pio Gaia in Nicolo Cusano, *Opere religiose*, Turin, 1971, pp. 115–546, and a French translation by Roland Galibois, Nicolas de Cues, *Concordance catholique*, Sherbrooke, Canada, 1977. A German version is being prepared by Hans Gerhard Senger of the University of Cologne.
[3] Nicholas himself refers to his "uncultivated style" in the Preface to the *Concordantia* (no. 2).

vii

World War II and it only appeared in 1959. In 1964 and 1965 Books I and II were reissued with a critical apparatus that incorporated more recent scholarship, and in 1968, on Gerhard Kallen's eighty-fourth birthday, a complete set of indices to the entire work was published.

In my translation I have occasionally (only rarely) departed from Kallen's interpretation, and corrected the very few mistakes that appeared in his text and footnotes. The references to Latin printed sources in the footnotes are taken from the Heidelberg edition, but I have added references to English translations where appropriate and noted the more important recent scholarly works that may help in understanding the text. In the interest of space I have included only those references that are directly relevant, and I have retained Nicholas' form of citing the canon and Roman law and added the modern equivalents in parentheses in the text itself. Migne's *Patrologia* has been used as the principal reference for the early Latin and Greek texts and Mansi's *Sacrorum conciliorum ... collectio* is referred to when the church councils are quoted, because they are the most generally available source collections. My translations of biblical quotations are influenced by both the Douai and King James versions in English but mainly by the Latin (Vulgate) text.

Both the introduction and the footnotes indicate my indebtedness to the host of German scholars who have contributed to a veritable explosion of Cusanus scholarship during the last twenty-five years. In addition to my obvious dependence on Gerhard Kallen's erudition, I should mention the excellent work being done by Rudolf Haubst and those associated with the Institut für Cusanus-Forschung, formerly located at the Johannes-Gutenberg Universität in Mainz and since 1981 at the University of Trier. All students of Cusanus are grateful to Erich Meuthen of the University of Cologne for his continuing contributions to a fuller knowledge of Cusanus' life and writings. The preparation of the translations was substantially assisted by grants from the Princeton University Committee for Research in the Social Sciences and the Humanities, and by a Senior Fellowship from the National Endowment for the Humanities. The final version of the text was prepared at the Rockefeller Foundation's Bellagio Study Center.

The Introduction will refer to my earlier work on Cusanus, in particular to *Nicholas of Cusa and Medieval Political Thought* (Cambridge, Mass.: Harvard University Press, 1963). It will also reveal the striking relevance of Cusanus' thought to the currents that have shaken church and state during the twenty-five years in which this translation has been in preparation. A reading of the original text with its heavy burden of references to canon law and theology, and its considerable emphasis on tradition and authority, should correct the mistaken impression, fostered by modern commentators[4] that Nicholas of Cusa was a precursor of modern liberal democracy. It will also reveal, however, that the later movements for expanded political participation and restraint on the arbitrary exercise of power have very deep roots in Western history and religion.[5] The checkered history of subsequent efforts to "constitutionalize" church and state has demonstrated how difficult it is to reconcile authority and freedom in matters political or religious. The conciliar movement was one of the first efforts to come to terms with this problem, and Nicholas of Cusa was the conciliarist who perceived most clearly its broader theoretical implications for both politics and religion.

This book is dedicated to my three children, Paul, David, and Stephen, whose appearance and development during the years in which I worked on it provided a constant reminder that the faith of the celibate Nicholas of Cusa in an underlying order in the universe runs contrary to the experience of every parent.

[4] See John Neville Figgis, *From Gerson to Grotius*, London, 1916, p. 69; Otto von Gierke, *Political Theories of the Middle Age*, Cambridge, 1900, p. 56; Paolo Rotta, *Nicole Cusano*, Milan, 1942, p. 27; Andreas Posch, *Die Concordantia des Nikolaus von Cues*, Paderborn, 1930, p. 94.

[5] Among the studies in English that have emphasized the importance of the political thought associated with the medieval church for the development of Western constitutionalism are Karl Morrison, *Tradition and Authority in the Western Church, 300–1140*, Princeton, N.J., 1969; Antony Black, *Monarchy and Community: Political Ideas in the Later Conciliar Controversy, 1430–1450*, Cambridge, 1970, and *Council and Commune: The Conciliar Movement and the Fifteenth Century Heritage*, London, 1979; and Brian Tierney, *Religion, Law, and the Growth of Constitutional Thought, 1150–1650*, Cambridge, 1982.

Introduction

Nicholas of Cusa, in Latin Nicolaus Cusanus, was born in 1401 at
Kues on the banks of the Moselle river between Trier and Koblenz.
His father was a moderately well-to-do boatman and vineyard owner
who served on juries and lent money to the local nobility.[1] There is no
proof that Nicholas studied with the Brothers of the Common Life in
Deventer, Holland, as many of his earlier biographers assert,
although he was influenced by the *devotio moderna* that they represented, and a scholarship, the *Bursa Cusana*, named after him, was
established in the seventeenth century at Deventer. Following a year's
stay at the University of Heidelberg in 1416, he pursued higher
education in canon law at the University of Padua from 1417 until
1423. After receiving a doctorate in canon law (*doctor decretorum*) he
returned to Germany and enrolled at the University of Cologne in
early 1425. He seems to have studied philosophy and theology at
Cologne and he practiced and probably also taught canon law. (In
1428 he turned down an offer of a professorship in canon law at the
University of Louvain.) In 1427 and 1429–30, Cusanus travelled to
Rome as the secretary of the Archbishop of Trier and established
contacts with the Italian humanists who were interested in his reports

[1] Biographical details have been taken from Edmond Vansteenberghe, *Le Cardinal
Nicholas de Cues*, Paris, 1920; Erich Meuthen, *Nikolaus von Kues 1401–1464*, 6th edn,
Münster, 1982; and the collection of original sources on Cusanus' life, edited by Erich
Meuthen and Hermann Hallauer, *Acta Cusana*, vol. 1 (1401–1437), Hamburg, 1976. I
have also drawn on personal conversations with Professor Meuthen of the University of
Cologne and with present and former associates of the Cusanus Institut, now located in
Trier, especially Rudolf Haubst, and I have consulted Nicholas of Cusa's library in
Kues, one of the oldest private foundations in Europe (established by his will in 1464).

of having discovered lost classical manuscripts in German monastic and cathedral libraries. In December 1429, he brought to Rome an eleventh-century manuscript of the comedies of Plautus that is still preserved in the Vatican library.

In 1430, Ulrich von Manderscheid, a member of the local nobility in the Moselle valley, made Nicholas his chancellor. Ulrich had been dean of the cathedral chapter in Cologne, and after the death of the Archbishop of Trier in 1430, he attempted to secure election to that post. (In addition to his spiritual functions, the Archbishop of Trier exercised temporal power over considerable territory in the Rhine and Moselle valleys, and was one of the seven electors of the Holy Roman Empire.) The first vote of the cathedral chapter went to another candidate but after the dispute was appealed to Rome and the pope named another candidate, Ulrich succeeded in persuading the chapter to vote for him. The dispute was then appealed to the Council of Basel which had begun to meet in July 1431. In February 1432, Nicholas of Cusa was formally incorporated into the council as a member of the delegation representing the claim of Ulrich to the Trier archbishopric.

Since its opening, the council had been embroiled in disputes with the pope. The Council of Constance (1414–1418) had voted in its decree *Haec sancta* (April 6, 1415) that it held its power "directly from Christ [and] every man, whatever his estate or office, including the pope, is obliged to obey it in matters concerned with the faith, the extirpation of schism, and reform of the church in head and members . . ." It also stated that it could not be dissolved until the necessary reforms had been carried out. On October 9, 1417, the council had adopted the decree, *Frequens*, which called for a new council in five years, another seven years later, and councils every ten years thereafter. The council had met at Constance in order to end the schism created by the existence of three rival claimants to the papal throne. After persuading the Roman pope to resign and deposing the other two, it had elected a new pope who took the name of Martin V. Following his election, Martin swore to observe "whatever has been defined, concluded, and decreed in a conciliar fashion [*conciliariter*] in matters of faith by the present council." Whether that oath included the doctrine of conciliar supremacy contained in *Haec sancta* is a matter of dispute to this day (centering principally around the significance of the word *conciliariter* in relation to the assertion of conciliar supremacy)[2] but in observance of *Frequens* Pope Martin called a council which met at Pavia and Siena in 1423–24. After an inconclusive discussion of possible reform decrees the meager representation (two cardinals, twenty-five bishops) in attendance at Siena voted to hold another council at Basel in 1431.

The papal legates had acted as chairmen at the Council of Siena and the pope had given them power to transfer or dissolve the council if they saw fit. As the date for the meeting at Basel approached, the Basel Council was seen as a possible site for discussions with the representatives of the Greek Church who were interested in negotiating a reunion with the West, and also as an occasion to deal with the Hussite heresy in Bohemia (modern Czechoslovakia) which had continued to spread even after Jan Hus had been burned at the stake at Constance. Before he died in early 1431, Pope Martin appointed Cardinal Giuliano Cesarini to preside over the council, and gave him the same power to dissolve or transfer it that had been given to the papal legates at Siena. Soon after the Basel assembly opened, Pope Martin's successor, Eugene IV, decided that it should be transferred to a site in Italy, both so that he could be in attendance, and because the Greeks had indicated their preference for an Italian city. In late 1431 he attempted to dissolve the council and to call a new one at Bologna, but by the time the papal bull of dissolution arrived in Basel (it took as long as two months for messages to travel between Rome and Basel) it had already organized itself and renewed the *Frequens* decree of Constance. At its second session in February 1432, the council reissued *Haec sancta* asserting conciliar supremacy, and it interpreted *Frequens* and *Haec sancta* as prohibiting papal dissolution or transfer of a council without its consent. Thus it was in a period of intense conflict between the council and the pope that Nicholas arrived at the Basel Council.

The disputed Trier election was referred to the Committee (*Deputacio* – the Basel Council was divided into committees, rather

---

[2] For the controversy on whether the claim of conciliar supremacy has "ecumenical" standing, see Francis Oakley, *Council over Pope?*, New York, 1970, and the literature cited there. On the dogmatic status of *Haec sancta*, see the literature cited in Erich Meuthen, "Der Dialogus concludens Amedistarum Errorum," in *Mitteilungen und Forschungsbeiträge der Cusanus-Gesellschaft* (*MFCG*), vol. 8, Mainz, 1970, p. 43.

than "nations" as at Constance) on Matters of Common Interest (*pro communibus*) and to the Committee on Peace (*pro pace*). Nicholas, already known to several participants in the council, was made a member of the Committee on the Faith (*de Fide*). He remained in Basel in February and March, but in April he returned to Koblenz where he was dean of the Church of St. Florin to give an Easter sermon, which is still preserved.[3] He returned to Basel in May, preached in Koblenz in August, returning thereafter to Basel, preached in Koblenz at Christmas, and was back in Basel in January 1433. (The Rhine river made it relatively easy to go back and forth between Koblenz and Basel.) In February 1433, Nicholas of Cusa was one of those named by the council to negotiate with the Hussite delegates from Bohemia and in this connection he wrote a work, *De usu communionis* on the disputed issue of communion under both species, i.e. bread and wine.

Pope Eugene continued to maintain that a council could only be valid with the pope's approval and that its chairman should be the representative (*legatus*) of the pope. The council answered that it alone was infallible and that the pope was only the minister of the church as a whole. In April 1433 the council threatened the pope with suspension and deposition; in June, it refused to recognize the papal representatives; and in July the council threatened to cite the pope for contempt (*contumacia*) and set deadlines for him to recognize its validity. It also voted that all church offices should be filled by election with papal rights of appointment and reservation to be strictly limited to those specified in canon law. In August 1433 under pressure from the newly-crowned Holy Roman Emperor Sigismund, Pope Eugene formally annulled his earlier bull of dissolution and recognized the council's decrees except for those that "prejudiced the rights of the Holy See." A subcommittee of the Committee on the Faith which included Nicholas of Cusa in its membership examined the papal bull of submission and pronounced it insufficient, and the council began to move in the direction of a formal break with the papacy. On the papal side, Pope Eugene issued a bull that condemned as heretical the doctrine of conciliar supremacy. The arrival of the Emperor on October 11, 1433, introduced a moderating influence as he pressed for reconciliation with the pope, and in December, Eugene accepted

[3] See Nicolai de Cusa, *Opera omnia*, XVI, fasc. 3, *Sermones I* (1430–1441) edited by Rudolf Haubst and Martin Bodewig, Hamburg, 1977, Sermo XII, pp. 229–251.

all the demands of the council. The pope revoked all previous bulls against the council, declared it legitimate from its inception, and recognized as one of the council's purposes "the general reform of the church in its head and members."[4] Although he may have appeared thereby to accept conciliar superiority, it was clear from Eugene's letters of the time and from his subsequent actions that he had no intention of subordinating the pope to the council, a doctrine which he viewed as heretical.

The Composition of *De concordantia*

During this period Nicholas wrote his major work of political theory, *De concordantia catholica* (the *Catholic Concordance*). Nicholas refers in the Preface (no. 2) to his use of original sources located in "ancient cloisters" and later (III, 3, no. 316) cites a manuscript that he has seen in the Cologne Cathedral library, so that he seems to have used materials from other locations than Basel. The *Concordantia*, however, was probably written in Basel, following Nicholas' return from Koblenz in early 1433. The early discussions in Book I of predestination, membership of the church, and the validity of sacraments administered by sinful clergy seem to have been influenced by the debates with the Hussites (Bohemians) at the council between January and April 1433. Book II uses records of early church councils that were probably only available there[5] and in the same Book, he refers to

---

[4] For details, documentation, and chronology, see Joseph Gill, *Constance et Bale-Florence*, Paris, 1965 (vol. IX of *Histoire des conciles oecumeniques*), Johannes Haller, *Concilium Basiliense*, vols. I–II, Basel, 1896–1897; and Johannes Helmrath, *Das Basler Konzil, 1431–1449*, Cologne, 1987. The major documents relating to the Council of Basel have been translated into English by C. M. D. Crowder, *Unity, Heresy and Reform, 1378–1460*, London, 1977, Part IV.

[5] John of Segovia's *History* of the Council of Basel mentions Cardinal Cesarini's use of an ancient collection of the records of earlier councils (*librum de antiquis conciliis antique scriptum*) and notes that Nicholas of Cusa, a close friend (*singulariter dilectus*) of Cesarini's, argued from an even older collection. Nicholas' argument as summarized by Segovia is similar to that of the *Catholic Concordance* in distinguishing different types of councils and emphasizing the role of the patriarchs in the earlier history of the church. See Ernest Birk (ed.), *Historia gestorum generalis synodi Basiliensis*, Book VII, chs. 14 and 18 in *Monumenta conciliorum generalium seculi XV*, vol. II, Vienna, 1873, pp. 605 and 612–613. Book I, ch. 12, no. 54 of the *Catholic Concordance* refers to the Council as "gathered there" (*ibi congregatis*) which may argue for composition of that chapter outside of Basel. There are also minor parallels between passages in Book I, chapters 1 and 3 and Cusanus' Christmas 1432 sermon in Koblenz, (*Opera omnia*, XVI, fasc. 3, *Sermones*, Sermo XVII, p. 271) including a reference to "*graduatione concordante et harmoniaca.*" However the bulk of the evidence favors composition in Basel in 1433.

"this council" (II, 20, no. 184), mentions decrees adopted in August 1432 (II, 17, no. 155) and in July 1433 (II, 18, no. 162), and alludes (II, 26, no. 211) to "a certain little work against the Bohemians," presumably *De usu communionis*, which we know he wrote in Basel in March or April 1433.

The manuscript evidence indicates that initially there was a shorter version of the *Concordantia*, comprising Book I and chapters 1–7, 16–21, and 26–33 of Book II, which was entitled *Libellus de ecclesiastica concordantia (Little Book on Concordance in the Church)*.[6] It was more directly focused on the relations of the pope and council, and did not include the more general philosophical discussions of consent or the analysis of the constitution of the Holy Roman Empire which are contained in the final version of the work. This would explain the shift of interest in the course of the work from the attempt in Books I and II to describe the patterns of harmony (*concordantia*) among the spiritual authorities to the analysis in Book III of the temporal power and its relation to the priesthood.

A short tract on the superiority of the councils to the pope (*De maioritate auctoritatis sacrorum conciliorum supra auctoritatem papae*) which has been identified as written by Nicholas is similar in argument to, and identical in some of its quotations with, parts of Book I, chapter 16 and Book II, chapters 2, 3, 7, 16, and 20. Since the tract was one of a number of such works written in the first part of 1433 when several council committees at Basel were discussing the

---

[6] The Basel manuscript of the *Catholic Concordance* contains an earlier introduction (*prohoemium*) which gives the title of the work as *Libellus de ecclesiastica concordantia* and summarizes the argument in a way that corresponds to the chapters cited. In addition, two sections appear in Book II that are located in Book III, ch. 35 in the final version – a quotation from an imperial decree calling the Council of Arles which in the Basel manuscript appears in Book II, ch. 7 as well as in Book III – and the description of a suggested electoral procedure in Book II, ch. 33 which appears in a slightly different form in Book III, ch. 37. On the dating and order of composition, see Gerhard Kallen's preface to the Latin edition of the *Concordantia* (*Opera omnia*, vol. XIV, *De concordantia catholica*, Book I, Hamburg, 1964, pp. ix–xii) and his article, "Die Handschriftliche Überlieferung der Concordantia des Nikolaus von Kues," *Sitzungsberichte der Heidelberger Akademie der Wissenschaften*, Philosophisch-historische Klasse, 1963, no. 2, pp. 51–59. See also the review of the Latin edition by Werner Krämer in *Historische Zeitschrift*, no. 209 (1969), pp. 143–150. Krämer believes (p. 146) that the *Libellus* continued to exist as a separate treatise. He bases his argument on the presence of a work entitled *Concordantia ecclesiastica* in the description of the books accompanying Nicholas at the time of his death in 1464.

council's response to the papal bulls including the possible use of a decree of nullification (*irritans*) against papal appointments to church offices, the first draft of the *Concordantia* must have been written after this time. That draft includes the aforementioned reference to a conciliar decree adopted in July 1433 (II, 18, no. 162) so that it could not have been completed until mid-1433.[7]

Additions were then made to Book II, including the chapters that are of most interest to modern students of political philosophy – the discussion of the requirement of consent as a prerequisite for legitimate law and government (Book II, chapters 8–15) – along with four chapters (22–25) on provincial councils and additional canon law references elsewhere in Book II. Then, the news of the impending arrival of the emperor and the announcement in September of the convocation of the Reichstag later in the year led Nicholas to extend his argument for legislation in councils and elective government (although not for conciliar supremacy) to the empire in an additional section (Book III). The last part of Book III from its frequent references to the emperor's presence in Basel (III, 24, nos. 465–468; III, 40, no. 565; III, 42, no. 596) must have been written after October 11, 1433, the date of the emperor's arrival. There is no reference to the papal submission to the council in December 1433 which was known in Basel at the end of January 1434, so that the work was probably completed before that time. The use of new sources, principally Marsilius of Padua's *Defensor pacis* (without acknowledgment), and a different style indicate that the preface to the third book

---

[7] See Erich Meuthen, "Nikolaus von Kues in der Entscheidung zwischen Konzil und Papst," *MFCG*, vol. IX, Mainz, 1971, pp. 19–33; Meuthen, "Kanonistik und Geschichtsverständnis" in Remigius Bäumer (ed.), *Von Konstanz nach Trient*, Munich, 1972, pp. 147–170, and his careful analysis of the relation of *De maioritate* and *De concordantia* in the introduction and notes to the published edition, "Cusanus Texte, II, Traktate 2. De majoritate auctoritatis sacrorum conciliorum supra auctoritatem papae," *Abhandlungen der Heidelberger Akademie der Wissenschaften*, Philosophisch-historische Klasse, Heidelberg, 1977. Nicholas' report on February 16, 1433 of discussions in the Committee on the Faith of the legal form to be used against the pope is mentioned in the records of the proceedings of the Council published in Johannes Haller (ed.), *Concilium Basiliense*, vol. II, Basel, 1897, p. 350. The council's debates on the nullification (*irritans*) decree in late 1432 and early 1433 are cited in Haller, *Concilium*, vol. I, Basel, 1896, p. 111. On the date of composition, and the role of Helwig of Boppard, a fellow Padua-trained canon lawyer at Basel, as collaborator with Cusanus in the composition of *De majoritate* and the *De concordantia*, see Werner Krämer, *Konsens und Rezeption: Verfassungsprinzipien der Kirche im Basler Konziliarismus*, Münster, 1980, ch. 6.

was added after Book III had been completed. The manuscript evidence also shows that new final chapters were added to Books II and III as well as additional documentation in Cusanus' hand.

It seems then that Book I and the two versions of Book II were written after Nicholas' return to Basel in early 1433, and Book III was written in the latter part of the same year. The entire work, with the possible exception of the preface to Book III and the final chapters of Books II and III, would then have been submitted to the council at the end of 1433 or the beginning of 1434. It is referred to in a work that Nicholas wrote in February 1434 so that it had been completed by that time, although minor additions may have been made thereafter.[8]

Despite its appearance in the midst of a profound constitutional crisis in the church, the *Catholic Concordance* is more than a canon lawyer's brief for conciliar supremacy. Faithful to its title, and to the theologically-inspired outlook that characterizes all of Nicholas' writing, it is an attempt to synthesize and harmonize many different and apparently conflicting strands in ecclesiological and political theory. While Nicholas argues for conciliar supremacy, he also grants that the pope possesses an independently-derived position as the divinely-intended head of the church. He relies on canon law, the writings of the fathers of the church, and the history of the early church councils for much of his analysis, but he also relates his argument to general philosophical principles of consent and representation that are of interest to modern political theorists and to students of the political and institutional development of the West. While the *Catholic Concordance* was occasioned by a conflict over the internal constitution of the church, the last book makes practical suggestions for the reform of the empire including an ingenious preferential voting system that would be of interest to modern political scientists (III, 37, nos. 535–540). In many ways the work appears rigidly formal and traditional in substance and form, but it also contains striking anticipations of modern concepts and practices – including themes that have received renewed attention during the last twenty-five years in the Roman Catholic Church in connection with the reforms introduced by the Second Vatican Council.

[8] See "Cusanus Texte, II, Traktate I. De Auctoritate Presidendi in Concilio Generali," *Sitzungsberichte der Heidelberger Akademie der Wissenschaften*, Philosophisch-historische Klasse, Heidelberg, 1935, p. 27, and English translation by H. Lawrence Bond, Gerald Christianson, and Thomas Izbicki, "Nicholas of Cusa, 'On Presidential Authority in a General Council'," *Church History*, 59, 1 (March 1990), 19–34.

The structure of the argument

Because of the way in which the *Concordantia* was written, a simple outline or table of contents is not sufficient to make clear its basic structure. It is not as contradictory or confused as some observers have claimed, but the basic unity of its argument is sometimes obscured, and the reader who begins with Book I and reads through to the end of the work may find its argument difficult to follow. Book I begins with an elaborate outline of the hierarchical structure of the universe and of the church. This is followed by an analysis of the relation between the pope and the bishops and the place of Rome in the church constitution. Book II focuses at greater length on the disputed issue of the relation of the pope to the council and the need for consent to church law and government. Book III on the reform of the Holy Roman Empire seems in many respects to be an after-thought to the argument already developed. It is less elaborate in its argumentation, its sources are cited either too briefly, or at too great length (or – in the case of the dependence of the Preface to Book III on Marsilius – not at all). Yet it is necessary to consider the work as a whole, both in order to understand Nicholas' fully developed theory with its intricate system of harmonies and parallelisms, and to explain his subsequent change of loyalties to the side of Pope Eugene IV after 1437 when he became, in Aeneas Sylvius Piccolomini's phrase, "the Hercules of the Eugenians."

On the basic issue, Nicholas upholds the doctrine of conciliar supremacy over the pope. "Even in the decision on matters of faith which belongs to him by virtue of his primacy he is under the council of the Catholic Church" (I, 15, no. 61). It is not required that the council be called by the pope; in cases of necessity or danger to the church the emperor can do so (III, 15, no. 402). In the face of the pope's persistent refusal to attend, the council once it has met "should provide for the needs and welfare of the church" (II, 2, no. 73; II, 13, no. 125). "The council has power both over abuses and the one who causes the abuses . . . Its power is immediately from Christ and it is in every respect over both the pope and the Apostolic See" (II, 16, no. 148). It can remove him for heresy and "when he governs incompetently" (II, 18, no. 159). The council's "judgment is always better than the individual judgment of the Roman pontiff" (II, 18, no. 158). "The canons of the ancients [in the early church councils] are

of greater authority than decretals of the popes which contradict them
– despite what modern writers say" (II, 18, no. 177). "The universal
council . . . has supreme power in all things over the Roman pontiff"
(II, 34, no. 249).

Yet Nicholas' theory is not as simple as the above quotations may
appear to indicate. The papacy as an institution does not depend on
the council; it is part of the divinely-established constitution of the
church with rights and prerogatives of its own. Christ made Peter and
his successor, the pope, the head of the church "to maintain unity"
and "to avoid schism" (I, 6, no. 35; II, 34, nos. 259, 261, and 264).
The pope is "prince of the bishops" and "he has a rulership over all
men in the church, for he is captain in that army" (I, 15, no. 61). He is
"first over the others" (II, 13, no. 126) with inherent powers of
administration which in Nicholas' opinion (although, as he admits,
not that of the Councils of Constance and Basel) cannot be taken
away from him on a temporary basis (suspension) but only by remov-
ing him from office (deposition) (II, 16, no. 162). He can grant
dispensations from church law out of his "personal prerogative" (II,
20, no. 187). In ordinary circumstances, the pope calls the council
into session. After waiting "a long time" for him to appear, it can
proceed without him, but it cannot define an article of faith without
considering the views of Rome (II, 2, no. 74). The pope is obliged to
yield to the majority view in the Council, but decisions on matters of
faith should be unanimous (II, 15, no. 137). He is "judge of the faith";
and on matters of faith "the Roman See", understood as the pope
acting with his patriarchal council, "can not err" (II, 7, nos. 94–95),
and declarations on matters of faith by the synod of the patriarchate of
Rome can not be reversed by the universal council (II, 5, no. 81).

Nicholas developed his ecclesiological theory in order to resolve
the apparently contradictory statements in the written records of the
church concerning the relationship of the pope and the council. Some
of the early church councils, as well as the recent Council of Constance, seemed to assert a general theory of conciliar supremacy over
the pope. Yet statements of the papacy and in church law (including
the forged Pseudo-Isidorean Decretals) seemed to enunciate a theory
of papal supremacy. Nicholas, confident as any orthodox medieval
churchman of the basic underlying harmony and rationality of the
universe, convinced that the Holy Spirit was providing the guidance
to the church that had been promised to it by Christ, and trained as a

canon lawyer in the interpretation and resolution of contradictory texts (the basic canon law text, Gratian's *Concordantia discordantium canonum*, usually referred to as the *Decretum*, was compiled in order to reconcile apparently contradictory canon law texts) was certain that a harmonious intermediate position (*medium concordantiae*) could be found.

His belief in an ordered harmonious universe was derived from the version of the Christian world view that was transmitted to the Middle Ages by the writings of "Dionysius the Areopagite", (or Pseudo-Dionysius), a fifth-century Syrian Christian disciple of the neo-Platonist philosopher, Proclus.[9] The opening chapters of the *Catholic Concordance* show the influence of the thought of Dionysius, who was mistakenly thought to be the Athenian convert of St. Paul mentioned in Acts 17:34. Dionysius wrote, among other works, *The Celestial Hierarchy* and *The Ecclesiastical Hierarchy* describing the hierarchical order of the universe beginning with God through nine choirs of angels, down to the sacraments, clergy, and people. The clergy, in turn, was divided into bishops, priests, and deacons, and the people into monks, the faithful, and catechumens.

Dionysius' hierarchical and triadic view of the world, as reflected and developed by Nicholas at the beginning of the *Concordantia*, begins with nine choirs of angels, continues through nine heavenly spheres from the prime moving sphere through the planets, sun, and moon to the earth. On earth all nature is divided into rational, sensate, and vegetative; man is body, soul, and spirit; and the church is made up of sacraments, priesthood, and the faithful. The sacramental power of the priesthood is distributed into nine ranks – bishops, priests and deacons; subdeacons, acolytes, and exorcists; and readers, porters, and tonsured clergy (I, 7, no. 41).

It is only in the sixth chapter of Book I that Nicholas reaches the subject of the structure of church government. Although all bishops

[9] On Nicholas' knowledge of Dionysius, see Paul E. Sigmund, *Nicholas of Cusa and Medieval Political Thought*, Cambridge, Mass., 1963, pp. 247–249. Among the more important mediators of the tradition of Dionysius was Albertus Magnus (1200–1280), whose works Nicholas came to know through his associate at Cologne, Heimericus de Campo. At Cologne and in a visit to France in 1428 he also developed a strong interest in the Majorcan neo-Platonic mystic, Ramon Llull (1235–1316). The definition of *De concordantia* in Llull's *Ars generalis* was borrowed by Cusanus, and he also adapted a system of preferential voting suggested by Llull (III, 37, nos. 535–541). For discussion, see Sigmund, *Nicholas of Cusa*, pp. 59–61.

are equal as to sacramental power "nevertheless there is a distinction of grades as to governing responsibility [*regitivam curam*]" (I, 6, no. 35). In the governmental hierarchy the nine ranks are: subdeacon, deacon and priest; above them, dean, archdean, and bishop; and on the highest level, archbishop, patriarch, and pope (I, 8, no. 42). At this point we would expect him to follow earlier conciliarists (e.g. John of Paris) to argue that the consent of the church is required for governmental authority, as distinct from the sacramental authority that is granted by laying on of hands in ordination. Instead, he turns to an analysis of the historical record of the church, mobilizes citations from canon law in favor of consent to law and government, and moves to an argument from original freedom and equality that extends far beyond the history and law of the medieval church.

The historical record shows, Nicholas argues, that the one *cathedra* or ruling authority in the church belongs to all the bishops as successors of the apostles in union with Peter as their head.[10] Peter was appointed by Christ to that headship with the consent of the other apostles, while Rome, Peter's last see, is the head of the church both because of its historical importance as the capital of the empire and because of consent of the church, as expressed by the bishops.[11]

When he looked at "the original sources, not some abbreviated collection" (as he says in the Preface) he found that the first eight councils had been called by the Eastern emperors, although papal consent and participation by the pope's representatives had been considered necessary to give them ecumenical status. He found that the popes repeatedly declared that they were bound by the canons of

---

[10] If Peter and his successors are to give the church unity and "prevent schism" (I, 6, no. 35), this seems to imply a final decision in matters of doctrine. However Nicholas, following the doctrine that he found in the writings of St. Cyprian, one of the Fathers of the Church, leaves this to a majority (*maior pars*) of the bishops and priests (I, 14, no. 58 See also II, 26, no. 211; III, preface, no. 270). For a linguistic analysis of the various meanings of "consensus" as it was used at Basel, and its relationship to majority rule, see Josef Wohlmuth, *Verständigung in der Kirche*, Mainz, 1983.

[11] For a similar argument, see Gulielmus Durandus, *De Modo Celebrandi Concilii Generalis* (1311), an annotated copy of which remains in Nicholas' library at Kues today. On the sources of Nicholas' theory in earlier conciliarist writings, see Paul E. Sigmund, *Nicholas of Cusa*, ch. 4. My chapter does not, however, give sufficient attention to the originality of Nicholas' effort to use the historical records of the early church councils as the basis for his conciliar theory. For a breakdown and analysis of the sources cited in the *Catholic Concordance*, see Hermann Josef Sieben, "Der Konzilstraktat des Nikolaus von Kues: De Concordantia Catholica," *Annuarium Historiae Conciliorum*, XIV (1982), 171–226, and Sieben, *Traktate und Theorien zum Konzil*, Frankfurt, 1983, ch. 2.

the early councils, especially those of the Council of Nicaea. He found that in A.D. 451 the Council of Chalcedon reviewed a decision of the papal synod and over Pope Leo's objection successfully raised the status of the Patriarch of Constantinople to a point immediately below that of the pope in Rome. And he found that the Eighth Council (Constantinople IV) held in 869–870 (not recognized by the Orthodox Church today), defended the authority of the patriarchs, and, while recognizing papal primacy, insisted that the pope was subject to the bishops assembled in the universal council and to the church laws (canons) that they adopted.

From Gratian's *Decretum*, the authoritative twelfth-century canon law collection, Nicholas frequently cites the statement in D.4.C.1 that a law must be approved by the practice of those subject to it, as well as Gratian's requirement that bishops and archbishops be elected by those under them (II, 18, nos. 163–164, and II, 32, nos. 232–233). He also draws an analogy between the canon law provisions that bishops and archbishops must consult their councils on matters that affect the diocese or province, and the need for the pope to secure the consent of the church as represented by the council, or when it is not in session, that of the cardinals acting as representatives of the provinces of the church (II, 18, no. 166).

Almost as an aside in his historical and legal argument (it was added in the second version of Book II) Nicholas also makes a broader philosophical argument – the one for which the work is best known – the derivation of consent from natural freedom, and equality. In Book II, chapter 14, after quoting Gratian to prove that all legislation is based on natural law, and arguing that since natural law is based on reason, the more rational ought to rule, Nicholas adds the following words:

> Therefore since all are by nature free, every governance – whether it consists in a written law or living law in the person of a prince . . . can only come from the agreement and consent of the subjects. For if men are by nature equal in power (*potentes*) and equally free, the true properly ordered authority of one common ruler who is their equal in power can only be constituted by the election and consent of the others, and law is also established by consent. (II, 14, no. 127)

The appeal to natural freedom and quality as the basis for partici-pation in government was something new in the history of political thought. It is true that the opening passages of Roman law contained the statement, "By the law of nature, all men from the beginning were born free" (*Institutes* I, ii), but this had not led the Roman lawyers or their later commentators to demand any popular role in legislation or government beyond a mythical original transfer of authority by the Roman people to the emperor. The belief in natural freedom and equality goes back to the Stoics, but its use to support the institution-alization of consent through the election of rulers and legislation by representative councils was new.

Corporate consensus vs. individual consent

Political and economic developments in the late Middle Ages made it possible for an argument for the institutionalization of consent to be made at this time. In the church quasi-representative corporate institutions played a significant role – the college of cardinals, the cathedral and monastic chapters; local, provincial, and patriarchal synods in the earlier history of the church, and the universal council itself which was now enjoying new prestige from having reestablished unity in the Western church. In the temporal sphere, the German empire had the Reichstag and the electors who chose the emperor. The Cortes of Castile had been meeting irregularly since the early thirteenth century. The English parliament had assembled with increasing frequency since the middle of the thirteenth century, and since the end of that century it had regularly included, in addition to the lords spiritual and temporal, the representatives of the shires (counties) and boroughs. In France the Estates General had been called at the start of the fourteenth century in order to strengthen the hand of Philip the Fair against Pope Boniface VIII. It was to continue meeting sporadically until the beginning of the seventeenth century – and then again, fatefully, in 1789.

These institutions were justified through largely implicit theories of corporate and community consent – not through appeals to natural equality or freedom. The community acted through corporate groups or by consensus rather than by counting heads. Hierarchical con-siderations counted for much, and the medieval representatives in the English House of Commons, for instance, were always properly deferential in their relations with the king and the lords.

Hierarchical and corporatist conceptions are important in the thinking of Nicholas and the other conciliarists too. We need only refer to his original cosmological "chain of being" outlined at the beginning of the *Catholic Concordance* or to the canon law controversies over the relative voting weight of the "larger" and of the "sounder" part, which became central to Nicholas' argument after 1437 when he joined the side of the pope against the Council of Basel. Yet here as elsewhere, political theory in the church anticipated later developments in the state. Controversies over the "sounder" part in the college of cardinals led to the adoption of the two-thirds rule in the twelfth century, on the assumption that the larger (*maior*) part would also be sounder (*sanior*) if its number was twice as large as the minority. The canon lawyers also discussed the relative weighting of the votes of head and members of ecclesiastical corporate groups, and the fifteenth-century councils (Pisa, Constance, and Basel) gradually extended voting rights to all those formally incorporated in the council without regard to hierarchical status. (One of Nicholas' later criticisms of the Council of Basel was that it admitted any simple priest to vote on the same basis as high church dignitaries.)[12]

There are a number of references to majority rule in the *Catholic Concordance*. In Book I, 14, no. 59 the true church is made up of a "majority" (*major pars*) of the faithful in union with Peter and his chair. St. Cyprian is cited several times to demonstrate that the "larger part" of the priesthood will remain free from error (I, 8, no. 43; II, 4, no. 79, and III, Preface, no. 270) although the actual quotation from Cyprian says "the larger and better part" – see no. 43. Nicholas also states that in the council the majority "ordinarily" (II, 4, no. 79) or "normally" (II, 15, no. 137) rules, although immediately following the second assertion, he seems to have some doubts on the question (II, 16, no. 138). Then, it appears, a reading of Marsilius's *Defender of Peace* rekindled his enthusiasm. At the end of Book II and in the Preface to Book III, written after the rest of the work, there are

---

[12] Arguing at the 1441 Reichstag, Nicholas cited a case in which the Basel Council had used the vote of a personal servant of one of the bishops in order to break a tie, and asked, "Does not one pope or prince have greater authority in his vote than one manservant?" (Hermann Herre [ed.], *Deutsche Reichstagsakten*, vol. xv, part 2, Gotha, 1914, p. 763). Nicholas also attacked the deposition of Pope Eugene IV by the Basel Council in 1439 on the grounds that it had only a few bishops and no archbishops present (Helmut Weigel [ed.], *Deutsche Reichstagsakten*, vol. xiv, part 1, Stuttgart, 1933, p. 348). At both Constance and Basel cardinals and bishops were considerably outnumbered by the lower clergy who once admitted as members had the right to vote (see Gill, pp. 207–208).

repeated favorable references to the rule of majorities (II, 34, no. 261, and III, Preface nos. 270, 276, 278, and 283). The anticipation of later ideas is all the more striking in the claim early in Book III that consent is required because of "the common equal birth of all men and their equal natural rights" (III, 4, no. 331).

It would be a mistake, however, to attribute modern democratic conclusions involving universal suffrage to his theory of consent based on natural freedom and equality. When he described his proposed conciliar structure for the church, it was distinctly hierarchical. Nicholas endorses legislation by an early Spanish council, quoted in the *Decretum* which appeared to mandate the election of priests. At the very least, he declares, priests should be appointed by the bishops with the consent (in the sense of absence of opposition) of the faithful. Bishops are to be elected by cathedral chapters representing the priests of the diocese with the (apparently tacit) consent of the laity. Archbishops would be elected by bishops with the consent of the clergy. They in turn would elect (i.e., appoint) cardinals as representatives of the church provinces to elect and advise the pope (II, 18, no. 164). In all cases and especially in that of the universal church, legislation on each level should be adopted by the appropriate conciliar body and the earlier practice of holding diocesan, provincial, and national councils should be revived. The result is an ambitious attempt – the first on such a broad scale – to give institutional expression on a regular basis to earlier inchoate ideas about consent to law and government.

Theories of representation – personification versus delegation

To move as Nicholas does from a general requirement of church consent to an argument for the councils as the expression of that consent requires a theory of representation. In *Haec Sancta*, its decree on conciliar superiority, the Council of Constance had based that superiority on the fact that "representing the Catholic Church [it] holds its power directly from Christ" and the Council of Basel had reaffirmed that decree. Yet as the unrepresentative character of the Council of Siena in 1423–1424 and the small initial attendance at Basel suggested, some kinds of guidelines had to be established to determine just when a council was truly representative, and when it was a pseudo-council (*conciliabulum*). On the basis of his reading of the records of the Eighth Council Nicholas cites among the requirements for a "full universal council" the participation of the five patriarchs which he then reinterprets as the "heads of the whole church". The council can proceed if all have been called and a majority (*plures*) are present (II, 3, no. 75).

Who are the heads of the church? Although at one point Nicholas allows the admission of "chosen and learned priests," church practice before the fifteenth century and Nicholas' own view restricted those with voting rights (*diffinitio et statuendi potestas*) to the bishops (II, 16, nos. 138–139. Cf. also II, 17, nos. 408–410). How do the bishops represent the faithful? Nicholas replies that they are united to him, since "the church is in the bishop" (St. Cyprian, quoted in the *Decretum* C. 7 q.l. c.7) and "as the universal church is the Mystical Body of Christ, so particular churches are the mystical bodies of those who preside over them as representatives of Christ." The bishop "represents and symbolizes (*figurat*) the church as a public person" (II, 6, no. 37).

This mystical or "virtual" theory of representation is then used to demonstrate that the council is superior to the pope. The council contains more "public persons" – patriarchs, cardinals, archbishops, and bishops – and "the more specific the headship, the more certain the representation" (II, 18, no. 163) so that it is more representative than the pope alone who only represents the church in a very general way (*confusissime*). Like the theories of tacit or implicit community consensus which had formed part of the common assumptions of medieval political thought, the theory of representation as impersonation (the ruler as the "personification" of his subjects – *l'etat, c'est moi*) could provide a rationale for the most oppressive tyranny. Indeed it only needed a bit of neo-Platonic philosophizing about absorptive hierarchy to provide a rationale for the papalist position that Nicholas adopted after 1437.

Yet his theory of representation contained more modern elements as well. Through a hierarchical system of councils the lower ranks would have a voice, although a limited one, in church government. The councils are described as made up both of the presiding officers (*praesides*) and of representatives (*legati*) of the various groups in the church who give the consent of all the faithful (II, 34, no. 248). The cardinals represent the church provinces and they take the place (*vices gerunt*) of the others in electing the pope and approving papal dispensations (II, 21, no. 93; II, 24, no. 202; II, 34, no. 262). The council and the cardinals derive their legitimacy from those below rather than from those above them, and from the laity (in an indirect fashion) as well as from the clergy. The promise of infallibility that Christ made to the whole church is fulfilled more directly by the universal council than by the pope alone because it more certainly represents the church and the majority (*maior pars*) of the priesthood which St. Cyprian had said would always maintain the true faith and law of Christ. Similarly in the empire and kingdoms "legislation ought to be adopted by those who are bound by it or by a majority of their representatives because ... what touches all should be approved by all" (III, Preface, no. 270).[13]

Like the movement from corporate, implicit, or quasi-unanimous consent (*consensus*) to individual voting on a regularized basis, the movement from representation as impersonation to representation as the result of the conscious selection of another to take action on behalf of an individual or group (delegation) marks an important transition in the development of modern political theory and practice that is anticipated in the *Catholic Concordance*. In words that sound strikingly modern Nicholas asserts that "all power both spiritual and temporal rests potentially in the people" (II, 19, no. 168) and "rulership comes from God through men and councils by means of elective consent" (II, 34, no. 249).

Parallel hierarchies in church and empire

A similar tension between authoritarian and "democratic" elements in Nicholas' theory can be found in the last book of the *Catholic Concordance* which deals with the German empire and temporal government in general. It too contains a theory of a hierarchy of offices reflecting the triadic organization of all creation. Yet where Pope Boniface VIII in his bull, *Unam sanctam* (1302) had appealed to "the Blessed Dionysius" in support of the strict subordination of temporal authority to the head of the spiritual hierarchy, Nicholas asserts not hierarchical subordination but parallelism. The emperor is

---

[13] On the history of the "quod omnes tangit" ("what touches all" ...) principle, see Gaines Post, *Studies in Medieval Legal Thought: Public Law and the State, 1100–1322*, Princeton, 1964, ch. 4.

the "one ruler of the world exercising his authority over the others in the plenitude of power, and in his own sphere he is the equal of the Roman pontiff in the temporal hierarchy on the model of the sacerdotal hierarchy" (III, 1, no. 293).

There were two problems, however, with any attempt to draw an exact parallel between the spiritual and temporal orders. The first was the existence in Christendom of kings like those of France and England who did not acknowledge a duty of subordination to the Holy Roman Empire. Already in the thirteenth century Pope Innocent III had recognized in his decretal, *Per venerabilem*, that "the king of France recognizes no superior in temporals." (At the council itself there had been problems with the order in which the representatives of the emperor and of the kings of other European countries would walk in formal processions.) To save the notion of the superiority of emperor, Nicholas relies on the emperor's religious role as protector (*advocatus*) of the church. While it is true that imperial jurisdiction that does not extend to kings and princes "who *de facto* or because of exemption do not recognize the overlordship of the empire" all are subject to imperial legislation on the enforcement of conciliar decrees (III, 7, nos. 355–356). Although the Roman empire originally included a major part of the world (in terms of area, although he also argues on the basis of population – see III, 6, nos. 343 and 346), Nicholas recognizes that its medieval successor controls a more limited area so that the medieval emperor's normal jurisdiction extends only to those who habitually obey his rule, and through the electors of the empire have given their consent to his election. However, when the emperor "exhorts the bishops and commands the laity" (III, 15, no. 399) in the convocation of the council and enforces its decrees, he is to be obeyed by all Christians, and because of his religious role he can participate in the council as the Eastern emperors in the early councils did. In this role he is "the minister of God" and "the vicar of Jesus Christ on earth" (III, 5, no. 341).

The second problem in Nicholas' structural parallelism between church and empire is that while he had seen the universal council as the instrument of reform in the church, in the empire he looked primarily to Emperor Sigismund. Even in church affairs, it was Sigismund who had been primarily responsible for the success of the Council of Constance and his arrival at Basel in October 1433 raised Nicholas' hopes that he would play a similar role there. He is thus not concerned to demonstrate the superiority of the Reichstag to the emperor – although at one point Nicholas asserts that it is "the common opinion of the doctors" that the emperor can be deposed by the people who elected him (III, 4, no. 339). Like the pope in the universal council the emperor in his imperial council (*Reichstag*) comprising the electors, princes, senators, judges, and representatives of the cities and towns is to meet to judge cases and work out common legislation for the whole empire (III, 25, nos. 469–472. See also III, 35, nos. 519–531 for a description of the smaller annual *conventus* comprising the emperor, the electors, and the judges of the empire). Like the pope too, the emperor would have a daily council "to advise him and defend the public good" (III, 12, no. 378).

The parallelism of church and empire is carried further. Nicholas lists three ranks in the empire, as in the church (III, 25, no. 471). He describes the emperor's relationship with the other kings as parallel to that of the pope as first among the patriarchs, and compares dukes to archbishops and counts to bishops "and so on with the rest" (III, 1, no. 293). Yet there is no mention of a hierarchical system of elected bodies like those that he had described in the church nor any discussion of the accountability of the emperor to the Reichstag. Nicholas' failure to complete his scheme of parallel concordances may be attributed to lack of time since it is clear that the last book of the *Catholic Concordance* was hastily written. It is more likely, however, that an emphasis on the restraining role of the Reichstag or other representative bodies did not suit his ultimate purpose in Book III, the reform of the empire. The problem in the church as he saw it was excessive centralization in the papacy; the problem in the empire was just the reverse. To remedy it he recommended the creation of a strong imperial standing army, a centralized treasury and tax system, and a common judiciary – based on district courts – all to be established under the emperor's sponsorship at the forthcoming Reichstag. Stronger limits on the emperor were not in his view necessary, and the extension of the conciliar structure to lower levels of the empire would have weakened the chances for the adoption of the reforms that were his basic concern.

Nicholas was also concerned to strengthen the empire by demonstrating its independence of the papacy. In this connection, he once again demonstrates a remarkable historical sense and an ability to marshal documentary evidence as he traces the constitutional

history of the German empire and criticizes the papalist arguments for the pope's superiority to the emperor. Best-known is his attack on the authenticity of the Donation of Constantine on the basis of the analysis of the historical documents (III, 2, nos. 300–308), but he also raises doubts about what later turned out to be forged papal letters included in the Pseudo-Isidorean collection (no. 309). His interest in geography and astronomy is also displayed in Book III, chapter 6 when he discusses the geographical extension of the empire – an interest that led to the production of one of the first maps of Western Europe in the late Middle Ages.[14]

At the end of the work, Nicholas' knowledge of medicine is demonstrated in an elaborate organic analogy comparing the officers of church and empire to the parts of the human organism, including an extended comparison (in somewhat questionable taste) between the process of legislation and the ingestion and digestion of food. The considerable lengths to which the analogy is carried are an indication of how thoroughly medieval is the outlook of the *Catholic Concordance* and how far it is from the modern democratic theory with which it has sometimes been linked. Nicholas was concerned with reform, not revolution. This reform was to be orderly, legal, and in a sense reactionary – that is, it should recapture the harmonious order that had existed in the church in the period of the great ecumenical councils in the East – especially the Eighth Council (Constantinople IV, 869–870) and in the German empire in the days of Emperor Otto II (955–983) when "everything tended to the common good" (III, 28, no. 495). While Nicholas believed in the possibility of a reconciliation of divergent tendencies, "a coincidence of opposites" to use the phrase that he made famous in his later work, *On Learned Ignorance* (1440), persistent dissension and incapacity to come to agreement was a sign that a church meeting was not inspired by the Holy Spirit, "the author of peace and concord," since one of the signs of a genuine council was that it was concluded in harmony, and on matters of faith, even unanimously (II, 15, no. 137, and II, 34, no. 248). "Where there is dissension, there is no council" (II, 1, no 69 quoting Gratian's *Decretum*).

---

[14] Cf. "Cusanus und die Geographie," in Nikolaus Grass (ed.), *Cusanus Gedächtnisschrift*, Innsbruck, 1970, part IV.

The shift to papalism

His belief in harmony, his attachment to law and order, his strong interest in reunion of the Eastern and Western churches, and the considerable authoritarian and hierarchical elements in his world view, all help to explain his change from the conciliarist to the papalist positions in 1437. When the Council of Basel, influenced by a growing French delegation hostile to the Pope, took an increasingly antipapal position and when it also became apparent that the Greeks had no interest in negotiating with the squabbling churchmen in northern Switzerland, Nicholas was more and more inclined to place his hopes for church reform in a strong pope working through a unity council in Italy, in a manner parallel to the hoped-for reform of the empire to be carried out by a strong emperor working through the Reichstag. In the Preface to Book III Nicholas had strongly endorsed elective monarchy as the best form of government, and as the Basel Council arrogated more and more papal prerogatives to itself (e.g. canonization of saints, payment of church taxes and fees, establishment of fast days, etc.) it seemed to exemplify that "plurality of rulers" which Nicholas described in the Preface as a bad form of government (no. 282, repeating the argument of Marsilius, *Defensor pacis*, D. 1, c. 17, no. 1). When the members of the council in favor of meeting the Greeks in an Italian city, including Nicholas, his former teacher, Cardinal Cesarini who had given up the chairmanship of the council, and three cardinals and twelve bishops, were heavily out-voted by those who supported Basel or Avignon in France, the atmosphere was compared by Aeneas Sylvius to the conduct of drunkards in a tavern.[15] On May 20, 1437, Nicholas left Basel along with two bishops and the two representatives of the Greek Church, and went to Bologna to get papal confirmation before going to Constantinople to assist in making arrangements for the Greeks to come to Italy for a unity council.

After 1437 Nicholas was an ardent papalist – but at the same time he made efforts to demonstrate a substantial continuity between his papalist and conciliarist thought. Thus in his appearances at the Reichstag where he endeavored to secure imperial support for the

---

[15] "... ut modestiores in taberna vinaria cernas bibulos," Letter to Peter of Nocetus, reproduced in J. D. Mansi, *Sacrorum conciliorum nova at amplissima collectio*, vol. XXXI, Venice, 1798 (reprinted, Paris, 1906), p. 223.

pope against the remnant of the Basel Council – an effort which was only finally successful in 1448 – he argued that Basel was no longer valid because it did not have the consent of the church.[16] Both at the Reichstag meetings and in 1460 when as a cardinal he submitted a reform proposal to Pope Pius II (himself the former conciliarist, Aeneas Sylvius Piccolomini), he described the college of cardinals as the embodiment of the consent of the church.[17] Even in the pro-papal letter that he wrote in 1442 to Rodrigo Sanchez de Arevalo, later used by post-Reformation defenders of the papacy like St. Robert Bellarmine, he maintains an emergency power for the church against an erring pope. While he describes the church as the "unfolding" (*explicatio*) of Peter and views the various church offices as particular expressions of a power contained (*complicata*) in its fullness in the pope, he still asserts that the power to govern the church was given by Christ to both the pope and bishops, the successors of Peter and the other apostles, and says that if the pope violates "the statutes of the holy fathers" thus "exceeding the limits of his authority," the church can "withdraw" from him.[18]

In fact this limitation was nearly meaningless. The cardinals continued to be named by the pope. After the Council of Ferrara–Florence in 1438–1439 that briefly reunited the Eastern and Western churches, no councils were held for the rest of the century. A dwindling number of participants in the Basel Council continued to meet until 1449 and even elected an anti-pope, but they were gradually

---

[16] For analysis of the arguments at the Reichstag, see Sigmund, *Nicholas of Cusa*, ch. 9 and A. J. Black, *Monarchy and Community: Political Ideas in the Later Conciliar Controversy, 1430–1450*, Cambridge, 1970, part III. Black has also analyzed the arguments at Basel itself in *Council and Commune: The Conciliar Movement and the Fifteenth Century Heritage*, London, 1979. The book devotes major attention to the writings of John of Segovia, but includes a discussion of Cusanus' role (pp. 51–57).

[17] The *Reformatio generalis* is printed in Stephan Ehses, "Der Reformentwurf des Kardinals Nikolaus Cusanus," *Historisches Jahrbuch*, XXXII (1911), pp. 281–297. In his reform proposal, Nicholas calls the cardinals the representatives (*legati*) of the "nations" (not, as in the *Catholic Concordance* the church provinces) who give the consent of the faithful to the election of the pope and form the daily full council of the church. Aeneas Sylvius' diary also records a confrontation between himself as pope and Nicholas over the naming of new cardinals without securing the consent of the present membership, a procedure which Nicholas said was contrary to the decrees of the Council of Constance. See Leona C. Gabel (ed.), *Memoirs of a Renaissance Pope*, New York, 1959, p. 228.

[18] *Epistola Nicolai de Cusa ad Rodericum de Trevino*, Appendix 3, in Gerhard Kallen (ed.), "De Auctoritate Presidendi in Concilio" (Cusanus-Texte), in *Sitzungsberichte der Heidelberger Akademie der Wissenschaften*, Philosophisch-historische Klasse, 1935–1936, no. 3, Heidelberg, 1935, pp. 110–111.

abandoned by most of Christendom. After the union with the Greeks in 1439. Pope Eugene IV was able to secure the endorsement at Florence of his bull, *Moyses vir Dei*, which condemned the doctrine of conciliar superiority. The conciliar theory seemed dead.

In fact, however, it was not. The Council of Trent discussed conciliarism and Cardinal Bellarmine quoted Nicholas. Appeals to the council were still made by the French church, and the Gallicanist theory as expressed in the writings of John Major in the sixteenth century, and of Bossuet a century later continued to assert conciliar supremacy over the Pope. The example of the actions and claims of Constance and Basel were not lost on later proponents of parliamentary supremacy in seventeenth century England.[19] Aside from some isolated references to his argument against the Donation of Constantine, however, Nicholas of Cusa's political writings were not directly influential on later theorists although there is a link to John Locke by way of the constitutionalist writings of George Lawson whose *Politica sacra et civilis* (1659) mentions "Cusanus" favorably.[20] Only in recent times, in connection with the renewed constitutional discussions within the Roman Catholic church during and after the Second Vatican Council, has his theory been used to argue for reforms such as the synod of bishops and the increased participation of laymen in church decisions.

The transition to modern constitutionalism

To the student of the history of political thought, the thinking of Nicholas of Cusa, the greatest of the conciliar theorists, is of continu-

---

[19] See Francis Oakley, "On the Road from Constance to 1688," *Journal of British Studies*, I (1966), 1–31, reprinted in *Natural Law, Conciliarism, and Consent*, London, 1984; Paul E. Sigmund, "Konzilsidee und Kollegialität nach Cusanus," *MFCG*, v (1965), 86–97, and Sigmund, "Das Fortleben des Nikolaus von Kues in der Geschichte des Politischen Denkens," *MFCG*, vii (1969), 120–128; Black, *Council and Commune*, ch. 16, and Brian Tierney, *Religion, Law and the Growth of Constitutional Thought, 1150–1650*, Cambridge, 1982, pp. 81, 97–98.

[20] Lawson only knew Cusanus indirectly as one of several conciliar theorists. Locke read Lawson's *Politica* in 1679, shortly before he began to write the *Two Treatises*. It included an argument from community consent similar to that of Locke. See Julian H. Franklin, *John Locke and the Theory of Sovereignty*, Cambridge, 1978, chs. 3–4. However, see Conal Condren, *George Lawson's Politica and the English Revolution*, Cambridge, 1989, who analyzes the important differences between the two theories on such topics as majority rule, individual consent, revolution, and property (pp. 181ff) and dismisses Franklin's claim that Locke "found" his central argument "ready-made" in Lawson as "sheer fantasy" (p. 5).

ing interest. It is the expression of a fascinating transitional period in political thought and practice. For the first time the considerable theoretical limits that medieval constitutionalism placed on the ruler were given concrete institutional expression. A political theory was developed to defend those institutions, and the aspiration of medieval Christendom to the rule of law was given a political application that moved it in the direction of modern constitutionalism and even of a version of the separation of powers.[21] The doctrine of original freedom and equality that had been asserted by the Stoics and given a Christian interpretation by the church fathers became in Nicholas of Cusa's theory something more than a part of the myth of a lost golden age. It was made the justification for continuing consent through permanent representative institutions. The theory of natural law that was part of the common heritage of the West began to acquire in his thought the critical role that was so important in its later development. In the *Catholic Concordance* this role was reformist rather than revolutionary, but this marked a shift from an earlier stage when natural law was used mainly to justify existing political and social arrangements.

The same kind of shift in the meaning and application of generally accepted terms takes place in Nicholas' theory of representation. However strong the religious and traditional justifications for his authority, the ruler had always been regarded as in some sense the representative of his people. The law too was viewed as inhering in the people as a whole and even in the early Middle Ages, the inquest was used to find out what the law of a given locality or group was. In Nicholas' theory, however, the people must give their consent – usually, but not always, implicitly – to their rulers, and the foundations were laid for the belief that legislatures can make legally binding new legislation through representatives who are responsible to the geographical or corporate group that has elected them.[22]

Moreover, these legislative bodies were to meet on a regular or continuing basis. The conciliar structure outlined by Nicholas was

---

[21] See II, 13, no. 123 and 14, nos. 129–130 on the separation of legislation and adjudication, and II, 15, no. 137 on papal subordination to conciliar legislation. Note, however, that the pope participates in church legislation as a member of the council (II, 15, no. 137).

[22] On the development of "proctorial" representation in the late Middle Ages, see Gaines Post, *Studies in Medieval Legal Thought*, ch. 3. On the late medieval basis of modern constitutionalism, see Quentin Skinner, *The Foundations of Modern Political Thought*, Cambridge, 1978, II, ch. 4.

not merely an emergency procedure but an integral part of the government of church and state. In the church, universal councils were to be held at least every ten years in accordance with the decree, *Frequens*, of the Council of Constance, and a representative and permanent college of cardinals in Rome was to limit the exercise of papal power. In the empire, the Reichstag, annual smaller meetings of the electors and judges, and a daily council of advisors were all part of Nicholas' scheme for constitutionalizing the exercise of power. It took three centuries for popular participation to be institutionalized in the temporal sphere and over half a millennium for it to become part of the constitution of the Catholic Church. (See the discussions at the Second Vatican Council of the role of "the people of God.") Nicholas' proposals were a remarkable anticipation of later developments in both realms.

He also saw a need for the decentralization of authority in the church. Thus, the bishops had an autonomous, not derivative, role; judicial appeals were to go no further than the church provinces or patriarchates (II, 31, no. 227); and legislation was to be adopted by decentralized diocesan, provincial, or national councils. He did not deal with the problems of federalism as we have seen them in the subsequent political evolution of the West but he clearly saw the advantages of a balance between centralization and decentralization in decision-making.

Since his theory is more constitutionalist than democratic it is something of an exaggeration to describe Nicholas of Cusa as Gierke does as "among the leading champions of popular sovereignty."[23] Nicholas' belief that the emperor backed by coercive force could be the agent of reform in the secular sphere foreshadowed his shift to the side of the papacy after he recognized that a deeply-divided council, however lofty its goals, could not carry out the needed reforms in the church. A strong ruler working in cooperation with a corporately-organized legislature was his chosen agent of ordered reform – not a populist omnicompetent body bent on subordinating the executive to its will, as the Council of Basel was threatening to become. The latter group could not have the unity, the determination, or the resources to carry out the reform within the framework of orthodoxy that Nicholas desired. Western Europe at the beginning of the modern period, like

---

[23] Otto von Gierke, *The Development of Political Theory*, trans. Bernard Freyd, New York, 1939, p. 149.

parts of the third world today, found authoritarian solutions more efficient than democratic ones and the movement in Nicholas of Cusa's political thought from a qualified conciliarism to a qualified papal absolutism helps to explain why this was the case.

There is a curious ambiguity in Nicholas' attitude towards the mass of men. Unlike Marsilius who has a certain confidence, based perhaps on his experience in the Italian city-state, in the soundness of the judgment of the ordinary man, Nicholas describes him as stupid, inclined to evil, and generally irrational in his decisions.[24] To support his view he quotes the Book of Ecclesiastes in the Old Testament, and it may be that the doctrine of Original Sin also has something to do with his attitude. Yet there is another religiously-inspired attitude in his thought that makes him more optimistic – his belief in the harmonious order of the universe as created by God, and in the continuing action of Divine Providence to assure that that harmony can make itself known. Thus, he believes that the less intelligent will accept the suggestions of their betters by a "certain natural instinct"; that "where two or three are gathered together, Christ is in their midst" (II, 3, no. 77, and II, 19, no. 101); and that the Holy Spirit will ensure that valid church councils will come to harmonious agreement on the truth.

This ambiguous attitude has been present throughout the history of Christian thought. Man's inclination to evil has been emphasized by Christian theorists both to justify authoritarian rule or in support of constitutional limitations on power. Yet the Christian belief in the action of God guiding the individual or the group to the truth has also inspired men to form self-governing religious communities and sects and it underlies many early attempts at democratic government. Nicholas' thought, here as elsewhere, combines these contradictory elements in a fragile synthesis.

From tradition to modernity

The movements from authoritarian rule to participation in decision-making, from hierarchy to equalitarianism, from implicit consent and virtual representation to the conscious election of responsible

---

[24] "The number of the stupid is infinite" (II, 16, no. 138); "We are drawn to the forbidden and prone to evil from adolescence" (III, 29, no. 454). See also III, preface, nos. 272–275.

representatives, are all part of a broader change in the West from a traditional to a more modern society. Theorists of modernization have defined this process in many ways. They have described it in terms of an increasing rationalization of relationships and thought, the replacement of ascriptive with achievement norms, a movement from status to contract, from dependence to autonomy, from particularism to universalism, and from fragmentation to centralization of authority. The *Catholic Concordance* can be viewed as a theoretical expression of one stage in this process of transition to modernity. Nicholas of Cusa is neither as thoroughly modern as some of his interpreters have made him nor as thoroughly medieval as others have described him. His political thought is indeed a "coincidence of opposites," and, in fact, his synthesis of papal monarchy and conciliar representative institutions remained viable even in his own thinking for only a little over three years. Divine-right monarchy triumphed for a time in church and state but the other part of his theory, the rule of law and regularized participation through representative instititions, became the basis of modern constitutional democracy. We may not have his faith in the possibilities of achieving a "universal concordance" but his attempt to do so combines many of the seemingly contradictory elements in ancient and medieval thought and points towards the new forms that they will take in modern times.

This discussion has been concerned with the interpretation of the complex synthesis that resulted from that attempt to combine opposing elements. It is hoped that making available to a modern audience an analysis and an English translation of the political thought of a writer who died over five hundred years ago "can help toward a deeper understanding of our political traditions in their relevance for the contemporary world."[25] The problems that Nicholas tried to resolve are still with us today. How can legitimate authority be reconciled with individual freedom? What is the proper balance between centralized and decentralized institutions and how can individuals and groups participate in decisions that affect their welfare? How can the relationship between religion and politics best be understood and given institutional expression? What do the history, tradition, and religious ideas of the West have to contribute to the search for beliefs and institutions adequate to the needs of the

---

[25] Alan Gewirth (trans.), *Marsilius of Padua, The Defender of Peace*, New York, 1956, p. xvii.

contemporary world? Study of the *Catholic Concordance*, like that of other great classics of the history of political thought, can "make us aware of what these unsettled questions are [and] present us with the best fruits of creative minds struggling to arrive at answers."[26] If there is a "Western Political Heritage," the *Catholic Concordance* is an important and original expression of its most central elements in a crucial period at the beginning of the modern age.*

[26] Robert Dahl, *Modern Political Analysis*, Englewood Cliffs, N.J., 1963, p. viii.

* The following chapters are recommended for course assignment: Bk. I, chs. 2, 7, 8, 15–17; Bk. II, chs. 1, 2, 8, 12–19, 21, 33, 34; Bk. III, Preface, chs. 1–6, 25, 29–33, 36–41.

Sources

Acta Cusana, ed. Erich Meuthen and Hermann Hallauer, vol. I, 1 (1401–1437), Hamburg, 1976– , (documentary sources on Cusanus' life).

Cusanus Texte, II, 1, *De auctoritate presidendi in concilio generali*, ed. Gerhard Kallen, in *Sitzungsberichte der Heidelberger Akademie der Wissenschaften*, Philosophisch-historische Klasse, 1935–1936, no. 3, Heidelberg, 1935.

Cusanus Texte, II, 2, *De maioritate auctoritatis sacrorum conciliorum supra auctoritatem papae*, ed. Erich Meuthen, in *Abhandlungen der Heidelberger Akademie der Wissenschaften*, Philosophisch-historische Klasse, 1977, no. 3, Heidelberg, 1977.

English translation, "On Presidential Authority in the General Council," trans. H. Lawrence Bond, Gerald Christianson, and Thomas M. Izbicki, *Church History*, 59, 1 (March 1990), 19–34.

French translation, Nicolas de Cues, *Concordance catholique*, trans. Roland Galibois, Sherbrooke, Quebec, 1977.

Italian translation in Nicolo Cusano, *Opere religiose*, trans. Pio Gaia, Turin, 1971, "La concordanza universale," pp. 115–546.

Nicolai de Cusa, *Opera omnia*, vol. XIV, *De concordantia catholica*, ed. Gerhard Kallen, Hamburg, Book I, 1964; Book II, 1965; Book III, 1959. Indices (with Ann Berger), 1968.

Select bibliography

Bett, Henry. *Nicholas of Cusa*. London, 1932.

Biechler, James E. "Nicholas of Cusa and the End of the Conciliar Movement: A Humanist Crisis of Identity." *Church History*, 44, 1 (March 1975), 5–21.

Black, Antony. *Council and Commune: The Conciliar Movement and the Fifteenth Century Heritage*. London, 1979.

Crowder, C. N. D. (ed. and trans.). *Unity, Heresy, and Reform: The Conciliar Response to the Great Schism*. London, 1977.

Gill, Joseph. *Constance et Bâle-Florence*. Paris, 1985.

Heinz-Mohr, Gerd. *Unitas Christiana*. Trier, 1958.

Helmroth, Johannes. *Das Basler Konzil, 1431–1449*. Cologne, 1987.

Krämer, Werner. *Konsens und Rezeption: Verfassungsprinzipien der Kirche im Basler Konziliarismus*. Münster, 1980.

Jacob, E. F. *Essays in Late Medieval History*, New York, 1968, chs. 5–6.

Meuthen, Erich. *Das Trierer Schisma von 1430 auf dem Basler Konzil*. Münster, 1964.

Nikolaus von Kues, 1401–1464, Skizze einer Biographie. 6th edn, Münster, 1982.

Oakley, Francis. *Natural Law, Conciliarism, and Consent*. London, 1984.

Posch, Andreas. *Die "Concordantia Catholica" des Nikolaus von Cues*. Paderborn, 1930.

Sieben, Herman Josef. "Der Konzilstraktat des Nikolaus von Kues: De Concordantia Catholica." *Annuarium Historiae Conciliorum*, 14, 1 (1982), 171–226.

Traktate und Theorien zum Konzil. Frankfurt, 1983.

Sigmund, Paul E. "Cusanus Concordantia: A Reinterpretation." *Political Studies*, 10, 2 (June 1962), 180–197.

Nicholas of Cusa and Medieval Political Thought. Cambridge, Mass., 1963.

Stieber, Joachim W. *Pope Eugenius IV*. Leiden, 1978.

Tierney, Brian. *Foundations of Conciliar Theory*. Cambridge, 1955.

Religion, Law, and the Growth of Constitutional Thought (1150–1650). Cambridge, 1982, ch. 3.

Vagedes, Arnolf. *Das Konzil über dem Papst?* 2 vols., Paderborn, 1981.

Vansteenberghe, Edmond. *Le Cardinal Nicolas de Cues*. Paris, 1920.

Watanabe, Morimichi. *The Political Ideas of Nicholas of Cusa with Special Reference to his De Concordantia Catholica*. Geneva, 1963.

"The Episcopal Election of 1430 in Trier and Nicholas of Cusa." *Church History*, 39, 3 (1970), 299–316.

For further bibliographies and current research consult the publication of the Cusanus Gesellschaft, *Mitteilungen und Forschungsbeiträge der Cusanus-Gesellschaft* (1961ff.) and the American Cusanus Society, *Newsletter* (1984ff.).

Chronology

1387–1417   Great Schism. As a result of a disputed election after the return of the papacy from Avignon to Rome there are two and, after 1409, three claimants to the papal throne.

1401   Nicholas Krebs (Cryfftz) born in Kues (Latin–Cusa) on the Moselle river near Trier.

1414–1418   The Council of Constance meets to end the schism. In 1415 adopts decree, *Haec sancta*, asserting conciliar supremacy in "matters of faith, extirpation of schism, and reform of the church in head and members." In 1417, council votes to meet at regular intervals in the future, one claimant to the papacy resigns, two are deposed, and the council elects Martin V as pope.

1416   Nicholas registers at the University of Heidelberg as "Nycolaus Cancer de Coesse," identified as "a cleric from the diocese of Trier." (Cusanus was in minor orders and was not ordained as a priest for another twenty years.)

1417–1423   Studies canon law at the University of Padua, receiving degree of *doctor decretorum*.

1423–1424   Council of Siena meets and adjourns, calling for another council in seven years.

1424   Cusanus visits Rome for the first time.

1425   Registers at University of Cologne as doctor in canon law. Teaches canon law and studies philosophy.

1426   Practices law in archdiocese of Trier.

1427	Italian humanists write of the discovery of classical manuscripts in Cologne cathedral library by "Nicholas of Trier" (Nicolaus Treverensis). Travels to Rome as secretary of the Archbishop of Trier where he obtains papal grants, confirmations, and dispensations allowing him to hold several benefices in the archdiocese of Trier, which carry endowed income. Henceforth he identifies himself as "dean of the church of St. Florin in Koblenz."
1428	University of Louvain offers Cusanus professorship of canon law which he declines. Offer repeated in 1435.
1429	Travels to Rome, bringing eleventh-century manuscript of sixteen plays of Plautus, now in Vatican library.
1430	Nicholas returns to Trier after the death of the archbishop, becomes chancellor of Ulrich von Manderscheid, a candidate for the archbishopric. Disputed election appealed to pope, who appoints an outsider, Raban, bishop of Speyer, as archbishop. Cathedral chapter elects Ulrich, with Nicholas as witness.
1431	Nicholas submits appeal to meeting of the Reichstag on behalf of Ulrich's candidacy, citing "divine and natural law" and "the will of the clergy and people" (Meuthen, *Acta Cusana* I, 41 and 43). Church Council opens in Basel to consider church reform and the Hussite heresy.
1432	On February 29, Nicholas is formally incorporated in the council to argue Ulrich's appeal of the papal decision. He is appointed to the Committee for the Faith.
1443	From February until April, Cusanus is involved in discussions with the Hussites (Bohemians) on the reception of the Eucharist under two species, leading to his treatise, *Opusculum contra Bohemorum errorem: De usu communionis.* In April he writes a legal brief on the supremacy of the council over the pope, *De maioritate concilii.* In mid-year writes *Libellus de ecclesiastica concordantia*, later incorporated as Book I and part of Book II of *De concordantia.* Late in the year he completes *De concordantia catholica*, submitting it to the council in December or January.
1434	In February, writes treatise *On the Authority of the President in a General Council* (*De auctoritate presidendi*).

1435	Council forbids payment of annates and other taxes to Rome.
1436'	Discussions at Basel with representatives of the Greek church on the site of a proposed union council. Nicholas votes for a site "favored by the pope and the Greeks."
1437	Council majority insists on Basel or Avignon, with the minority including Cusanus favoring a location in Italy. On May 20 along with other members of the defeated minority Cusanus goes to Bologna, is appointed by the pope as a member of the papal delegation to Constantinople, and negotiates the participation of the Byzantine emperor and representatives of the Greek church in a union council in Italy.
1438–1439	Council of Ferrara–Florence negotiates unification of Eastern and Western churches (immediately repudiated in Constantinople) and condemns doctrine of conciliar supremacy.
1439–1447	Nicholas argues the papal side against the representatives of the council at the meetings of the German Reichstag.
1439	Nicholas publishes his best-known work, *On Learned Ignorance* (*De docta ignorantia*).
1448	Reichstag and princes support the papal side, leading to 1449 vote by remaining participants to dissolve rump council at Basel. Nicholas is named cardinal of the Church of St. Peter in Chains in Rome.
1450	Nicholas named Bishop of Brixen (Bressanone) in the Tyrol. Sent on reform mission in Germany.
1452–1460	In Brixen, involved in continual conflicts with Sigismund, Duke of the Tyrol.
1453	Publishes *De pace fidei* (*On Peace in Faith*) – arguing possibilities of agreement among the principal religions.
1460	Submits reform proposal to Pope Pius II, calling for elective college of cardinals representing the "nations" of Christendom.
1464	Dies in Rome. His body is buried in the Church of St. Peter in Chains, his heart in front of the altar of the chapel

at Kues, built at his instruction along with a library for his books and a home for the aged. Still functioning today, it is probably the oldest private foundation in Europe.

Abbreviations

Hinschius   Hinschius, Paulus (ed.), *Decretales Pseudo-Isidoriana*, Leipzig, 1863.

Jaffe   Jaffe, Philip (ed.), *Regista Pontificum Romanorum*, Leipzig, 1885.

Kallen, *OCC*   Nicolai de Cusa, *Opera omnia*, vol. xiv, *De concordantia catholica libri tres*, Gerhard Kallen (ed.), Hamburg, 1959–68.

Mansi   Mansi, J. D. (ed.), *Sacrorum conciliorum nova et ampliissima collectio*, Florence, 1759.

MG   *Monumenta Germaniae Historica*.

PG   Migne, J. P. (ed.), *Patrologia Graeca*, Paris, 1857.

PL   Migne, J. P. (ed.), *Patrologia Latina*, Paris, 1844.

The Catholic Concordance

1. The matters being debated by this holy Council of Basel – which might easily be considered novel by those who when doubts arise rely unquestioningly on modern writers – demand that we make known some of the learning of the ancient authors, long neglected by those who are experiencing our current difficulties, and that we demonstrate the superior qualities of our more enlightened forebears. The discord that has arisen has produced this work by the action of heaven, overcoming our natural disposition and lack of preparation or previous notice.

2. Who, I ask, would not have been surprised, a few years ago, at the events which we have now seen that have demonstrated the great power of the universal councils – so long dormant, to the detriment of the public good and the orthodox faith? But we see that the past is being sought once more by those who pursue all the liberal and mechanical arts. As if the wheel had come full circle, we eagerly return to the weighty opinions of those authors. We see that all are delighted at the eloquence and style of ancient letters. This is especially true of the Italians who, not satisfied with the literary excellence that is appropriate to their nature as Latins, devote great effort, following in the footsteps of their ancestors, to the writings of the Greeks. We Germans, however, although not far behind in native ability, must – because of the different position of the stars, not through our own fault – defer to others in the pleasing exercise of eloquence – since we are able to speak Latin correctly only with great effort, overcoming, as it were, the force of nature.

Other nations should not be surprised to read in the documents quoted below things that they have not heard before. For I have collected many original sources that have long been lost in the armories of ancient cloisters. Those who read these things therefore should be aware that they have been quoted here from the ancient originals rather than from some abbreviated collection. I ask that my uncultivated style not deter anyone from reading, for an open and clear meaning, humbly expressed without disguise, is more easily understood even if it is less appealing. Nevertheless I hope that this collection will be pleasing to all, especially, however, to the participants in this holy Council, and in particular to you, Sigismund, our invincible emperor crowned by the will of God, as well as to the worthy Cardinal Giuliano [Cesarini], the most gentle [papal] legate to our nation. If this work is approved by two such lofty authorities, no one would be justified in rejecting what they have endorsed.

3. In my treatise on the Catholic concordance, I believe that it is necessary to examine that union of faithful people that is called the Catholic Church, as well as the parts that together make up that church – i.e., its soul and body. Therefore we will consider first the church itself as a composite whole, then its soul, the holy priesthood, and thirdly its body, the holy empire. And everything will be studied on the basis of ancient approved sources, as necessary to understand the substance, the nature, and the combinations and joinings of its members, so that we can know the sweet harmonious concordance that produces eternal salvation and the safety of the commonwealth.

BOOK I

BOOK I

THE CHURCH IS A CONCORDANCE OF ALL RATIONAL SPIRITS UNITED IN SWEET HARMONY WITH CHRIST, THE WAY, THE TRUTH, AND THE LIFE, WHO IS THE SPOUSE OF THE CHURCH

4. Since anyone endowed with the slightest intelligence can draw the proper conclusions if he knows the basic principles, I will begin with a few words concerning the underlying divine harmony in the church. Concordance is the principle by which the Catholic Church is in harmony as one and many – in one Lord and many subjects.[1] Flowing from the one King of Peace with infinite concordance, a sweet spiritual harmony of agreement emanates in successive degrees to all its members who are subordinated and united to him. Thus one God is all things in all things.[2] From the beginning we have been predestined for that marvelous harmonious peace belonging to the adopted sons of God through Jesus Christ who came down from heaven to bring all things to fulfillment.

5. The Apostle [Paul] writing to the Ephesians demonstrates this when he says at the beginning that a man shall leave his father and mother and cleave to his wife and they shall be two in one flesh.[3] This is a sacrament [which symbolizes the union] of Christ and the church. If then the union of Adam and Eve is a great sacrament in Christ and the church it is certain that just as Eve was bone of the bone of her husband and flesh of his flesh so also the church is made up of the members of Christ, bone of his bone and flesh of his flesh. Thus Ambrose in Letter XVI *To Irenaeus* praises this epistle of Paul, "No

---

[1] For the source of this definition in Ramon Llull, *Ars Generalis*, see Paul. E. Sigmund, *Nicholas of Cusa and Medieval Political Thought*, Cambridge, Mass.: Harvard University Press, 1963, p. 61.

[2] 1 Cor. 15:28.

[3] Eph. 1:15.

5

epistle has bestowed such blessings on the people of God as this one." And he says that Christ sits at the right hand of the Father and we all "will not only sit but will be seated together with Christ as his flesh in heaven." But in order for us to achieve that union of eternal harmony in faith, he has set up a concordance of the different grades in the church "making some apostles, others bishops, others teachers . . ." so that each one "united in faith and knowledge may be in touch with the head so that, so to speak, every member is present in Christ who is head of all. From him one body of the faithful, united and joined in rational harmony with the Word in every branch of the ministry, helps to increase his body proportionately in charity so as to produce one temple and one spiritual dwelling-place for all. Here I think we are to understand that there is a union in faith and the spirit, not only of the saints but of all the faithful and of all the heavenly hosts and powers so that by a certain concordance of powers and ministries one body made up of all spirits of a rational nature adheres to Christ, their head, forming the framework of the church edifice in such a way that the links between the individual adherents are not perceived by the senses."[4] This and other excellent things are said by Ambrose above. Jerome agrees in the next to the last section of his letter *To Algasia*, and in his letter, *On Monogamy*, he says: "Eve signifies the church, because she is the mother of all the living; Adam signifies Christ; their marriage is a spiritual union. Christ is the head of the woman, and the woman, that is the church, is formed from the side of the man and is flesh of his flesh."[5] There are many writings of the saints on this subject that I think I must omit for the sake of brevity.

6.   And since it is very evident that every living being has been created in harmony [*concordantia*], so also in the divine Essence where life and existence are one and completely equal there is a most infinite concordance because no opposition can be present where there is eternal life. But every concordance is made up of differences. And the less opposition there is among these differences, the greater the concordance and the longer the life. And therefore life is everlasting where there is no opposition. On this basis you can perceive the basic principles of the most holy Trinity and Unity because it is a unity in

[4] See St. Ambrose, *Letters*, trans. Sister Mary Melchior Beyenka O.P. New York: Fathers of the Church, 1954, no. 85, pp. 476–480.
[5] Cf. PL 22, pp. 1031 and 1053.

trinity and a trinity in unity, and there is no opposition internally since whatever the Father is, so also are the Son and the Holy Spirit. Behold the ineffable concordance that exists in a God who is three-fold and unitary. From it anyone who wishes to study further the way in which all the perfections that can be asserted or thought of God exist in the greatest concordance of one essence and three persons can derive the most lofty and incomprehensible truth to be seen with the eyes of the intellect.

7. Since this concordance is highest truth itself – but this is not our principal subject – it is sufficient to cite the comment of Albertus Magnus on the words, "Thou art Christ, the Son of the living God" (Matt. 16) that "the Father is the source of life, which is channeled through the Son and flows to all things in the Holy Spirit."[6] For in the unity of the spirit there is a marriage between Christ and the church. As Cyprian says in *On the Unity of the Church*, "Whoever wishes to have God as his father can not be born again to life except through the Church, the mother of all living men."[7] Then, since he is united in spirit to Christ, he is a member of Christ and with our adherence and agreement, Christ transforms each of us according to our rank. As Augustine says to Consentius concerning the Trinity, "God, since he is life itself, gives us life when we are in some manner made sharers in him. Since he is justice itself, he brings forth justice in us when we live justly in adherence to him, and we are more or less just in proportion as we adhere more or less to him. Therefore it is written of the only-begotten Son of God that as he possesses the wisdom and justice of the Father always in him, he has become for us the wisdom and justice and holiness and redemption of God. Accordingly it is written, 'He that glorieth in himself let him glory in the Lord.' "[8]

8. In summary therefore, we may say that Christ is the way, the truth, and the life, and the head of all creatures, the husband or spouse of the church, which is constituted in a concordance of all rational creatures – with him as the One, and among themselves, the many – in various [hierarchical] gradations.

[6] Albertus Magnus, *Commentarius in Matthaeum, 16:18* in August Bourgnet (ed.), *Alberti Magni Opera omnia*, Paris, 1890, 20, p. 638.
[7] St. Cyprian, *De unitate ecclesiae*, ch. 6 (PL 4, p. 519).
[8] St. Augustine, *Ad Consentium* (PL 33, p. 461).

CHAPTER II

THE RELATION OF THE MEMBERS OF THE CHURCH
TO CHRIST IS ONE OF DIFFERENT GRADATIONS.
THIS IS ILLUSTRATED BY THE EXAMPLE USED BY
SAINT AMBROSE OF A MAGNETIC STONE AND THE
ARRANGEMENT OF IRON RINGS THAT ARE
ATTRACTED TO IT. THE HIERARCHICAL ORDER [OF
THE CHURCH] IS ANALYZED ON THIS BASIS.

9.   Now let us investigate more closely how we should understand this fundamental principle, that the church is organized on the basis of union with Christ. First, all things in creation flow from one eternal and perfectly simple God and reflect him in varied ways and in different degrees of perfection. The highest first created things [angels] participate symbolically in the First Principle through a certain God-revealing concordance. However, since a finite creature is incapable of concordance with the infinite they are infinitely removed from the original infinite concordant essence in which the Son is the image and splendor of the Father and three persons are one God, the eternal Light. Nevertheless it [the angelic rank] is the highest in its own mode of existence since it adheres to the Supreme Being and is self-directing, and it exceeds other created things to the degree that it resembles the uncreated simple Infinite Being. From here, by an emanation of their nature, they transmit a lesser degree of the [divine] likeness, and the lower levels of creation are hierarchically ordered, so to speak, as shadows, figures, or likenesses of the preceding higher natures. At last this process of multiplication into lower and less worthy beings exhausts its life-giving force, coming to rest at a final point, with no remaining power but only enough for itself which it is unable to communicate further. And so the last member of that order ends in darkness. And such is the gradation from the Infinite down to nothingness, that all the intermediate gradations depend on the First Principle and nothing in the whole hierarchical order can be carried out by intermediaries except through the action of the originating Principle.

10.   To illustrate my point I shall cite the example that Ambrose gives in his letter to Sabinus.[1] To explain the decline of human nature

[1] St. Ambrose, *Ad Sabinum* (PL 16, p. 1193).

8

in subsequent generations, he gives the example of a magnetic stone which has such power to draw iron to it that it transmits its magnetism to that material so that if one carries out an experiment in which several iron rings are brought near that stone, it holds them all in the same way. Then if you should move another ring next to the one that is held to the stone and place the individual rings in order, while the natural attraction of the stone holds them all in order, it attracts the ones that are nearer more strongly, and those further away less intensely. Thus I think of the Word from above as like a magnetic stone the power of which extends through everything down to the lowest being. Its infinite power is not lacking down through the ranks, but there is a marvelous order of interconnection among finite and limited creatures.

11. In the overall order, all created things demonstrate the Trinity, since they are either spiritual, corporeal, or mixed. Spiritual things are divided into three orders and each order is divided into three choirs, so that throughout the heavenly choirs of angels there is a hierarchical unity and the sign of the Trinity – a unity in trinity and trinity in unity. And so who can capture the hierarchical subdivisions in each choir from the highest to the lowest angel, and then within each angel in terms of its constitutive principles?[2] If you look further, you can find this hierarchy repeated in its own way in corporeal nature – as three orders with three choirs in each. Just as the highest sphere in this hierarchy, the prime mover or ninth sphere, is like the shadow of the lowest angel, so the earth is its lowest reflection – the basest of the elements. There is also a third or mixed type of nature which is modeled on the others because it is composed of the rational, the sensate, or the vegetative, and in this there are also orders and choirs as among the angels. And [the realm of] the elements is the shadow of this hierarchy. We will discuss this elsewhere.

12. These matters are important because the investigation of all things in nature and the whole of creation depends on them. For when the concordance of differences in the whole universe is

---

[2] Cf. Dionysius the Areopagite, *The Ecclesiastical Hierarchy*, I, 3; *The Celestial Hierarchy*, 4, 2, translated in Pseudo-Dionysius, *Complete Works*, New York: Paulist Press, 1987. Many medieval writers including St. Bonaventure and Hugh of St. Victor, as well as Peter Lombard, *The Sentences*, spoke of the nine choirs of angels. For discussion by Nicholas of Cusa before the composition of the Concordantia, see his Christmas 1430 sermon printed in Nicolai de Cusa, *Opera omnia*, XVI, I, *Sermones* I, *1430–1441*, Fasc. I, Sermo I, no. 14, citing Dionysius.

examined, wise men perceive that there is a marvelous combination in nature, the whole world shares in a mutual spherical interaction, and everything is ordered to a single end. Suffice it for our present investigation to know that as all created things are constituted as such from created beginnings in a certain graded similarity to the First [Principle] and are preserved in union and harmony with their natural originating source, the church which is our subject is made up of the rational spirits [angels] and men who are united with Christ – although not all in the same way but hierarchically, as is evident from the example of the magnet.

CHAPTER III

FROM THE BEGINNING TO THE END OF TIME THE CHURCH IS ONE AS CHRIST IS ONE. CHRIST WHO ALONE IS THE TRUTH IS EXPRESSED IN VARIOUS SCRIPTURES, SIGNS, AND SACRIFICES APPROPRIATE TO THE TIME AND PLACE, ALTHOUGH IN A CLEARER MANNER AT ONE TIME THAN ANOTHER. THE MEMBERS OF [THE BODY OF] CHRIST WERE ENDOWED WITH INCREASING HOLINESS AND TRUTH UNTIL THE COMING OF CHRIST. FROM THEN UNTIL THE END OF THE WORLD, THEY HAVE SUCCESSIVELY BEEN OF LESS HOLINESS AND TRUTH. PARADISE SIGNIFIES THE REIGN OF THE CHURCH.

13. Now it is indicated above by Ambrose that the holy church which blessed Paul calls the heavenly Jerusalem, our mother, the lasting city established by God, a house not built with hands, consists of angels and men.[1] Part of the church reigns now with God in heaven, being made up of men who in different ranks enjoy the society of the angels. Part, however, is a wayfarer in various ranks on earth and aspires to the society above where there is a tabernacle not made by hands nor of this creation which is the model of the

---

[1] St. Paul, Galatians 4:26; Hebrews 13:14; II Cor. 5:1.

tabernacle made by Moses when God commanded him to do all things as he directed him on the mountain. And in this true tabernacle in heaven which God and not man has made, the Highest Bishop of our faith, the Eternal Pontiff in an everlasting priesthood, the High Priest according to the order of Melchisedech, has entered behind the veil, that is into heaven itself, by shedding his own blood to obtain a holy and eternal redemption.[2] He sits at the right hand of the Father in the glory of the Father's majesty and intercedes for us not with words but in acts of mercy. The King of Kings and Lord of Lords through whom kings reign and legislators determine what is just, rules a heavenly and earthly government – indeed the whole universe, whether a spiritual realm in heaven or a temporal realm on earth. He disposes and directs it in its various orders and he rules over a heavenly and earthly court. In accord with the needs of the times he assigns their duties to angels and men in a wondrous order and decrees what is to be done at each time whether by private inspiration or more public direction.

14. The holy doctors demonstrate in many passages that when the soul feeds on the food of wisdom it becomes a sharer in the divine nature.[3] For the Son is the Wisdom of the Father. And as Ambrose writes in his twelfth letter to Irenaeus, God revealed this Faith in Christ through the prophets and the apostles and the treasure of his scriptures, so that we might know here by faith and there see face to face.[4] There is more on this subject in that letter. Likewise Augustine in the second question of his *Letter to Deogratias* in which he speaks at length about the problem of the diversity of sacrificial rites, says that the one Christ is thus expressed in different sacrificial ceremonies in accordance with the time and place just as the same idea is expressed in a variety of languages.[5] And this variety was established and commanded for the salvation of men by God who is never lacking in justice and goodness to mortals. For one and the same religion is observed at one time by some customs and signs, at other times by others, earlier in a more hidden fashion and later more openly, earlier by a few and later by a larger number. Hence, as he adds on the same subject in the third question, there was a gradation among these

---

[2] Hebrews 7:9.   [3] 2 Peter 1:4.
[4] Galatians 3:26 in St. Ambrose, *Ad Horontianum* (PL 16, p. 1126).
[5] St. Augustine, *Ad Deogratias, Letters of St. Augustine*, trans. Sister W. Parsons, New York: Fathers of the Church, 1953, II, pp. 158ff.

sacrifices because the first ones were like foreshadowings and the later ones like figures of Christ who was truth. And, as was pointed out in the preceding chapter, since all created things exist because of Christ and for him and the one world is filled with the one God who is the Word Incarnate, from the beginning, perhaps his [Christ's] coming was revealed by degrees in sacrificial rituals and through the increasingly clear light of the prophecies of men. John [the Baptist] who pointed him out with his finger from among the sons of women was the most holy prophet before him, and the apostles followed after him. And as there was a gradation from Christ, true God and man, back to the first man at the beginning of time, so will it be from his time until the end. And Augustine [writing] *To Hesychius On the Last Day* says: "Although there have always been bad men, there will be many more as we approach the end. But we know that evil men now abound among us, and after this they will be even more in evidence and they will be everywhere when the end is at hand that will not be known beforehand ... But we know that we act as apostles in the world today, but much more so those who preceded us and we more than those who follow after us until those come who, if we may use the expression, will be the last of the last."[6]

15. And this is the essential truth – nothing else is shown in signs and sacrifices in all the scriptures but God and the Word made flesh which was crucified for us. Paul knew this alone, and we are invited to believe this in faith, so that we may cry out in spirit and in faith as adopted sons of God in the church, "Abba, Father," and may be as sons of God when we all rise again incorrupt, and see face to face that Eternal Light of which Ambrose writes at greater length in his 23rd letter, to Irenaeus. For, as he likewise writes in his 30th letter, to the same person, just as it was appropriate that man was made last among created animals as the end of nature, "so among men the end of the Law is Christ for the justification of everyone who believes. And thus we are as beasts of burden in the contemplation of the Lord, as the Prophet says, 'I have been considered as a beast of burden before Thee.' "[7]

16. Thus he is the Good Shepherd and we are the sheep of his flock.[8] And this is our fundamental premise – that the Word is the wisdom of Father, and wisdom is life (Proverbs 8). Thus every

[6] St. Augustine, *Ad Hesychium* (PL 33, p. 913).
[7] St. Ambrose, *Ad Horontianum* (PL 16, pp. 1126 and 1184).   [8] John 10–14.

rational creature that has been or will be on earth must adhere to the Word, and sin which was the cause of death both among the angels and men was contrary to the wisdom of God. For the angel who wished to be like the Most High raised himself up against wisdom. And the same was true of man, who wished to be like gods in the knowledge of good and evil. And so for all of human nature since the fall, life comes from adherence to faith in the mediator, the Incarnate Word.

17. Hence it is not inappropriate to consider that Paradise as God created it in the beginning was a symbol of the reign of the church, for in its center was the tree of life which would have offered unfailing life to rational creatures in heaven and on earth. From the beginning the unfailing fountain of the Holy Spirit that nourishes the Church flowed over its roots and that fertile tree always bore the fruit of life to nourish those united to it. But heaven's creature [Adam] opposed this life and turned to the tree of knowledge since he wished to be like the Most High, although not by participation in the wisdom which was from all eternity, since he had desired to know and wished to eat of the Tree of Knowledge. Thus man rejected faith as the way to be like the Most High; he wished to know before he believed.

18. Observe that the wisdom which is life (Proverbs 4) and the life which is Christ, was lost by those creatures. As Ambrose says in *On Faith*: The Son of God is the wisdom of God, "for coming from the heart of the Father, he has opened the hidden secrets of heaven to believers."[9] He says, "to believers," because, as he also writes to Simplicianus, only the Son knows the Father – and those to whom he has revealed him.[10] And no one apprehends the mysteries of heaven without the revelation of the Son. "For the apostles or prophets who have dared to speak of the majesty of God or of heavenly things have done so because of a revelation granted to them." On Christ as wisdom, justice, holiness, fortitude, etc., see St. Jerome as quoted in [the *Decretum*], [C.] 11 q. 3 [c. 84] *existimant*. Hence it is clear how wrong were the earlier spirits and men who attempted to come to life and truth without using that Way. From this we conclude that the Catholic Church is established in union with Christ by faith, for without faith it is impossible to achieve the longed-for eternal glory or the vision of God and the Lord Jesus, the Savior.

---

[9] Phoebadius, *De fide* (PL 20, p. 42) – not Ambrose.
[10] Matthew 11:27 in St. Ambrose, *Letters*, no. 56, p. 3081.

CHAPTER IV

THE CHURCH IS COMPOSED OF THREE PARTS – THE
CHURCH TRIUMPHANT, THE CHURCH SLEEPING,
AND THE CHURCH MILITANT. THE CHURCH
MILITANT MAY BE CONSIDERED IN DIFFERENT
WAYS – EITHER AS LEADING TO THE CHURCH
TRIUMPHANT IN HEAVEN AND THUS MADE UP OF
THE PREDESTINED [FOR SALVATION], OR AS THOSE
UNITED AT THE PRESENT TIME WITH GOD IN FAITH
AND CHARITY, OR ONLY IN FAITH. THE CHURCH
MAY BE COMPARED TO AN ARMY AND TO OTHER
EXAMPLES. THIS IS AN ESPECIALLY VALUABLE
CHAPTER TO ELIMINATE MANY DOUBTS AND
CORRECT ERRORS.

19.   Brevity requires me to speak at less length than I have done at
the outset. And so coming directly to our purpose – to find the
symbolism of the Trinity in the church – we now find that the church
has three orders; namely, the church triumphant [in heaven], the
church sleeping [in purgatory] and the church militant [on earth] and
that every order again is divided into three choirs with many additional threefold gradations in each choir. Passing over the hierarchies
of the church triumphant and sleeping and turning to the church
militant, I think we should consider what [Pope] Leo IX writes in the
37th chapter of his letter against the claims of Michael of Constantinople in which he says: "The very structure of the parts of the body
should teach us about the structure of the church, for it is the Body of
Christ. And the Apostle [Paul] says; 'You are one body, and members
of each other.'[1] And as there are many members in one body but they
all do not perform the same functions, so we are many as one body in
Christ and members individually each of the other." And below: "If
the eye were the whole body, where would the hearing and other
senses be? But in accordance with his will, God has assigned to each
of the individual members of the body their proper function. However
a member that is not content with its function but desires to take over
another disturbs the total order of the body, as if the sight attempted

[1] 1 Cor. 12.

14

to hear sounds or the hearing to see colors. Thus the adornments of some individual members do not suit others but each requires its own and rejects what is unsuitable for it. For the foot refuses the helmet and crown, and the head sandals, and so there is a concordance of differences [*discors concordia*] among them so that each of them absolutely refuses to give over its function to another. They enjoy together the good of one member just as they suffer in common any evil, and they carry out their functions not only for themselves alone but rather for mutual benefit. Thus the Apostle clearly says: 'If one member is glorified, all the members rejoice together'."[2]

20. The above quotation is sufficient along with the one at the beginning of the chapter where speaking to the Patriarch Michael and to the Archdeacon Leo, he [Leo IX] writes: "Let us be one body and spirit, just as we have been called in one hope." From this it is evident that the pope and the patriarchs and all Christians constitute one body in which there are various members – each content with his office so as not to disturb the whole order. Hence in the diversity of members we can perceive the hierarchical order in harmonious unity without which a hierarchy cannot exist, since there must be a concord of one and many, in one head and many members.

21. And – to say a few appropriate words out of the many that could be said – in this body of the church which thus adheres to Christ in the spirit dwells the Spirit which gives life to the whole body and to every member of it. The whole soul is in the whole body and in every one of its parts, as Augustine argues at length [in his letter] to Dardanus, *On the Presence of God*.[3] And therefore this animal body derived from Adam has been made spiritual through regeneration in Christ. In this regeneration, the dead body in Christ has risen as a new more spiritual man like a spotless bride who has been betrothed.[4] In the battle he has achieved victory over death, and a new-risen spiritual incorruptible spouse is brought to an everlasting matrimonial union.

22. It is evident that the body of the church which has these characteristics is made up only of the predestined, for only those called before the establishment of the world will come to that inheritance. And because this decision is unknown to all men – for no one knows

[2] Leo IX, *Ad Michaelem, Patriarcham Constantinopolitanum* (PL 16, p. 1275).
[3] St. Augustine, *Letters*, New York, Fathers of the Church, IV, p. 187.
[4] Eph. 5:27.

whether he is worthy of [God's] hatred or of love[5] – and considering that any believer who does the will of God becomes one in spirit with him by consent and thus contracts a betrothal for a future marriage, we say that the church is made of the predestined [for heaven] and the foreknown [as lost]. For God, since he acts for the best, distributes saving grace to whoever is disposed and capable [of receiving it]. But because not every member of this church militant will succeed in consummating this marriage, man is on trial since by his misdeeds he may lose the final victory over death. The hour of death tells who is predestined and who foreknown. Before that time the foreknown can sometimes be in grace, and the predestined in mortal sin, although one of the foreknown could not have had the grace of God without adhering to the faith. Therefore he is in the church at that time, and in this way all those who are now in the state of grace are considered as members of the church.

23.   We may also consider the church as a faithful bride, obedient to her loftier and nobler part and confined and restrained in order to remain faithful to the bridegroom. And in this way one who constrains his intellect to believe that Christ is God and man, savior etc. is considered to be a member of the church. Hence, according to Augustine in *On the Creed,* man is constituted of spirit, soul, and body, in the image of the Trinity.[6] But the spirit, as the higher, nobler, and more elevated part of the intellect, represents the figure of the Father, and the body, the person of the Son, and the soul, participating as it were in the nature of both [and] proceeding from each, represents the person of the Holy Spirit.

24.   And so the man who subdues his intellectual spirit and believes that Christ is the Way, the Truth, and the Life, is said to be a member of the church even if the spirit has not yet subjected the soul to itself nor through the soul the body. Hence for a man to be a faithful image of the divine Trinity, [and] to achieve that vital concordance his spirit must be perfected through faith, hope, and charity, and joined to the Holy Spirit as its life and truth. His soul must be perfected so that it obeys the spirit which it often resists not by nature but because of a habit of sin so that "the animal nature of man does not perceive the things which come from the spirit of God."[7] And so when the soul obeys the spirit and the spirit obeys Christ, there is no reason not to

---

[5] Ecclesiastes 9:1.   [6] 1 Cor. 2:14.
[7] St. Augustine, *De fide et symbolo* (PL 40, p. 193).

16

hope that the body also will be restored to its own nature at the resurrection so that the whole spiritualized man will be united with God, as Augustine says above.

25. Thus the church militant in that victory which is by faith, is like an army that acknowledges Christ, true God and true man, as its king and emperor, its life and truth, although while they do not think that anyone else can be king, not all the members obey his commands. And although faith without works is dead,[8] no member is cut off while his faith lasts, but there continues to be a connection like that with a withered member, [C.] 1 q. 1 [c. 47] *Sicut urgeri* and [C] 23 q. 7 [c. 4] *Quemadmodum*. Hence it is said that this church is a spotless bride in faith despite the fact that different terms are applied to it because of disobedience in soul and body of many – like a community which, because it has many good and many bad inhabitants is sometimes called totally good, sometimes totally bad, as Paul sometimes calls the Corinthians good and sometimes bad.[9] Paul was a member of the church when he said: "With my mind I serve the law of God; with the flesh, the law of sin."[10] And because God alone is a searcher of hearts, no human judgment about the membership of the church is certain, except that concerning newly baptized infants. But with regard to adults there can be deception, – see Augustine, *On the Correction of the Donatists* where he says that many only appear to be in the church.[11]

26. From this we conclude that the betrothal of Christ to the church militant and to any of its members is like an agreement by the emperor to marry the queen of France while she is queen and ruler of France, on condition that she work to get her kingdom to obey him and to convey it to her spouse – or otherwise the marriage will not take place. Then although the queen remains faithful to her pledge, the marriage does not take place because at some point she does not put down the resistance of the kingdom and bring it back to obedience when she could have done so. For her spouse did not oblige her to do the impossible but asked her to do what was difficult. And the same thing is true in general for the church militant. From here let us move to the explanation of the body described above, and consider its condition.

[8] James 2:17.   [9] 1 Cor. 5:6 and 2 Cor. 2:8.   [10] Romans 7:25.
[11] St. Augustine, *De correctione Donatistorum*, ch. 7 (PL 33, p. 806).

CHAPTER V

THE CHURCH IS COMPOSED OF BOTH GOOD AND
EVIL MEMBERS. THE OFFICIAL ACTIONS OF EVIL
PERSONS SINCE THEY DEPEND ON THE OFFICE AND
NOT THE PERSON ARE STILL VALID. THE CHAPTER
ALSO DISCUSSES THE SYMBOLIC REPRESENTATION
OF THE TRINITY IN THE CHURCH MILITANT, AS
WELL AS THE RELATION OF SUBORDINATION
AMONG THE CHURCH TRIUMPHANT, THE CHURCH
SLEEPING, AND THE CHURCH MILITANT. MANY
FINE AND NOTEWORTHY THINGS ARE SAID THERE.

27.   Furthermore since it is called a church [*ecclesia*] because it is a
gathering together in unity and concord, the church is characterized
by a spirit of fraternity which is the opposite of division or schism. It is
joined together by a common belief, but an occasional difference of
opinion if it is not held in a spirit of obstinacy is consistent with unity.
For Cyprian and the whole council of seventy bishops differed from
the faith of the Catholic church, but as Augustine states in Book II of
his work, *Against the Donatists*,[1] they were not cut off from the church
because they did not prefer their own opinion to fraternal unity and
they were not obstinate about it. For it is very difficult to judge
matters of faith. Ambrose writes in his 37th letter, *To Constantius*: "It
is wise not to make rash judgments, especially in a matter of faith
which is rarely perfect among men."[2] Therefore the church militant
since it can only make human judgments has many in the body of the
church who do not appear from external indications to be unbelievers
but are secretly in disagreement on the faith. They are not expelled or
condemned, unless what has been hidden becomes known. And since
such men do not corrupt the whole of the church militant if they are
not known, what they do for the salvation and guidance of others is
still valid.[3] For since man is not obliged to the impossible, what is not
known is rightly excused; and therefore the ministry of a secret
heretic which one believes is being carried out properly in unity with

---

[1] St. Augustine, *De baptisma, contra Donatistas*, II, 6 (PL 43, p. 130).
[2] St. Ambrose, *Ad Constantium* (PL 16, p. 925).
[3] This was denied by the Hussites, whose representatives came to Basel in January 1433.

the church, while it injures the one who carries it out, does not adversely affect the recipient if he is rightly disposed and in communion with the church. This is Catholic doctrine which all believers hold and which Augustine discusses at length in *Against the Letter of Parmenianus*, Book II.[4]

28. And so [Christ], the most perfect God and man and the mediator between God and men, so ordained it in a perfect and infallible command that, as Augustine writes in his letter 42, *To Paulinus* and as Ambrose wisely agrees in his letter 56, *To Justus*,[5] Christ is all that is to be sought after, the instrument of concord with God in whom alone all things exist. Therefore a bad minister does not do harm, for the Holy Spirit works through the appointed prelate, even if he is a false minister. Although he is not really a member in the church, he acts validly in evangelizing, consecrating, and regenerating to bring salvation to the recipient through his ministry, since it is not man but Christ who acts through the Holy Spirit and a human agent. This is the infallible truth which Augustine discusses in his work against Parmenianus, as quoted in C. 1 q.1 [c. 98] *Per Ysaiam* and in many other chapters [of the *Decretum*] including D. 19 [c. 8] *Secundum*. And Ambrose in the first book of *On Penance* writes that the priestly office receives its power from the Holy Spirit.[6] Now from this we conclude that those who only appear to be in the church militant can exercise a valid ministry for the salvation of the members of the church.

29. And so from this point of view the church militant is composed of those who are true believing Catholics and those who only appear to be. Let us consider this last conception of the church more closely. Note how the church symbolizes the Trinity. For if it is considered from the point of view of divine judgment, only those who are united to God in love are in the church, and God alone knows them. If it is considered from the point of view of the judgment of the angels, then only all believers are members and the angelic spirits know the inner decision by which the intellect is converted to the faith. Indeed the faith is like a continuous spiritual line connecting all Christians to the Head. Therefore when this chord is struck in secret in a kind of

---

[4] St. Augustine, *Contra epistulam Parmeniani* (PL 43, pp. 53–61).
[5] St. Augustine (and Alypius), *Ad Paulinum* (PL 33, p. 816), and St. Ambrose, *Ad Justum* (PL 16, p. 950).
[6] St. Ambrose, *De poenitentia*, I, 2 (PL 16, p. 950).

spiritual harmony, it is perceived by those angelic spirits and increases the joy of all the spirits in heaven. Human judgment is different. It presumes on the basis of outward human opinion that they are reborn in Christ until it is established otherwise by an external act or sign. For men hope that a good man will continue in the faith and they never would wish him to be disappointed in his hope of eternal glory, nor should they presume to make a judgment concerning matters which are hidden. Thus the church militant is like an army that carries the sign of the cross as its flag, an outward sign of its opposition to the Anti-Christ, the adversary of Christ, – yet not all may possess the inward dispositions indicated by the external sign.

30.   And in this immortal army of Christ as in a single body a harmonious unity of true and presumed faith requires differing grades – a subject on which more should be said. And we ought at least to allude briefly to the things that are relevant to our purpose, although since they are most profound they could perhaps be more fruitfully discussed in greater detail than our purpose here may require. To explain the continual concord between the one groom and the one bride, we must first consider that the whole church is one in three, i.e., it is a church triumphant, sleeping, and militant. The church militant occupies the lowest position. Just as the lowest hierarchical rank in the church triumphant is passively enlightened without communicating further because the influence terminates there, while the middle rank is enlightened and enlightens and the highest rank [only] enlightens, so the church militant is the point at which the influence terminates, and the church sleeping is in the middle, and the church triumphant is the highest. This is a marvelous continuity through disparate intermediaries, since the whole church sleeping is subordinate to the church triumphant, the higher part of the church sleeping is immediately subordinate to the lowest part of the church triumphant, and the higher part of the church militant is subordinate to the lowest part of the church sleeping. The whole of the church sleeping is made up of those predestined [for salvation] but the membership of the church militant is always in doubt until it joins the church sleeping and triumphant. The passage from the church militant occurs in such a way, that not everyone enters the church triumphant by way of the church sleeping, but many do so without going through the church sleeping, since they do not need to be purified [in purgatory]. Hence the [pattern of] harmony in the

church sleeping cannot be examined although it is not without its proper order which is directed toward the church on high.

31.   And because Christ is all things, as noted above, the church is fundamentally made up of God, the angels, and those men who are united through Christ to God. The church sleeping is considered as in an intermediate position between angels and men. It is a reflection of that of the angels, and the church militant is a reflection of the church sleeping, although the church sleeping is like the human church on earth in being directed toward the church triumphant. Thus on this point the church sleeping should be considered as linked to the church militant because the souls that are henceforth to be among the blessed are exiled in purgatory – although they cannot earn merit, while those on earth can still perform meritorious acts.[7] However, among the wayfarers [to heaven] the members of the church sleeping come first for "death has been caught up into victory"[8] and they are certain of their reward. Therefore with firm and undoubting hope they are spiritualized in accord with their merits ahead of the militant below who proceed in a state of doubt with gross bodies as shadows as it were [of those above]. Although since they have not been purified so as to be able to enter heaven, all of the members of the church sleeping are below the lowest ranks of the church triumphant, in the whole gradation of those on pilgrimage [to heaven] there is no order of ascent which requires that one rise through the ranks from the lowest members of the church militant through the church sleeping and be placed on the last level of the church triumphant. The ascent to union with the true Head is swift or tardy, high or low, according to the degree of one's inner adherence [to God] which is based on the merit or demerit which is earned by the inherent free will of the individual, so that anyone has equal access to the means through which he can become an adopted son of God, just as someone can rise on the basis of merit from the lowest grade of the clergy or laity to a ruling post as duke or archbishop or higher without [passing through] the intermediate ranks. But let us end this discussion so that we may turn our attention to the church considered as composed of living men.

[7] On the development of the theology of purgatory, see Jacques LeGoff, *The Birth of Purgatory*, Chicago: University of Chicago Press, 1984.
[8] 1 Cor. 15:54

CHAPTER VI

THE CHURCH TRIUMPHANT UNITES GOD, THE
ANGELS, AND THE HOLY SOULS. THE CHURCH
MILITANT FOLLOWS THE MODEL OF THE CHURCH
TRIUMPHANT BECAUSE IT IS MADE UP OF
SACRAMENTS, PRIESTHOOD, AND CATHOLIC
PEOPLE. THE SACRAMENTS ARE SUBJECT TO GOD,
THE PRIESTHOOD TO HIS MINISTERS, THE ANGELS,
AND THE PEOPLE TO THE BLESSED SOULS. THE
CHAPTER ALSO DISCUSSES THE RELATION OF
SUBORDINATION BY WHICH THE PRIESTHOOD IS
JOINED TO CHRIST THROUGH THE SACRAMENTS
WHICH ARE LINKED TO GOD, AND THE PEOPLE
COME TO THE SACRAMENTS THROUGH THE
PRIESTHOOD, AS WELL AS THE GRADATIONS IN
EACH PART. IN ANY PART THE HIGHEST MEMBER
INCLUDES ALL THE LOWER MEMBERS REPRESENTED
IN HIMSELF. THIS IS A MOST IMPORTANT CHAPTER.

32. We should examine the way in which the concordance in the body of the church signifies the Trinity since three great orders are found to be marvelously linked to a single head, Christ. First, the sacraments are subordinated to the divine concordance of Trinity and Unity. Secondly, the holy priesthood is subordinated to the divine concordance of the angels, the ministers of the Holy Trinity, since the priests are the ministers of the sacraments. Thirdly, the faithful on pilgrimage on earth are subordinated to the blessed spirits in heaven. The sacraments enlighten and purify, the pastoral priesthood purifies and is purified, and the faithful are purified and do not purify. All are arranged in harmonious order on the model of the threefold order among the angels, and through them of the Divine Trinity. In the admirable hierarchy of the sacraments, Christ as the Head communicates himself to all beings in this life through symbols and as a mystery in conformity with our mortal life, just as he communicates himself face to face without concealment[1] to the church triumphant, for this is what is proper to the capacity of each state.

[1] I Cor. 13:12. The entire chapter is strongly influenced by Dionysius, the Areopagite, *On the Ecclesiastical Hierarchy* (see Pseudo-Dionysius, *The Complete Works*, New York: Paulist Press, 1987).

33. And so the sacraments are communicated by God in a hierarchical order, for there are so many sacraments that Augustine says
writing to Volusian, "It would take too long to discuss adequately the
various signs that are called sacraments when they relate to the
divine."[2] The sacraments thus divinely imparted for our salvation,
since they are directed ultimately to the one Christ, possess a holy
concordant order up to the highest sacrament, the Eucharist, just as
in the church triumphant every rank is directed in a marvelous
harmony to Christ, the head, in whom the whole court [of heaven]
rests eternally in God. Thus in the sacrament of the one head, Christ,
all other sacraments achieve their goal since he is the "sacrament of
sacraments."[3] Also every sacrament symbolizes the Trinity since in
each there is the sacrament itself, what it signifies, and the thing
signified together with the sacrament. Who can investigate fully the
sweet concordance from the lowest sign to the highest sacrament
down through the intermediate ones and within any particular sacrament? No one with certainty. Let it suffice therefore to have touched
on these few points.

34. The rank of priests follows. It is characterized by its power to
administer the sacraments so that there is a continuity in the whole
church without any intervening break. The priesthood thus wears an
indelible sacramental sign of its harmonious ordering towards divine
things above. And in this priesthood there is a hierarchical order from
the highest pontiff down to the laity, which Dionysius the Great
describes in his *Ecclesiastical Hierarchy*.[4] And as man is made up of
spirit, soul, and body, so the sacraments are the one spirit of this body
of the church, the priesthood the soul, and the faithful like the body.
For as the soul adheres partly to the body and partly to the spirit and
is the intermediary through which the spirit flows into the body, so the
priesthood acts on the faithful. Therefore the priesthood is like a
single soul in the one body of the faithful. Hence Gregory Nazianzen
in the beginning of his *Oratio Apologetica* when he discusses how the
body of the church is made up of the rulers and the ruled says: "He
assigned others as pastors and teachers for the perfection of the
church – those who because of their outstanding virtue are closer to
God. They carry out the function in the church that the soul carries

[2] St. Augustine, *Ad Marcellum* (PL 33, p. 527).
[3] Dionysius, *The Ecclesiastical Hierarchy*, ch. 3, para. 1.
[4] Dionysius, *The Ecclesiastical Hierarchy*, chs. 5–7.

out in the body or the mind and reason in the soul. What is insufficient or in excess among the various members is harmonized by the spirit as a perfectly integrated body adapted for all purposes and worthy to have Christ as its head."[5] Ruling, life-giving, and illuminative power is given to the priesthood because it is the light of the world and the salt of the earth.[6] Hence as Cyprian says in his letter *On the Dice-Player* (*De Aleatore*) priests are called the salt of the earth since they distribute to the whole brotherhood the salt of heavenly wisdom.[7]

35. There are hierarchical ranks in the priesthood as to responsibility for government and rule. For although all members of the highest rank in the hierarchy, the bishops, are equal as to orders and their priestly office, nevertheless there is a graded differentiation as to governing responsibility. In this government the hierarchy exhibits a certain concordance of one and many. "For there is only one episcopate in which each has a part," and a differential order with respect to responsibility for ruling. "All the other apostles assuredly participated in the same fellowship of honor and power as Peter," but Peter was set over the others so that there might be a unity in concordance, as Cyprian argues, writing to Novatian.[8] And Jerome writing *Against Jovinian* says that among equal apostles Peter was chosen to preside so that with an established head there would be no possibility of schism.[9]

36. Hence just as there is one episcopate, so there is one *cathedra* [lit. – chair] and one rule established in hierarchical grades. On this unity of the *cathedra*, Optatus of Milevis in Book II of his work *Against Parmenianus* (against whom he wrote seven small books) argues in elegant fashion that all Catholic bishops must occupy a single *cathedra*.[10] And because this rulership was instituted by Christ, the head, to avoid schism and to preserve the unity and peace of the faithful, it is hierarchically organized in a way analogous to temporal governments. Thus Jerome observes that a presiding bishop is established in the same way as a captain is chosen in an army to act as

---

[5] Gregory Nazianzen, *Oratio 2, Apologetica*, ch. 3 (PG 35, p. 410).

[6] Matthew 5:13–14.

[7] Cyprian, *De aleatore*, 2 (PL 4, p. 903) – not written by Cyprian.

[8] Cyprian, *De unitate ecclesiae*, 5 and 4 (PL 4, p. 515); *Ad Antonianum* (PL 3, p. 815).

[9] St. Jerome, *Adversus Jovinianum*, I, 26 (PL 23, p. 258).

[10] St. Optatus of Milevis, *De schismate Donatistorum*, II, 2 (PL 11, p. 947). St. Optatus was was a fourth century bishop who opposed the Donatist heresy and influenced St. Augustine.

a ruling public official with the consent of all, D. 93 [c. 24] *Legimus.* Therefore "as the commonwealth is the common concern of the people, and the common concern is the concern of the state [*civitas*] and a state is a body of men united in any bond of agreement" as Augustine writes to Volusian in *On Changes in the Divine Laws*[11] so one who rules as a pastor follows the example of one to whom the commonwealth is entrusted. Hence all who are under his care are understood to be united in the ruler as the body is united with the one soul which gives it life.

37. Hence those united to the pastor constitute the church, as Cyprian writes in elegant fashion to Florentius Pupianus; part of which is included in C. 7 q. 1 [c. 7] *Scire debes,* where he says, "These, they say, are the church: the people united to their priest and the flock following its shepherd. And you know that a bishop is in his church and the church in its bishop. And if anyone is not with his bishop, he is not in the church."[12] Cyprian says the same thing in his letter to Cornelius, *On the Five Priests,* "Hence as the universal church is the Mystical Body of Christ, so particular churches are the mystical bodies of their heads who act in place of Christ."[13] Thus Pope Anastasius when he writes to John of Jerusalem against Rufinus, speaks of the Roman church as follows: "It will be my concern to guard the faith of the Gospel among my people, and to keep together the parts of my body in various places on earth with whatever letters I can, so that no profane interpretation may creep in which might attempt to disturb the minds of the devout."[14] And this agrees with D. 19 [c. 7] *Ita dominus.* Our basic point is that the church is united in the bishop. And so the bishop symbolizes and represents them [the members of the church] because for that collectivity he is a public person. And this will be useful in later discussions.

38. But there is a gradation [among the bishops] as Leo IX mentions in his letter to two African bishops, when he says: "There is one order of bishops, although some are set over others whether from the fact that they are located in capital cities and those that are more famous in power or secular law, or because they have some special privilege from the holy fathers as an indication of their worth. Just as

---

[11] St. Augustine, *Ad Marcellinum* (PL 33, p. 529).
[12] St. Cyprian, *Ad Florentium pupianum* (PL 33, p. 529).
[13] St. Cyprian, *Ad Cornelium* (PL 3, p. 821).
[14] Pope Anastasius I, *Ad Joannem* (PL 20, p. 72).

every earthly power is different from every other in rank, that is, Augustus or the emperor may be first, then the Caesars, then kings, dukes, and counts and tribunes, so according to the holy fathers ecclesiastical power is hierarchically ordered. As blessed Clement says: 'In those cities in which there once were high priests and leading doctors of the law among the pagans, primates and patriarchs have been established who have the right to pass judgment on the rest and carry out the more important business of not one but several provinces.' Thus where there were archpriests among the pagans, Christian archbishops have been established to head individual provinces. Where there was a metropolis – which is translated as a 'mother city' – there were metropolitans who ruled over the greater mother city of three or four cities in a province. Hence sometimes these are simply called metropolitans, and elsewhere archbishops if there were no higher officers in that province. In lesser important cities which had only priests or counts, bishops are established. And the tribunes of the people are correctly understood to be the equivalents of priests or other clerics of lower rank. The Roman pontiff has been set over all of these by divine and human law."[15] This is also the opinion of [Popes] Anacletus, Clement, Anytus, Julius, and of other Roman pontiffs.

39. And this argumentation is to be noted well for it demonstrates that church government was added to the temporal power as the soul to the body so that where there was temporal rule and earthly government, a Christ-directed rulership was added to lead all things in peace and harmony in the appropriate way to the one Head of highest power. It remains to give fuller consideration elsewhere to what has been said. Now let us touch on certain fundamentals, and then specifically on the subject of the priesthood.

[15] Pope Leo IX, *Ad Petrum et Joannem Episcopos* (PL 143, p. 730).

CHAPTER VII

THE ECCLESIASTICAL HIERARCHY HAS ORDERS AND RANKS LIKE THOSE OF THE ANGELS. THIS IS PROVEN BY EXAMPLES AND INTERMIXTURE.

40. Earlier when we were discussing the hierarchic orders and choirs we said that just as in the hierarchy as a whole there is a highest, intermediate, and lowest rank, in the highest part of each created hierarchy there are also different ranks up to the one that is first in rank. Just as there are three orders in the angelic hierarchy, so also in the first order again there are three choirs. And although there is a gradation in this manner in any choir, I now wish to show that a continuous ordered relationship of concordance is found throughout the whole hierarchy. In the last choir of the first order the illumination carried out in the first order remains within it without being communicated, so that its influence ends there. Yet that choir is still connected with the upper part of the succeeding first choir of the second order so that without communicating the radiance belonging to the first order, it actually communicates a radiance sufficient for the second order so that there is an unbroken sweet melody in a continuous hierarchical order. On this basis, let us imagine that the first order has 21 degrees of spiritual illumination which act there and are more than are necessary for the first choir. The first choir attempts to share these with the second choir but cannot wholly do so. Thus the second choir receives only 20. And that choir cannot communicate the totality of what it has received, and hence it communicates 19. And because the order consists of three degrees of light, the lowest choir in that rank cannot communicate them further and therefore it remains purely passive as far as that order is concerned. Hence the 18 degrees which it can communicate pass down to the next lower order and thus successively down to the last choir of the third order which will have twelve.

41. And from this we may conclude that since God is infinite light, every light outside of God, being created and finite when it is compared to God, is considered reflection of the Infinite Light. And the more distant it is from God, the darker it is, although in heaven the eternal divine Light embraces every spirit with a radiance that com-

pletely fulfills the desire of each. Thus returning to our argument, in the orders of religion and that part of the church which is considered more spiritual there are nine choirs from that of bishops down to that of monks. The highest order consists of the bishop, priests, and deacons, all consecrated. The intermediate order is made up of the subdeacons, acolytes, and exorcists, who are mixed. The lowest are the readers, the porters, and the tonsured, who are not consecrated. Likewise the order of deacons, subdeacons, and acolytes possesses comparatively more holiness because it contains two consecrated choirs. Again the order of the priests, deacons, and subdeacons is consecrated but extends below the first order. And so with other mixtures. But monks are linked to the tonsured choir, since they are midway between the laity and the clergy.

CHAPTER VIII

THE PRIESTHOOD IS A TRINITY OF ORDERS, GOVERNING POWER, AND *CATHEDRA* WHICH ARE ITS SPIRIT, SOUL, AND BODY. AS IN ORDERS, SO ALSO IN GOVERNING POWER AND *CATHEDRA*, THERE IS A HIERARCHICAL GRADATION. THE CHAPTER ALSO DISCUSSES THE HOLINESS OF THE PRIESTHOOD.

42.   Similarly, in accordance with what appears above, the ruling power that is the basis of government and pastoral care is divided into orders. The first order is made up of the pope, the patriarchs, and the archbishops; the second order, of the bishops, archdeacons, and deans; the third, of priests, deacons, and subdeacons. And they have mixed gradations and subordinate connections among themselves. D. 89 [c. 7] *Ad hoc* tells us that as in the case of the heavenly ranks, such a diversity of grades must work to preserve the whole so that a great differentiated order is maintained. Also on the subject of the unity of the whole *cathedra*[1] it should be noted that the whole priest-

---

[1] *Cathedra* – literally, the chair or throne of a bishop. It symbolizes the bishop's teaching authority. The First Vatican Council (1870–71) declared that the pope is infallible when speaking on faith and morals, *ex cathedra*, that is, in his official teaching capacity.

hood constitutes the church as one body, and the orders of the priesthood are like its soul and the Holy Spirit is its spirit, so that the priesthood in the church is made up of body, soul, and spirit. And because the Holy Spirit performs the actions of the priests through the imprint [*character*] received at ordination, the priesthood is holy. That the Holy Spirit works through the priest has already been shown above by Augustine in Book II of *Against the Letter of Parmenianus*,[2] and by Albertus Magnus discussing the creed in his work, *On the Sacrifice of the Mass*,[3] and by others, nearly all of them doctors.

43. Therefore although many priests may become schismatics and heretics now and in the future, the words of Christ remain true that promised that the holy priesthood would remain in him and he in it until the end of the world. Hence the body of the priesthood, although it is weak and mortal and subject to error in its members, is still not (so) as a whole since the majority always remains in the faith and law of Christ, as Cyprian concludes in his letter to Novatian where he says: "Although every man is a liar, God is still truthful. Hence the greater and better part of the confessors stand firm in the faith and the truth of the Lord's law and teaching." And as "the worthiness of the other apostles was not diminished by the fall of Judas, so also the other priests do not lose their worth on account of the departure of some priests from the faith."[4] From this I deduce a proposition which is not unimportant for our purpose that the majority of the priests always remains in the [true] faith and law. And this is an additional important basis for what follows.

[2] See chapter 5.
[3] Albertus Magnus, *De sacrificio missae*, II, 9 (*Alberti Magni, Opera omnia*, ed. A. Bourgnet, Paris, 1890, 38, pp. 64 ff.)
[4] St. Cyprian, *On the Unity of the Church*, trans. Roy J. Deferrari, Washington, D.C.; *The Fathers of the Church*, ch. 22 (p. 177).

CHAPTER IX

IN THE SAME WAY THAT THE PRIESTHOOD IS
SUBORDINATED TO GOD, THE POWER TO GOVERN IS
UNDER THE ANGELS. THROUGH THE *CATHEDRA*
THE PRIESTHOOD IS LINKED TO THE ANGEL WHO IS
SET OVER A CHURCH TO GUARANTEE THE TRUTH
OF THAT *CATHEDRA*. THIS IS AN EXCELLENT
CHAPTER.

44.   Next we should consider that [church] rulership is characterized by its angelic spirit, its *cathedra,* and its body. Just as the sacerdotal power draws its strength from the Trinity itself and is directed by the Holy Spirit through the imprint of orders because the priesthood is subordinated to the Highest Priest and the Supreme Divine Concordance, so the [ecclesiastical] rulership, which flows from the priesthood in a descending and comparative fashion as it governs the faithful, is subordinated to the hierarchy of the angels and the priesthood is connected to the power of the angels by means of the *cathedra.* Now it is clear from the Apocalypse that angels preside over and are put in charge of churches.[1] Catholic doctors also hold that they are set over the commonwealth and principalities, since the angel said to Daniel: "I have come because of your words. But the prince of the Persians resisted me for 21 days. And behold, Michael, one of the first princes [of the angels] came to my aid." and a little later: "Now I shall return to do battle with the prince of the Persians. For when I was leaving, the prince of the Greeks appeared."[2] And St. Gregory says: "What shall we call the princes of the other nations but angels? Among the mysteries to be taught concerning the angels is the fact that angels are placed over each individual nation and different ones for the same people. For the angel that spoke to Daniel was placed over the Jewish people who were in captivity in Persia and Michael over the other Jews not in captivity."[3]

45.   And from this it is evident that this holy guardianship is exercised by the angelic spirits through the *cathedra.* Hence in its

[1] Apocalypse (Revelation) 2:1.
[2] Daniel 10:13 and 20.
[3] Pope Gregory I, *Expositio veteris et Novi Testamenti,* VI, 9 (PL 79, p. 1001).

power to rule, the priesthood has the soul of its rulership in the *cathedra*, and its spirit in an angel, on the model of the example above. From this we conclude that although pernicious persons often may sit in the episcopal chairs [*cathedris*] the truth taught by the ruling *cathedra* is infallible for this reason – as Augustine declares when he discusses the words of Christ "In the chair of Moses . . ." in *On the Correction of the Donatists*.[4] And from this comes another fundamental proposition for our work – that the truth adheres to the *cathedra*.

[4] St. Augustine, *Contra litteras Petiliani Donatistae*, II, 61 (PL 43, p. 304), on Matthew 23:2.

CHAPTER X

THE EFFICACY OF THE POWER OF INTERCESSION OF
THE PRIEST IS AIDED BY THE INTERCESSION OF
THE BLESSED IN HEAVEN. AN EPILOGUE ALSO
SHOWS THAT TRUE PRIESTHOOD IS BASED ON A
THREEFOLD CONCORDANCE IN HEAVEN – WITH
THE DIVINE THROUGH ORDERS, WITH THE ANGELS
THROUGH THE *CATHEDRA*, AND WITH THE BLESSED
IN HEAVEN THROUGH THE [PRIESTLY] OFFICE.
THUS THE PRIESTHOOD IS ONE SOUL IN THE ONE
BODY OF THE FAITHFUL. THIS LITTLE CHAPTER IS
TO BE KEPT VERY MUCH IN MIND, ESPECIALLY THE
CONCLUSIONS AT THE END.

46. Thirdly, we shall consider the priesthood in its function as intercessor, which derives from a combination of orders and governing power. For this purpose it is subordinated to the blessed spirits in heaven who offer up the copious prayers, which have come from the [priestly] office which has orders and governing power, on behalf of those for whom they have been said. The actions so aided are accepted because of the holiness of the office, even though the person who offers it may not be acceptable. The basic point to be considered here is that the prayer of the priest is more acceptable because by virtue of the priestly office it is continued by the saints in heaven and

reaches Christ who is Truth. And this should be noted. Hostiensis speaks of it in his *Summa de remissione* towards the end: "The church is one. Part of it is the church militant on earth and another part is the church triumphant in heaven. And the whole church wishes devout souls to be helped, *De penitentia* [*De consecratione*] D. 1, [c. 55] *Hi duo*." And in the same place he notes that "there are three things in the church which always retain their efficacy, however sinful the one who performs them – the power of the words, the power of the sacraments, and the desire of the church, [C.] 15, final qu. [8] final c. [5]; 13 q. 2 [c. 21] *Pro obeuntibus*. For God is moved by the supplication of the church triumphant and the petitions of the church militant."[1]

47. We now can describe the way in which the true priesthood is based on a threefold concordance with heaven. It is related to the divine through orders so that Gregory Nazianzen says in his *Oratio Apologetica* that the sacred mysteries are celebrated on earth following the model of those in heaven, and through them, although still on earth, we are associated with the orders in heaven.[2] It is related to the angels through the *cathedra* and to the blessed in heaven through the office. And so the priesthood is like one soul in the body of the faithful which communicates life, growth, and sensation to its members. A ranking is assigned to a presiding see [*cathedra*] on the basis of the rank of its members. But the hierarchical grades of the body [of the church] are arranged on the basis of the ranks of earthly government at the head of which is the Roman republic. From the above it is easy to deduce the divisions into orders and choirs of the earthly hierarchies of the body [of the church]. Hence I now pass over this for reasons of space since I will discuss it in Book III.

48. And the only thing to be kept in mind is this. As the soul in the head is compared to the pontiff in the city of Rome, the highest-ranking commonwealth in the world, so dwelling in the other members on a similar hierarchical basis it represents the other bishops according to their rank, as Leo IX notes above.[3] And let it suffice for now to know that, as Cyprian says to Rogatian, "There is one church in the whole world divided into many members, and one episcopate divided into many bishoprics in a harmonious plurality." And,

---

[1] Hostiensis, *Summa aurea de remissionibus*, Lyons, 1537, p. 289a.
[2] Gregory Nazianzen, *Oratio 2 Apologetica*, c. 75 (PG 351, p. 482).
[3] See no. 38 above.

"whoever is not in the church is far from Christ, the life and the truth," as he says.[4]

49.   After the above, we should examine the words of Christ that are to be applied to the church and to the successors of the apostles so as to establish in this way the basis of ecclesiastical power.

[4] St. Cyprian, *Ad Antonianum*, ch. 24 (PL 3, p. 815).

CHAPTER XI

NEXT WE SHOULD INVESTIGATE THE WORDS OF
CHRIST THAT REFER TO THE CHURCH AND THE
SUCCESSORS OF THE APOSTLES IN ORDER TO FIND
IN THEM THE BASIS FOR THE POWER OF THE
CHURCH. FIRST, CHRIST OFTEN SAID THINGS TO
HIS APOSTLES THAT APPLIED NOT TO THEM BUT
TO THEIR SUCCESSORS. OFTEN HE WISHED TO
DIRECT HIS WORDS TO THE CHURCH AS ACTUALLY
GATHERED TOGETHER, AND SOMETIMES AS STILL
DISPERSED. PETER'S ROLE AS A REPRESENTATIVE
OF THE CHURCH IS DISCUSSED AND THE LETTER
OF ALYPIUS, AUGUSTINE, AND FORTUNATUS IS
QUOTED WHICH HAS POINTS WORTH NOTING.

50.   Now we should see what we can conclude from the sound fundamental principles set forth above, in order to know the answers to questions which can arise in the church. First let us note the opinion of Augustine [writing] to Hesychius, *On the End of the World* concerning the words that Christ spoke to the apostles. He says that the words that Christ spoke to the apostles are to be understood as applying to their successors – words such as the following: "All nations will hate you for my name's sake." And the following: "You will be witnesses in Judea and Samaria and even to the ends of the earth," and the following: "Behold I am with you all days even to the consummation of the world." Everyone knows that he made these promises to the whole church which would exist, with some dying and others being born, until the end of the world. "And thus he says to

them (it does not wholly apply to them, and nevertheless it is said as if it applied to them alone): 'When you shall see the abomination' etc. and 'When you see this, know' etc."[1]

51. From this we must conclude that the words that Christ spoke to the apostles are to be applied to the church. And on this it should be noted that sometimes Christ wished to reveal mysteries to the church as a single united body, and sometimes as dispersed in the world. Because Peter was the oldest of the apostles and he had placed him over the apostles to avoid schism and preserve peace, as Jerome says in his first book against Jovinian,[2] Christ often spoke to Peter, the chief of the apostles, as the ruler who symbolized and represented the unity of the whole church which had been committed to him. For there is no doubt that the whole church has the power of the keys, to bind and loose, as long as it is united, but we find that Christ only granted that power when he said to Peter: "I shall give thee the keys," and "Whatever thou shalt loose etc."[3] Augustine discusses this in the 22nd chapter of *The Christian Combat* along with the saying of Christ, "Peter, I have prayed for thee, that thy faith fail not," and the following: "The gates of Hell shall not prevail against it."[4] Hence, because as Ambrose says in D. 50 [c. 54] *Fidelior*, Peter was called a rock because of the strength of the church and "because he first established the foundation of the faith among the nations and like a steadfast rock was to uphold the whole structure of the work of Christ," Christ when he wished to speak about the church spoke to him as one who stood for it. Therefore we should draw the firm privileges of the church from what Christ granted, promised, and said to Peter.

52. And to touch on another matter, let us note the letter which Alypius, Augustine, and Fortunatus wrote to Generosus which says: "The Gospel has been preached to you by the voice of Jesus Christ himself because his 'Gospel will be preached to all nations, and then the end will come.' The Gospel has been preached to you through the prophets and the letters of the apostles that a promise was made to Abraham and to his seed, Christ, when God said: 'In thy seed shall all

---

[1] St. Augustine, *Ad Hesychium* (PL 33, p. 923).
[2] St. Jerome, *Contra Jovinianum*, II, 26 (PL 23, p. 258).
[3] Matthew 16:19.
[4] St. Augustine, *De Agone Christiano*, ch. 30 (PL 40, p. 308) on Luke 22:32 and Matthew 61:18.

nations . . . be blessed.' Therefore if an angel from heaven should say to you as you keep these promises: 'Give up universal Christianity and take the side of Donatus . . .' he should be anathema for he would be trying to cut you off from the whole, to lead you astray, and to separate you from the things which have been promised by God. For if the succession of bishops is important, how much more true and useful is it to count from Peter himself to whom, as representative of the whole church, the Lord said: 'Upon this rock I will build my church, and the gates of hell will not prevail against it?' Linus succeeded Peter, Cletus, Linus, etc., and Miltiades, Eusebius . . . But in the sucession which goes from Peter to [Pope] Anastasius who today sits in the same chair [*cathedra*] even if some traitor might have been led astray in that period, there is nothing that can hurt the church and innocent Christians. The Lord foreseeing this says about bad rulers: 'What they say do, what they do, do not do: for they say things and do not do them.' And thus he made certain that the hope of the faithful, being placed not in man but in God, would never be shaken by the storm of sacrilegious schism."[5]

[5] Augustine, Fortunatus, and Alypius, *Ad Generosum* (PL 33, p. 196ff.).

CHAPTER XII

EXCELLENT TEACHING ON OTHER SUBJECTS MAY
BE DRAWN FROM THAT LETTER. THE CHAPTER
ALSO DISCUSSES THE SPREAD OF THE CHURCH
THROUGH THE WORLD BEFORE THE SECOND
COMING OF THE LORD AND THE MEANING OF HIS
COMING IN THE CLOUDS OF HEAVEN.

53. Excellent teaching is contained in the aforesaid letter. In the first place it demonstrates that the true church is the one that is universal and spread everywhere, and that it will extend throughout the whole world before the day of judgment. Augustine also discusses this at great length in the letter To Hesychius, *On the Last Day*.[1] Therefore, although the day of judgment will not come before the

[1] St. Augustine, *Ad Hesychium* (PL 33, pp. 908ff.).

Anti-Christ has appeared and the saints, such as Cyprian and Lactantius, wrote a variety of things about the end of the world and the coming of the Anti-Christ, and Cyprian even believed that he would come very soon in his own time, as he wrote in two letters to Demetrian and Fortunatus,[2] nevertheless, whether Christ will come earlier or whether the world will last for seven thousand years as Lactantius seems to hold in the seventh book of his *Institutes*[3] or when this will happen is completely uncertain. For Christ said to the apostles who were the church, "It is not for you to know the times and the moments that God has established in His power."[4] Nevertheless according to St. Jerome's letter to Algazias, last question, we know from the [letter of the] Apostle [Paul] to the Thessalonians that first the whole Roman empire must be destroyed and all its subjects withdraw from it.[5] And similarly in the Gloss on those words of Paul many doctors say that before the coming of the Anti-Christ, there should also be a departure of the clergy from obedience to the Roman see. Hence in view of the present situation in the papacy and the empire, the wise man will conclude from this prophecy that there is not much time left. Nevertheless although today we see persecution and many of the evils that are to precede the end, we know that the end is not in the immediate future – although there may be signs of the end – because the name of the Lord and the church must be first spread throughout the whole world and all its islands.

54. Hence when Augustine in his discussion speaks of the coming of Christ on high in a time of persecution, this is to be understood not in the superficial literal meaning of the day of judgment but in the more subtle interpretation of the coming of Christ to the church, that he will come "in the clouds of heaven" in the church with all his power in a time of great persecution, and "then he will send forth his angels and will gather the elect." He writes in more detail on this in the aforesaid letter to Hesychius. Elsewhere in a little book which is an extensive investigation of truth and goodness, I have come to the conclusion that more than 600 years still remain and that in this time the world ought to be prepared for reform.[6] O God, if only we could

---

[2] St. Cyprian, *Ad Thiberitanos* (PL 4, pp. 359ff.).
[3] Lactantius, *Institutiones*, VII, 4 (PL 6, p. 1085).
[4] Acts 1:7.
[5] St. Jerome, *Ad Algaziam* (PL 22, p. 1036) on 2 Thess. 2.
[6] The book mentioned by Cusanus has been lost.

lift up our heads at this time and see that our redemption is at hand, for we see that the church has never fallen as low as it now is. God grant that his elect may meet in the holy synod of Basel, and gathered there amid such adversity and perplexity, may manifest the coming of his majesty in the heavens.

CHAPTER XIII

THE TRUE CATHOLIC CHURCH IS NOT LIMITED IN GEOGRAPHICAL EXTENSION. MATERNUS, THE BISHOP OF COLOGNE, IS ALSO MENTIONED.

55. And so this letter can set all doubts to rest, for it shows that the Catholic church and the true faith is the one that is least limited geographically and the most widely diffused throughout the world. Thus Optatus in the second book of his work, *Against Parmenianus*, tells how Eunomius and Olympius were sent from Rome by Pope Miltiades and by Maternus of Cologne, Reticius of Autun, Marinus of Arles, and 10 other bishops and stayed at Carthage for forty days. There was fierce argument every day and the final decision was that the Catholic church was the one that was spread throughout the world.[1] On this Augustine, Cyprian, and the holy Fathers have left us many writings.[2] And so from this we can conclude that since our faith today is in agreement with the faith that was spread throughout the world at that time, it must be true because the unvarying faith is one. Despite the fact that neither among the 205 bishops who dwelt in parts of Africa and signed the (African) conciliar decrees, nor in the East was there a single orthodox Christian [and] in spite of the many schisms and different heresies in our Christian faith, the one true faith is more widespread than any sect of the schismatics and heretics. And this argument alone is sufficient to defeat every wicked heresy.

[1] St. Optatus of Milevis, *De schismate Donatistorum*, I, 23 and 26 (PL 11, pp. 931 and 935).
[2] St. Augustine, *Ad Bonifacium; de correctione Donatistorum*, (PL 33, p. 794, and 34, p. 509).

CHAPTER XIV

THERE IS ONE TRUE AND CERTAIN *CATHEDRA* OF
PETER WHICH IS THE CHAIR OF ALL HIS
SUCCESSORS. A DISCUSSION FOLLOWS ON THE
UNITY OF THE CHAIR [*CATHEDRA*] WHICH ALL
CATHOLIC BISHOPS MUST OCCUPY, AND IT IS
ASSERTED THAT THE POPE IS FIRST IN THAT
CHAIR. HOW WE ARE TO UNDERSTAND THE
STATEMENT THAT HE WHO DOES NOT ADHERE TO
THE CHAIR OF PETER IS NOT A BELIEVER. THIS IS
AN IMPORTANT CHAPTER.

56.   Next we affirm that Peter represented the church [when Christ
promised] the gates of hell would not prevail against it. All the venerable fathers held this opinion and gave their reasons for so doing. On
this there is more below. We also affirm that the true and certain chair
[*cathedra*] of Peter in which all his successors sit, is one. Hence, since
the unity of the *cathedra* is the first privilege of the one church,
according to Optatus, *Against Parmenianus,* Book II,[1] it follows that
whoever does not adhere to the unity of the *cathedra* is outside the
unity of the church, see D. 93 [c. 3] *Qui cathedram.* In the same way
Optatus says in the book mentioned above, "The *cathedra* is one. You
cannot deny that you know that the episcopal chair [*cathedra*] in the
city of Rome was granted first to Peter who occupied it as head of the
apostles. This is also why he was called Cephas. In him the unity of
the *cathedra* was not recognized by all so that no one could claim that
any other apostle had a separate *cathedra,* since this would make
anyone a schismatic who wished to set up an alternative to the one
cathedra. Thus there is a single *cathedra* which is first of the endowments [of the church]. Peter occupied it first; Linus succeeded him;
Clement succeeded Linus; and then Anacletus etc. etc., and Siricius
succeeded Damasus and he is our associate today." And below, "We
read that Peter, our prince, received the saving keys against the gates
of hell when Christ said: 'I shall give thee the keys . . .' Why therefore
in your presumption and audacity do you strive to usurp the keys of

---

[1] Optatus, *Contra Parmenianum,* II, 3–9 (PL 11, pp. 947–962).

the kingdom for yourself by warring against the chair of Peter?" etc. "Therefore the *cathedra* is the first of the endowments of the church which we have proved is ours through Peter and it has an angel watching over it." For the angel given to a church is not assigned to one that is not in union with the chair of Peter. And below: "I say that you are branches cut off from the vine, a stream cut off from its source. For a stream that is small and does not begin of itself must have a source and a tree cannot grow from a branch which has been cut off, for when it is cut off, it withers." These are important examples for there is but one *cathedra* by succession to Peter upon whom the church was founded, and we are certain that the gates of hell will not prevail against it. From this we should conclude that whoever says that he is a Christian must of necessity say that his chair is joined to the chair of the successors of St. Peter and is united in association with that chair. Otherwise he is not a Christian, see [C.] 24 q. 1 [c. 27] *Quicumque* etc. and [c. 33] *Pudenda* at the end, and the chapter headed *Schisma* [c. 34] and D. 93 [c. 3] *Qui cathedram* along with many similar passages.

57. And so it is true that there is one chair of Peter, for the chair [*cathedra*] signifies the power to rule the church. And as the three first patriarchs, those of Rome, Alexandria, and Antioch, are said to have occupied that chair of Peter, the same is true of all the subordinate bishops along with them. Hence Pope St. Gregory in the 199th letter in the [Papal] Register says to Eulogius of Alexandria: "Your most sweet Holiness has said many very pleasing things to me in your letters about the chair of St. Peter, the prince of the apostles, – observing that Peter still occupies it today through his successors – although I consider myself unworthy to be among those sitting in it, or even standing [near]. But everything that you have said on that subject I have freely accepted because the one who speaks to me of the chair [also] sits in the chair of Peter." And below: "Therefore, although there are many apostles, only the head see of the apostles has been authoritative for government, a see that is one in three places. For he glorified one see [Rome] as the one where he deigned to remain and to end his life. He honored [another] see [Alexandria] when he sent it an evangelist, his disciple [Mark]. He confirmed [a third] see [Antioch] by presiding there for seven years, although he was to leave it. Since therefore there is one see belonging to one man [Peter] over which by divine authority three bishops now preside, whatever good I

hear from you I impute to myself. If you believe anything good of me impute it to yourself for we are one in him who says: 'That all may be one as thou, Father, in me and I in thee, and these are one in us!' "[2] And this letter is to be especially noted because three bishops sit as rulers in one chair of Peter, and of these the highest is the bishop of Rome. And as all bishops were joined to these sees at the time of the Council of Nicaea[3] and before, and after that time all bishops went out from them, so there is one *cathedra* for one episcopate made up of all the bishops, in which the Roman bishop sits in the first place.

58. And again, although some popes such as Liberius, Honorius,[4] and others who sat for a time in the chair of Peter fell victims to the error of schism, the see remained unblemished. It should especially be kept in mind, I think, that it is a certain rule and secure strength that the sees which have been founded by the Roman see when they are united to it as its daughters are considered [part of] one see and *cathedra,* although certain pontiffs, both in the direct succession in a straight line from the Roman pontiffs and in collateral ones [from other bishops] have fallen into heresy. For the generations from Abraham to Christ are named by Matthew in succession, [and] although not all in the line were holy, it reached to Christ. So in the church, which this succession symbolizes, a straight line of pontiffs reaches to Christ despite the evil conduct of intermediate popes. For that line or holy *cathedra* will endure without defect even to the consummation of the world. Hence whoever thinks that he is in the Christian faith should observe the infallible rule of Cyprian that the majority always continues in the faith and true law, and whoever separates himself from it [the majority] separates himself from the church of the faithful. Hence Cyprian says to Florentius and Pupianus: "If certain ones have fallen away from the faith, has their unbelief disproved the fidelity of God? No! God tells the truth and every man is a liar. It is said in the Gospel that when his disciples left him as he was speaking, he turned to the Twelve and said: 'Do you not also wish to go?' Peter answered him saying: 'Lord, to whom shall

---

[2] Pope Gregory I, *Ad Eulogius* (PL 77, pp. 898–899).

[3] The Council of Nicaea (A.D. 325) is recognized as the first Ecumenical Council. It condemned the Arian heresy and adopted the Nicene Creed.

[4] Pope Liberius (352–366) was forced by the emperor to subscribe to Arianism. Pope Honorius (625–638) was condemned by the Council of Constantinople for subscribing to the Monothelite heresy that asserted that Christ had only one will, rather than a human and a divine will.

we go? Thou hast the words of eternal life. And we believe and know that Thou art the Son of the Living God.' Peter upon whom the church had been founded, teaches in this passage that although the obstinate and proud multitude of those who do not wish to hear may depart, the church does not withdraw from Christ. And these are the church: the people united to the priest and the shepherd to his flock."[5]

59.   This is correct doctrine, for Peter spoke in the name of the whole church as its representative. And still many fell away from the church; even among the apostles there was Judas. Therefore the true church of the faithful is made up of those who consider themselves to be in the faith of Christ and constitute a majority in union with their pastor and with Peter and his chair. Leaving this conclusion which is evident from the above, I will try to add a few more general observations on this matter. For the passage in which Christ prayed that Peter's faith would not fail[6] – and he was heeded because of his holiness – is explained as referring to the faith of the church. Others however, for instance, Albertus Magnus writing on the same passage, also understand it as indicating that the faith of Peter and his successors will not ultimately fail.[7] Still others, as Gorra explains, understand it as referring to the faith of the Roman church.[8]

[5] St. Cyprian, *Ad Florentium Pupianum* (PL 4, p. 418ff).
[6] Luke 22:32.
[7] Albertus Magnus, *Commentarius in Lucam*, 22 (in A. Bourgnet (ed.), *Alberti Magni, Opera omnia*, XXIII, p. 685).
[8] Nicholas de Gorra, *Commentaria in quattuor evangelia*, Cologne, 1537, f. 456v.

CHAPTER XV

THE PRESIDING BISHOPS REPRESENT THE
CHURCHES UNDER THEM, AND IN THIS WAY THE
CHURCH IS IN ITS BISHOP. THERE IS ALSO
DISCUSSION OF THE RULERSHIP OF THE ROMAN
BISHOP – IN WHAT WAY HE IS FIRST AMONG THE
BISHOPS OF THE FAITH.

60.   To give a clearer understanding of our meaning, let us recall the things touched on above when we quoted St. Cyprian and Leo IX to the effect that every ruler is assigned a rank for his office according to

the law and privileges of the place over which he rules, and also that the ruler represents the whole church united to him – as Cyprian says, the church is in its ruler.[1] On that subject we say first that, as Ambrose writes in [C.] 2 q. 7 [c. 37] *Beati,* "Rome has the rulership and the headship of the nations" and this was done by divine intention so that "the center of holiness would be located in the place where the center of superstition had been." Therefore the Roman bishop has the rank in [church] government that Rome had among the pagans. On this, see D. 80 [c. 1] *Urbes* quoting Pope Lucius, and Pope Clement in the chapter [c. 2] *In Illis* of the same Distinction. And this arrangement was divinely inspired according to Leo in the chapter [c. 4] *Illud* of the same Distinction, on which see also D. 99 [c. 1], *Provinciae.*

61. Although Peter was set over the others by divine grant, according to Anacletus and to St. Jerome in the first book of *Against Jovinian* this was done with the concordant agreement of the apostles.[2] As Augustine says above, the successors of Peter occupy the same chair; therefore the special privileges of the chair are the same now as then. Hence just as Peter was prince of the apostles, the Roman pontiff is prince of the bishops since the bishops succeeded the apostles. There is almost an infinite number of writings of the saints on this. This rulership is over all men in the church of the believers, for he is the captain of that army, as Emperor Leo wrote to Theodosius. Emperor Valentinian also wrote to Theodosius: "The most blessed bishop of the city of Rome to whom antiquity gave the priestly rule over all has the power of judgment in matters of faith." And below: "Because of this power and according to the solemn decree of the councils, the bishop of Constantinople also appealed to him in writing on the dispute which had arisen concerning the faith."[3] Likewise Emperors Marcian and Valentinian wrote: "To Leo, the Archbishop of Rome, the glorious city: Your holiness possesses the rulership in the episcopate of the holy faith . . ."[4] On this, see D. 12 [c. 2] *Praeceptis*; [c] 24 q. 1 [c. 12] *Quotiens*; and C. 16 q. 1 [c. 52] *Frater noster.* Hence I understand C. 9 q. 3 [c. 14] *Aliorum* as meaning that every believer is

---

[1] Cf. nos. 34–38.

[2] St. Jerome, *Adversus Jovinianum,* I, 26 (PL 23, p. 258). Pope Anacletus is quoted in the *Decretum,* D. 21 c. 2.

[3] Valentinianus, *Ad Theodosium* (PL 54, p. 859).

[4] Valentinianus and Marcianus, *Ad Leonem,* I (PL 54, p. 899).

subject to the pope as long as he is head of the whole body, i.e., in the faith, for the body [of the church] is made up of the believers. Jerome also speaks in this way to Damasus in the tenth question of *De Cathedra*: "If anyone is united with the chair of Peter, he is united to me."[5] However a matter of faith is not always defined by the arbitrary will (lit. – at the nod) of the Roman pontiff alone for he could be a heretic – on which more will be said below.[6] Indeed in decisions on matters of faith which is why he possesses the primacy, he is subject to the council of the Catholic church.

[5] St. Jerome, *Ad Damasum* (PL 22, p. 355).
[6] Book II, chapter 18.

CHAPTER XVI

THE ROMAN CHURCH SOMETIMES MEANS THE SEE OF ROME; WHEN THIS IS THE CASE; HOW MANY SEES THERE ARE; AND WHICH IS FIRST. ROME'S PRIMACY WAS DERIVED FROM THE PAGANS SINCE THE ROMAN BISHOP POSSESSES HIS POSITION OF EMINENCE BECAUSE OF THE POSITION OF THE CITY OF ROME. THIS IS SUPPORTED BY MANY ARGUMENTS, NOT LEAST OF WHICH IS THE PRIVILEGE GRANTED BY CHRIST.

62. Hence it should be noted that the Roman church is sometimes – even usually – understood as meaning the Roman see. In the time of the Nicene Council, there were three sees, those of Rome, Alexandria, and Antioch, although the bishop of Elia, that is, Jerusalem, was always honored, as appears in chapter 6 of the Nicene Council[1] and in D. 19 [c. 9] *Anastasius*; D. 66 [65] [c. 7] *Quoniam Mos*; and D. 22 [c. 2] *Sacrosancta*. After that council, the sees of Jerusalem and Constantinople are also found in the acts of the councils, and because Constantinople was the new Rome the bishop of Constantinople called himself the universal patriarch in a particular council before Chalcedon, and these five are called the patriarchal sees in D. 22

[1] Council of Nicaea, canons 6 and 7 (Mansi 2, pp. 67off.).

[c. 7] *Diffinivimus*. The question, we read, was settled in the following way in the Council of Chalcedon: Henceforth in the canons mentioning both the vicar of the Apostolic See and the patriarch of Constantinople it was defined by the decree of the judges of the council that the Apostolic See should hold the first place because it was the old Rome, and Constantinople the second place as the new Rome, see D. 22 [c. 3] *Constantinopolitanae*, although Constantinople was to enjoy the same privileges of primacy, see D. 22 [c. 6] *Renovantes*. And although at that time Pope Leo tried in many letters to reverse the part of the definition which said that the patriarch of Constantinople would have second place – on the grounds that it went against the laws of the Council of Nicaea which, he wrote, were inviolable[2] – nevertheless this usage was established over a long period of time. Hence in the actions of the universal councils which followed, Constantinople always preceded Alexandria, see D. 22 [c. 6] *Renovantes* and the following chapter [c. 7], and [*Decretals*, v 33] *De privilegiis*, [c. 23] *Antiqua*. I find these five sees called the heads of the church in the seventh action of the acts of the Eighth Universal Council in Constantinople,[3] and they are called apostolic sees in [C] 1 q. 7 [c. 4] *Convenientibus* and those occupying them are also called popes, as appears in the same place, as in Para. *Item Tharasius*. In what way they are considered heads is discussed below. And just as the Pope of Rome is often called a patriarch, as is done practically throughout the acts of the councils, especially those of the Eighth Universal Council,[4] the other patriarchs are also called popes, as the Gloss on D. 40 [c. 6] *Si Papa* notes as well as the text of [the Gloss on] [C.] 22 q. 2 [c. 6] *Sane* Para. *Item: Si Romanorum*. But this is not very relevant to our purpose.

63. Now it should be noted that the Apostolic See has the first place over all, see D. 22 [c. 4] *De Constantinopolitana*, Hincmar, the Archbishop of Rheims, in the 15th chapter of his work against the bishop of Laon, quotes from the brief [but] important definition of the Council of Nicaea in which, he said, the ancients held that every hierarchical gradation of primacy which existed among the pagans was established by the inspiration of the Holy Spirit.[5] And therefore

---

[2] See Pope Leo I, *Ad Marcianum* (PL 54, pp. 991ff.).
[3] Eighth Council, Constantinople IV, Action 8 (Mansi 16, p. 140).
[4] Eighth Council, Constantinople IV, c. 17 (Mansi 16, p. 17).
[5] Hincmar of Rheims, *Opusculum contra Hincmarum Laudunensem*, ch. 15 (PL 126, p. 332).

the definition of the Council of Chalcedon says that Rome has the primacy according to the canons, but the ancients would observe the rule regarding a city's privileges that it should keep the governmental rank held by the high priests and others in the pagan cities.[6] But there is no doubt that the pontiff in the Capitoline of Rome was the highest officer in the temple of Jupiter and so it is [today] in the time of grace. Hence Empress [Galla] Placidia, when she wrote to her son, the emperor, said: "Because Rome is the greatest of cities and the mistress of all lands, Peter established the first rank of the divine episcopacy there."[7] That the ancients argued primacy from the rank of the cities involved is also evident in the dispute in the 12th action of the Council of Chalcedon, where the attempt is made in many arguments to prove on this basis that the bishop of Nicaea had been placed by the court over the bishop of Basianopolis.[8] In the first chapter of the Council of Turin it is also defined: "Whoever has proved that his city is and has been of metropolitan rank, let him hold the primacy."[9]

64. Note that primacy is derived from, and primarily based upon, the ranking of the city. The definition by 150 fathers and also afterwards by the Council of Chalcedon that placed the see of Constantinople after that of Rome is based on this, when it said: "The fathers were right to return its prerogatives to the see of old Rome on account of the ruling power of that city. Guided by the same intention, 120 most reverend bishops acted correctly in giving equal privileges to the holy see of the new Rome [Constantinople] since they judged that the city honored with the presence of the emperor and senate should enjoy privileges equal to those of the old Rome and have an importance in church affairs like it, and rank second after it."[10] This is the incontrovertible argument which was approved at the Council of Chalcedon. And although the emperors gave exemptions to certain prelates, nevertheless as is indicated there, this ancient right has always remained unaffected and secure. Hence, insofar as what we say approaches the truth, it can be concluded that if we were to argue the primacy of a see on the basis of the sanctity of the first one to exercise authority there or out of reverence for its location, there is no

[6] Council of Chalcedon, Action 16 (Mansi 17, p. 443).
[7] Galla Placidia, *Ad Theodosum* (PL 54, p. 861).
[8] Council of Chalcedon, Action 13 (Mansi, 7, p. 302).
[9] Council of Turin, c. 2 (Mansi 3, pl 861).
[10] Council of Chalcedon, c. 28 (Mansi 7, p. 370). See also c. 16 (Mansi 7, p. 41).

doubt that Jerusalem would be first for there the Highest Pontiff washed the church in His blood. It was also the see of the Apostle James, the first archbishop, as appears in the first action of the Eighth Universal Council, about whose see [*cathedra*] Eusebius writes well in Book VII, chapter 16.[11] Also the writers on the canonical epistles [of the New Testament] assert that those of James are placed first because he was the first to hold the see of Jerusalem which was the first in Christendom. Paul also puts James first when he speaks of the pillars of the church. Alexandria is not allotted the first position because its first bishop, Mark, is not placed ahead of Saint John, the Beloved [Disciple], and Mark presided in Alexandria and John in Ephesus. Yet neither is Ephesus preferred over Alexandria because of its importance as a bishopric since Alexandria was of greater secular importance than Ephesus. But we should believe that both factors, not only secular importance but also religious reasons were involved in determining the pre-eminence of these sees – as Pope Innocent writes to Alexander concerning the see of Antioch, where he says: "Hence we note that this rank was given to it both because of the importance of the city and because it was shown to be the first see of the first apostle."[12]

65.   Nevertheless, although in the beginning the ranks in the church were assigned by the sacred councils and holy fathers according to the [secular] importance of the place, the rank of the bishop of a given locality does not increase with an increase in temporal power unless there is a decision of a council to this effect. Hence when Acatius said that he was bishop of the royal city and therefore of such high rank that he could not be judged by the Apostolic bishop, Pope Gelasius wrote to the bishops in Troy that he laughed at this, saying: "Was the empire not ruled for lengthy periods from Milan, Ravenna, Sirmium, and Trier? Have the bishops of these cities assumed more than what was allotted to them in antiquity?"[13] There is more on this there. Also on this topic Pope Anastasius says in a letter to Bishop Alexander which begins: *Onus et honor,* that the church of Antioch has yielded to that of Rome and that metropolitan bishops should not be named by the emperors but according to the ancient custom of the provinces.[14] On this, see D. 10 [c. 1] *Imperiali.*

66.   Because there has been a lengthy discussion of this above, I

---

[11] Eighth Council, Constantinople IV, Action 1 (Mansi 16, p. 27), and Eusebius of Caesarea, *Ecclesiastical History* (PG 20, p. 68).
[12] Pope Innocent I, *Ad Alexandrum* (PL 20, p. 548).
[13] PL 59, p. 71.   [14] PL 20, p. 48.

think that we may conclude that the Roman see rightly possesses the primacy by the statutes of the councils, because of its secular importance, [and] by divine grant, for the increase of the faith and the preservation of peace, and on account of having had so many holy popes, more than thirty of whom in succession were crowned as martyrs for the faith.

CHAPTER XVII

THE ROMAN CHURCH IS SOMETIMES UNDERSTOOD AS MEANING ALL THOSE DIRECTLY CONNECTED TO IT; AND SOMETIMES THE SEE IS TAKEN AS MEANING THE PONTIFF. THE [ROMAN] CHURCH SOMETIMES MEANS THE POPE, THE CLERGY, AND THE FAITHFUL OF HIS DIOCESE, SOMETIMES IT REFERS TO HIS SUBJECTS AS A METROPOLITAN, SOMETIMES TO THOSE SUBJECT TO HIM AS A PATRIARCH, AND SOMETIMES TO THE CHURCH OF THE FAITHFUL. THERE IS ALSO A DISCUSSION OF WHAT IT MEANS TO SAY THAT THE ROMAN CHURCH CANNOT ERR.

67.   Sometimes however the Roman church is taken for those most directly connected to the Roman church. See, for example, the pamphlet of Leo IX against the claims of Michael of Constantinople, chapter 32, where he says that the Roman church is like "the hinge on which the door of the church turns and it will always remain firm."[1] His clergy are called cardinals because they are close to that hinge [*cardo*]. The Emperor Constantine writes to Pope Agatho at the beginning of the acts of the Sixth Universal Council to send three persons from his church and twelve metropolitans from his full council.[2] From this example we can conclude that sometimes "the Apostolic See" means the Roman pontiffs, [and] that sometimes "the Roman church" means the pope with the clergy and laity of his diocese and sometimes all those under his see as metropolitan and archbishop – since many universal councils call him the archbishop of

[1] PL 143, pl 765.   [2] Sixth Council, Constantinople III, Action 1 (Mansi 11, p. 199).

Rome. At times it also means all the metropolitan churches united to him as their patriarch and head in his patriarchal see. For example in the seventh action of the Eighth Universal Council when he speaks of the opinion of the council of Rome the representative of the Patriarch of Jerusalem says: "The Holy Spirit which has spoken in the church of the Romans, has also spoken in ours."[3] At times "the Roman church" means the church made up of all the faithful united with the Roman church as its head. Hence when we say that the Roman church can never err, this is true of the whole universal church considered in this last way. And after that it is also true of the patriarchate of Rome. Then it is true of it as an archbishopric. And finally it is true of Rome as a bishopric.

68. But these possess the truth in varying degrees. The first is infallible and always was and always will be. The second is infallible today for the reason that the universal church is almost completely reduced to the patriarchate of Rome. Then in considering the patriarchal sees, the faith is also always more true in the patriarchate of Rome and so it was and will be, although by the promise of Christ the universal church possesses greater certainty. The belief of the archbishopric of the city of Rome is still more fallible, and that of the bishopric more fallible, although from the beginning of the faith the patriarchate of Rome among all the patriarchates, the archbishop of Rome among all the archbishoprics, and the bishopric of Rome among all the bishoprics were more certain and less fallible. And it will be this way until the last day. It appears in the acts of the Eighth Universal Council that Bahanes, a most renowned prefect of the court and patrician, said that the patriarchal sees ought to be reduced successively to one patriarchate and that through it God ought to create the other patriarchates anew.[4] Alas, now we see that the first part of his statement has come true. May God grant that we may see the second come true in our lifetimes! And because, as I have said, the Roman church (and also another, Constantinople) is often taken for the subordinate churches united with it, and this union is called by the Greeks a synod, and by us a council, it remains now to add some things about the council. The discussion of the councils follows.

END OF BOOK I

[3] Eighth Council, Constantinople IV, Action 8 (Mansi 16, p. 86).
[4] Eighth Council, Constantinople IV, Action 8 (Mansi 16, p. 140).

BOOK II

CHAPTER I

A SYNOD IS A MEETING OF BISHOPS AND PRIESTS
WHO STRIVE TO COME TO AGREEMENT AS ONE.
THOSE THAT DISAGREE DO NOT CONSTITUTE A
COUNCIL. COUNCILS ARE OF VARIOUS RANKS FROM
THE PARTICULAR TO THE UNIVERSAL, AND THE
TERM, UNIVERSAL COUNCIL, HAS VARIOUS
MEANINGS. THE CHAPTER EXPLAINS THE
GRADATIONS FROM THE LOWEST SYNOD UP TO THE
HIGHEST.

69. My intention is briefly to examine and compare the various synods to determine their authority, and from this to resolve certain doubts. First of all, a synod properly speaking is a gathering of bishops and priests.[1] It is called a synod from *syn* which means "at the same time" and *hodos* or "way" because all travel in one way towards the same end. Synod is a Greek word. It is translated as an "assembly" [*coetus*] see D. 15 [c. 1] *Canones* para. *Synodus*, and is called in Latin *concilium* [council]. Isidore tells us why it is called a council in D. 15 [c. 1] *Canones Concilii*, and its distinctive characteristic is concord. As is said there, those who disagree among themselves do not form a council. There are different kinds of synods since they take place on different levels from the local to the universal through various intermediate grades. According to Bartholomew of Brescia, who follows Huguccio in the interpretation of D. 16 c. 1, a council or synod is universal if it is composed of the pope or his legate together with all the bishops.[2]

70. But perhaps this definition is insufficient [for the council of the

---

[1] The Latin is *"senum et presbyterorum"* – elders and priests, but the context seems to indicate that the *senes* are bishops.

[2] Bartholomew of Brescia wrote an *Apparatus* to Joannes Teutonicus' *Gloss* on Gratian's *Decretum* that is in the library at Kues (no. 224). Huguccio wrote his *Summa* on the *Decretum* earlier. Bartholomew's comment is on *Decretum* D. 17, not D. 16.

universal church] since it can also apply to the universal council of the Apostolic See [Rome] which I discuss in the next chapter. But it is true that it is essential to a council if it is to be full and perfect that the legate of the Apostolic See must at least be present, as appears in D. 3 [c. 2] *Porro* and D. 17 [c. 2] *Regula.* But Hincmar of Rheims in his 20th chapter discussing this holds that the fourth volume of a book on a certain general council on the veneration of images which was held in France in the time of Charlemagne contained the following: "It is called one corporate body [*universitas*] from the fact that it proceeds by bringing many tendencies to unity. For a multitude becomes a corporate body [*universitas*] when it is united as one. And as the universal church is called Catholic in Greek, so it is certain that whatever does not depart from that unity can be called Catholic. For every Christian doctrine, decree, or tradition ought to apply to the universal church. Heretics have never maintained this universality in the smaller meetings [conventicles] that they have held in various geographically restricted parts of the world, for by their actions they have separated themselves and many others from the fellowship of the church. Therefore when the bishops of two or three provinces meet and legislate on things that are appropriate for the Catholic church, the meeting can perhaps be called universal even though it does not involve all the [church] authorities in the world. It is sufficient that it not differ from the faith and tradition of all."[3] And there is more there.

71. Moreover a gathering of the church fathers can be called a universal council for various reasons: either because the fathers discuss and define as true a doctrine of the Catholic church, or because they deliberate about the state of the universal church, or about a general case affecting the entirety of a certain large province and obedience. For depending on what the council decides that decision acquires a universal character. If it concerns a case which is common to all, as I have said, it is properly and generally called universal when the full assembly makes a universal Catholic definition. But another council although it is called universal because of its general subject matter may still not be a universal catholic council properly speaking. Thus the Council of Africa when it legislated on this latter type of universal council said: "So that the requirement of an annual meeting

---

[3] Hincmar of Rheims, *Opusculum contra Hincmarum Laudunensem,* ch. 20 (PL 126, p. 360) in the library at Kues (no. 52).

may not tire the brethren, it has been decided that whenever there is a subject of common interest to all Africa, there will be a universal gathering. However cases that are not of general interest should be judged in each province."[4] And it is right to call the councils in which some definition of the faith against heretics was made, universal councils, as the text of D. 100 [c. 4] *Optatum* proves, although every universal council should also publish canons, see D. 16 [c. 6] *Habeo.* But there are different conciliar gatherings ranking from the lowest through various intermediate grades up to the highest universal synod. A curate gathers a synod of his parish, and there is a diocesan synod above him, above which is the metropolitan synod, and above that the provincial synod in the kingdom or nation, over which is the patriarchal [council] and the greatest of all is the council of the universal Catholic church. And as [Pope] Leo says to [Emperor] Marcian in the letter in which he writes about the delegation sent to represent him at the Council of Chalcedon, "Nothing that is not based on the truth of faith should be considered a council. It is more accurate to call any other meeting a pseudo-council [*conciliabulum*]."[5]

---

[4] Canon 62 of the Council of Carthage (A.D. 419) in North Africa, also cited by Hincmar (PL 67, pp. 213ff., and Mansi, 3, p. 79).
[5] Paulus Hinschius (ed.), *Decretales Pseudo-Isidoreana*, Leipzig, 1863, p. 608. Subsequent footnotes will cite Hinschius.

CHAPTER II

ANY PRESIDING AUTHORITY NORMALLY HAS THE
RIGHT TO CALL THE SYNOD SUBJECT TO HIM.
THEREFORE THE POPE HAS THE RIGHT TO CALL
THE UNIVERSAL COUNCIL. WHAT IS MEANT BY
SAYING THAT NORMALLY THE UNIVERSAL COUNCIL
CANNOT TAKE PLACE WITHOUT THE
AUTHORIZATION OF THE POPE.

72. Any presiding authority in the church of whatever rank has the right to call together those under him. Without him or his representative, a council is not considered fully valid or properly assembled. Hence since the Roman pontiff is the highest officer in the church

militant and ranks first among the bishops of the faith, ordinarily it is not legitimate to hold a universal council without him or his authorization, D. 96 [c. 4] *Ubi Nam,* D. 17 [c. 6] *Hinc Etiam* and the chapter [2] *Regula,* and [Pope] Leo IX writes on this in a letter to Peter of Carthage[1] to the same effect, see C. 3 q. 6 [c. 9] *Dudum,* and the same thing appears in many places. A provincial council likewise cannot be celebrated without the metropolitan [of the province] nor a universal patriarchal council without the patriarch, nor a diocesan council without the bishop. The reason is obvious and the decrees of the holy councils demonstrate this in various passages, see D. 17 [c. 2] *Regula* with the chapters which follow and D. 18 [c. 4] *Propter,* and the chapter [12] *Si Quis* and the following chapter. The convocation of the universal council belongs to the universal patriarch. Therefore [Pope] Pelagius [II] writes to the bishops called together by John of Constantinople, "It has been reported to the Apostolic See that John of Constantinople describes himself as the universal bishop and in his presumption is calling you to a general synod etc." Marcellus, pope and martyr, speaks as follows in chapter 5 of his decrees: "By divine inspiration, the apostles and their successors decreed that no synod should take place outside the authority of the Roman see. For the bishop of that see is the judge of the whole church and no judgment is valid without a legitimate judge." Pope Damasus also affirms this in chapter 9 of his decrees. Likewise the Roman pontiffs, Anastasius, Athanasius, and Julius.[2]

73. Therefore it is not necessary to insist too much on this. Although we often read that universal councils were called together by emperors – in fact all eight [of the ecumenical councils] were called by them as can be seen from their acts up to the Eighth which was called at the time of Emperor Basil at Constantinople, see D. 15 [c. 1] – nevertheless, the presiding authority of the Roman pontiff was always present in the councils and without it there would have been no universal council, provided that he was at least willing and able to be present. Hence just as there is no perfect provincial synod without the metropolitan, as appears in the next to the last action of the Council of Chalcedon[3] – and this is the common opinion of all the

---

[1] PL 143, p. 730.
[2] Hinschius, pp. 720, 223, 502ff, and 456.
[3] Mansi 7, p. 378. Emperor Basil I (867–886) whom Nicholas repeatedly praises was an illiterate Armenian who murdered his predecessor in order to become Byzantine

ancients – so in the case of the universal council, the pope [must be present] provided that he is at least willing and able to be present. Otherwise, if the council waits for him and he does not send anyone or does not come or does not wish to do so, the council ought to provide for its needs and for the welfare of the church. This is well proven by the text of the Eighth Universal Council which is entitled: "A Decree by the Council Before the Arrival of the Representatives of Old Rome" where after further discussion indicating that they had been waiting for the representatives of the bishop of Rome for a long time and that it was not right to wait longer, the Council adds: "We hold it altogether unsuitable to take no action on the precarious state of the church of Christ, our Saviour, by putting off needed decisions. For this reason, constrained by necessity, we denounce etc . . ."[4] On the same subject we read in the acts of the Second Synod of Ephesus that when the council notified Bishop Julius, Deacon Hilary and the Notary Dulcitius who were the ambassadors of Pope Leo, that the council would sit on the day after the next and asked them to come quickly and they did not come, Thalassius, bishop of Caesarea in Upper Cappodocia said, "For us to delay in this city brings considerable harm to all the most devout and holy bishops and the holy churches. Furthermore our most devout Christian emperor wishes to hasten the end of the synod so that he may take specific legal cognizance of the things that are decided. Because therefore we have done what is fitting for a holy synod – those who represent the holy Archbishop Leo, most beloved of God, have been advised by messengers sent to them, and they have refused to meet with us –, I think that postponement is not necessary. However if the holy synod wishes to do so, let us not delay beyond the customary waiting period."[5]

74.   Thus he said that it is sufficient for a synod to give a formal warning, especially when the papal representatives refuse to come. Nevertheless as the text of the Eighth Council cited earlier proves,

---

emperor. The Fourth Council of Constantinople (869–870) is recognized by the Roman Catholic church but not by the Orthodox churches, as the Eighth Ecumenical Council. It was important for Nicholas as the last occasion at which the Eastern and Western churches were in agreement, settling the Photian schism.

[4] Mansi 16, pp. 30ff.

[5] Kallen notes in the Heidelberg Latin edition (p. 99) that there is no Latin text of the "Robber Council" of Ephesus (A.D. 449) extant today although Nicholas seems to have used one. That Council's decisions were reversed by the Council of Chalcedon (A.D. 451) and the pope described it as a "latrocinium" (robbery).

nothing should be done in haste and the council should wait for the representatives of the Roman pontiff for a long time – as they waited in this case for a year and more. And in matters of faith, even a legitimately assembled council if it still lacks the authorization of the Apostolic See, may not proceed without considering the opinion of the Roman church.

CHAPTER III

THE FULL UNIVERSAL COUNCIL IS MADE UP OF THE
FIVE PATRIARCHATES. IT IS ESSENTIAL FOR A
COUNCIL TO BE CELEBRATED IN PUBLIC AND NOT
IN SECRET, IN COMPLETE FREEDOM WITHOUT
FEAR, AND IN AN ORDERLY AND CANONICAL
FASHION WITHOUT DISTURBANCE. OTHERWISE IF
IT IS NOT CELEBRATED IN PROPER FORM, IT CAN
BE IN ERROR, AND ONE CAN APPEAL FROM IT TO
ANOTHER COUNCIL. MANY THINGS ARE SAID THAT
SHOULD BE ESPECIALLY NOTED.

75.   The acts of the Eighth Council clearly teach that a full universal council is constituted of the five patriarchal sees. For it is said at the end of that Council that Emperor Basil "by divine help and grace" brought together the five patriarchs, "the builders of the tabernacle of the church, from the ends of the earth."[1] And there is more on this subject there. The text is contained in Book III below. And in the ninth action of the same Council we read that the synod, on receiving the representative of the see of Alexandria who arrived last, said, "We glorify God, the creator of the universe, who has provided what was lacking to the universal synod, rendering it now most perfect, etc."[2] From this we conclude that a fully perfect synod is made up of the heads of the whole church. Hence I do not think that [all the] emphasis should be placed on the [form of the] convocation of the council in determining its validity, provided that at least the fathers are there who represent the universal church. But if neither the

[1] Mansi 16, p. 179.
[2] Mansi 16, p. 147.

54

fathers who are the heads of the churches are there nor is there a legitimate convocation by the highest power, there is no doubt that the universal church cannot be represented in that council. But where it has already been legitimately called together and the fathers who are the heads [of the churches] have not yet come together, I do not believe that one should proceed immediately, for we read that many councils including those which had been properly called have been in error. Rather it is necessary to wait for the fathers, although not all of them, for it is sufficient for a majority to be there if all have been called. This, we read, was the reply to St. Ambrose in the Council of Aquileia to the heretic Palladius when he refused to answer concerning his beliefs because the Eastern bishops were not present. When Palladius said that he only was required to answer for his faith in a full council, which was not true of the present meeting, St. Ambrose concluded: "The Eastern emperors summoned them and so they could have come, so that this claim is an evasion."[3] In addition for a universal council to be valid it must be celebrated in public, not secretly – as is evident in the fifth action of the Eighth Universal Council.[4]

76. Likewise everyone in it should be able to speak freely, as appears in the first action of the Sixth General Council held in the time of [Pope] Agatho, and at the end of the letter to the council by Agatho.[5] Thus when an objection was put to Pope Nicholas concerning the large numbers at the council called by Photius, he said, "We follow the conciliar legislation of the holy fathers at Nicaea, Chalcedon, and other councils and revere their decisions, not just because of the numbers of bishops assembled there but because they were free, just, and divinely inspired."[6] From this we conclude that the number of the fathers together with freedom of speech confer great authority [on a council], for more support is given to what is decided by many rather than by few, see D. 19 [c. 6] *In canonicis*; D. 20 [c. 3] *De quibus*; [C.] 2 q. 7 [c. 35] *Puto*, and freedom and unanimity are as necessary as numbers, see [C.] 24 q. 1 [c. 19] *Alienus*. Hence Agatho when he writes to Constantine, in the place noted above, about the fathers to be assembled in the Sixth Council says, "Give permission to speak freely to everyone who wishes to speak on the faith that he believes and holds so that all may recognize

---

[3] Mansi 3, pp. 602ff.   [4] Mansi 16, p. 78.
[5] Mansi 11, p. 283.   [6] PL 119, pp. 792ff.

clearly that no one who wished to speak about the truth was in any way impeded or dissuaded by fear, power, threats, or rejection." And again, "Private matters ought not to be dealt with under the pretext of religion."[7] Thus Pope Leo wrote to Emperor Theodosius on the errors of the Synod of Ephesus: "When private matters are dealt with under the pretext of religion, the impiety of a few harms the universal church. We have learned from a not unreliable source that many priests met at the synod whose participation would at least have been useful in the discussion and decisions if the one who claimed the presiding seat for himself had been willing to preserve sacerdotal moderation so that, as is customary, the decision could be arrived at freely by everyone in the tranquil and just spirit proper to the faith for the assistance of those in error. But we have found out that not all the council members participated in this decision. For we have learned that some were excluded and others were brought in who, by the intention of the above-mentioned priest, signed the unholy decisions under compulsion because they knew that it would adversely affect their positions if they did not do as they were commanded. The decision announced by him, although directed at one man, appeared as a direct attack on the whole church. Our representatives sent from the Apostolic See saw this as indeed unholy and contrary to the Catholic faith, and no pressure could compel them to consent. In vain they kept protesting in that synod, as was their duty, that what was being decided would not be accepted by the Apostolic See." And further on he says, "All the priests in our part of the church beseech Your Grace with sighs and tears to order a general council in Italy, since our representatives registered protests in good faith and Bishop Flavian has submitted a formal appeal." And below, "As is considered necessary when an appeal has been made, the decrees adopted at the Council of Nicaea which were adopted by the clergy of the whole world are cited in support."[8]

77.   Now this is an essential requirement for a universal council at which general matters are to be discussed that a hearing be given to all in complete freedom, not in secret but publicly. If anything is then defined by general agreement it is considered to be inspired by the Holy Spirit and infallibly decided by Christ who is present among those gathered in his name. This was the way it was at the Council of

[7] Mansi 11, p. 283.
[8] PL 54, pp. 827ff.

Nicaea, where we read in the acts of the Council of Chalcedon the Holy Spirit was clearly present among the fathers. The Council added that the Holy Spirit commands what is commanded in councils of this kind, so that he who violates them rejects the grace of the Holy Spirit. The holy synod said, "We all say this. Anathema be he who rejects it."[9] This is the way it was with all orthodox councils. And therefore at the end of the Eighth Council when the reason was given that it should be obeyed, the Council said, "By the power given to us by the Holy Spirit who is our most high and mighty pontiff." And below, "Who does not know that Christ the Lord, infinite and incomprehensible, who said, 'Where two or three were gathered' etc., was in the midst of the sacred synod?"[10] That the power of the council is most high is evident from what Elpidius, a man of respectable rank, said to the Council of Chalcedon, as it appears in the first action: "Today the God of all, the Word, the Saviour, has given himself to you for judgment. He accepts those who decide, and he honors the authority of their decision."[11] The first and fifth actions of the Eighth Council contain the statement which is the basis of the fathers' power in council when they say: "The most holy representatives of old Rome and we who are representatives of the other sees decide all these things today by the grace of Jesus Christ who granted us the power of the highest priesthood, that of binding and loosing, etc."[12] Hence the power of binding and loosing was given to Peter as the representative of the church. This is the statement on which the decision of the synod bases its force. Isidore [of Seville] writes well about the authority of the councils, as can be seen at the beginning of the book that he wrote on the synods.[13]

[9] Mansi 6, p. 627.   [10] Mansi 16, pp. 199ff.
[11] Mansi 6, p. 619.   [12] Mansi 16, p. 86.
[13] Cusanus is referring to the section of St. Isidore of Seville's *Etymologies* that deals with conciliar legislation (VI, 16, printed in PL 82, p. 243).

57

CHAPTER IV

FOR THE DEFINITIONS OF A UNIVERSAL COUNCIL TO BE CONSIDERED AS INSPIRED BY THE HOLY SPIRIT, ITS PRONOUNCEMENTS AND DECREES MUST BE ADOPTED WITH THE CONCORDANCE AND COMMON CONSENT OF ALL.

78. I have said that if a [conciliar] definition is made with [general] agreement we believe that the Holy Spirit who is the author of peace and concord has acted. For it is not human but divine that various men brought together in complete freedom of speech should come to agreement as one. And this should be presumed in all cases. This is the way it appears in the fifth action of the Eighth Council where the fathers, when they speak of the decision of the council, assert that they were prompted by divine inspiration because the decision was promulgated with the unanimous agreement of the holy synod.[1] And after the end of the Eighth Universal Council at Constantinople, Emperor Basil said to the synod, "Now let the holy and universal synod say whether the present conclusion has been reached with the consent of all the holy bishops in agreement. For religious matters should be proclaimed and confirmed in church bodies with the consent and concordance of all." The holy synod replied, "We all understand it this way. We all proclaim this. We all readily subscribe to this in harmonious agreement. This is the judgment of truth. This is the decree of justice."[2] There is more there on this.

79. Note that agreement [*concordantia*] is particularly required on matters of faith and the greater the agreement the more infallible the judgment. Hence, as appears in the Council of Chalcedon, ordinarily the majority always rules and its decision is presumed more certain.[3] Nevertheless the opinion above indicates that a decision on a matter of faith is not certain unless the greatest possible number of priests has agreed to it. The opinion of St. Cyprian is that since by the decree of Christ the majority will always remain without error, the opinion of the majority has a great presumption in its favor so that if that opinion remains fixed and unchanged among them, the presumptive judg-

---

[1] Mansi 16, p. 80.   [2] Mansi 16, p. 185.
[3] The Council of Chalcedon did not speak of majority rule (Kallen, *DCC*, p. 106).

ment is very great.[4] For truth remains for ever and ever and falsehood cannot endure for a long time.

80.   Although many things are necessary for universal synods, the common decision of all, as indicated above, is the most important. Hence Pope Leo says to the Synod of Ephesus, "In an act of true religious piety, our most Christian emperor wished to hold a council of bishops so that a decision by a larger number could eliminate every error. I have sent our brethren, Bishop Julius, Renatus the priest, and my son, Hilary the deacon, and with them Dulcitius, a notary of proven faith, who are to attend your holy meeting, my brethren, as my representatives and they are to decide by common agreement with you whatever may be pleasing to God."[5] Note that the business of the sacred council was to be decided by the common agreement of the legates and the others.

81.   Especially in matters of the faith, which is necessarily one and unchangeable – as it has been and will remain – the holy universal council should always be guided by the rules that the Holy Spirit has now clearly expressed in the canon of the Holy Scripture and in past councils. It should search the Scriptures when in doubt, as was done in the Sixth Universal Council and in many others, and then from what has been said the [resulting] definition will necessarily be free of error. However if these conditions are not observed, especially a free hearing for all, and if attempts are made in synods to adopt things that are opposed to the faith of the Roman church, it is proper to issue a protest and to appeal to a future council, as is demonstrated above. And this is demonstrated more clearly still in the letter from Pope Leo and the Roman synod to Empress Pulcheria which says that the legates of the Apostolic See at the Synod of Ephesus protested its invalidity because of the force and intimidation employed, and stated that no physical pressure could cause them to depart from the faith which they had brought from the see of Peter to the holy synod.[6] From this it can also be concluded that the faith of the Roman church can be overruled by no universal synod – this being true, as will be explained below,[7] of the faith of that whole church expressed in its patriarchal synod.

---

[4] Cyprian is also cited on majority rule in Book I, ch. 4, no. 43, and ch. 14, no. 58.
[5] PL 54, p. 799.
[6] Pope Leo, *Ad Pulcheriam Augustam* (PL 54, pp. 833ff.).
[7] Cf. no. 140.

CHAPTER V

ALTHOUGH WE READ THAT MANY COUNCILS WERE
IN ERROR THAT WERE ATTENDED BY THE LEGATES
OF THE APOSTOLIC SEE, NONE OF THEM WAS
CARRIED OUT PROPERLY. THIS IS PROVED FROM
SPECIFIC PSEUDO-COUNCILS. IN WHAT WAY
UNIVERSAL COUNCILS CORRECT LOCAL COUNCILS
IS DISCUSSED AS WELL AS THE GREAT STRENGTH
OF THE UNIVERSAL CATHOLIC CHURCH.

82.   Having considered these things, if we turn to the various acts by pseudo-councils [*conciliabula*] we will find that none actually fulfilled these basic conditions. For either they were held in secret or the results were arranged beforehand or they were compelled to act out of fear. Therefore although it could be said that the Council of Rimini consisted of 330 bishops, an objection that was put to Augustine when he wrote against Felicianus on the Trinity, it was found that it was not properly, openly, and freely gathered together nor fixed in its conclusion.[1] On this Pope Liberius and the western bishops write in a letter to Eustachius and Cyril which begins *Optabile nobis*, that those who had been in Rimini had returned to the declaration of faith of the Council of Nicaea.[2] Ambrose in Book I, chapter 8 of *On the Father and the Son* [*De Patre et Filio*] says, "You have heard, O holy emperor, that those who assert such things have been rightly condemned. 318 bishops came to Nicaea not by human effort or arrangement but so that the Lord Jesus might prove that he was present in their consent from the fact that their numbers were a sign of his passion and his name, since the number 300 is the cross [T in Greek numerals] and 18 is the first two letters of "Jesus" in Greek [IH in Greek numerals]. The profession of faith of the Council of Rimini and the statement of correction issued after the Council of Rimini both showed this. A letter sent to Emperor Constantius bears witness to the profession; subsequent councils attest to the correction."[3] Ambrose also writes in

---

[1] St. Augustine, *Collatio cum Maximino Arianorum episcopo* (PL 42, pp. 710ff.). The Council of Rimini was held in 359.
[2] PL 8, p. 1585.
[3] St. Ambrose, *De fide*, I, 18 (PL 16, p. 579). The signature lists are defective so that the actual number of participants is not known.

his 77th letter against Auxentius, that the "Robber Council" of Rimini was gathered in secret and was corrected.[4] Augustine in the aforementioned work against Felicianus says that the decrees of that pseudo-council [*conciliabulum*] have disappeared with the same facility with which they were decreed. How this was done he explains in the same place.[5] And many writers assert that the council issued decrees that were signed under compulsion due to interference and pressure from Constantius. Liberius was pope at that time, and, as Augustine writes to Crescentius, he subscribed to the Arian sect.[6] At first he resisted and was therefore sent into exile. (There is an interesting disputation on the subject between Emperor Constantius and Liberius.) However he returned from exile and was forced to consent to false doctrine, as St. Jerome writes in his *Chronicles*.[7] But we do not find that he was present at that council either in person or through representatives. Hence Pope Damasus and the other bishops who were assembled in Rome write to their "most beloved brethren" in Illyria: "The numbers assembled at the Council of Rimini do not constitute an objection to its invalidity since it is clear that neither the Roman bishop whose decision they should have awaited before taking any action, nor Vincentius who was bishop without interruption for so many years, nor others gave their consent to these things – especially since, as we have said before, the very ones who seemed to have yielded in the meeting have now followed wiser counsel and indicated their disapproval."[8] Hence that pseudo-council [*conciliabulum*] had many defects. The same thing is clear in the case of the Second Council of Ephesus, since, although it was properly assembled in the presence of the representatives of Pope Leo, there was no freedom, an erroneous decision was taken without agreement, and the papal representatives protested and appealed as is clearly indicated in the acts of the Council of Chalcedon. The fathers who subscribed to its decisions confessed that they had done so out of fear of bodily harm, as Pope Leo also writes on this subject to Emperor Theodosius and Empress Pulcheria.[9] We also know from the acts of the Eighth Universal Council that the legates of the Apostolic See and others

---

[4] PL 16, p. 1057.
[5] See note 1.
[6] Not in the published works of St. Augustine.
[7] PL 27, p. 501.
[8] Hinschius, pp. 518ff.
[9] Hinschius, pp. 601–602.

who were present at the council organized by Photius, could not act freely.[10] The same thing appears in [C.] 16 q. 6 [7, c. 15] *Sane.*

83.   Augustine writes, however, that local councils of one bishop or province are corrected by universal councils, and this is contained in C. 2 q. 7 [c. 35] *Puto Item: Cum Petrus.* Also the council of 86 bishops including St. Cyprian, which Augustine mentions in his letter to Vincentius Rogatista, and also in Book II of *Against the Donatists,* was corrected by a later universal council.[11] Augustine says in Book I of his work *Against the Donatists* when he wishes to prove that the faith is firmly based on the decision of the universal council, "Do not think that I am using human arguments since in earlier times in the church before the schism of Donatus the obscurity of this question compelled many men and bishops of great charity to debate and disagree among themselves while keeping the peace, so that for a long time differing conciliar statutes were adopted and amended in each area, until the view which was considered more salutary was confirmed and doubts were removed by a full council of the whole world."[12] And likewise to prove that local councils are corrected by plenary ones as well as plenary councils by subsequent plenary ones in cases of an error of fact, see Book I of *On Baptism,* "Who does not know that councils that take place in individual regions or provinces unquestionably yield to the authority of plenary councils which are made up of the whole Christian world, [and] that earlier plenary councils are corrected by later ones since experience may make available what was inaccessible and reveal what was hidden?"[13]

84.   From this two things are to be noted: first, that a plenary council is made up of the whole church. The paragraph, *Item,* para. *Cum Petrus* is to be understood in this way; namely, that a plenary council overrules every [other] authority. Secondly, it is to be noted that the universal plenary council may be deficient as to its knowledge of the facts. That several such councils erred in judgment appears in the letter sent by Augustine to Eleusius and Glorius and others on the side of Donatus,[14] as well as in other places. Thus in all these things the opinion of Ambrose is correct that secret meetings are corrected

[10] Mansi 16, p. 86.
[11] PL 33, 340 and 43, pp. 128ff.
[12] PL 43, p. 114.
[13] The quotation is also from Book II of *Against the Donatists* (PL 43, pp. 128ff.).
[14] PL 33, pp. 162ff.

by universal ones, following the teaching of Augustine in *On Christian Doctrine*, Book II, chapter 8, that the things that are universally accepted ought to be preferred to what is held by particular areas.[15] You see now the authority of universal councils that are properly carried out. Hence Augustine in the first part of his sermon against the Pelagians says that the authority of Mother Church is such that its canon of fundamental truth is so firm that anyone who butts against this impregnable wall will himself be shattered.[16] Augustine also says the same thing in the 11th book of *Against Faustus*,[17] and more quotations could be given on the subject but it is not necessary here.

[15] PL 34, p. 40.   [16] PL 38, pp. 1335ff.   [17] PL 42, p. 246.

CHAPTER VI

THE BRIEF FORM USED BY THE ANCIENTS IN CELEBRATING UNIVERSAL COUNCILS.

85. In summary, from the records of the councils we should note that universal councils were assembled by the emperors to discuss articles of faith, with the consent of the Roman pontiff and of the other patriarchs. The Holy Gospels, a piece of the wood of the Holy Cross, and other relics were placed in the middle of the meeting. All Catholic bishops and abbots were admitted, together with those laymen whom the representatives of the [episcopal] sees brought along and those whom the emperor himself wished to represent him or to be at his side. Matters were treated in different actions each day and settled in [public] sessions and each proposal was submitted in writing and read from a high pulpit. Matters of faith were discussed first and the synod heard the authorities quoted by each side, checked the original copies and opening sections of the books and the contents of the whole of the chapters quoted, to prevent the meaning of the quotation from perhaps having been altered by abbreviation. All of these things were carried out in good order, openly and publicly after a review both of the books and the quotations, and the synod issued its decrees in accordance with the testimony of the Scriptures. After this it went into questions of peace, the return of heretics, and the

settlement of questions between litigants by consent of the parties. Finally it concerned itself in formal judicial proceedings with those cases where an agreement among the parties involved had already been arrived at in the synod, so that there might be less possibility for an appeal. And at the end of each action a notary arose who spoke the praises of the emperor in many glowing terms, comparing him either to Constantine or Marcian and extolling his good works and zeal for religion. He also praised the five patriarchs and said that the senate and the synod would be remembered forever.

86.   At the end before the closing, the statutes were read in a loud voice by the bishops or metropolitans at the same time in the upper and lower sections of the synod. The closing followed with agreement to all the acts. The reason that the council had been called and a brief summary conclusion were inserted there, together with a profession of faith. Laymen and princes did not participate in the definitions of the faith but were present to advise and exhort and direct. Lastly the signatures followed which vary as to their order from one council to another, as also does the seating order. At the Eighth Council Emperors Basil and Constantine signed after the representatives of the patriarchal sees, followed by the other bishops, and the senate also declared that it accepted the synod and this was noted by notaries. More writings could be quoted on this subject, but it is not necessary here. Therefore let us move to other subjects.

After these words let us consider the general councils which are often called universal, in order to show why many modern writers have been mistaken.

CHAPTER VII

SOMETIMES COUNCILS OF SEVERAL PROVINCES, OR
A COUNCIL OF THE WESTERN CHURCH AND THOSE
THAT ARE ATTENDED BY A PAPAL REPRESENTATIVE
BUT ARE NOT COUNCILS OF THE UNIVERSAL
CHURCH ARE CORRECTLY CALLED PROVINCIAL OR
LOCAL COUNCILS. HOWEVER WHEN THE POPE
PRESIDES OVER THEM THEY MAY SOMETIMES ALSO
BE CALLED GENERAL OR UNIVERSAL COUNCILS,
ALTHOUGH THEY SHOULD BE CALLED
PATRIARCHAL COUNCILS. THERE IS DISCUSSION OF
THE GENERAL OR UNIVERSAL COUNCIL OF THE
ROMAN CHURCH OR OF THE POPE. IT IS ASSERTED
THAT SUCH COUNCILS ONLY TAKE PLACE IN THOSE
REGIONS SUBJECT TO HIS SEE AS PATRIARCH. THE
CHAPTER DISCUSSES IN WHAT MATTERS AND HOW
IT IS SUBJECT TO THE POPE, AND BY WHAT
AUTHORITY IT EXISTS – AS WELL AS OTHER USEFUL
MATERIAL ON ITS CONVOCATION AND THE SIGNING
[OF ITS DECREES].

87. We also find that a council of some large province or of two provinces meeting together is often called a universal council, as in one case in Toledo as well as a certain council in Africa, which is mentioned above.[1] We also find that a council of the Western church is called a universal council – as St. Ambrose answers in the records of the Council of Aquileia to a heretic who objects that it is not a universal council.[2] Hence although all councils except those of the universal church are called provincial councils as in D. 3 [c. 2] *Regula* or para. *Porro* – even when a representative of the Apostolic See participates, as it says in the same place, or when a patriarch participates, as in the last action of the Council of Chalcedon which describes as an action by a provincial council the deposition of Athanasius by the council of the Patriarch of Antioch when he did not appear after being called three times,[3] – all councils other than the

[1] The Fourth Council of Toledo (Hinschius, p. 364). On the African Council, see no. 71.
[2] Mansi 3, pp. 1602ff.   [3] Mansi 7, p. 314.

councils of the universal church are also called local councils. On this, see the text, [C.] 1 q. 7 [q. 4] *Convenientibus*, which quotes the Second Council of Nicaea and says that only seven universal councils preceded it, the others being local in character. Although the Gloss says on that point that they were general councils because the representatives of the Apostolic See were there,[4] nevertheless even if it is true that a council cannot be universal without the authorization of the Apostolic See, it does not follow that a universal council of the whole church takes place whenever the pope or his legate presides over a council. The Sixth Council of Carthage at which the papal legates, Bishop Faustinus and the priests Philip and Asellus, were present, and a certain council at Arles which some writers claim was attended by Theodore, the bishop of Dalmatia, and Agatho, the deacon, as legates of Pope Sylvester, and similar meetings are called provincial councils.[5] Thus Pope Leo writes to Emperor Theodosius, "May Your Grace [lit. – Your Clemency] allow a universal council in Italy granting my request and that of the synod which has met in Rome for this purpose."[6] Observe that a universal synod is sought in Italy from the emperor by the synod over which the pope presided, and this is to be noted. And the text of the 17th canon of the Eighth Council given below clearly proves this, when it distinguishes between the universal council and the one over which the pope presides as patriarch.

88.   Nevertheless the patriarchal council of the pope is often called a universal or general council, as is evident in the chapter [23] *Antiqua* of [the *Decretals*] *De privilegiis* [x, 5, 33] where the heading calls it "general" and the text "universal" although it is called "general" more often than "universal". And similarly although a council of the universal church is properly called universal and this term is frequently used, at times it is called a general council. For instance, Pope Leo in the letter concerning the approval of the [decisions on] faith of the Council of Chalcedon which begins *Omnium*, calls Chalcedon a general council and Gregory, in D. 50 [c. 16] *Quia sanctitas*, calls all five universal councils, general councils.[7] But on that, Emperor Constantine [III] when he writes to Pope Agatho con-

---

[4] The Gloss to the *Decretum* was written by Joannes Teutonicus. The *Decretum* text refers to *six* universal councils.

[5] Hinschius, pp. 308 and 321.

[6] Hinschius, p. 604.

[7] Hinschius, p. 577. Pope Gregory's letter is apocryphal.

cerning the Sixth Council says that he should send three persons from his church and twelve metropolitans from his council "to our general council". In reply Agatho writes that he will obey as far as possible given the limited time and abilities of the province subject to him, and he says that he would have summoned the representatives and sent them more quickly except for the extensive area of the provinces over which his humble council was set. These things appear in the acts of the Sixth Universal Council.[8]

89. From this we conclude that the pope like any patriarch has his own patriarchal council subject to him as appears in the same place in the first action in the chapter headed *Piissimus*.[9] And the northern and western parts of the church are in that council, as is contained in more detail in the same place. Agatho and his council write to Constantine [IV] as follows: "Bishop Agatho, servant of the servants of God, with all the synods subject to the council of the Apostolic See – to Constantine, the great Emperor, [and] to imperial Heraclius and Tiberius: The hopes of all good men seem fulfilled when His Imperial Highness faithfully seeks and earnestly desires to embrace the true faith, prized above all gifts, which comes from the One who has crowned him and set him to govern men well. It is a gift most pleasing to God from whom proceeds all that is good and to whom it returns in our acknowledgement of his majesty. By its spirit the radiant light of the holy will shines forth all around, penetrating secret places of the mind with a growing spiritual flame, and a sweet odor ascends from the sacrifice of the heart to the Lord who is pleased with this homage. May he grant him success in earthly matters and subjugate all nations to him so that he may bring them to believe in and to know God. As subjects of the Christian empire may he free them from the power of darkness and make those happy who had been humiliated because unhappily he had permitted them to be cast down from their exalted positions."

"O most holy and powerful of princes, august emperor, we admire and praise the pious and worthy proposal which you deign to direct towards our apostolic faith. It pleases God in a more subtle way than flowing words or false loquaciousness. Prompted by divine grace and without ambiguity you wish to know the truth of the orthodox and

[8] Mansi 11, pp. 199 and 234ff. The Sixth Ecumenical Council, Constantinople III, was held in 680–681, and dealt with the Monothelite heresy.
[9] Mansi 11, pp. 214ff.

apostolic faith. Therefore all of us, the humble leaders of the church and the servants of your Christian empire in the northern and western parts, limited in knowledge but by the grace of God firm in our faith, are overjoyed by what we have learned of the holy imperial command. With deep heartfelt emotion we have given thanks for this pious proposal to God, the creator and ruler of all things, who reigns and rules along with you. We believe that Your Highness [lit. – Tranquillity] wishes to carry out a work which is praiseworthy, marvelous, salutary, and more acceptable to God than any sacrifice. It has indeed been desired by many pious and just kings but only a rare few have carried it out in a way pleasing to God in the purity of the apostolic faith."[10]

90. And below there follows in the style of another writer, "Furthermore we, your lowly servants, should explain to you, our most serene and gracious lord, the reasons for the delay in sending the persons from our council etc. whom Your Most Pious Highness in your sacred and most august letter commanded to be sent. First indeed is the fact that our numbers extend to the regions of the Atlantic Ocean, which is a great distance to travel. We hoped that from Britain our associate and fellow bishop Theodore, archbishop of the great island of Britain, as well as Philip and others who up to this time are delayed there would join our humble self so that at our lowly suggestion there might join us in a full council different bishops belonging to the council from various regions, so that all and not only a part would know what was done. In particular we know that situated among the nations of the Lombards and the Slavs, the Franks, the Galls, and the Goths or Britons are many of our fellow bishops who do not cease to be concerned to know what is being done on the subject of the apostolic faith. These can be of great assistance if they are kept in harmony in faith with us and think in agreement with us, but if – God forbid! – they were to be scandalized by the head of the faith, they would become hostile and contrary. But we, although most lowly, strive with all our energies that your Christian empire – in which the see of Blessed Peter, the prince of the apostles, was founded, the authority of which all Christian nations venerate and cherish along with us – may be shown to be exalted over all peoples. We have arranged for persons to go from our lowly position to the

[10] Mansi 11, pp. 286ff. Heraclius and Tiberius, Constantine's younger brothers, had been granted the title of *Augustus* by their father before his death.

court of Your Highness, who is protected by God. They are to offer the suggestions of all of us, that is, of all the bishops of the northern and western regions. We have also prepared the confession of our apostolic faith, not so as to dispute on uncertain matters but to put forward what is certain and immutable in a brief definition."[11]

91. From this it is clear that a general patriarchal council subject to the Roman pontiff was established in the northern and western provinces. Africa too is subject to the patriarchate of Rome – see D. 12 [c. 11] *Quis Nesciat* where the provinces subject to the Roman see are enumerated. Hence Flavian, the patriarch of Constantinople, writing to Pope Leo says: "To all the devout bishops who have been established under your reverence, etc."[12] And on this, see also the letter of Leo to Theodosius which begins: *Olim ab initio.*[13] The text of [C.] 2 q. 4 [5 c. 19] *In omnibus* also agrees with this where it says: "Of all of our bishops" as do D. 43 [93 c. 4] *juxta*, where it says, "All the bishops who are subject to the command of this Holy See" and a certain letter of Deacon Hilary to the Empress Pulcheria.[14] Nevertheless as is indicated in a letter of Pope Nicholas [I] to Emperor Michael, at that time [the bishop of] Thessalonica represented the Apostolic See in its authority over old and new Epirus, Illyria, Macedonia, Thessaly, Achaia, Dacia on the [Danube river] and on the Mediterranean, Mysia, and Praevalis.[15] Thus the Roman patriarchate had the greatest part – practically the whole of Europe and a great part of Africa – under it.

92. But this patriarchal council has the highest privilege in that being called "the Roman church," since it is united to the one Roman see, it never has and never will err on matters of faith. For it appears in the seventh action of the Eighth Universal Council that "what the Apostolic See has decreed in a regular synodal manner, ought to be more zealously embraced and more carefully observed, since you will know that this universal church has always held to what has been decided by that see, so that when individual errors arose in the church, it gave its decision first in accordance with its authority as primatial see, and the universal church then followed in the same way.

[11] Mansi 11, pp. 294ff.   [12] PL 54, p. 727.
[13] PL 54, p. 823.   [14] Mansi 6, p. 26.
[15] Jaffe, p. 2686. The dioceses enumerated included all of present-day Greece and Albania, the southern half of Yugoslavia, and a portion of the coast of Turkey, opposite Greece.

Although sometimes the universal church may have resisted it in certain matters for a time, it always finally approved what it had approved and rejected what it had rejected."[16] From this and other statements in the same place we conclude that the pope in his council ought to decide matters of faith with the unanimous agreement of his fellow-bishops. For it is said there: "To our most holy brother fellow-bishops, who are deciding and deliberating together with us." On this see D. 19 [c. 19] *Anastasius* and the Gloss on [C.] 24 q. 1 [c. 18] *Loquitur.*

93. The fact that this council is called the Roman church is evident from the above. Also in the first action of the Eighth Universal Council where the legates of the pope say: "Let the document be read which the Holy Church of the Romans has produced" and the document was read before the council. A similar passage appears in the sixth action in the chapter which begins: *Multae quidem* which says that Pope Nicholas pronounced an anathema in a synod of the whole church of the Romans. "This Roman church will always remain steadfast in the faith so that those who do not adhere to it are outside the Catholic church" is what appears in the first action according to the records of the same council in a document signed by all the participants.[17] We also read there a document which Pope Nicholas issued in the synod, which begins: "The first rule for salvation is to keep to the rule of correct belief, and then never to depart from what has been established by God and the fathers." And further on: "And you cannot ignore the statement of our Lord the Saviour which says: 'Thou art Peter and upon this rock, I will build my church.' His words are verified by the results since the Apostolic See has always kept the doctrines of religion unstained." And at the end: ". . . this see firmly possesses the whole truth of the Christian religion."[18] This was sent by [Pope] Hadrian to the Eighth Ecumenical Council of Constantinople and all subscribed to it as follows: "We follow and embrace the holy synod which Pope Nicholas of happy memory celebrated before the most sacred relics of the great apostle Peter. You yourself, our angelic lord and supreme pontiff, have subscribed to it and have held a synod there as well, and we observe and venerate all the things which were decided in those matters by your wise decree, accepting

16 Mansi 16, pp. 110ff.
17 Mansi 16, pp. 27 and 93.
18 Hinschius, p. 704.

those whom you accept and condemning all those who are condemned there."[19]

94. Note two things: First, that the term, Apostolic See, is understood as meaning the whole Roman synod, and when it says that the Roman see cannot err it means by "see," the whole synod. Secondly, it is to be noted that the see of Constantinople comes after that of Rome in making definitions, especially in matters of faith. And as was noted by the nuncio [*apocrisarius*] of the Apostolic See when he took care to bring the signatures and records of the council to Rome before the representative of the Apostolic See [at the council] arrived, Emperor Basil and the Patriarch Ignatius regretted the fact that the bishops of the see of Constantinople had signed as they did because the Apostolic See of Rome could argue from those signatures that it was greater than that of Constantinople since the professison of faith stipulated that they would follow the Apostolic See in all matters. Therefore the emperor saw to it that those signatures were taken away from the representatives of the Apostolic See by guards sent by him. Afterwards at the insistence of the [papal] representatives they were given back, and the emperor confessed that the Apostolic See was the teacher in matters of faith. And, as indicated above, so that there would be no danger of losing them the nuncio secretly took them along with the acts of the council to Rome ahead of the representatives – who were robbed of them on the way. The constancy of the faith of the Roman church is also proven in the first action of the Sixth Council and in many other places.[20]

95. From this, two things are to be noted: First, that the universal or general patriarchal council is under, and subject to, the Roman pontiff, and this is seen in the documents signed by the legates of the pope and those of his council in the Sixth and Eighth Councils,[21] since the signatures of the legates of the council follow [those of the papal legates]. D. 17 [after c. 6] *Hinc etiam* v. *Illud* indicates this [as well]. Just as he [the pope] is first in matters of faith and is judge of the faith, as indicated above, so his council is first in matters of faith among all the patriarchal councils. And from this there is a second conclusion that the decision on matters of faith which is made by the pope and this council is the most certain of all the decisions of

---

[19] Mansi 16, p. 28.
[20] Mansi 16, p. 29 and 11, p. 215.
[21] Mansi 11, p. 667 and 16, p. 140.

particular meetings, although the decision of a universal council of the whole church is more infallible and more certain. For we read in the first action of the Council of Chalcedon that Emperor Marcian says: "It is not safe to discuss a question of faith without a council of those in charge of the Sacred Scriptures throughout the world."[22] But today alas, the universal council of the Catholic church and the patriarchal council of the Roman see are the same, since the whole church has been reduced to a single patriarchate. Therefore since the decision of the Roman church, in the sense described above, has always stood as the true faith, so now the promise of Christ that the gates of hell will never prevail against it remains still more infallible and true. This is the second basic point that we wish to make.

96.   I will say a word about the procedure utilized by the Council of Africa to assemble a council since it was also later followed by the Apostolic See.[23] The location was fixed beforehand, and the metropolitans were informed as to the subject to be discussed. After a provincial council had met and the matter discussed the metropolitans sent one or two representatives of the province representing the whole (provincial) council to the meeting place. The Roman pontiff was frequently accustomed to convene a patriarchal council in the city [of Rome] and often outside it as well. Among those held outside the city at the time of Constantine was the Second Council of Arles, at which the legates of the Apostolic See and of Pope Sylvester were the priests Claudianus and Habitus, and the deacons Eugenius and Quiriacus, and we read that representatives were present from all of Africa, Mauritania, Sicily, Italy, Gaul, Spain, Germany, and all the other provinces under the patriarchate of Rome.[24] For we conclude from the acts of the Sixth Council that a synod or council of the Roman church takes place when representatives from its provinces meet at its command. Then as appears in the same place, the signatures of the others in the patriarchal council [of Rome] were affixed in the following way: First Agatho signed as follows: "I, Agatho, bishop of the holy, Catholic, and apostolic church of God in the city of Rome along with the whole council of the Roman see have consented to and signed the proposal contained above as the true apostolic faith." And after that: "I, Andrew by the grace of God

---

[22] Mansi 6, p. 598.

[23] Hinschius, pp. 297, 307.

[24] The *First* Synod of Arles met when Constantine was emperor.

bishop of the holy church of Ostia, have likewise signed this resolution which we have unanimously adopted as our apostolic faith." And in that way, all [of them] sign in order. And there follows: "I, Adeodatus, humble bishop of the holy church of Toul, the legate of the venerable synod of the provinces of Gaul, have likewise signed this proposal which we have established unanimously as our apostolic faith." And Wilfred, bishop of York, the venerable legate of the synod of Britain, signed in exactly the same way. And as it appears there, Felix of Arles and Taurinus, deacon of Toulon, were representatives of all Gaul in addition to Adeodatus and they all signed.[25] From this you have the manner of calling a council and then of signing, and the fact that decisions are made by unanimous consent – which is particularly to be noted. There follows now a further difficulty on another question.

96a. [Basel Codex only.] Nevertheless we read that the council of the Roman patriarchate was often held outside of Rome, especially in Arles. Hence the following appears in chapter 18 of the Second Synod of Arles in which the legates of the Apostolic See and of all the provinces under it participated; "A synod is to meet at the decision of the bishop of Arles in which city, we read, a council made up of participants from all parts of the world was held and convened at the time of St. Marinus."[26] And it was already defined before the time of Constantine and the other Caesars that a council should be held each year in Arles, which was called the city of Constantiniana. Thus there appears in the imperial command to the illustrious prefect of the Gauls, Agricola, which begins *Saluberrima*, after many other matters: "We command that a council be held every year in the city of Constantiniana. For it is so well-located, commerce so flourishes there, there is so much traffic in foodstuffs, that products of other regions are easily brought there. No other province enjoys the fertility that the soil of Arles seem to have. Indeed anything outstanding that the wealth of the Orient and perfumed Arabia, the delicacies of Assyria, the fertility of Africa, the beauty of Spain, or the strength of Gaul can possess seems to abound there, as if everything that is marvelous elsewhere were produced there. The southern flow of the Rhône and the northern flow of the nearby Durance are necessary to bring hither whatever the one or the other flows by or around. Whatever agri-

[25] Mansi 11, pp. 298 and 306.
[26] Hinschius, p. 322 (A.D. 353).

cultural products may be useful for that city are brought there by sail, oar, wagon, land, sea, and river. . . . In that city we command that there be a meeting . . ."[27]

This is the reason that it was determined that the annual meeting was to be held in Arles. And these considerations should be respected in all meetings. And it happens that in the edict on the holding of councils there at the time of Bishop Marinus and Emperor Constantine we read that at the same time that the Council of Nicaea was being held the fathers met [at Arles] and decreed universal regulations even without the presence of the Roman pontiff or his legate. At the beginning of the record of that council it says, "The meeting of bishops who have been assembled in the town of Arles, to our most holy lord bishop, Sylvester: What we have decreed in common council, we signify to Your Holiness [lit. – Charity] that all may know what should be observed in the future . . ."[28] Observe that by the authority of the councils to be assembled at the appointed place the fathers meeting together issued statutes to be observed by all. Note in particular that a properly assembled council can legislate with universal force against a contumacious pope.

However so that the form of a universal patriarchal council might be more perfect and as an indication of how the representatives of all the subjects of the Apostolic See were accustomed to meet together at the appointed place, note the form and signatures of another later Council of Arles which indicate that Pope Sylvester sent the priests, Claudius and Habitus, and the deacons, Eugenius and Quiriacus, and that legates were named from Sicily, Campania, Apulia, from the province of Dalmatia, from Trier, from Cologne, from Aquitaine, from Mende, from Bordeaux, from Toulouse, from Britain, from Romagna, from Andalusia, from Tarragona, from Saragossa, from Baza, from the province of Mauritania, from Sardinia, from Africa, and other provinces under the Roman see are listed along with all the legates sent – bishops, deacons, and exorcists – whose names for the sake of brevity I omit.[29] Suffice it only to know that legates from the

---

[27] Imperial order from Emperors Honorius and Theodosius in A.D. 418 (printed in G. Haenal, *Corpus legum*, Leipzig, 1845, no. 117).

[28] First Synod of Arles (A.D. 314), see Hinschius, p. 320.

[29] See discussion in Kallen, *DCC*, p. 129 and text in Hinschius, p. 321. Sylvester was not pope at the time of the Second Synod of Arles.

provinces were accustomed to meet together in this patriarchal council – and from which provinces they came.

For the sake of brevity I must omit discussion of the other provincial councils made up of one or many provinces, which also met in antiquity. It is not of great interest to us to discuss them here, since the point is clear.

But we can see how much power is given to these synods by the Nicene Council since the synod is to govern and administer everything in the province and appeals are made to it, as is done in the letter of the Council of Africa to Pope Innocent and in C. 9 q. 2 [c. 9] *Non invitati.* For when Innocent intervened in African affairs to absolve those who had been excommunicated in Africa the fathers in the Council wrote back that no definition of the fathers [in the universal council] had withdrawn this power from the African church, and the Nicene decrees clearly committed the lower clergy and the bishops to their metropolitans, for they saw it as most prudent and just that matters should be settled in the areas where they had arisen. The providence of the Holy Spirit would provide, they wrote, wise and firm justice for everyone from the priests of Christ, especially since if anyone was dissatisfied with the decision of the judges he was permitted to appeal to the council of his province or to a universal council – unless perhaps anyone believed that God could inspire one individual to carry out a just judicial procedure but deny it to vast numbers of priests meeting in council.[30] This text is to be noted because it says that the pope should not put himself above the judgment of the [universal] council and also that a provincial council can appeal to it. Nevertheless note what the Archdeacon says on this subject when he discusses D. 18 [before c. 1] *Episcoporum* and D. 17 [before c. 1] *Generalia*[31] and observe that after the gloss on the chapter, *Episcoporum* it says that difficult matters cannot be decided in provincial councils but must be settled by the pope.

[30] Letter to Pope Celestine, Mansi 4, p. 516.
[31] The Gloss referred to is on D. 17, C. 1, *Constituendum.* The Archdeacon is Guido de Baysio, author of the *Rosarium*, an important commentary on the *Decretum.*

CHAPTER VIII

THE AUTHORITY OF COUNCILS DOES NOT DEPEND
ON ITS HEAD BUT ON THE COMMON CONSENT OF
ALL. IT IS DECLARED THAT THE MANY SIGNATURES
TO THE ACTS OF THE COUNCILS PROVE THAT THE
POPE DEFINES AND LEGISLATES ON THE BASIS OF
CONSENT [OF THE OTHERS] NOT MERELY OF THEIR
ADVICE. ALL THE BISHOPS ARE JUDGES AND
AUTHORS OF CONCILIAR DEFINITIONS AND
LEGISLATION, AND THEIR SIGNATURES SHOULD
STRENGTHEN AND CONFIRM THE ACTS OF THE
COUNCILS.

97.   And to raise another serious problem – always subject to correction – there is a question as to whether statutes that are adopted in universal or other councils where the pope is presiding, either personally or through a legate, are adopted by the authority of the pope himself with the advice of the council, or with the concordance of the council. For this we should look to the subscribing signatures on other subjects besides the matters of the faith about which Agatho speaks above, and thus we may draw our basic conclusions from these and other writings. First, I find that in all the universal councils of the universal church the legates of the pope signed in the same form as the others without any difference. Each bishop either says: "Assenting," or "Consenting," or "Decreeing," or "Defining, I have subscribed." The papal legates used the same form, and I say "the papal legates" because I do not find that the pope was present at the eight universal councils.[1] To prove that this is not in doubt I will quote a few excerpts from the acts of the Council of Chalcedon concerning the deposition of Dioscorus. When Dioscorus refused to appear after three warnings, Paschasinus, the legate of Pope Leo, said to the Council: "We wish to learn from your holinesses what punishment he

---

[1] Seven councils are generally held to be ecumenical: Nicaea (A.D. 325), Constantinople I (381), Ephesus (431), Chalcedon (451), Constantinople II (553), Constantinople III (680–681), and Nicaea II (787) The Eighth Council, Constantinople IV, is not recognized by the Eastern Church – but was useful for Cusanus' argument, since it was the last Council (before Ferrara–Florence, 1438–1439) at which both the Eastern and the Western churches were represented.

deserves." The holy synod said: "Let what is in accordance with the canons be done." Paschasinus said: "Do your reverences command that we apply the canonical punishment to him? Do you agree or do you wish to do something else?" The holy synod said: "We also consent. No one disagrees and the will of the holy synod is unanimous." Julian, the bishop of Hippo, said to the legates of [Pope] Leo, "We beseech your holinesses, since as representatives of the holy Pope Leo you have a more eminent place than the rest, to promulgate a just punishment against the contumacious person and to pronounce the sentence against him contained in the canonical regulations. All of us in the holy synod are in agreement with the sentence of your holiness." Paschasinus said: "Let what pleases your excellencies be unanimously carried out." Maximus, the bishop of Antioch, said: "We are all also in agreement with what your holiness thinks should be done." After this the apostolic legates pronounced the sentence by which Pope Leo had deposed and condemned Dioscorus, and they added: "Let not this holy synod hestitate to issue a decree in accordance with the canonical rules concerning the celebrated Dioscorus." Anatolius, the bishop of Constantinople, and everyone in the council passed sentence saying: "I judge him to be removed from every priestly or episcopal ministry."[2] Note that the apostolic legates at the council since they sit in the first place pass sentence first if the synod commands it, and after them each one does so according to his rank, and that the force of the sentence depends on the unity and agreement of wills. Note also that the sentence of deposition of Dioscorus adopted by the Apostolic See was reviewed again by the universal synod in a new citation of Dioscorus in accordance with the canonical rules – which should be kept in mind in what follows. This is the form for the universal councils.

98. I find that the signatures of subscription of the Roman pontiffs in other councils were also given in the same form. Thus in the Council of Pope Martin [I] which preceded the Sixth Universal Council, I find that Martin signed as follows: "I, Martin, the bishop of the holy, Catholic, and apostolic church of the city of Rome, have signed this definition into law which confirms the orthodox faith and condemns Sergius of Constantinople and Pyrrhus and Paul."[3] And this is the way that Maximus of the holy church of Aquileia signed

[2] Mansi 6, pp. 1043ff.
[3] Mansi 10, p. 1162.

confirming, condemning, and decreeing, along with 103 bishops using the same form. I find that the signatures were given in this way in the council at Rome over which Pope Gregory II presided at the time of Emperors Leo and Constantine the Younger: "I, Gregory, bishop of the holy, Catholic, and apostolic church of the city of Rome, have signed this, as adopted and promulgated by us."[4] And bishops, 21 in number, 14 priests, and 4 deacons signed in the same way. We read the same thing in the synod of Symmachus. We read in the sixth action of the council over which Symmachus presided in the time of King Theoderic that 218 bishops said: "In confirmation of the statutes of the holy fathers, we have expressly decreed ..." Symmachus, bishop of the Catholic church, said: "Show a like unity however as to what should be done if anyone should dare to transgress or act against these decrees" and when the bishops had risen together and afterwards were seated again, they said: "If anyone should dare to infringe the prohibitions of this holy synod, if he is a cleric, let him be deprived of his office; if a monk or layman, let him be forbidden communion." And below: "When they were seated, and silence was established, the whole synod said: If any cleric or monk or layman, whether of greater or lesser rank, presumes to contravene the decrees in the form put forward by us, let proceedings be carried out against him as a schismatic in accordance with the holy canons." And they signed: "I, Caelius Symmachus, bishop of the holy Catholic church of the city of Rome have signed this, adopted by us at the inspiration of the Lord. I, Lawrence, bishop of the holy church of Milan, have signed this, adopted by us at the inspiration of the Lord. I, Eulalius, bishop of Syracuse, etc." And everyone signed in the same way. And in the sixth action Pope Symmachus said that some statutes were to be reissued and certain ones corrected, and added: "Because God has granted your presence in my support, I believe that it is necessary that the matter be confirmed in a way appropriate to ecclesiastical authorities." And he subscribed, "I, Caelius Symmachus, etc. have signed what has been adopted by the synod and approved and confirmed by us."[5] And everyone signed in the same way.

99. I find analogous signatures in the council of Pavia held by Pope Boniface against clerics living in concubinage.[6] Note that every

---

[4] Mansi 12, p. 264.   [5] Mansi 8, p. 298.
[6] Mansi 19, p. 314. (The Council was called in 1022 under Pope Benedict VIII.)

signature indicated consent and confirmation. This is the way it appears in the sixth chapter of the Council of Africa where Gennadius said: "What has been said by all we should confirm with our own signature." And all the bishops said, "So be it, so be it."[7] Also as we see at the end of the acts of the Eighth Universal Council, the representatives of old Rome said: "Because by the providence of God all church matters have been brought to a happy conclusion, we should confirm these things in writing by our own hand in order in the synod." Therefore in order to indicate confirmation and consent and to reinforce all of what was formally concluded, the signatures of the bishops were affixed at the end in order in the synod.[8] The following is found in a certain Council of Toledo: "Concluding and confirming all these things with our signature" and thereafter: "I, Eugene, metropolitan bishop of Toledo, have signed giving my assent to these common decrees." And the other bishops signed in the same way. Another council [in Toledo] at which Isidore was present, said: "We confirm all these things with our own signatures so that they may endure."[9] And this is found at the end of all the councils.

100.   From this it follows that the signatures cited above prove that the force of canons adopted in council is derived not from the pope nor from the head of the council but only from a single concordant consent. The Nicene Council directed that heretics who returned to the faith should profess those decrees that had been adopted by common consent and no others see [C.] 1 q. 7 [c. 8] *Si qui voluerint.* And if sometimes it is found that the pope decreed something "with the advice" of the council [this usage never appears, however, in the ancient councils], this is to be understood as advice which was also an approval which is equivalent to consent. For there is no doubt that a provincial council cannot legislate on matters that concern the whole province without its head, the archibishop, who is judge of the province as the Archdeacon notes on D. 17 [before c. 1], *Generalia*, [C.] 9 q. 3 c. 1 and 2, unless he does not wish to be present or cannot participate, for instance because he is dead, as is noted in D. 18 [c. 10] *Placuit.* However statutes that are adopted in these provincial councils are not for that reason ascribed to the metropolitan with the consent of the council, but to the various learned men in the council who were the authors of the canons, as appears in the procedure in D.

---

[7] Mansi 3, p. 873.   [8] Mansi 16, p. 188.
[9] Fifth and Fourth Councils (A.D. 633) of Toledo (Mansi 10, pp. 656 and 641).

16 [c. 9] *Sexta*, para. *Annotatio*.[10] And those canons were not based on the authority of their authors but on the fact that the counsel as well as the consent of the others concurred – which is proven by their signatures.

[10]D. 16 c. 11.

CHAPTER IX

NO CANONICAL LEGISLATION IS VALID UNLESS IT
HAS BEEN ADOPTED WITH EXPRESS OR TACIT
CONSENT OR ON THE BASIS OF SOME OTHER
CANON. IF OTHER DIRECTIVES ARE ISSUED BY ANY
INDIVIDUAL THEY ARE NOT CALLED LAWS
[*CONSTITUTIONES*] AND THEY ARE NOT BINDING
EXCEPT FROM ACCEPTANCE OF, AND PREVIOUS
CONSENT TO THE AUTHORITY OF THE LEGISLATOR.

101.   It has been demonstrated above that the council derives its authority from the power of binding and loosing given to the church and to the priesthood by Christ, as well as from the fact that there is no doubt that Christ is present in the midst of those brought together in his name and the spirit of the Lord inspires those assembled together.[1] The Nicene Council decided that the synod of the province is to decide the things that concern each province, [C.] 9 q. 2 [c. 8] *Episcopi*; [C] 3 q. 6 [c. 16] *Neminem* para. *Illa*. The same definition by the Nicene Council declares that it is to govern and administer everything [C.] 9 q. 2 [c. 9] *Non invitati*, and, as the paragraph *Illa* cited above states, whatever arises within the province should be heard and finally decided by fellow members of the province. From this it is evident that since a council is established by consent, because where there is dissent there is no council, see D. 15 [c. 1] *Canones* para. *Synodus*, no more basic foundation for the canons can be discovered than that of concordance. For church canons can only be adopted by the church gathering called a synod or meeting. And therefore if anyone whether he be pope or patriarch, promulgates decrees that are

[1] Matthew 18:20 and Acts 15:25.

not in accordance with the church canons, those statutes cannot be called canons or church laws and they have no special binding power whatsoever except to the extent that they are confirmed by acceptance and use or consent or they agree with the canons. Hence the texts of Pope Leo concerning the letters of his predecessors, in D. 19 [c. 1] *Si Romanorum*, and those of Pope Damasus in [C.] 25 q. 1 [c. 12] *Omnium*, speak of decretals and letters promulgated concerning the teachings of the canons.

102. I do not wish to deny that by the authority and power of God who commanded us to obey those set over us and to be subject to kings,[2] rulers have the power to legislate and command in accordance with the responsibility entrusted to them. But I say that the obligatory force of the statutes also requires consent through use and acceptance. The [church] laws of Africa would not have bound the Gauls if Charlemagne had not applied them to Gaul when he received them in two summary collections from Pope Hadrian and if Gaul had not then accepted them.[3] Hence the [third] Council of Toledo, held in A.D. 627 when all had been converted to the faith from the Arian heresy, said: "We have subscribed with our whole heart and soul to the decisions of the holy councils of Nicaea, Ephesus, Constantinople, and Chalcedon, which we have heard with a most favorable ear and approve with true consent."[4] Notice that the synod says: "With our consent." Another Council of Toledo says: "We decree that if anyone who knows the acts of the Council of Nicaea presumes to act otherwise and thinks that he need not follow that Council, he should be treated as excommunicated unless he mends his ways when he is corrected by his brethren."[5] And it is frequently found in all councils that the canons of past councils are confirmed in order to renew their force, to show that they are agreed to and accepted, and to renew any canons that may have abrogated through non-observance.

---

[2] 1 Peter 2:13.
[3] PL 67, pp. 136ff.
[4] Mansi 9, p. 987; Hinschius, p. 357.
[5] Hinschius, p. 350.

CHAPTER X

GENERAL STATUTES NEVER BIND PARTICULAR
PROVINCES UNLESS THEY ARE ACCEPTED. THE
FORCE OF STATUTES DEPENDS RATHER ON
ACCEPTANCE THROUGH USAGE AND CONSENT, SO
THAT ONLY WHAT HAS BEEN PROMULGATED IN A
COUNCIL IS PROPER [CANONICAL] LEGISLATION.

103. In addition it is clear that since the direction of a province in all
matters is up to its synod, no law is binding unless it is approved by
the synod. For every law ought to be appropriate to the country or
place and time, see D. 4 [c. 2] *Erit autem* [as well as] D. 29 in its
entirety, and the synod of the province has to determine this – I am
speaking of positive human laws. All binding obligations should be
based on the authority of the Holy Scriptures, the statutes of the
bishops issued in the councils, and the custom of the universal
church. Everything else should be eliminated; see D. 12 [c. 12] *Omnia
[talia]*, which is a text of Augustine. Note that he [Augustine] excludes
all other obligations. Therefore the binding force of particular
statutes as they apply to subjects depends on usage and acceptance.
Hence laws are confirmed in usage and approved by the custom of
those using them, see D. 4 [after c. 3] *Leges.* And it is also true of the
statutes of the Roman pontiff that they lose their force through non-
usage. This is proved in the same place in the chapters [c. 4 and 6]
Statuimus and *Denique.*

104. And it should be known that church laws [*constitutiones*] are like
common resting places [*stationes*]; see [*Decretals* 5 39] *De Sententia
Excommunicationis* [c. 31] *Inter alia* – although Hostiensis says
otherwise in his *Summa* on [*Decretals* 1 2] *De constitutionibus unde
dicatur.*[1] And those laws are properly called canons that must be
observed by all, as is said in c. 1 of [*Decretals* 1 2] *De constitutionibus.* In
all the ancient books only those church laws are called canons which
have been adopted by synods because although the metropolitan has
the responsibility and care of the province, [C.] 9 q. 3 [c. 2] *Per
singulas,* he does not have the power to issue general statutes for the

---

[1] *Stationes* is a corruption of *statuitio,* "decision" or "determination." Hostiensis denied
that consent was necessary for church laws (*constitutiones*). See Kallen, *DCC,* p. 139.

whole province, but he should constitute them, that is, legislate together with other suffragan [bishops], for God rejoices in this concord and is glorified in his members, see [C.] 9 q. 3 [c. 5] *Archiepiscopus*, as with one voice the Trinity is glorified in concord in the church, see the same chapter and question [c. 7] *Nullus primas*. For God is present where there is simple consent without deformity, as Pope Hormisda says in his letter to the bishops of Spain.[2]

[2] Hinschius, p. 690.

CHAPTER XI

THE DECREES OF THE ROMAN PONTIFF MUST ALSO DERIVE THEIR FORCE AND BINDING POWER FROM USAGE AND ACCEPTANCE. OTHERWISE CHRISTIANS WOULD BE IN PERIL. THEREFORE THE LAWS ADOPTED BY THE COUNCIL HAVE THE GREATEST BINDING FORCE, AND THE REASON FOR THIS IS GIVEN. IN ADDITION WHAT THE CANON LAWYERS SAY ABOUT THE DECRETAL LETTERS OF THE APOSTOLIC SEE SHOULD BE UNDERSTOOD AS APPLYING TO DECREES ADOPTED IN COUNCIL OR ACCORDING TO THE CANONS.

105. Although we ought to obey salutary papal [lit. – apostolic] commands, see D. 12 [c. 2] *Apostolicis*, and although we must admit that the Roman pontiff has legislative power from God, as the Gloss on [c. 13] *Generali* of [I, 6] *De electione* in the *Liber Sextus* notes, and no one can take this power from him, as is noted in the comments by the Archdeacon on D. 2 [c. 2], and those of Antonius de Butrio on [*Decretals* I, 7] c. 1 *De translatione* – which should be understood, however, in a limited sense, as is explained at the end of this second book[1] – nevertheless, in order for his statute to be binding it is not sufficient for it to be publicly promulgated but it should also be accepted and approved in usage as we have said above. See also the

[1] See no. 249. The Archdeacon (Guido de Baysio) and Antonius de Butrio (d. 1408) both defended unlimited papal legislative power.

comments on the heading of [*Decretals* I 2] *De constitutionibus,* by the doctors who say that for a statute to be valid three things are necessary: authority in the legislator, the approval of the statute through usage, and its publication.[2] Thus we see that even at the beginning many apostolic statutes were not accepted after they were issued. The principle of interpretation for all these appears in D. 4 [after c. 6] *Haec etsi* which reads: "Although these have been established as laws, those who do not observe them are not guilty of a crime because they have not been approved by common usage. Otherwise those who did not obey them would be punished unjustly." No one is said to ignore or break such a law or statute because the law is not operative. But if there is a law which has also been accepted, then anyone who does not observe it and will not submit his will to the reasoning of the law is in criminal contempt – although not if he is driven by passion or desire – as the Archdeacon says so well, discussing D. 81 [85 c. 5] *Quicumque.*

106. From this we conclude that the statutes which have been adopted in synod are rightly considered as canonical because depending on its rank, the synod represents either a province or a kingdom or the universal church. Whatever is thus adopted in the synod carries with it both acceptance and confirmation, although its force grows with usage. Therefore all the laws that speak of the statutes of the Apostolic See, D. 19 esp. c. [5] *Nulli fas,* ought, I think, to be understood as speaking of the statutes of the synod of that see, as the text quoted seems to say – or at least of that see understood not as the pope alone but with the cardinals as well, who act today as the representatives of the whole Roman church and even of the universal church.

107. Indeed the pope is said to be the spokesman of that see, because that see speaks through the pope. The letters of the Roman pontiffs are called apostolic letters that have statutory force because at some time the pope issued them with the consent of a synod made up of the metropolitans who came once a year to [his] see. Hence in the Synod of Toledo made up of all the bishops of Spain and Gaul in the year A.D. 627 in the reign of King Recaredus, the first chapter of the statutes after the chapters on the orthodox belief (since they were all coming back from the Arian heresy to the Catholic faith) reads as follows: "But now since peace has returned to the Church through the mercy of Christ let everything which the past canons prohibited be

---

[2] The most frequently cited source of the requirement of confirmation through usage is the *Decretum* D. 4 para, *Leges* which cites "the custom of the users" as necessary.

restrained by a new binding force and let everything be done which they have commanded. Likewise let all the definitions of the councils remain in force as well as the letters of the synods of the holy bishops of Rome."[3] And in another council held at Toledo in the time of King Sisenandus, it says in ch. 17: "The authority of many councils and the decrees of the synod of the holy bishops of Rome describe the Book of the Apocalypse as written by John the Evangelist and they have decreed that it should be included among the divine books"[4] etc.

108. Note that the letters of the synod are called decrees. From this we conclude that the approval of books [of the Bible] which is ascribed to Pope Gelasius was carried out by a synod, as is contained in the third book of Burchard where it is said that seventy bishops were in that council.[5] The text, D. 96 [c. 13] *Constantinus*, also proves this. In addition the texts of Pope Nicholas and of Gelasius and others which say: "Decrees promulgated by the Roman pontiff on pain of excommunication for the correction of morals and discipline," ought to be understood, says Hincmar, the most subtle archbishop of Rheims – who is praised by the same Pope Nicholas in [C.] 11 q. 3 [c. 102] *Excellentissimus* – as concerning the decrees that have been promulgated – that is, those of the binding decisions of the sacred canons and of the Apostolic Synod, which is often called the Apostolic See, whose spokesman is the pope, which he manifests to the people.[6] This is the way that I understand D. 19 c. 1 and similar passages in the *Decretum* about which more will be said at a certain point below. And when they clearly refer to the pope alone, as has been said above, they must be understood as referring to statutes which have been accepted and confirmed in usage – which amounts to the same thing as legislation by a synod. For the practice of the universal church can be equated with the decrees of the bishops in council, see D. 12 [c. 12] *Omnis*.

109. Nevertheless I do not deny that the pope has always been able to respond, advise, and write when consulted, but I say this about statutes which have the force of canons and decrees which bind universally in the church. Whether today as a result of customary practice over a long period the pope can also legislate by himself for

---

[3] Third Synod of Toledo (A.D. 589) – see Mansi 9, p. 992.
[4] Fourth Synod of Toledo (A.D. 633) – see Mansi 10, p. 624.
[5] Burchard of Worms, PL 140, p. 175.
[6] PL 126, pp. 384ff.

the universal church, I will not discuss for the present. Nevertheless I do say: Even if he could do this, it is not contrary to our position, which amounts only to saying that the authority to adopt canons does not depend solely on the pope but on universal consent. And against this conclusion no prescriptive right or custom can have any validity, just as it cannot do so against divine or natural law from which this is drawn as a conclusion.

CHAPTER XII

THE FORCE OF CUSTOM PROVES THAT THE BINDING
POWER OF STATUTES DEPENDS ON CONSENT. IT IS
CORRECT TO EQUATE THE LEGISLATIVE POWER OF
THE POPE AS CHAIRMAN OF THE UNIVERSAL
COUNCIL WITH THAT OF THE PRESIDING
METROPOLITAN IN A PROVINCIAL COUNCIL. AND
THEREFORE THE POPE IS NEARLY ALWAYS CALLED
ARCHBISHOP BY THE ANCIENTS.

110. Anyone can see that it is true that the force of a law comes from the concordance of the subjects who are bound by it, by observing the force of custom based only by usage. On the validity of custom see the discussion in D. 12 in its entirety and especially in D. 11 [c. 5] *Ecclesiasticarum.* Thus we respect what has been introduced by custom even when it is not known whether it had the consent of any ruler with the power to legislate. And even if the force of custom also depends in part on the tacit consent and permission of the superior, as is the case with many legitimately established customs including particular customs that are opposed to general binding human laws, it should not be said that the source of its force does not still come from usage and preceding consent. Even when it discussed the power of patriarchs, we see that the Holy Council of Nicaea argued from custom, see D. 65 [c. 6] *Mos est* and [c. 7] *Quoniam Mos*, saying: "This custom is like that of the Roman Church. Just as the Roman pontiff has power over all his bishops, so also the Church of Alexandria should have this power throughout Egypt on the basis of custom." Thus it commanded that custom be considered in the case of the

power of patriarchs, see [C.] 9 q. 3 [c. 8] *Conquestus*. We also see how much power beyond the holy ancient observances the Roman pontiff has acquired from the usage and customary obedience of his subjects today.

III. We wish one brief conclusion to be drawn and rationally proved from the above concerning the significance of the practice of signing conciliar decrees – that in the councils the Roman pontiff does not have the power to adopt general statutes which certain of his adulators attribute to him, i.e. that he alone has [the right] to legislate with the others acting in an advisory capacity. Rather the presiding role of the Roman pontiff is not very different in its effect in a general or universal council from the presiding role of the metropolitan in a provincial council. Indeed in a universal council of the whole universal Catholic church, this presiding role possesses *less* authority to act than in a patriarchal council. In a patriarchal council, however, his role is correctly compared to, and equated with, that of the metropolitan in a provincial council, as has been concluded above. Therefore among the ancients the Roman pontiff was often called an archbishop. In the universal council of the universal church, however, not as much power should be attributed to the presiding role of the Roman pontiff as is allotted to him in his patriarchal council or to a metropolitan in a provincial council, as will be explained below.

CHAPTER XIII

ALL THE ARGUMENTS THAT MAINTAIN THAT THE
POPE HAS THE PLENITUDE OF POWER FROM GOD
AND SIMILAR POINTS ARE INVALID. THIS IS
DISCUSSED AT LENGTH. THE EXERCISE OF
ADMINISTRATIVE POWER BY SUPERIORS IS BASED
ON THE SUBMISSION OF THOSE UNDER THEM SO
THAT THE POWER OF SUPERIORS DEPENDS ON
THEIR INFERIORS. THIS IS WORTHY OF NOTE.
PAPAL ADMINISTRATIVE POWER HAS THE SAME
BASIS AS THAT OF BISHOPS BECAUSE ALL
ADMINISTRATIVE POWER IN THE CHURCH COMES
FROM ABOVE AND BELOW, SINCE THE PASTOR IS A
MEDIATOR BETWEEN GOD AND HIS FLOCK. ALL THE
CONTRARY ARGUMENTS ARE ANSWERED FULLY,
ONE AFTER ANOTHER.

112. This may perhaps seem novel to those who have read the
writings of the Roman pontiffs arguing (1) that there is a plenitude of
power in the Roman pontiff and that all others are called in an
advisory capacity, see [*Decretals* 1 8] *De Usu Pallii* [c. 4] *ad honorem*,
and (2) that Gelasius, Sylvester, and Nicholas, and Symmachus and
other Roman pontiffs say that the pope judges all the other churches
and no one judges him, (3) that since the power of the pope is divine,
it is given to him by God in the words "Whatsoever you shall bind," as
Franciscus Zabarella notes in his *Commentaries* on [*Decretals* 1 2] *De
constitutionibus* [c. 6] *Cum omnes* (4) that therefore he presides as the
vicar of Christ over the universal church, see [Zabarella] *Commentaries* on [*Decretals* 1 7] *De translatione* c. 1 and 2,[1] and (5) that since he
has the highest power we find that he has judged and absolved the
subjects of many bishops even when their bishops were not guilty of
negligence and appeals are made to him without going through an

---

[1] On the influence on Cusanus of Zabarella, a leading conciliarist at the Councils of Pisa
(1409) and Constance (1414–1417) and a teacher of canon law at Padua before Nicholas
studied there, see Sigmund, *Nicholas of Cusa*, pp. 110–113. The passages cited do not
represent Zabarella's own views. See also Thomas E. Morrissey, "Cardinal Zabarella
and Nicholas of Cusa: From Community Authority to Consent of the Community,"
MFCG, 17 (1986), 157–176.

intermediary. Pope Damasus in his letter to Stephen, the Archbishop of the Council of Mauritania, and to all the bishops of Africa which begins "When the letters from you, my brethren, had been read . . ." says that the pope has episcopal ministry over the universal church, the Roman church is the highest of the churches, and that any Roman pontiff takes the place of Peter as representative of Christ. He also says that in the metropolitan council cases ought to be discussed with the agreement of all but to decide "the most important cases or to condemn bishops is not permitted without the authorization of the Apostolic See which all ought to call upon if necessary for support and help. For a synod cannot be Catholic without its authority and a bishop cannot be definitively condemned except in a legitimate synod congregated at the proper time by Apostolic authority, and all other councils are not to be considered as ratified without authorization by the Apostolic See."[2]

113. Similar statements are made by many Roman pontiffs. Furthermore because the power of legislation depends on the power of jurisdiction the Cardinal [Zabarella] notes in his statement on the chapter *cum omnes* that it is absurd to say that anything more than the will of the pope is required for a statute to have force. For what pleases the prince has the force of law. Besides there is no doubt about the statement of the doctors on the chapter [8] *Cum accessissent* and also on *Cum omnes* [c. 6] of [*Decretals*, 1, 2] *De Constitutionibus*, that the rector of any corporate body [*universitas*] has the exercise of jurisdiction although that jurisdiction itself also remains potentially [*in habitu*] in the corporate body. But no one doubts that the pope is also the master of the ship of St. Peter and of the universal church. Therefore the force of church laws depends on him since a corporation cannot legislate without its rector.[3]

114. Such things and others like them can be argued at length but to answer briefly, suffice it to say that they are all reduced to these basic principles – which can be answered. Arguing especially on the basis of those points [and] citing the actions described in his letter to all the bishops in Dardania, Pope Gelasius concluded that by ancient tradition the Apostolic See acting without a council absolved those unjustly condemned by a council and also that without a council it had

[2] Hinschius, pp. 502ff (False Decretals).
[3] On the significance of the power of jurisdiction, see Brian Tierney, *Foundations of Conciliar Theory*, Cambridge, 1955, pp. 31–33.

the power of condemning those who should be condemned. Nevertheless – before I proceed – he was speaking of the condemnation of the heretic Acatius and the pope based his action on the action of a general synod which had condemned the heresy into which Acatius had fallen. It was as if the pope acknowledged that Acatius would not have been condemned by the Apostolic See without a synod if he had not fallen under the sentence of condemnation of the synod which condemned the heresy into which he fell, – as if the Apostolic See had carried out a sentence already passed – [C.] 24 q. 1 [c. 1] *Acatius* with the two chapters that follow [c. 2 and 3].

115.   But to investigate the truth of this matter as to whether indeed as a matter of positive law all prelates below the pope have their power of jurisdiction by derivation from the pope himself, as the doctors, especially my Lord Franciscus Zabarella, assert regarding [*Decretals* 1 2 c. 7] *quam ab ecclesiarum* – if this is true, Peter ought first to have received something special from Christ and the pope should be his successor in this respect. But we know that Peter received no more power from Christ than the other apostles, see D. 21 [c. 2] *In novo* [and] [C.] 24 q. 1 [c. 18] *Loquitur.* For nothing was said to Peter which was not also said to the others. Just as Peter was told, "Whatsoever thou shalt bind upon earth" etc. Christ also said to the others – "Whatsoever you [plural] bind. . . ." And when Christ said to Peter "Thou art Peter and upon this rock," etc., we understand the word, rock, as a reference to Christ in whom he [Peter] had confessed his belief. And if the word, rock [*petram*], is to be understood as a reference to Peter's role as the foundation stone of the church, according to Jerome the other apostles were also foundation stones of the church. When these things are discussed in the next to the last book of the Apocalypse no one doubts that it refers to the apostles when it speaks of the twelve foundation stones of the city of Jerusalem. And if Christ said to Peter "Feed my sheep," it is clear that this feeding is by word and example. Similarly according to St. Augustine's gloss on the same passage, the same command was given to all [when Christ said] "Going into the whole world" in the last chapter of Matthew and Mark.[4] Nothing else is said to Peter which implies any power. Therefore we are correct in saying that all the apostles are equal to Peter in power.

[4] The scriptural passages quoted are Matthew 16:19; Matthew 18:18; Matthew 16:18; Apocalypse (Revelation) 21:14; John 21:17; Matthew 28:19; Mark 16:15.

116. In addition it should be remembered that in the beginning there was only one general episcopate in the church diffused throughout the world without any division into dioceses, see [C.] 7 q. 1 *Novatianus Item episcopatus*. For this reason c. 1 of [VI 1 7] *De Translatione Praelaturae* notes that it is not essential for the episcopacy that a bishop be attached to this or that place but it is sufficient for him to be a bishop of the whole church, as were Paul and Barnabus who were sent out generally to the whole church, see D. 75 [c. 5] *Quod die dominico*, as Hostiensis notes in his *Summa* on *De Translatione* – on which subject more is also said earlier in another place.[5] Hence since the power of binding and loosing which is the basis of the whole jurisdiction of the church comes immediately from Christ, as Joannes Andreae notes in his comments on c. 1 of *De renuntiatione*[6] and see also [the *Decretum*] *De poenitentia* D. 1 [c. 51] *verbum* and similar statements, and because the power of jurisdiction is derived from that power of binding and loosing, it is evident that all bishops – and perhaps even all priests – are of equal power as to jurisdiction, although not as to actual execution. The exercise of executive power is kept within certain limits by positive law in order better and more peaceably to bring all men to their final end; namely, God, to which final end all power and jurisdiction and human statutes ought to tend by means proportionate to the time and the place. Hence when, on account of the negligence of those in the lower ranks or because of necessity, the reasons for the law that sets geographical limits and decrees that no one should enter into the territory of another no longer apply, those positive laws cease to bind. And we see that in times of necessity we go beyond human positive laws into the area of natural law, because in that situation any priest can absolve anyone from any sin, even someone excommunicated by the pope. Hence administration necessarily depends partly on positive law as to the grades of superiority and inferiority. The fact that to maintain unity there are separate dioceses and that a single bishop is established over the priests of each diocese is a matter of positive law, although this was done by the inspiration of God, see D. 93 [c. 24] *Legimus* and D. 95 [c. 5] *Olim*. Therefore, following Hostiensis in his *Summa* on [*Decretals* 1] *De Maioritate et Oboedientia*,[7] we say that all the bishops

[5] See no. 48.

[6] Joannes Andreae (d. 1348) wrote a standard commentary on the *Liber sextus*, the canon law collection issued by Boniface VIII in 1302.

[7] On Hostiensis, see Brian Tierney, *Foundations of Conciliar Theory*, pp. 149–153.

are equal in power and the higher offices such as that of archbishop, patriarch, and pope are administrative in character, as is stated in the Gloss on [D. 21 c. 2] *In novo* mentioned above as well as that on [C.] 2 q. 7 *Puto.*

117. But administrative rank which is derived from the possession of jurisdiction is established in part on the basis of the consent of the subjects. And so we say that an elected officer has ordinary jurisdiction over those who elected him by virtue of his administrative power over them. Thus on c. 1 of *De renuntiatione* in the *Liber Sextus*, it is observed [by Joannes Andreae] that the cardinals elect the pope in the name of the universal church and from the submission through them of the universal church to the one who is elected, the pope receives the administrative power together with the power of jurisdiction transmitted to him by election, which makes him pope. However I do not deny that the power of God is also involved, who authorizes and confirms their action, as is noted in the same place and discussed at a certain point below at the end of this second part.[8] On this basis it is clear that the jurisdiction which the Roman pontiff possesses is established by divine privilege and by election – as is that of the others who have ecclesiastical administrative power. Just as the hierarchical rule of the highest authority is established both by divine ordination and the election or consent of his subordinates, as appears in the text [D. 31 c. 2] *In Novo* which asserts that Peter was established as ruler by Christ with the agreement of the apostles, so also are the others who have administrative power. This administrative power is held to be distributed and ordered throughout the church, as Hostiensis notes in his *Summa* discussing [*Decretals* 1 7] *De Translatione* and the chapter [9] *Pastoralis* of [*Decretals* III 10] *De hiis qui fiunt a praelatis* and [C.] 13 q. 1 [c. 1] *Ecclesias.* Therefore we find the sole difference in the case of Peter is that he was chosen by Christ with the agreement of the apostles to have greater administrative power because he was older, as St. Jerome asserts in his first book against Jovinianus.[9]

118. However while the Roman pontiff is the principal successor of St. Peter, we cannot deny that all the bishops are also his successors. Peter was the first to have the pontificate over the apostles, as noted in the aforementioned chapter [D. 21 c. 2] *In novo*, but since the episcopate involves rulership over the priesthood as already indicated we

---

[8] Book II, nos. 249 and 262.
[9] PL 23, pp. 258ff.

have to say that all ecclesiastical power to rule exists by a kind of succession from the first ruler, namely Peter. And as Peter's power to rule was derived from the fact that he represented Christ, so also in the case of the ruling power of the other bishops, as Anacletus says in the same chapter *In novo*. "Therefore he who hears them, hears Christ." He does not say "He who hears them, hears the pope or Peter."[10] Indeed all the bishops have an apostolic command to rule the flock over which the Holy Spirit placed them for the good governance of the church. And they make decisions in the synod because they are the princes and rulers of the church. That the episcopal authorities who are chosen to be archbishops or primates are also the successors of Peter is evident from what Anacletus says in a letter to all the bishops and priests which begins: *Benedictus deus*. He says "The blessed apostles decided among themselves that the bishops of the various nations should know who was to be first among them, so that responsibility over them would be his. For there was also a certain difference of rank among the apostles and although all were apostles, it was granted to Peter by the Lord – and the apostles wished this to be the case – that Cephas, i.e., the head, should rule over all the other apostles and act as the foundation of the apostolate. They also prescribed this same form to be observed by their successors and the other bishops."[11] See D. 22 [c. 2] *Sacrosancta*. Note that this form was transmitted by the apostles that as they had put Peter over themselves, so also a primate ought to be established over the other bishops. Thus the primate succeeds Peter as the other bishops succeed the other apostles and what is said of the primate ought also to be said of the archbishop – that he is a successor of St. Peter.

119. Certain modern writers say that Peter sent the apostles out to the individual provinces. They wish to conclude from this that the exercise of the power of binding and loosing was given by Christ to Peter and through Peter to the others. Pope Anacletus in the letter above does not say this. He says that the apostles were chosen by Christ and sent out at his command. The Roman pontiffs, especially Pope Symmachus and others, write that the Roman pontiff is judged by God alone,[12] but does not Anacletus in a letter to the bishops of Italy which begins *Quoniam apostolicae* likewise say that the high

[10] Hinschius, p. 79 (False Decretal) – *Quoniam Apostolicam*, n. 12.
[11] PL 130, p. 78 (False Decretal).
[12] See C. 9, 9.4 c. 14 and c. 13 (False Decretal).

priests, that is the bishops, are judged by God?[13] See also Pope Pius in [C.] 6 q. 1 [c. 9] *Oves.* Hence whatever is understood to apply to the pope, e.g. that he cannot be judged by his subjects, also applies to the bishops. Similarly if a text says that the pope has the plenitude of power and others are called in an advisory capacity, we can also say this concerning any archbishop or patriarch as appears in the [introductory] paragraph to [C.] 9 [19] q. 3.

120.   If you say that the pope looses and binds those who are subject to the bishops, I say the same thing is true of other cases when the consent of the proper bishops is given. For an act which otherwise would be invalid is rendered valid in a given case with the consent and agreement of the appropriate member of the clergy, see [C.] 9 q. 2 [c. 10] *Lugdunensis,* and the chapter [c. 6] *Nullum,* and the chapter [c. 7] *Episcopum.* Since therefore this practice has been introduced by common usage and consent is given through usage, it is obvious that its efficacy comes from consent. Hence since no one is obligated to obey except as authorized in a canon, see [C.] 18 q1. 2 [c. 1] *Hoc Tantum,* and [C.] 9 q. 3 [c. 8] *Conquestus* and since no canon of any council can be found [that says] that the pope can do this when a case is not appealed to him, the matter ought to be resolved through custom, usage, and consent. For canon law gives the pope no power to violate the jurisdiction of bishops, since this would be a disturbance of order, see [C.] 11 q. 1 [c. 39] *Pervenit* – at the end, *igitur* etc.

121.   We do not read that the Roman pontiffs of old intervened in these matters and granted confessional and similar rights and perhaps it would not have been allowed. The decision of the Council of Africa to which St. Augustine agreed did not allow an appeal from a synod to the pope because this was not allowed in the canons.[14] On the contrary it was defined by the Council of Nicaea that a case should terminate in the synod where it began, as appears in [C.] 6, q. 4 [c. 5] *Si quis episcopus criminaliter* which includes the letter of the same council to pope Zosimus.[15] Likewise they refused to recognize the text, [C.] 2, q. 6 [c. 36] *si episcopus,* ascribed to the Council of Sardica, which allowed appeals and provided that the legate of the pope was to be sent to the province, as we see in the same letter and in the letter written to Pope Boniface by the same council. They even said that

---

[13] Hinschius, p. 76 (False Decretal).

[14] The Council of Carthage (A.D. 419) – see no. 71.

[15] Hinschius, p. 311 prints a similar letter by Pope Zosimus.

they had not found it in any council, although Faustinus, the legate of the Apostolic See, said that the text was that of the Nicene Council and in the place mentioned above it is said to be that of the Council of Sardica.[16] How could they have taken these positions then and allowed the outrageous things which are being done today? But because consent and long usage have now introduced this practice, these things are useful for the salvation of souls as long as they are tolerated. However they can be repealed by the council, and this reform is necessary.

122. If you go on and argue from the papal power to dispense from canons to a power to legislate, you are proving nothing, for a bishop and priest can dispense from the penitential canons, see [C.] 27 q. 6 [c. 2] *Tempora poenitudinis* and a bishop from other penal canons, see D. 50 [c. 22] *Si quis presbyter*, [C.] 1 q. 5 last paragraph; [C.] 9 q. 2 [c. 10] *Lugdunensis*. And a dispensation does not revoke the canons, see [C.] 9 q. 1 [c. 5] *Ordinationes*, and q. 2 [c. 10] *Lugdunensis* and the argument of D. 50 [55] c. [1] *Priscis*. Hence the argument proves nothing.

123. And what is said about the [powers of a] rector, is no objection since if a corporate body cannot legislate without its rector, the exercise of jurisdiction being his, the converse does not follow – that a rector can legislate without the corporate body which possesses a potential power [to legislate]. Nor is it correct to argue from [the power of] jurisdiction since the power to legislate, although it is linked to that of judging, does not follow from it. Not everyone with the power to judge has the power to legislate, although everyone with the power to legislate can make judicial decisions. Thus we say that every synod of the fathers because it has the power to adopt laws, has the power to make judicial decisions as well.

124. Hence it is clear from the above that the binding power of the canons is derived from consent, for unless we could argue validity from usage and a law could be abrogated by not being observed, there would be no salvation. Who can know in what ways our teaching has been added to, or changed from, that of the Four Councils[17] without

---

[16] The Council of Sardica (A.D. 343) – today's Sofia – was boycotted by the bishops of the Eastern church. Its canons were once believed to be those of the Council of Nicaea, and were thus cited by Pope Zosimus in his letter to the Council of Carthage in 418. See Hamilton Hess, *The Canons of the Council of Sardica*, Oxford, 1958.

[17] I.e., Nicaea, Constantinople, Ephesus, and Chalcedon.

our incurring condemnation, or when certain sacraments were introduced in the councils, or how we could evade the numberless penalties of automatic excommunication, deposition and the like contained in the canons, if in all of these matters concord and consent, usage and non-usage, did not help us? Hence in chapter 1 of the same Council of Toledo it is said, "If any earlier decrees have been neglected, let them receive a new binding force so that because we devote our attention to the religious observance of matters relating to the practice of the faith which have been decreed in the councils but have fallen into disuse over time, we may more easily obtain the mercy of God."[18] Note that decrees that have been ignored lose their binding power and they acquire it again when they have been accepted once more. Thus long-standing customs approved by the consent of those who observe them are similar to law, see D. 12 [c. 6] *Diuturni,* and where a legal authority is lacking, the customs of the people and the practices of one's ancestors are observed as the law, see D. 12 [D. 11 c. 6] *In his.*

Indeed the statutes of the synods are based on this type of consent. Hence Pope Gregory [I] in professing his belief in the Four Councils says that since they were constituted by universal consent, anyone who presumes to loose those whom they bind or to bind those whom they loose, acts to his own destruction, not that of the statutes. For a synod makes its definitions by the authority of all, not only of those who are present, as Gregory says when he declares that the statutes adopted by the bishops who were present representing the others, were adopted by universal consent.[19] Hence at the end of the Council of Toledo, we read: "If however anyone of us or of those in the province who are not present now in the sacred synod should dare to violate this sacred decree or neglect to comply with it devoutly, let him be excluded for a time from the community of brotherly love."[20] By the above reasoning, if the others who are concerned with the council have been summoned to it, those who are present are considered to act as the representatives of all. And this is proved in the eighth canon of the Second African Council, discussed below, where it is said that the representatives grant full authority to the council in the name of the others.[21]

---

[18] Second Council of Toledo (Mansi 8, p. 784).
[19] PL 77, p. 478.   [20] Mansi 8, p. 787.
[21] *Third* Council of Carthage, c. 2 (Mansi 3, p. 787).

125. And there is no doubt that both the universal councils of the whole church and those of the kingdoms of Spain, the Gauls, and of Africa, as well as of an individual province have always been able to legislate for themselves – just as Boniface writing to Rusticus of Narbonne says that the fathers who were assembled in Nicaea adopted canons for themselves, that is for the whole world or the universal church which they represented there.[22] We read in the records of the council held at Rome in the ninth year of the reign of Emperor Constantine III under the chairmanship of Pope Martin with 105 bishops in attendance that to show that Pope Leo's message had been approved by the Council of Chalcedon Pope Martin said at the beginning, "The holy Council of Chalcedon, that is to say the assembly of all the holy fathers, made this definition. For what one synod of the holy fathers is seen to decide, all the synods and all the fathers together confirm in indissoluble harmony in one and the same expression of faith."[23] And just as a provincial synod when it meets decides on the canons necessary for the province, so if the seven provinces of Gaul were to meet they could legislate for the seven provinces. And if all the provinces in the world were to meet, just as any one province can provide for itself so all together can legislate by common agreement on all matters. And it is surprising to say that all of them gathered with full power as representatives cannot do what any one province can do for itself. But there is no doubt that any one province can provide for its needs without the pope. Therefore all of them can so provide, provided that following the normal procedure the pope or anyone else belonging to the synod is not excluded, if willing and able to come. For a synod of many provinces has more authority than that of one, as is said in the following chapter.

126. And although we insist that the pope is not the universal bishop but the first over the others, and we base the force of the holy councils not on the pope but on the consent of all, at the same time since we defend truth and maintain the rights of everyone, we rightly give honor to the pope, see D. 99 [c. 5] *Ecce.*

[22] Boniface I to Hilary, Bishop of Narbonne (PL 20, p. 773).
[23] Mansi 10, p. 875.

CHAPTER XIV

ALL LEGISLATION IS BASED ON NATURAL LAW.
SINCE BY NATURE WE ARE ALL EQUALLY FREE, ALL
COERCIVE POWER IS DERIVED FROM THE ELECTION
AND CONSENT OF THE SUBJECTS. THE
JURISDICTION THUS CREATED IS NOT VALID IN
ITSELF UNLESS IT IS IN ACCORDANCE WITH THE
LAW AND CANONS. THIS IS A FINE OBSERVATION.

127.   In order for everyone to be better convinced, I add another consideration to these arguments. Although one might wish it to be developed at greater length, in the interests of brevity and to please the reader I will limit myself to a summary discussion. All legislation is based on natural law and any law which contradicts it cannot be valid, see D. 9 [after c. 11] *Cum ergo* and [D. 10 c. 4] *Constitutiones.* Hence since natural law is naturally based on reason, all law is rooted by nature in the reason of man. The wiser and more outstanding men are chosen as rulers by the others to draw up just laws by the clear reason, wisdom, and prudence given them by nature and to rule the others by these laws and to decide controversies for the maintenance of peace, as is contained in D. 2 [c. 5] *Responsa prudentum.* From this we conclude that those better endowed with reason are the natural lords and masters of the others but not by any coercive law or judgment imposed on someone against his will. For since all are by nature free, every governance whether it consists in a written law or is living law in the person of a prince – by which subjects are compelled to abstain from evil deeds and their freedom directed towards the good through fear of punishment can only come from the agreement and consent of the subjects. For if by nature men are equal in power [*potentes*] and equally free, the true properly ordered authority of one common ruler who is their equal in power cannot be naturally established except by the election and consent of the others and law is also established by consent. See D. 2 [c. 1] *Lex,* [and] D. 8 [c. 2] *Quae contra* where it says "An agreement of every race and city among themselves" etc. and "There is a general agreement in human society to obey their kings" etc. Note that for the convenience of human society men wish to make a general agreement to obey their kings.

Since in a properly-ordered government an election of the ruler ought to take place by which he is set up as judge of those who elect him, rightly-ordered lords and rulers are established by election, and through election they are established as general judges over those who elect them. As I have noted elsewhere, this follows Hostiensis in his *Summa* and other doctors.[1]

128. And because they are general judges, appeals can be made from them to the highest authority, because they were not specifically elected to have the final decision in every case. But if judges are chosen in a particular case by the parties involved, appeals are not normally allowed as the tenth canon of the Council of Africa states: "Certainly if judges have been chosen by consent of the parties, even if by a smaller number than prescribed [by the law] there should be no appeal,"[2] see C. 2 q. 6 [c. 34]. A judge ought to decide in accordance with justice, so that a sentence is legally invalid if it is pronounced in violation of laws and canons, see [*Decretals* 2 27] *De sententia et re judicata* c. 1 with the cross-references mentioned in the Gloss on that passage.

129. Moreover we do not read that the Apostolic See ever made a decision that was contrary to the canons, as is noted in the letter of Pope Boniface to Zacharias which begins *Confitemur*[3] and in many quotations given below. Yet the papal decision is reviewed once more by the plenary council, as is stated below on the basis of the works and authority of Augustine.[4] But such a review would be in vain if everything that the Roman pontiff wished were law because then it would be impossible for him to act against the law. Hence it is proper that his judgment should be limited by the canons, to which he is subordinate and in accordance with which his decision is reviewed in order to determine whether it does or does not follow them.

130. Furthermore the canons are based on natural law. Even the ruler has no power to violate natural law, and therefore he also has no power over a canon based on, or incidentally following from, natural law. And because this is the case, how can we say that it is in the power of a judge to adopt canons and statutes? If this were so, if he

---

[1] Book I, no. 117.

[2] Third Council of Carthage (Mansi 3, p. 882).

[3] PL 130, p. 1,163, written in A.D. 742 by St. (not Pope) Boniface, the Apostle of Germany.

[4] Book II, no. 149.

himself had the power to make the canons, a judge could not be charged with an unjust decision, since the decision would be the law, and therefore it would always be just. But because law ought always to be reasonable, possible, and not against the custom of the country, see D. 4 [c. 2] *Erit autem*, we cannot call something a law which is not accepted by the usage of the users – whether in the civil or canon law, see D. 4 [c. 3] *Leges*, and chapters which follow. Hence if approval through use is required of laws as is said in the chapter, *Leges*, it cannot be right to condemn someone as guilty for violating a new law because he could not violate something which did not yet exist. Thus he must have broken a law that has been adopted and accepted in custom and usage. And from this it is clear that the law or canon is a standard for every judge, and that any judge who makes a decision is subject to all the laws and canons.

131. Furthermore, if it is true that a canon is approved by agreement, usage, and acceptance, then the strength of all legislation comes from acceptance. Hence the canons of the common council are rightly called those of the church. For the church is a congregation. One person cannot properly issue church canons. Thus we see that canons are issued in the councils by harmonious acceptance, consent, and subscription, but the decretals of judicial decisions of the Roman pontiffs or those on doubtful points in new situations have been confirmed as just, not out of pure authoritative will [of the pope] but because the canons agree that those decisions should be made, – a point which ought to be noted. This is the way I understand D. 15 [c. 3] *Sancta Romana* para. *Item decretales*, and D. 19 [c. 6] *In canonicis* along with similar passages, and there is more on this subject elsewhere, especially at the end of this Second Book and at the beginning and end of Book III.

CHAPTER XV

ON THE BASIS OF WHAT HAS BEEN SAID ABOVE WE
CAN SAY THAT JUST AS THE BISHOP SHOULD NOT
LEGISLATE WITHOUT HIS CHAPTER NOR THE
METROPOLITAN WITHOUT HIS SUFFRAGAN
BISHOPS, SO THE POPE SHOULD NOT ISSUE
UNIVERSAL STATUTES AFFECTING ALL HIS
SUBJECTS WITHOUT HIS CARDINALS. NO
[CONCILIAR] DECISION IS FINAL UNLESS IT IS
RATIFIED BY THE APOSTOLIC SEE SINCE APPEALS
HAVE BEEN MADE TO THE ROMAN SEE FROM ALL
DOCTRINAL DEFINITIONS – EVEN THOSE BY
SYNODS – EXCEPT FOR THOSE OF THE UNIVERSAL
COUNCIL OF THE UNIVERSAL CHURCH. HOW THIS
COMMON DICTUM IS TO BE UNDERSTOOD IS ALSO
DISCUSSED.

132.   From the above it is now clear that the binding force of every law consists in concord and tacit or express consent which is given either through usage or by the action of those with others under their authority, because they represent them or rule over them. For just as the bishop and his chapter are said to make up the diocesan church because that gathering potentially contains all the others who belong to the same church so that they are all considered to be represented by them, so also a metropolitan and his suffragan bishops constitute the church of a province and a patriarch with his metropolitans, the church of a patriarchate. Hence the authority of any gathering extends to all represented in potentiality in that gathering. We say that according to ancient practice the Roman church was made up of the pope and his associated metropolitans since each year they used to meet with him as the head of their patriarchate. And because as a result of the agreement of the metropolitans and by universal practice the cardinals of the various regions have become their representatives and take the place of all, both in electing the Roman pontiff and in advising the universal Roman church, we are justified in saying that the Roman pontiff can take no action in any matters affecting the universal Roman church without the cardinals, and that if he should

do anything without them, it cannot be accepted with impunity. It is true that this power belonging to the cardinals to represent the tacit consent of the universal Roman church needs to be reorganized so as to enable them to act as representatives who give its express consent. This is treated in another place.[1]

133. From the above it is also easy to understand what is often asserted by the Roman pontiffs; e.g., by Pope Damasus in a letter to Stephen, the Archbishop of the Council of Mauritania,[2] as well as other Roman pontiffs in D. 17 [c. 2] *Regula,* – that no synod is valid unless it is confirmed by the authority of that Apostolic See – since they are speaking of the [Roman] see. It is true that no synodal decision is certain in which the Apostolic See does not participate because there is always the possibility of an appeal from the decision of that synod to the Apostolic See. Thus we read that the cases of the Patriarchs Flavian and Ignatius and others in Constantinople and Athanasius in Alexandria were appealed to the Apostolic See.[3] Hence if a synod has condemned anyone, including a patriarch, the decision of that synod is not ratified until it is confirmed by the Apostolic See since it can be appealed to that see. And when it is said that by itself without a synod, the Apostolic See can reinstate those unjustly condemned in a synod, this is true, if [by "without a synod", we mean] without a meeting of the universal synod of the whole church. For if someone is condemned by a patriarchal synod, whether of Constantinople or Alexandria or some other large provincial synod in France or Spain, the Apostolic See which, as has often been said, is made up of those comprising and representing the Roman church as outlined above, has a higher jurisdiction and can take judicial cognizance of what has been decided by the synods. Thus we read that Pope Nicholas in his Apostolic See assembled in synod examined the case of Ignatius who had been condemned by Photius. Pope Martin acted in this way in the case of Pyrrthus and Sergius, as did Pope Julius before them in the case involving Eusebius and Athanasius of Alexandria.[4] This is how we read that they acted in all cases.

134. Hence it is true that the Apostolic See is superior in jurisdiction to all synods except the universal council of the whole church of which that see is a part, and that therefore it can review the decisions of all lower synods without action on the part of the council of the

---

[1] Book II, no. 191.   [2] See Book II, no. 112.   [3] See Book II, no. 76.
[4] PL 119, p. 1073; 87, pp. 119ff.; 8, p. 879.

universal church. For example in the sixth action of the Eighth Council in the answers of Metrophanes, bishop of Smyrna, to the arguments of Zacharias of Chalcedon concerning the absolution granted to Apiarius by the Roman church contrary to the decision of the Council of Africa, we read that it was not accepted [at first] in Africa and that later the decision of Pope Zosimus in his synod to absolve Apiarius who had previously been condemned in the synod of Africa was finally accepted.[5] However he was not admitted to his former church on account of the possibility of scandal but letters of recommendation were given to him by the synod so that he might act as a priest in all the other churches. And note this case on account of certain points related to this subject which are discussed above and below.

135. And on the same point, note the letter of Pope Boniface to Bishop Eulalius of Alexandria on the topic of the reconciliation of the Africans which says that at the time of Boniface and Celestine, Aurelius of Carthage and his colleagues rose up in pride at the instigation of the devil against the Roman church but that now all professed [belief in] the document of the synod held at the time of Justinian, beginning, *Prima salus*, which you have above.[6] And although there is much that is worthy of note in that letter – as when it says so well at the beginning that the church contains a hierarchical concordance of inequality on the model of the heavenly army in which all are subordinate to one first [ruler], i.e. the Roman pope – it seems hard to say, as it does, that Valerius and his colleagues were in error, because 216 bishops including Augustine agreed as one to its decisions which they also signed in writing, as is noted above. And if they were later led to the recognition of the rights of appeal and jurisdiction belonging to that see, it should not be said that they were in error earlier unless this means that the African church itself was in error in not accepting the legislation of the Council of Sardica, since, as is mentioned at a certain point above, Augustine did not consider that council Catholic but Arian.[7] Nevertheless because the whole church accepted its decisions, as is clear in the actions of the Eighth Universal Council,[8] the Africans were also obliged to accept those statutes as Catholic without considering those who did the legislating. However the Council of Sardica adopted a statute in honor of the memory of

[5] Mansi 16, pp. 90ff.   [6] Book II, nos. 93 and 121.
[7] St. Augustine, *Contra Cresconium* (PL 43, p. 516).   [8] Mansi 16, p. 71.

St. Peter which provided that one could appeal to the Bishop of Rome. It was proposed and moved by Hosius, Bishop of Cordoba, the legate of the Apostolic See, and this is discussed in C. 6 q. 4 [c. 7] *Quod si aliquis* which is to be noted carefully. This text proves from the decision of the synod in honor of the memory of St. Peter, that the Roman pontiff has the power to judge local councils but only in the form set down there, i.e., he can approve a decision but cannot disapprove one except by means of a new synod – so that that text proves that the administrative power of the pope depends very much on positive law and the consent of the synod.

136. You may perhaps say that the legislation of the universal council of the universal church must also be ratified by the authority of the Apostolic See, i.e. the Roman pontiff, to be valid. I admit that in the case of legislation on matters of faith it is true that unless the authorization of the Apostolic See is secured, the laws are not valid. Indeed the consent of the Roman pontiff himself must also be given, since he is chief-bishop of the faith. This is also true of all other church laws because they receive their force from the agreement of the synod and even the lowest-ranking suffragan bishop in a provincial synod or canon in an episcopal synod or metropolitan in a patriarchal synod is essential to his synod because its validity depends on the agreement of all. Pope Damasus, for example, argued that the Council of Rimini was invalid for this reason, for Vincentius who was bishop for a long time, and other bishops did not give their consent.[9] Indeed I think that no one doubts that an act which otherwise has the essential form required is invalid if this is not observed. Therefore I would think that if the pope is assembled with his cardinals as representatives of the provinces, as I have touched upon elsewhere, and even one cardinal is missing they should take no action on any universal statute for the whole Roman church. There is no doubt [that this is true] of the head of the synod, i.e. the metropolitan in the patriarchal synod, and the pope in general or universal synods. Hence just as a decision of a synod can be contested if anyone who is supposed to be present is not permitted to participate while willing and able to do so, since it violated the proper order of charity, so also with even more validity for the head [of the synod].

137. It is not true however that the legal authority of a synod which

---

[9] PL 13, p. 349.

has been properly called and is carried out according to correct procedure with those in attendance that ought to be admitted, is also so dependent on its head that unless he consents to a decision, no decision can be made. For this would then imply that it would not be a decision of the synod but only of one man. And since anyone who goes to a synod is bound to submit to the decision of the majority because he assumes that normally the majority rules, the synod finally makes its definitions with the agreement of all in deciding by majority vote even if the opinions of particular persons may differ. Nevertheless no conclusion, especially on a matter of faith, can be certain unless the vote is made unanimous as was the case, we read, in all the councils. And with this interpretation we think we can satisfy anyone who wishes to understand correctly the authorities whom the Roman pontiffs cite in their letters. I say, the Roman pontiffs, because I could find very little in the records of the councils on all these subjects which did not fully agree with the positions that I have taken above.

CHAPTER XVI

FROM THE SIGNATURES APPENDED TO [CONCILIAR] DEFINITIONS WE CONCLUDE THAT BISHOPS HAVE THE POWER TO MAKE DEFINITIONS, BUT OTHERS INCLUDING ABBOTS AND MONKS ALSO GIVE THEIR CONSENT AND SIGN – LAYMEN ALSO DO SO BUT AS AUDITORS AND WITNESSES. ALSO CLERICAL EXPERTS [PERITI] NOT IN ADMINISTRATIVE POSITIONS SHOULD NOT BE EXCLUDED FROM THE COUNCILS.

138. Since the question has arisen as to which persons should be admitted to the council and also who should be allowed to sign its decrees, we should consider that although the Egyptians who came to Chalcedon from Alexandria with Dioscorus raised this question along with others in the Council of Chalcedon and, as appears in the acts of that council, repeatedly claimed that a council is made up of bishops and that the others ought to be excluded, we do not read there that

non-bishops were excluded for this reason.[1] In the Fifth Universal Council we read that everyone down to the rank of lector signed,[2] in the Sixth and Eighth Councils that priests and monks, the emperor and the senate and deacons signed, and that they were always accepted in the sessions and in the signing at the place where their superiors were located, as is indicated in D. 93 [c. 26], *Praecipimus* which contains the text, and in D. 94, c. 1.[3] However in the Sixth Council of Constantinople where the signatures of Pope Agatho and his council appear, we do not read that anyone besides bishops and their representatives signed the definition [of dogma]. Hence the power of definition and legislation has perhaps always belonged to bishops *de jure*, see D. 12 [c. 12] *Omnia* where the text says that statutes ought to be adopted in councils of bishops, and although others summoned such as abbots and monks also sign, we read that this is not generally done with the power to make dogmatic definitions on which see [C.] 1 q. 7 [c. 4] *Convenientibus*. Hence when a universal council speaks on matters of faith, I wonder why, since lay people are allowed to enter, non-bishops ought not be admitted – and not merely in an advisory capacity – but to legislate and sign, if they are at least qualified and knowledgeable. But in other matters, where a decision is made not by unanimity but by majority vote, discretion and prudence and authority ought rightly to lead us to consider whether the judgment of fools whose number is infinite might not outweigh the votes of the wise.[4]

139. Hence I do not think that the laity or clergy should be admitted indiscriminately, but I think that qualified learned churchmen should be included in making decisions since the common good of the church is being sought and it does not matter from what source it come, providing only that it is found. But as appears below, we read in the seventeenth canon of the Eighth Universal Council and in D. 96 [c. 4] *Ubi nam* that lay people were admitted to the universal council when a question of faith was to be defined, and subscribed to the other acts in the council as witnesses. Thus we read in the Fourth Action of the records of the Eighth Council. "The most excellent

---

[1] Mansi 6, p. 602.
[2] Mansi 9, pp. 389ff. (Only bishops signed at the Second Council of Constantinople, A.D. 553.)
[3] Mansi 11, pp. 667ff. and 682ff., and 16, p. 190.
[4] Ecclesiastes 1:15. Note this limitation on earlier discussions of majority rule (no. 137).

senators and glorious princes said to the council through the patrician and president, Bahanes: 'Our holy emperors have sent us, his servants who make up the senate, which by the will of God is honored in every way, so that we might act as auditors of what is done. Therefore if you wish to ask us for our signatures at the end of this holy universal synod, as is proper for a synod, all my brothers and fellow patricians say through me, the unworthy servant of our holy emperors, to our most holy lord, the patriarch, and to the most holy representatives of old Rome and those of the eastern sees: Unless we have heard in person both from Photius and from his bishops and in front of us that their mouths are closed because of the precepts of the canons and the synod, our hands will not sign one word of that synod. Let them hear what has been decided by Pope Nicholas in the Synod of Rome and if they say nothing in reply, the schism will be healed by their submission. But if this is not done, we know that you would not want us to sign at the end of our actions etc.' "[5] Note that the laity since they are to sign as witnesses in the council can demand what reason and justice requires from the council in order for them to sign properly. And this should suffice on that subject.

[5] Mansi 16, p. 55.

CHAPTER XVII

A PATRIARCHAL COUNCIL IS NORMALLY NOT
SUPERIOR TO THE POPE BUT IS SUBJECT TO HIM,
UNLESS HE DEPARTS FROM THE FAITH.
NEVERTHELESS IT CAN CORRECT HIM IN THE SAME
WAY THAT A PROVINCIAL COUNCIL CAN CORRECT
ITS METROPOLITAN. THE COUNCIL OF THE
UNIVERSAL CHURCH IS NOT ONLY OVER THE POPE
BUT IT IS ALSO CLEARLY SUPERIOR TO HIS SYNOD
AND TO THOSE OF ALL THE OTHER PATRIARCHS.
THE ARGUMENT IS ANSWERED WHICH IS USUALLY
MADE THAT THE ROMAN SEE IS OVER THE WHOLE
CHURCH BY THE GRANT OF CHRIST. WE SAY THAT
DESPITE CHRIST'S GRANT, FOR THE GOOD OF THE
UNIVERSAL CHURCH THE UNIVERSAL COUNCIL HAS
JURISDICTION AND SUPREMACY OVER THE PERSON
WHO OCCUPIES THAT SEE WHEN HE ABUSES HIS
POWER. EXAMPLES ARE GIVEN.

140.   From what we have said above a sufficient answer can easily be
given to the supposedly difficult question as to whether the universal
council is indeed above the pope. For the universal or general
patriarchal council, as we always read, is subject to the Roman pontiff.
This is evident from the above and from what follows, and is defined
in the sixth chapter of the Council of Nicaea referring to the see of
Alexandria and other sees, see D. 65 [c. 6] *Mos*, and all the councils
after this say the same thing. Therefore in the case of this universal
council [i.e., the patriarchal council], I think that it is true that the
Roman pontiff cannot be judged by the council unless he is in error
on [a matter of] faith since as long as he remains in the faith he
remains as its head. Therefore he cannot be judged by a lower power
because he has the power of all the others, as the definition in the
sixth chapter of the Nicene council says. In addition he remains the
head, in the unity of the Catholic church which is [a unity] in faith, of
the other patriarchs in all the rest of the church. Therefore it is
correct that as a metropolitan he cannot be judged by his synod unless
he is in error on [a matter of] faith, as is defined in the 10th canon of

the Eighth Ecumenical Council[1] and note in [*Decretals* III 5] *De prebendis*, [C. 29] *Grave*, and in [C.] 11, q. 1 [c. 46] *Si clericus* – on which the Archdeacon comments that a metropolitan since he is head of the provincial council cannot be punished by that council.[2] Hence Pope Anacletus in a letter to all the bishops which begins, *Benedictus Deus*, says, "The teacher and shepherd of the church if he should depart from the faith ought to be corrected by the faithful. However for bad conduct he is rather to be tolerated than coerced."[3] And he understands by the faithful, his subjects, as is evident in the text immediately following. And it is clear why this should be understood this way, for the shepherd of the church cannot be corrected by the church which is his flock of sheep, but if he is not in the faith he is not the shepherd and then he should be corrected with anathema and withdrawal of obedience.

141. And there is no doubt concerning the case of condemned heresy since he falls under the sentence of already condemned heretical teaching, as Pope Gelasius wrote to Emperor Anastasius and to all the bishops in Troy concerning Acatius. For he says, "The universal church in observance of the ancient law considered that all those who held an already condemned heresy were refuted once it was condemned, just as the Nicene Council included all Arians in its condemnation of Arius."[4] But if a heresy has not [already] been condemned, then, according to the tenth canon mentioned above, one should not withdraw from him until it is formally established that he is a heretic.[5] However a pastor can be corrected privately by those under him for an error in faith and he can be denounced to his superior. Hence Pope Fabian in his letter to the eastern bishops which begins, *Exigit dilectio*, says: "If a bishop should deviate from the faith, he should first be corrected privately by his subordinates. But if it appears that he cannot be corrected (may it never happen), then he should be denounced to his superiors or to the Apostolic See. But in his other actions he ought to be tolerated by his subjects rather than denounced."[6] But if he is a heretic, then since he is excommunicated

[1] Mansi 16, p. 166.
[2] Guido de Baysio held that the metropolitan council could judge its head (Kallen, p. 176).
[3] Hinschius, p. 85 (False Decretal).
[4] PL 59, pp. 44ff. and 62ff.
[5] Mansi 16, p. 166.
[6] Hinschius, p. 166 (False Decretal).

ipso facto for that heresy rather than because of any positive law because he is a heretic on account of error in the intellect and obstinacy in the will, he has separated himself from the whole body of the church, as Saint Cyprian says in [C.] 1 q. 1 [c. 70]: If anyone, he says, has left the church in the presumptuousness of heresy, he has condemned himself, see [C.] 4 q. 5 c. 1; [C.] 24 a. 1 cc. 1, 2, and 3.

142. Everyone, even a simple layman, is also obliged to separate himself from that heretic and by that separation he says anathema upon him. In this way we read that the laity in the council declared publicly condemned heretics to be anathema and also individuals outside the council declared heretical Roman pontiffs anathema. Thus superiors and those in higher office when they are heretics are said to be deposed by their inferiors when they separate themselves from them on account of the anathema that comes as a result of heresy.

143. Hence since his exercise of his administrative duties as superior ceases because of the withdrawal of obedience and because the ruling office of a bishop, primate, or pope consists in the exercise of administrative duties, when that ceases they are rightly considered to be deposed, as Joannes [Andreae] in his *Novella* notes on chapter 1 of [1 7] *De renuntiatione* of the *Liber Sextus*. When it is clear that a pope does not wish to carry out his administrative duties then he is considered to have already given up the papacy since the papacy consists in the exercise of administration, as is noted in D. 21 [c. 2] *In novo* and [C.] 2 q. 1 [c. 35] *Puto*. The exercise of administration ceases once the obedience of all has been withdrawn because of heresy. Therefore the papacy also ceases to be located in its material subject; namely, the heretic. In this way we read that Popes Liberius and Marcellinus were deposed by separation and withdrawal of obedience. So also any patriarch, including the patriarch of Rome, is deposed indirectly by his former subjects if he falls into a condemned heresy. This is the way in which I think the following relevant provisions of canon law should be understood: D. 40 [c. 6] *Si papa*; D. 17 [c. 6] *Hinc etiam*; D. 21 [c. 4] *Inferior*; and the chapter *Nunc autem* [c. 7] and similar provisions.

144. Nevertheless although a metropolitan may not be judged by his council, as is contained above, he can be corrected by it. This is proved by the text and heading of [C.] 2 q. 1 [c. 46] *Sicut inquit*, and by [C.] 9 q. 3 [c. 6] *Si autem* and the chapter *Salvo* [c. 4]. In the same

way, I would think that the general council of the Roman see can correct the pope, in accordance with the same text which says that the head of a council should be corrected by his council. On this point [D.] 18, [before c. 1] *Episcoporum* is useful which proves that a council, although in a given case unable to make formal definitions, is able to correct and reform its head in accordance with the ancient canons. On this point there does not seem to be any doubt in the case of the canons of the universal councils of the Catholic church involving automatic excommunication, since all Catholics are obliged to observe them, as will be discussed more fully below.[7] In the case of the authentic punitive legislation of those councils and all other statutes of any other councils, it is clear that they do not apply to the pope unless he has formally bound himself to observe them. And the same thing should be said for other patriarchs and archbishops – if they violate a statute of automatic excommunication adopted by a higher authority, they can be corrected even in their own councils by a declaration that the statute applies [*de incidisse*], in a way similar to what has been said about the pope – but otherwise only by way of exhortation.

145.   But I do not think there is any doubt that a universal council properly understood, that is, one that represents the whole Catholic church, is over the patriarchs and the Roman pontiff. Hence although we read in various places that the power of the Roman pontiff comes from Christ, it also appears in many places that the primacy of the Roman church over all churches comes from the decisions of the apostles and their successors, as appears in [C.] 3 q. 6 [c. 9] *Dudum*. And the judges in the Council of Chalcedon, when the question of the primacy arose between the churches of Rome and Constantinople ordered the canons to be produced and decided that according to the canons old Rome had the primacy, as D. 17 [after c. 6] *Hinc etiam* says. And likewise although we find in the records that the pope is described as the vicar of Christ, we also find it said that he takes the place of, and represents Peter, see [C.] 2 q. 7 [c. 4] *In sancta*. And much can be said regarding the different expressions used in similar passages. For some bishops called the pope their "associate," as did Optatus, others their "fellow priest," as did Ambrose, and the fathers in the Council of Ephesus, and the Council of Turin, and some

---

[7] Book II, chapter xx.

"brother," others "bishop," some "archbishop," or others "patriarch."[8]

146.   But it is enough for us [to conclude] that although the Roman pontiff as successor of Peter has received great privileges from Christ and possesses high power derived from his see and *cathedra* – privileges that are associated permanently with that see – the primacy which the Roman pontiff exercises over all the churches comes partly from men and the canons, as is said above. Pope Anacletus says that while Peter was established as prince of the apostles by Christ, it was done with the consent of the apostles, see D. 22 [c. 2] *Sacrosancta*; D. 16 [after c. 6] *Hinc etiam*; C. 24 q. 1 [c. 15] *Rogamus*; [C.] 7 q. 1 [c. 34] *Mutationes*. And the text of D. 99 [c, 2] *Nulli* proves this when it says that the primates were established by the apostles and their successors. The Gloss says that the primates are those of Rome, Alexandria, and Antioch, see D. 21 [c. 1] *Cleros* etc.

There is no doubt that the patriarch of Antioch has succeeded to the see of Peter, but he does not possess the primacy by virtue of this since the patriarch of Antioch defers to the patriarch of Rome. Therefore Pope Marcellus in a letter to the inhabitants of Antioch which begins: *Sollicitudinem omnium* says, "If your church in Antioch which once was first has yielded to that of Rome, there is no church which is not subject to its authority. To it as head all bishops who wish to do so can have recourse and can appeal."[9] Hence in the synodal letter of Leo IX to Peter, the Patriarch of Antioch, he writes, "From the fact that your apostolic see is consulting ours, we conclude that [you in] your prudence do not wish to depart from the decree of the Lord and all the holy fathers by which the apostolic see of the holy Roman church is established as the inviolable head of all the churches in the whole world to which the more important and difficult cases are to be referred by other churches for decision. This has been proclaimed by all venerable councils and human laws, this the Holy of Holies Himself, the King of Kings and Lord of Lords, confirms – that the venerable summit of ruling authority and of all church discipline should be located in the place where Peter, the very center and chief of the apostles, awaits the blessed resurrection of the flesh on the last day. Surely he alone is the one for whom Our Lord and Saviour declared that he prayed that his faith would not fail, saying: 'Simon,

[8] See PL 11, p. 949, 16, p. 1004, and Mansi 5, p. 1070, 3, p. 861.
[9] PL 7, p. 1093 (False Decretal).

Simon, behold Satan has sought that he might sift thee as wheat. But I have prayed for thee that thy faith fail not and that thou being once converted should confirm thy brethren.'[10] And the result of this venerable and efficacious prayer has been that until now the faith of Peter has not failed and we believe that it will not fail on the throne of Peter until the end of time. Rather he will strengthen his brethren when they are shaken by various trials of their faith, as until now he has not ceased to strengthen them."[11]

147. Hence I do not think that the universal council would ever wish to take away those privileges of the primacy from the Roman see as they have been defined by other councils. [Pope] Leo says the same thing in answer to the claims of Michael of Constantinople in chapter 36: "Whoever attempts to destroy or diminish the authority and privileges of the Roman church plots the subversion and destruction not of one church but of all Christianity. What other mother will give mercy and sustenance to her daughter under oppression if that one mother church has been crushed? To what refuge will they appeal? With whom will they have shelter? For that church received, protected, and defended Athanasius and all the Catholics, and restored them to their own sees after they had been driven out."[12]

148. But because those who sit in that see are human beings subject to error and sin, and especially because at present with the world moving towards its end and evil on the increase they abuse their power using what was granted for the building up [of the church] to destroy it, who of sound mind can doubt that without any diminution of the true power and privilege of that see the universal council has power both over abuses and over the one who commits them – to act for the preservation and the well-ordered rule of the whole church? I believe that it is wrong to say that the universal council also cannot take judicial cognizance of, and make decisions concerning the primacy of the Roman church for we read in the records that the Council of Chalcedon expressly involved itself in this and passed judgment on it.[13] Hence it can be said in general that a universal council that represents the Catholic church has power directly from Christ and is in every respect over both the pope and the Apostolic See.

149. And many conciliar actions and canons and proofs from reason

---

[10] Luke 22:31.   [11] PL 143, p. 770.
[12] PL 143, p. 767.   [13] Mansi 7, pp. 354ff.

support this opinion. For the dispute over the primacy which took place in the Council of Chalcedon proves this; as does the definition by the Nicene Council which was produced in the same Council of Chalcedon in defense of the Roman see, and also the fact that the actions and judgments of the Roman pontiff even in his synod are often reviewed and examined in the plenary councils. The Council of Chalcedon reviewed the decision of [Pope] Leo against Dioscorus and the Sixth Council reviewed the decision in synod of Pope Martin against Pyrrhus and Sergius, and the Eighth Universal Council reviewed the decision of Popes Nicholas and Hadrian against Photius – and there are many similar cases.[14] Hence Augustine in his letter to Glorias and Eleusius which begins *Dixit quidem apostolus*, after he has discussed the decision of 70 bishops against Cecilianus and noted that that decision was reversed by Pope Miltiades and certain other bishops sent by Emperor Constantine, says that those who opposed the decision of Pope Miltiades and his associates said that they had supposedly suffered a decision by biassed judges. "This is the excuse of all bad litigants when they have been refuted by the obvious truth. Could it not properly be said to them on this point: 'Let us assume that the bishops who made the decision in Rome were not good judges. There was still the plenary council of the whole church where the case could be discussed with those judges and if they were convicted of having judged wrongly, their sentences could be annulled.' Let them indicate whether they did that. That they did not, we can easily prove from the fact that the whole world is in communion with him [Cecilianus]. If it was done, they were also defeated in the council."[15] It is the opinion of Augustine that even after a decision by the Roman pope, the universal council of the whole world is superior to him for the purpose of approving or absolving those who make the decision. Augustine holds this opinion in many places, [for instance] D. 19 [c. 6] *In canonicis*; [C.] 2 q. 7 [c. 35] *Puto*, para. *Item: Cum Petrus* and in other places cited in this work.

150.   There is no doubt on this point since Christ says to Peter: "If he will not hear the church, let him be to thee as an outcast and a publican."[16] Hence it is evident that he who does not obey the church and the council which represents it, is to be considered as an outcast and a publican by Peter and his successors. And this can be proved by

[14] Mansi 7, pp. 302ff., 7, p. 370, 6, pp. 1046ff., 11, pp. 554ff., 16, p. 189.
[15] PL 33, p. 169.   [16] Matthew 18:17.

the authority of Pope St. Gregory in letter 214 in the [Papal] *Register* where, after he criticizes John, the Patriarch of Constantinople, for describing himself as the universal patriarch [he says] at the end: "And we against whom in rash presumption this offense is committed will put into practice what Truth commands when it says: 'If thy brother has sinned against thee, etc.' And so I a sinner who once through my emissaries and twice in humble words have striven to refute this in the whole church, write personally. Whatever I should have humbly done, I have done, but I am rejected for that correction. It remains for me to turn to the church."[17] Note that Pope Gregory admits that fraternal correction in this way is his duty as Christ commands and that as a last resort he should turn to the church as the supreme judge etc.

151.   The same is also true of many other ordinances concerning the Roman see which were made in various ecumenical councils, and it is clear that those ordinances received their force from the fact that they were made by a higher authority. Hence the authority of the ecumenical council is greater [than that of the pope]. This is proved by the canon of the Eighth Council concerning the power of patriarchs which also speaks of the Roman patriarch.[18] Likewise it is proved by the tenth canon of the same council which begins *Divina*, which says: "This holy and universal synod rightly and properly defines and decides that no layman or monk or clergyman may separate himself from communion with his patriarch before a careful examination and decision by the synod, even if he claims to know that he is guilty of a criminal act."[19] It [the canon] does not discuss heresy, since, although one should not separate oneself [from communion with one's patriarch], as that text and [C.] 2 q. 7 [c. 8] *Sacerdotes* and [C.] 8 q. 4 [c. 1] *Nonne* state, these texts do not apply in the case of heresy because even if he has been tolerated, you should note that he was excommunicated at that time for falling into a condemned heresy, see [C.] 24 q. 1 [C. 1]. The Gloss also makes statements that agree with this when it discusses the aforesaid chapter *Sacerdotes* [c. 8] and the chapter *Anastasius* [c. 9] of D. 19 and one should always withdraw from a heretic, as is stated in the same place in the Gloss and as Pope Hadrian in synod also states in his third message which appears in the seventh action of the Eighth Council.[20] And because that text refers to

---

[17] Jaffe, p. 1357.   [18] Mansi 16, pp. 170ff.
[19] Mansi 16, p. 166.   [20] Mansi 16, p. 127.

other crimes, the pope can also be judged by the council concerning other crimes besides heresy.

152. This can also be proved from what was said by St. Peter to Clement, as appears in the letter of Clement to James where he says that Peter said to him when he established him as his successor: "For Christ did not wish to constitute you today as a judge with jurisdiction over secular affairs for fear that because of the burden of the human cares of the moment you could not dedicate yourself to the word of God. For if you were occupied with worldly concerns, you would deceive yourself and those who hear you. For you could not perceive what pertains to salvation more clearly than other men, and therefore you would be deposed as one who did not teach the way to the salvation of men, and your disciples would perish in ignorance."[21] Nevertheless I do not wish to assert that Clement actually did write in this way to James because it is sufficiently established as true that James died as a martyr eight years before Peter, as is discussed below in Part III.[22] But since the church does not reject this letter, it is also clear that the pope can be deposed for negligence, for it says: "You would be deposed," etc., and so this supports our proposition.

153. Note therefore that the canon that discusses judgments by the council speaks of all patriarchs in the same way.[23] From the acts of that council it appears that the pope is always called the Patriarch of Rome. If there is no doubt that a criminal case involving any other patriarch can be decided by the council, the same is true in the case of the Roman patriarch. [D.] 22 [c. 7] *Diffinimus* says that all patriarchs are equal as to [the possibility of] their deposition. Likewise the text of the tenth canon of the Eighth Council proves that all representatives are equal for the purpose of the deposition or correction of metropolitans. The acts of the Council of Chalcedon in its last action and in other places as well as other acts of the councils also prove that other patriarchs besides the Roman pope [acting] together with their councils have deposed bishops and archbishops.[24] The laws which say that the pope alone can depose a bishop should therefore be understood to apply only in his own patriarchate. And the aforesaid acts of the Council of Chalcedon concerning the deposition of Anastasius seem to prove that a patriarch should carry out depositions not [merely] with the advice but with the consent of his council. For the

---

[21] Hinschius, p. 32 (False Decretal). [22] Book III, no. 309.
[23] See no. 151. [24] Mansi 7, pp. 314 and p. 291.

bishops of the Council of Antioch say: "We deposed Athanasius who was accused by the clergy of his church because he did not come when he had been called three times."[25] Hence when the Archdeacon commenting on [D.] 22 [c. 5] *Qua traditione*, says that the pope can depose anyone without action by a council, this should be understood in accordance with what is contained below. It is true [that he can act] without a council of the universal church or even a patriarchal council when the one to be deprived of office or deposed falls under a penalty for an offense involving automatic imposition of punishment [*latae sententiae*].

154.   But to cite a clearer definition by the same Eighth Universal Council to the effect that the pope is subject to the ecumenical council of the whole church, it says in canon 21 which begins *Dominicum sermonem* para. *Porro* part of which is contained in [D.] 22 [c. 7] *Diffinimus* – that the universal synod is obliged to hear with due reverence any question that arises concerning the Roman see, and to go into those things, and to take action on them, but it could not pass judgment rashly on the Roman pontiff.[26] Note that although the ecumenical council has to decide every question that arises concerning the Apostolic See, it should do this with due reverence and not pass judgment rashly, on account of the primacy [of Rome] and [the council's] reverence for its head.

155.   Hence it is evident from these [examples] that the universal council is clearly [*simpliciter*] superior to the pope. And it is not necessary to produce further examples of this since we have the various decrees of the Council of Basel as well as those of Constance, [declaring] that the pope is subject to the council. And although Constance only speaks of superiority in three cases, it is clear that all the canons which have been adopted and those that could be adopted further, can be reduced to these [three].[27] Was it not defined in the fifth session of this Council of Basel that no one, either in person or through his recognized representative, could leave the place where the council was meeting, even by the authority of Rome?[28] Why was this prohibition adopted if not because to allow it would work to the prejudice of the council? If therefore the authority of the Roman

[25] Mansi 7, p. 354.   [26] Mansi 16, p. 174.

[27] Mansi 29, p. 21 and 27, p. 585. The three cases were "faith, the extirpation of schism, and reform of the church of God in head and members."

[28] Mansi 29, p. 38.

pontiff cannot extend to particular persons when it is presumed that this could operate to the prejudice of the council, who doubts that the council as a whole is over the pope? There are more such decrees of this council that prove this, such as those citing and warning the pope and decrees of this kind.

CHAPTER XVIII

THE ASSERTION THAT THE COUNCIL IS OVER THE POPE IS BASED ON AUGUSTINE'S STATEMENT THAT THE CHURCH WHICH WAS PROMISED TRUTH AND [DIVINE] ASSISTANCE IS REPRESENTED MORE CERTAINLY AND INFALLIBLY IN THE UNIVERSAL COUNCIL THAN IN THE POPE ALONE. THE CHAPTER DISCUSSES THE BASIC PRINCIPLES OF REPRESENTATION AND ADMINISTRATION, WHY PRELATES SHOULD BE ELECTED, AND WHAT PROCEDURE SHOULD BE FOLLOWED AND IT DESCRIBES HOW CARDINALS SHOULD BE ELECTED BY THE [CHURCH] PROVINCES AS THEIR REPRESENTATIVES. FURTHER SPECIFIC POINTS ARE MADE ABOUT THEM – THAT THEIR POWER HAS ARISEN FROM COMMON CONSENT, AND IN WHAT SENSE THIS IS TRUE.

156.   But so that we may see more profoundly that this is true, let us recall to mind what is said above concerning the representativity of the presiding officers of a council. And we may say that by the assistance of Christ the power of binding and loosing and infallibility and freedom from error are in the true Catholic church until the end of time. But since the Roman pontiff is a member of the church which is the Mystical Body of Christ, and infallibility was not promised to any member but to the whole church, there is no doubt that the unerring power of binding and loosing belonging to the whole church is superior to the power of the Roman pontiff, although the power of binding and loosing in both the church and the pope flows from the same source. And I say that this is true not only of the whole church

but also of the priesthood in the church which is like one soul in the whole church. It is true by the promise and delegation of Christ, because the priesthood was established by the Holy Spirit to rule the church of Christ, as the Apostle Peter says: "Feed the flock which is among you"[1] etc. Therefore the priesthood, whether actually or potentially gathered together, exercises the power to feed the whole church which is delegated to it by Christ over the whole church and all its members including the pope. But because the universal council is a congregation or church gathering composed of the members of the whole Catholic church and for this reason represents the whole church, we should then consider that the Roman pontiff because he is the highest pontiff also acts as the figurative representative of the one universal church.

157.   Hence Augustine says in *Sermon 7 on the Gospel of John* concerning the passage, "Thou shalt be called Cephas." "It is a wonderful thing that he changed his name from Simon to Peter. For Peter is from *petra* [rock], and the rock is the Church. Thus the name of Peter is a figurative representation of the church."[2] He says the same thing in Sermon 11 and in his last sermon where, when he speaks of the church, Augustine says: "The Apostle Peter was the representative of the church as a whole since he was first of the apostles. Considered as a person by nature he was a man, by grace he was a Christian, by more abundant grace he was an apostle – and at the same time the first of the apostles. When it was said to him: 'I shall give thee the keys of the kingdom of heaven and whatsoever thou shalt bind etc.' – he represented the whole church, and this is why he received the name of Peter. For it was not *petra* from Peter but Peter from *petra*, just as it is not Christ from Christian but Christian from Christ. Hence the Lord rightly says, 'Upon this rock I will build my church,' because Peter had said, 'Thou art Christ, the son of the living God.' Upon this rock therefore, which thou hast confessed, I will build my church. But the rock was Christ upon which foundation Peter himself also built. But the church that was founded by Christ, received the keys of the kingdom of heaven, that is the power of binding and loosing, from him through Peter. Peter's relationship to the rock symbolizes the church's relationship to Christ, since the rock symbolizes Christ and Peter the church."[3] For this, see the text of Augustine in [C:] 11 q. 3

[1] 1 Peter 5:2.   [2] PL 35, p. 1444. The scriptural quotation is from John 1:42.
[3] PL 35, p. 1763 (Tractatus 50).

[c. 87] *Illud*; and that of Leo in [D.] 19 [c. 7] *Ita Dominus*; and the Archdeacon discussing [C.] 24 q. 1 [c. 6] *Quodcumque* and the chapter *Quicumque* [c. 27], D. 21 [before c. 1] *Decretis*, and *De poenitentia*, D. 2 [c. 40] *Si es* [*enim*] v. *Petrus*. See also Augustine, *The Christian Combat*, c. 20 and his *Homily on the Transfiguration* and *On the Words of the Lord*, Book I, Sermon 13, and *On the Apostles Peter and Paul*, Sermon 13, and Book II q. 79 of *Questions on the Old and New Testament*, and Homily 46 in the *Book of Homilies* and *Sermon 13* on Psalm 108, and Ambrose, *On Pastoral Care* and Anselm on the passage of Matthew, "For the poor you have always with you."[4]

And because Peter is from *petra* [rock] and the rock is the church which signifies Christ, and for this reason is his Mystical Body, it is evident that as Christ is truth, the rock – which is the image [*figura*], or sign of Christ – is the church, and the image or sign of this rock is Peter. Hence just as Christ is the truth which the rock or the church represents or signifies, so the rock is the truth which Peter signifies or represents. From this it is clear that the church is over Peter just as Christ is over the church. Just as we say that the Old Testament prefigures the New and that the New Testament is the truth in relation to the Old Testament and is therefore superior to it and the representation [*figuram*] of the future glory where alone there is the truth so that the New Testament is both truth and representation, truth with respect to that which is below it, and representation with respect to that above, the same thing is also true of the Catholic church.

158.   Hence it is clear that as Peter represents the church as an individual in an obscure way and subject to error, there are many grades of representation and signification between the rock and Peter so that we move from the weakest representation and sign through intermediate representations that are more certain and true, to the rock which is truth. But only one person or one gathering which the Greeks call a synod can signify and represent the one church. Therefore in the case of a universal synod we should ask whether it is a properly-ordered gathering that can represent the universal church united as a synod because it includes, for example, the pope, the patriarchs, and the heads of the provinces etc. According to what has

---

[4] PL 40, p. 308; PL 158, p. 604 (Anselm of Canterbury); PL 38, pp. 479 and 1348ff.; PL 35, p. 2273 (False Decretal); PL 38, p. 1148; PL 37, p. 1537; PL 139, p. 171 (False Decretal). Anselm's Commentary has not been printed.

been said above, when it happens that a universal synod is properly congregated in this way, there is no doubt that the more certainly and truly that synod represents the church, the more its judgment tends towards infallibility rather than fallibility, and that this judgment is always better than the individual judgment of the Roman pontiff who represents the church in a very uncertain way [*confusissime*]. There is an old proverb that what many look for is found more easily. Hence the individual judgment of a pope should be presumed to be less stable and more fallible than that of the pope along with others – and there is no doubt about this.

159.   What has been said above seems to be proved by Letter 62 of St. Ambrose – which was written by a Roman pontiff and not by St. Ambrose as is proven by comparing that letter with the one immediately preceding it. For Letter 61 of St. Ambrose to Theophilus begins, "Evagrius does not have a basis for what he urges, and Flavian has reason to fear a trial and therefore avoids it. Let the brethren pardon our justified grief. Because of these men the whole world is disturbed, yet they do not share our sorrow." And below, "Serious discord has arisen in the whole world. In the shipwreck of precious peace, the holy Synod of Capua finally offered a haven of tranquillity when it declared that communion should be established with all those throughout the East who profess the Catholic faith, and that these two men should be tried by Your Holiness with the participation of our brethren and fellow bishops of Egypt – for we felt that your judgment would be a true one. We think that you should certainly consult our holy brother, the bishop of the church of Rome, for we presume that you will make decisions which in no way displease him. A decision on the sentence will be useful and assure peace and quiet – if it is decreed by your council." And he proceeds further, "What the Roman church has undoubtedly approved, we gladly approve as the result of this trial."[5] Following this there is a letter with the answer of the pope himself to what had been written by the judges appointed by the council, as Ambrose had advised. And at the beginning the pope, whose name I have not found in my manuscript, says that they asked his decision concerning Bishop Bonosus in all truth and modesty. And below: "We note that the procedure for making such a decision is not available to us. If the full synod were meeting today, we would

---

[5] PL 16, p. 1220.

be right in deciding on the matters to which your writings refer. But it is now your duty to decide everything since you have been given the responsibility for judging the case." And below: "You are the representatives of the synod whom it chose for the investigation. Finally since after your decision bishop Bonosus asked our brother Ambrose to give his advice as to whether he should enter the prohibited church by force, he answered him that nothing should be done rashly, but everything with modesty, patience, and in order. And nothing was to be attempted in violation of your decisions, so that you to whom the synod had given the authority might decide what seemed just to you. Therefore the first thing is for those to whom the power to decide has been given to make a decision. For, as we have written, you are the representatives of the whole synod, and it is not proper for us to judge as if we had the authority of the synod." And finally at the end: "Hence we await your decision."[6]

160. Here the pope declares that if the synod were acting as a whole, that is, if it had not delegated the power of judgment to others, he could have decided on the case himself. But because the synod delegated it to others he says that he cannot decide the case and it is not fitting for him to act with the authority of the synod. Note this, for it clearly proves that the authority of the synod is over the pope and also that those assigned to act as representatives of the whole synod have greater power than the pope in a matter assigned to them. The Pope who wrote this was St. Damasus, I believe, because the immediately following letter, No. 63, says that Damasus was pope at the time since Ambrose says: "Also two years ago, St. Damasus, bishop of the Roman church, elected by the judgment of God, sent me, etc."[7]

161. Hence we conclude that a universal council if properly assembled although its decisions may vary in degree [of authoritativeness] is always of greater authority and less fallible than is the pope alone. From this it follows as a corollary that the universal council also has the power to depose [the pope] in cases other than heresy as, we read, was true in the cases of Benedict XII and John XXIII.[8] And this is proved from ch. 1 [of 1 7] *De Renuntiatione*, in the *Liber Sextus*. For if as stated there, the papacy can be taken away from the material subject, i.e. the person involved, by the decision of the pope himself

---

[6] PL 16, pp. 1222–1224 and PL 13, p. 1176 (Pope Siricius).

[7] Pope Damasus died in 384 and was succeeded by Siricius, who wrote the letter.

[8] Mansi 27, pp. 1141ff. and 652ff. (the Council of Constance).

when he decides that he is incapable of ruling, and if, as we have argued, the decision of a council is of greater authority and less fallible than that of the pope alone, then it is clear that just as the pope can for legitimate reasons resign from office, so his subjects in common council can cease to give obedience for the same reasons when he is guilty of misrule. For when a prelate is elected, he is chosen to rule well, see [C.] 1 q. 1 [after c. 43], *Ecce cum honore*; [C.] 8 q. 1 [c. 11] *Qui episcopatum*; [C.] 28 q. 1 [c. 8] *Iam nunc*; and *Decretals* 1 9 *De renuntiatione* [c. 10] *Nisi cum pridem* para. *Porro*; and [C.] 23 q. 4 [c. 5] *Quisquis*. So when he rules badly the tacit condition on the consent given is put into effect and since the reason for which he was elected ceases to exist, those who elected him then give that authority to the council itself, *a fortiori*, – although the pope says that he possesses it in that first chapter [of *Liber Sextus* 1 7 *De renuntiatione*]. No rational person can doubt that a council which represents the church has power over the papacy to direct its occupant in accordance with the needs of the church which is greater than the decision of one man concerning a papal office which has been given to him in the name of the church and for its benefit.

162. There may perhaps be some doubt that the council can deprive a single legitimate pope of the exercise of administration temporarily or at will, not because the council does not have power but because it is a contradiction in terms, since it is clear from the above and also from later passages that an essential element in the papal office is the free exercise of administration so that if that is taken away, the papacy is taken away. However since the Council of Constance and this Council of Basel issued certain decrees against the pope under pain of suspension,[9] I cannot deny that the pope can be suspended, although at first glance, I would want to assert that despite that suspension a person who has received absolution in the area of conscience, where the pope has special power from God, as long as he is pope would be truly absolved. This suspension ought not to extend to that power because it appears to be attached to the papacy by divine intention, although besides that power he would not have the exercise of any others which depend on law or men or involve externals. But if the council wanted expressly to take away from him by suspension the exercise of the power of binding and loosing in the penitential sphere,

---

[9] Mansi 27, pp. 625ff. and 29, p. 59. The Basel decree was adopted on July 13, 1433, which is helpful in dating this part of the *Concordantia*.

then one should either say that he was deposed at that time or that the papacy is something other than the free administration of the power of binding and loosing – but this would contradict what is said above and would be a novelty.

163. From this and from what has been touched on above it is clear that any ruler represents his subjects in proportion to the generality of the representation, so that the pope represents the whole church in a vague way, and he represents his patriarchate in a more direct way, his metropolitanate still more directly, his diocese still more certainly, his clergy yet more certainly, and finally he represents his daily council, as it were, in a single body. So it is that the cardinals as representatives of the provinces who assist the Roman pontiff are called the principal members and part of the body of the pope. From this it is also clear that the more specific the rulership, the more certain and less vague the representation by the ruler. Therefore since, as Jerome says to Rusticus in [C.] 7 q. 1 [c. 41] *In Apibus*, every ecclesiastical order has rulers who finally bring them together as one, by natural and divine law those rulers ought to be established by consent, and as Pope Anicetus has said, it is proper that the one who is to be over all should be chosen by all, see D. 66 [c. 1] *Archiepiscopus*, and no one should be set up over unwilling subjects, as will be said below because, according to St. Leo, there is no reason which permits someone who is not elected to be a bishop.[10]

164. On this point for one body to be established in a harmony of subjects and ruler, reason and natural and divine law all require that there be mutual consent in this spiritual marriage which is demonstrated by the election by all and the consent of the one elected, just as a spiritual marriage is rightly established by consent between Christ and his church, as is said in [C.] 7 q. 1 [c. 11] *Sicut* and in other chapters in the same place, and in many similar passages of D. 62 and 63, and in [C.] 24 q. 1 [c. 33] *Pudenda* and D. 63 [c. 19] *Metropolitano*. Thus although the sacraments can be given to someone against his will, this is not the case with matrimony since consent is of the essence there, see [C.] 27 q. 2 [before c. 1] para. 1 and [C.] 32 [31] q. 2 [before ch. 1] para. 1, and as the Gloss notes on [C.] 1 q. 1 [c. 3] *Constat*. But the church is the wife or spouse of the bishop, see [C.] 21 q. 3 *Sicut* and similar passages, and therefore etc. On this more will be

---

[10] PL 54, p. 120. The reference to unwilling subjects is from the *Decretum*, D. 61 c. 13.

said below.[11] Hence if right order is to be preserved, the text of the Council of Toledo in D. 51 [c. 5] *Qui in aliquo* and those in D. 62 [c. 1] *Nulla* and D. 23 [c. 1] *In nomine Domini* and similar texts should be observed so that parish priests and curates are elected or at least some convenient provision is made for consent to their appointment, as is stated in D. 67 [c. 1] *Reliqui*, D. 63 [c. 20] *Si in plebibus*. Then the clergy should elect the bishop with the consent of the laity, see D. 63 [c. 11] *Plebs* and [c. 12] *Nosse*, and the bishops the metropolitan with the consent of the clergy, see D. 66 [before ch. 1] *Archiepiscopi*. The metropolitans of the provinces with the consent of the bishops should elect the representatives of the provinces who assist the pope and are called cardinals and those cardinals should elect the pope, if possible with the consent of the metropolitans. But if it does not seem useful to wait for their consent because of the danger that the papacy will be vacant for too long, then the present procedure should be followed [but] in better order. This would mean that the Roman pontiff would have with him a continuing council which legitimately represents the whole church. With this council, there is no doubt the church would be ruled in the best possible fashion.

165.   Hence when canon 26 of the Eighth Universal Council commanded under the pain of automatic excommunication that the decision of the patriarch should be strictly observed, it said that it was just, reasonable, and above suspicion because a number of honorable men were associated with him.[12] And the canon did not speak of the Roman cardinals because, as is clear from the canon *Praesul* [c. 2] as well as the canon [c. 3] *Nullam* of [C.] 2 q. 5 [q. 4], bishops at that time always took precedence over cardinals because they were more important than the cardinals – as appears in the Gloss on [C.] 2 q. 7 [c. 34] *Quamquam* because the cardinals were priests and deacons of the Roman clergy, as appears in the same place and in D. 79 [D. 78] [c. 9] *Si quis pecunia* and the chapter [c. 3] *Oportebat* and the chapter [c. 5] *Si quis ex episcopis*. For as the text of D. 24 [c. 3] *Presbyteri* proves, the title of cardinal stands for a certain eminence, where "cardinal pontiff" is the title given to the metropolitan etc. And this is also proved by D. 93 [c. 5] *A subdiacono* and by the statement of Leo IX above. Also the Archdeacon commenting on D. 22 [c. 2] *Sacrosancta* says that the pope is counted among the cardinals and that

[11] Book II, ch. 32, no. 232.
[12] Mansi 16, p. 178.

bishops are also to be called cardinals as is stated in [C.] 21 q. 1 [c. 5] *Relatio*; [C.] 7 q. 1 [c. 42] *Pastoralis*; and D. 71 [c. 5] *Fraternitatem*.

166. But the text mentioned above speaks of the metropolitans and representatives of the provinces who were obliged to come to the patriarchal council in accordance with canon 17.[13] Therefore since it is difficult to assemble a plenary universal council, I would think that the first essential reform for good government would be that the cardinals be chosen from the representatives of the provinces and that anything important or against the general content of the canons be decided in a council of cardinals and signed both by the pope and the cardinals. The signing is to show that this is done with clear knowledge and careful examination so that in this way the canons can be observed with due reverence, and provision can be made for particular cases of utility and necessity. For the cardinals act in place of the metropolitans, see D. 23 [c. 1] *In nomine Domini*, and Hostiensis notes this in his *Summa* [commenting on *Decretals* v 38] *De Poenitentia et Remissionibus* para. *Cui papa* v. *Alii dicunt*. Therefore just as the metropolitans of the provinces are established through election by the members of the provinces, so the cardinals who represent them should also be constituted in the same way, as described above. And this seems to be especially necessary at this time because the metropolitans and bishops do not make an annual visit to the pope as they did of old, although perhaps they still swear to do so according to the ancient form, as is mentioned in the canon *Episcopi* [after c. 3] and subsequent passages of D. 92. The Roman pontiffs were also accustomed to make use of their advice in deciding difficult cases. Of old this was strictly observed, especially by the metropolitans, as we read in canon 17 of the Eighth Universal Council, since they could not be excused either on account of conflicting provincial synods or being summoned by a secular prince. Today however even if they are present at the Roman *curia*, as foreigners they are not summoned to the papal council. This is absurd, especially when a case involving the universal church or a matter in some way affecting the whole church is under consideration. Hence it seems necessary to create such representatives of the provinces as cardinals for many worthwhile reasons as any intelligent person who has any knowledge of the procedure of the Roman *curia* will easily recognize.

---

[13] Mansi 16, p. 171.

CHAPTER XIX

FREE ELECTION IS THE BASIS OF ALL PROPERLY ORDERED POWER – A BRIEF BUT WELL-EXPRESSED DISCUSSION.

167.   If the laws and decrees of the holy fathers were observed which say that no one should be appointed to ruling responsibility who is not elected by those over whom he is to rule – so that he may recognize that his rulership comes from those over whom he is ruling and thus act as a loving pastor without pride – we would see how properly ordered elections on each level would produce the result described above by St. Augustine – Peter would be based on (lit. – originate from) the rock [*petra*] that is the church of the faithful. Not that the power to rule which is in rulers comes in its entirety from the people, but, as is said above, just as the moving and sensible parts of the soul are produced out of the potency of matter but its rational part comes from God, so the priesthood which is the soul of the church militant derives its moving, vegetative, and sensible power to rule from the faithful subjects – a power which comes from the potency of matter of the faithful by way of voluntary subjection – but the power of the rational soul which comes from above, it receives from God through the sacraments. In this way power from on high can flow in sweet harmony to the body of the subjects through the mediation of a power which comes from it and is granted by it in order to bring about a salutary union [of the faithful] with Christ, the head. Hence Pope Hormisda says to the bishops of Spain: "Let not the blessing which we believe comes from God through the laying-on of hands be sold for money. Who would think that something is valuable if he has sold it? Let the election observe proper reverence for the priests to be ordained, keeping in mind that the weighty decision of the people is the judgment of God. For God is present where there is genuine consent without irregularity."[1] And although God has reserved the deposition of the most high priests for himself, he has given their election to the faithful, see D. 79 in the final chapter [c. 11] and divine grace appoints the one who is chosen by common consent, see [C.] 8

[1] PL 63, p. 424.

q. 2 [c. 2] *Dilectissimi.* On this there is more at greater length below. 168. And it is a happy thought that all power, whether spiritual or temporal and corporeal, is potentially in the people, although in order for the power to rule to be activated there must necessarily be the concurrence of that formative radiance from above to establish it in being since it is true that all power is from above – I speak of properly ordered power – just as from the potential of the earth, the lowest of the elements, various vegetable and sensible beings are produced through the mediating influence of heaven. Hence it was not inappropriate for the Abbot Joachim when he discussed the Apocalypse to say that the people represent the Father, the secular clergy the Son, and the religious the Holy Spirit, because as the Son comes from the Father, so the clergy comes from the laity, and as the Holy Spirit comes from both so the religious proceed from the laity and the clergy.[2]

[2] Joachim of Flora, *In Apocalypsim* (Venice, 1527). On the influence of Joachim, see Eric Voegelin, *The New Science of Politics*, Chicago, 1952, reprinted 1987.

CHAPTER XX

THE POPE CANNOT ABROGATE, CHANGE, OR
REPEAL UNIVERSAL CANONS. THIS IS PROVED BY
AUTHORITATIVE TEXTS, EXAMPLES, AND
DOCTRINAL STATEMENTS, AS WELL AS MANY
ARGUMENTS. DISPENSATIONS AND A DECLARATION
THAT A CANON DOES NOT APPLY IN A PARTICULAR
CASE CAN TAKE PLACE WITHOUT ADVERSELY
AFFECTING THE CANON. THIS IS DISCUSSED AT
LENGTH AS APPROPRIATE.

169. From what has been written above it is easy to answer another current problem – whether the pope can be bound by the decrees of the universal council so that he cannot act against them. For if the universal council, properly speaking, is above the pope, as is said above, the problem is resolved. Hence although the pope in the chapter [c. 4] *Significasti* of [Decretals I 6] *De Electione* says he is over the council and in the chapter [c. 4] *Proposuit* of [Decretals III 8] *De*

Concessione Praebendae says that he is above the laws, this is true [only] of his own general council over which he presides as patriarch, and of the laws adopted there or in other particular councils or laws made by him – although I grant that because of its rulership over all men in the church the Apostolic See has the power of equity [*epieikeia*],[1] and this cannot be taken away in particular cases since he often has to dispense from, and interpret [the law] in cases of utility and necessity for the welfare of the church – but only for that purpose. That he cannot abrogate or change the canons of the universal councils or adopt anything to the contrary is proved by the noted text, [C.] 25 q. 1 [c. 7] *Contra statuta* where Pope Zosimus says: "The authority of this see can neither adopt nor amend any law contrary to the statutes of the fathers." And Zosimus also says the same thing to Aurelius and all the bishops established in Africa, Gaul etc., "When action is taken contrary to the statutes of the holy fathers, injury is done not only to the wise decision that they decreed should govern forever, but also in a certain way to the discipline of the Catholic faith itself. For what can be more holy and venerable than never to depart from the way of our ancestors whose canonical statutes act as a kind of foundation for the burdens of our faith which we must bear?"[2]

170.   These points are also proved from the fact that Pope Damasus when he wrote to Paulinus commanded that those who came back to the faith be required to subscribe not only to the declaration of faith of the Nicene Council, but also to its canons, as appears in D. 100 c. 1, 2, and 3.[3] The text [of Pope Zosimus] quoted above says: "Against the statutes of the fathers, that is, the canons," as the text of D. 20 [c. 1] *De libellis* says. The end of this latter text agrees completely with that of Zosimus above since it says: "It is clear that no one genuinely believes and holds the holy gospels to his benefit if he does not observe the statutes of the holy ones that we call canons." And Pope St. Gregory in the [Papal] *Register* says to John, bishop of Larissa, at the end of the letter which begins, *Frater noster Adrianus*: "We decree and define that in accordance with the holy fathers anyone who does not obey the sacred canons may not minister at the sacred altars or receive communion."[4] And the canons which are thus to be revered by all should be adopted in universal councils, D. 16 [c. 6] *Habeo librum*, and they are called general canons, as Gregory says of the

[1] On *epieikeia*, see Aristotle, *Nicomachean Ethics*, v, 10.
[2] PL 20, p. 661.   [3] PL 56, p. 686.   [4] PL 77, p. 611.

canons of the Council of Chalcedon in the *Register* in his letter to Secundinus which begins: *Dilectionis tuae,* where he says: "The holy synod of Chalcedon spoke in order to define the faith and promulgate canons on general matters. After the canons were adopted, it concerned itself with the settlement of particular disputes among the bishops."[5] The Archdeacon notes that the pope cannot repeal statutes that affect the universal state of the church. See his comments on D. 19 [after c. 7] *Ita Dominus* at the end, and the chapter [c. 6] *Sunt quidam* and other chapters in [C.] 25 q. 1 cited there make the same point.

171. Again the pope is the shepherd of mankind. To him it has rightly been said: "Feed my sheep."[6] But the rules and canons of the ecumenical councils have been issued for our moral betterment, see D. 31 [c. 12] *Nicaena igitur,* and the pope is obliged to obey them and should employ them in feeding his flock, for the saving canons were adopted by divine inspiration, as Pope Leo IV says in [C.] 25 q. 1 [c. 16] *Ideo.* Therefore the Universal Council of Constance also added that if he did not obey them he could be punished because no see should follow the legislation of all the synods more than should the Roman see, as Pope Gelasius says in [C.] 25 q. 1 [c. 1] *Confidimus.*[7] And Pope Leo who is described in the Eighth Council as the trumpet of truth says to Emperor Marcian that the Nicene canons cannot be uprooted by wickedness, nor abridged by innovation, and adds: "And in the faithful performance of my duties, with Christ as a guide, I must carry out my service with perseverance since [the power of] dispensation has been entrusted to me and I would be judged guilty if the norms contained in the sanctions of the fathers which were established by the inspiration of the spirit of God were violated – God forbid! – by my acquiescence."[8] A text of Pope Leo says this in [C.] 25 q. 1 [c. 3] *Quae ad perpetuam.* In addition when Leo refers to his approval of the [decrees on] faith of the General Council of Chalcedon, in a letter which begins *Omnem,* sent to all the bishops, he says that anything done against the Nicene canons of which, he says, he is the guardian, is worthless and invalid. But the reason that he cannot act against them and he above all is obliged to follow them is that, as the text *Violatores* [c. 5] says in the same place, they were established by the spirit of God for the good governance of the

[5] PL 77, p. 986.

[6] John 21:17.

[7] Mansi 27, p. 590.

[8] Mansi 11, p. 66; PL 54, p. 995.

universal church, and it is the responsibility of the Roman pontiff to advance them in the spiritual plane.[9] Hence the Archdeacon notes in his comment on D. 19 [c. 7] *Ita dominus*, that the pope cannot repeal the statutes that concern the universal state of the church.

172.   And so the canon of the universal council is the guide and rule for the governance and progress of the church which the first builder should use if he wishes to exercise his power properly. For no one could create more just or unerring rules than the Holy Spirit who inspires the universal councils. Hence in the sixth action of the Eighth Council, Zacharis, the bishop of Chalcedon, when the opinion of the Roman pontiff was put before him, said: "The canon is the rule for Pope Nicholas and the other patriarchs, and if they act in accordance with it, they will do nothing which is not proper. But when they do something against it, whether it is Pope Nicholas or anyone else, we will not acquiesce." And below: "If these things were done by Nicholas in accordance with the canon, we follow, agree, and confirm them, and we do not recognize anything which is contrary to them. But if they were done contrary to law and the canon, it is not we who censure or reject them, but the canon." Then when Metrophanes answered, he did not claim that the pope was above the law but said: "In a different case a different evaluation and opinion should also result," and he answered that he had decided according to the regulations and no alleged custom to the contrary concerning the promotion of laymen or even of catechumens to the high position of patriarch or archbishop could prevail against them. He said: "This is obvious, for what is done as a rare exception does not subvert the established laws."[10] For there was very great concern among the ancients to preserve the canons and frequently there is a statute placed at the beginning of the canons of a given synod concerning their observance, as in [C.] 25 q. 1 [c. 14] *A sanctis*, and in the canons of Carthage where we read: "We must observe what has been done or said above or written by other councils. If anyone violates them, if he is a layman let him be denied communion, if a clergyman deprived of his position." Everyone said: "We approve; we approve."[11] And this is stated still more strongly in the 20th chapter of the general council which was held previous to the Sixth Universal Council in the reign of Pope Martin – who according to the Gloss on D. 18 [c. 15] *Propter* had

[9] PL 54, p. 1031.   [10] Mansi 16, pp. 87–90.   [11] Hinschius, p. 94.

reissued the canons. Its words are reproduced as follows in the eighth action of the Eighth Universal Council: "If anyone, following criminal heretics in violation of the law, changes in any way by word, time, or place, the terms which the fathers and saints of the holy Catholic church and the five universal synods have so clearly established, rashly inventing novel doctrines or altering the expositions of the faith or propounding other creeds or laws or definitions, or formulations . . ." and below, ". . . or dispositions which are inconsistent with, or unknown to, ecclesiastical procedure . . ." and below, "against the holy paternal conciliar teachings of the orthodox [believers] in the Catholic church . . . let the one who impiously does this if he has not repented, be condemned forever and let all the people say: So be it, so be it."[12] And Pope Martin signed together with the others. From this you see that the canon was speaking of the universal councils, since the Roman pontiffs are obliged by them. Hence we read that the popes signed the canons in the ecumenical councils – as they also did in their own general councils as noted above.

173. But that canon does not speak of all the canons and laws and definitions of the fathers but of those of the five ecumenical councils which were the only ones held previous to that time. Thus [Pope] Leo writes to Maximus, the patriarch of Antioch, that the canons of the Nicene Council are inviolable.[13] That the Roman pontiffs who like the other patriarchs are obliged to hold the profession [of faith] of the universal councils, are also obliged to observe the canons by reason of that profession is proved by the text *Sancta* [c. 8] of D. 16. In the profession of faith located there the pope declares that he will observe the eight councils to the letter, and follow in every way what they command and teach. And the text of D. 15 [c. 2] *Sicut* also proves this, and the text of D. 50 [c. 16] *Sicut sanctitas*, demonstrates that in that canon *Sicut* St. Gregory referred not only to the faith but also to the canons [of the councils]. The same thing is also proved by the declaration of [Pope] Leo IX to Peter of Antioch in which, after seven universal councils had been held, he says, "Whatever the aforesaid seven universal councils have felt and approved, I feel and approve."[14] And in the *Panormia* of St. Ivo, bishop of Chartres, the declaration of faith of the Roman pontiff from the Book of the Roman Pontiffs appears in this form: "I declare that I will diligently and carefully

---

[12] Mansi 10, pp. 1159 and 1162.
[13] Mansi 54, p. 1043.   [14] PL 143, p. 773.

confirm and maintain undiminished and enforce as adopted, all the canonical decrees of all our preceding apostolic pontiffs which they have adopted in synod and confirmed. Likewise I will condemn and abjure whatever and whomever they have rejected and condemned." And after this [in the *Panormia*] there follows another declaration [of faith] from the book of the Popes which is called the *Liber Diurnus*: "I declare that I will not make any diminution or alteration or innovation in any of the traditions that I have found handed down and preserved by my most worthy predecessors, but as their true and fervent disciple following in their footsteps with my whole heart, I will observe and revere what has been handed down to me in a canonical manner."[15]

174. From this it is clear that of old the holy Roman pontiffs were not so presumptuous about their power but were humble, even [to the point of] confessing their sins before their own synods – not that of the universal church [since] the synod of the universal church is the universal council. On these confessions, see [C.] 2 q. 4 [q. 5] [c. 10] *Mandastis*, where the Gloss compares the pope to the dean who can confess his sins before his [cathedral] chapter as Sixtus did before his synod.[16] See also the canons, *Auditum* [c. 18] and *Omnibus nobis* [c. 19]. Indeed Pope Leo [I] said that he would submit to all the penalties contained in the laws of [Emperor] Marcian, if he did not observe them after he had approved them – as he himself writes to Emperor Leo concerning his consent to the laws: "If I have violated them," he says, "I submit to the conditions of punishment which were established by the authority of Emperor Marcian of happy memory and I have confirmed by my own consent."[17] From this we conclude that when the pope submits himself, there is no doubt that he is bound by his decisions, as the Gloss notes on the chapter [c. 6] *Si Papa* of D. 40. But we are arguing here that the pope has submitted to the laws to which he has given his consent in writing, and since it has been clearly proven above from his own declaration that the pope has approved the canons in the records of the universal councils, he is therefore also subject to them.

175. In addition, anyone who has violated what he has professed

---

[15] PL 161, pp. 1130ff. St. Ivo of Chartres (*c.* 1040–1116) wrote works on canon law before Gratian's *Decretum*, the most important of which was the *Panormia*.

[16] Cusanus is referring to the unprinted Old Gloss (*Glossa Antiqua*) which is manuscript no. 223 in the hospital at Kues.

[17] PL 54, pp. 1144ff.

and signed, is to be deposed in council as the title of the sixth chapter of the Council of Africa says. And the text says: "At the request of Bishop Gennadius all the bishops said: 'Whoever violates what he has professed and signed will separate himself from this meeting.' "[18] Note that, as Pope Leo says above, if the pope either promises to observe or signs the statutes and does not keep them, he condemns himself. See also the promise of Leo IV concerning the observance of the laws [made] to Emperor Lothar whom he also addresses as "pontiff" in the manner of the ancients in D. 10 [c. 9] *De capitulis.* And on this basis and in view of the way in which the popes signed the decrees of their patriarchal councils as reviewed above, it would not be absurd to say that the pope also cannot take away or change the statutes issued in synod by the Roman church, because I have found that he subscribed to these in the same way as he did to the statutes of the universal council of the whole church. On this point however, although he should not change the patriarchal statutes because he has signed them – if he did, it should not be said that the revocation or change had as little value as if he had changed a statute of an ecumenical council of the Catholic church because the pope is obliged to observe this latter kind of statute not only from his having subscribed to it, but because it was issued by an authority which is superior to him. Therefore it should be said all the more emphatically that he is under the universal canons to which the Roman pontiffs through their legates have subscribed. This is well put in the text, [C.] 2 q. 7 [c. 41] *Nos si*, which proves this sufficiently, along with the following paragraphs *Item Hieronymus* and *Item Symmachus* which seems to say – contrary to *Hinc etiam* [after c. 6] in D. 17 – that Symmachus was deposed in the Roman synod. In fact this was the case but he was reinstated because according to *Hinc etiam* of D. 17, it did not have the right to do so. And these things can be seen in the original acts of that council transcribed in solemn and eloquent form by Deacon Ennodius.[19] The next chapter [c. 42] also speaks on the above points. And we also conclude that the Roman pontiff is subject to a council of the universal church from the fact that we read that the legates of the Apostolic See who attended the universal councils stood up when they spoke to the council, following the example of Peter who stood up in the council of Jerusalem when he spoke as a sign of

---

[18] Second Council of Carthage (Hinschius, p. 294).
[19] PL 63, pp. 183ff.

his subordination and reverence. Thus we read in the Sixth Ecumenical Council held in Constantinople, in its first action: "And rising to their feet, those who were representing the Apostolic See of Rome . . ."[20] And we read the same things in other councils.

176. We also find that the universal council examined the letters and writings of the Roman pontiffs sent to the council. In the third action of the Eighth Council when the letter of Pope Hadrian had been read by the council, the representatives of old Rome asked whether the letter had been composed in a canonical and synodic fashion. The holy synod said: "The letter of the most holy Pope Hadrian which has been read is canonical and in good order and correct throughout." And Metrophanes, the worthy bishop of Smyrna, stood up and said: "We have taken cognizance of the wise message of the most holy pope of Rome and of the concern which he has for the observance of the holy canons." And Pope Nicholas says to the Emperor Michael that "this holy apostolic church is the head of all churches which in all its actions always follows the unfailing authority of the holy fathers."[21] This appears in the fourth action of the same Eighth Council and subsequently in the letter of Pope Nicholas to Photius which begins, *Postquam*, which appears in the same place. In this letter after Pope Nicholas proves the primacy of the Apostolic See, and demonstrates that because of that primacy the Roman pontiff is responsible for all who are called by the name of Christ for whom he has to give an accounting in an eternal judgment, he adds that all the faithful seek the teaching of the Roman church and ask it for sound doctrine and the pardon of offenses which by the grace of God should be given to them, for it [Rome] is the head of the churches from which all churches demand right order in all ecclesiastical activities, because the Roman church keeps the canonical and synodal decrees of the holy fathers inviolate and unbroken, and for this reason its judgment is certain.[22] Note that the reason given for the certainty of the decision of the Apostolic See of Rome is its unbroken observance of the inviolable canons. In the same way in chapter six of his own council made up of the whole Roman church, he says: "Because we should keep securely in mind the doctrines of our ancestors and always venerate the dogmas of the holy fathers in all things . . . ," and this is also contained in the seventh action [of the

---

[20] Mansi 11, p. 215.   [21] Mansi 16, p. 53.   [22] Mansi 16, pp. 65–70.

Eighth Council of Constantinople].[23] On the basis of the same principle, the [canon law] texts of the same Nicholas, C. 9 q. 3 [c. 10] *Patet* [and] C. 17 q. 4 [c. 30] *Nemini*, say that the opinion of the pope can be overruled by no one. If it were incorrect, it could be overruled and in [case of] doubt, it is reviewed by the universal council. Hence in the fourth action of the Eighth Ecumenical Council when the representatives of the Apostolic See opposed a review of the judicial decisions of Pope Nicholas in his synod, the princes and senators insisted upon it saying that they would not subscribe as witnesses to the acts of the Council unless those who had been judged by the [papal] synod were admitted to answer for those decisions. And Metrophanes, the metropolitan of Smyrna arose and said, "When we consider the words of the most excellent princes, we find them just and fitting. All the bishops of this holy synod also favor this."[24] Note that by decree of the universal council, the decision of Pope Nicholas and his council on [the case of] Photius was reviewed and approved again, despite the opposition of the representatives of the bishop of Rome.

177. This clearly proves the supremacy of the universal council over the pope and his patriarchal synod. Thus Pope Leo writing to all the bishops in all the provinces says of the letters of all his predecessors: "We command that you observe all the decretals adopted both by Innocent of blessed memory and by all my other predecessors, which have been promulgated concerning ecclesiastical legislation and the teachings of the canons. If anyone contravenes them, he will know that pardon will be denied him," see D. 19 [c. 1] *Si Romanorum*. Pope Damasus speaks in the same way in [C.] 25 q. 1 [c. 12] *Omnium*. And Hincmar, discussing this letter in his work against the bishop of Laon says that it should be noted that to promulgate is to reveal to the people [*vulgo promere*].[25] Those popes do not speak of the simple promulgation of laws and canons but of decretals promulgated concerning the teachings of the canons. Hence when they go against the canons, it is the canons that are rather to be obeyed, see D. 19 *Ita Dominus* [after c. 7] para. *Hoc autem* with the gloss and the canon [c. 8] *Secundum* para. *Quia ergo*, where it is proved that the canons of the ancients are of greater authority than the decretals of the Roman pontiffs that go against them, however much modern canon lawyers may criticize Gratian on that point.

[23] Mansi 16, p. 109.   [24] Mansi 16, p. 55.   [25] PL 126, p. 316.

178.   And this is a further proof: It is obvious that the decree of a
synod which includes the authorized representatives of the Roman
pontiff, possesses an authority which is greater than, or at least equal
to, the decretals of the pope. But these councils are called provincial
councils in D. 3 [after c. 2] para. *Porro* or by another designation, local
councils, in [C.] 1 q. 7 [c. 4] *Convenientibus*. But there is no doubt that
provincial councils can be corrected by universal councils, as is shown
above. The text is [C.] 2 q. 7 [c. 35] *Puto* para. *Item: Cum Petrus*, in
which St. Augustine says that the statute of a universal council is to be
preferred to the authority of one bishop or a provincial council. That
text is very pertinent to this point as is clear from the following
quotation: "If Paul corrected Peter, therefore, *a fortiori*, the authority
of the universal council, etc." [Pope] Innocent [I] writes in the same
way of the canons of Nicaea and Sardica, and [Pope] Boniface writes
to Rusticus of Narbonne that all must believe that the holy fathers in
Nicaea adopted their canons by the inspiration of the Holy Spirit, and
adds: "So that your holiness [lit. – charity] may observe there that we
keep the precepts of the canons and so that our legislation may define
matters in a similar way. . . ."[26]

179.   This is also said in the letter of Celestine to all the bishops in
Calabria.[27] And Pope Leo [I] says to Anatole of Constantinople, "The
Nicene canons will remain until the end of the world as adopted by
the holy fathers who live on among us through their laws, and if
anyone presumes to legislate otherwise, the law is nullified immediately." In the same letter he says, "The clauses of the Nicene canons
which have been ordained by the Holy Spirit are never to be relaxed
in any way since that holy synod is endowed with such divine privilege
that any ecclesiastical decision whether made by few or many, which
departs from their content is completely devoid of all authority."[28] He
also writes to Maximus of Antioch: "Any case involving synodal matters can be examined and decided by the bishop if nothing was
defined on the subject by the holy fathers at Nicaea. But nothing that
departs from their laws and rules can have the consent of the Apostolic See."[29] And he also writes to Anastasius: "There can be no
departure from the rules adopted earlier, either by reason of negligence or of presumption."[30] And [Pope] Gelasius in a general decree

[26] PL 20, pp. 503ff. and 20, pp. 773ff. (to Hilarius).
[27] PL 50, p. 436.   [28] PL 54, pp. 1005 and 1003.
[29] PL 54, p. 1045.   [30] PL 54, p. 672.

to all the bishops says: "Since for our part we wish to allow nothing contrary to reverence for the norms of salvation,..."[31] – see [*Decretals*] *De consecratione,* D. 1 [c. 6] *Basilicas,* where the accompanying text has a gloss which declares that the whole body of the church should observe the canons since the Roman church which is supreme strives with pious and devout purpose to preserve the canons and would not relax them for anyone even for a possible good reason. Likewise [Pope] Hormisda writes to Remigius, the holy archbishop of Rheims: "We command that the regulations of the fathers, the decrees defined by the most holy councils should be observed by all. Guard them with the proper reverence. Their strict observance allows no possibility for blame. They prescribe right and wrong. They prohibit what no one would dare desire."[32]

180. From this it is sufficiently clear that the opinion of the ancients was not that the pope cannot be bound by the ecumenical councils, but rather that he of all men, as the head, has always observed the rules handed down by the universal councils; and the popes have also acknowledged that they ought to observe them. Pope Fabian says in [C.] 11 q. 3 [c. 95]: "He who has feared almighty God does not consent to do anything against the gospel of Christ, the apostles, the prophets, or the statutes of the holy fathers." Observe that the Roman pontiffs who fear God do not consent to do anything against the statutes of the holy fathers.

181. In addition the same point is proved by another argument. It is clear that Pope Leo did not accept what appears in certain parts of the decrees of the Council of Chalcedon, in particular the decree that Constantinople should precede Alexandria.[33] He always protested as did other popes after him but still the decree of the Council prevailed, as is clear from [*Decretals* v 33] *De privilegiis,* [c. 23] *Antiqua* and D. 22 [c. 6] *Renovantes* and the sessions and signatures of the councils after Chalcedon. But if the pope had it in his power to revoke the decrees of the universal councils, Leo and some of his successors would have prevailed. But this is not true, as indicated above. It is to be noted that although as Hincmar relates at length in the book referred to above, Pope Leo was opposed to three canons in the decrees of the Council of Chalcedon, he did not oppose them on the basis of his own authority but on that of the canons of the Nicene council which he

---

[31] PL 56, p. 692.   [32] PL 63, p. 369.   [33] PL 54, pp. 1001ff.

wished to preserve from violation, and he said that the observance of those canons was his responsibility and that the later canons contradicted them.[34] Similarly the Council of Africa opposed [Pope] Celestine because he wished to act in violation of a canon of the Nicene Council, and Celestine did not say that he could do this but alleged that the council cited the [Nicene] Council incorrectly in support of its argument because it did not have a properly translated text, as appears in the letter of the Council of Africa to Pope Celestine, bishop of the city of Rome, which begins: *Domino dilectissimo*.[35] Furthermore, returning to the case of Leo, since the authority of all universal councils is one, see D. 16 [c. 8] *Sancta*, he also did not prevail on the point concerning the order of listing of the patriarchal sees, as is clear from the above.

182.   In addition, to introduce a more recent example, the universal Council of Basel decreed in its second session that the Roman pontiff also may not violate the canon *Frequens* of the Council of Constance by transferring its location, although there is no decree of invalidity [*irritans*] against [an action of] the Roman pontiff in that same canon, *Frequens*.[36] It is well to emphasize here that there is no doubt that this happened under the inspiration of the Holy Spirit. This can be concluded from the firm character of the conciliar actions, for St. Augustine in his book, *On the Trinity*, against Felix, argues against the Council of Rimini from the inconstancy of its defenders.[37]

183.   We see that by the grace of God the Council of Basel has now been strengthened in a marvelous way – although at the beginning it was convulsed by doubt and fluctuation –, and this can come only from God who is lasting truth. Therefore let us firmly believe that all its actions from the beginning were inspired by the Holy Spirit. It is sufficiently marvelous that on the basis of the canon *Frequens* of the Council of Constance, it turned in its first session to three matters; the uprooting of heresies, the reformation of the morals of the whole church, and peace among Christians.[38] The Holy Spirit undoubtedly inspired these actions so that if perhaps the pope wished to resist,

[34] PL 126, pp. 369ff.

[35] Mansi 4, p. 515.

[36] Mansi 29, pp. 3ff. and 564ff. The debate at Basel in the first part of 1433 on whether the council could nullify papal actions through a decree of invalidity (*irritans*) was one of the reasons for the writing of the *Concordantia*. See Introduction.

[37] See discussion in II, ch. 5, no. 82.

[38] I.e., variations on the three topics cited by the Council of Constance in *Frequens* (1417).

there would be no doubt as to the universality of the council. On these three matters there had already been a definitive and immutable decree in the Council of Constance. And so by divine inspiration the Council [of Basel] concerned itself with this before any difficulty arose. There followed the supposed transfer or, more accurately, dissolution of the Council by the pope. Afterwards the second session of the Council took place which concluded its argument in an admirable syllogism as follows: The pope is bound to obey all reform decrees. The canon, *Frequens*, is a reform decree. Therefore he is obliged to obey it. The major premise is the decree of the Council of Constance and the minor premise is proven by the text of the decree, *Frequens*. Thus the conclusion is that he is bound to obey it. Therefore he is subject to it. Therefore he cannot abrogate or change it.

184. If there is no doubt that the Holy Spirit dictated this syllogism to this holy Council, what need is there to doubt or dispute further whether the pope can be bound by the reform decrees so that he cannot contravene them? Likewise if the Council of Constance says that a pope who does not obey can be punished,[39] then its force as a council does not depend entirely on the pope because if there were no council whenever he did not wish there to be one, how could he ever be punished since only a council can punish him? Likewise the decree adopted by the Councils of Constance and Siena says that the fathers gathered at Basel at this time are a true council.[40] The pope says that since he does not wish there to be a council, it is not a true council. Who then is so insane as to say that the opinion of the council, in which necessarily the authority of the Roman pontiff was included, is false and the will of Pope Eugene true? If when the decrees of the aforesaid councils were reissued at Basel, the Holy Spirit said that it wished to inspire the Council at this time, how can Pope Eugene say that this is true [only] if he wishes it to be and not otherwise? As if the inspiration of the Holy Spirit were in the power of the Roman pontiff so that it would grant its inspiration only when the pope wished. If you recall that the holy fathers live on in their laws, and that the church is one, with some dying and others succeeding in their place, and that the universal councils also succeed one another in the same way, then you [will] easily understand the foregoing.

185. We should not deny, however, that the Roman pontiff can

[39] Mansi 27, p. 590.   [40] Mansi 27, p. 1195, and 28, p. 1070.

make sure of the power of equity [*epieikeia*]. For we read in the first action of the Eighth Council that Hadrian wrote as follows: "To quote Pope Gelasius, it is necessary and convenient for the government of the Apostolic See for us to weigh the decrees of the canons of the fathers and to judge the precepts of our predecessors so that as far as possible after careful consideration we may modify what present necessity requires to be relaxed for the renewal of the church. For we too can act with equity for the benefit of the brethren and imitate him [Gelasius] directly in considering the requirements of the times."[41] This appears in [C.] 1 q. 7 [c. 5] *Necessaria* and in the paragraph *Nisi rigor*.

186.   Note that as it says, it is to be understood that the law's provisions are to be modified "as far as possible after careful consideration" as to whether it is necessary and useful for the renewal of the church. And on this, note the paragraph [after c. 8] *Sed sciendum* of D. 61 along with the gloss upon it, as well as the gloss on [C.] 1 q. 1 [c. 41] *Quod propter necessitatem* to the effect that when ecclesiastical prohibitions are made for certain reasons, if those reasons cease and the law does not cease to oblige since it is general, suspension of the law is appropriate. For to go against a general prohibition in a particular case when necessity or utility advises it because the reason for the law is no longer present is not really a suspension of the law, but a declaration that that case is not included in the scope of the law, see D. 28 [c. 13] *De Syracusanae*. But because the reasons given for a declaration, interpretation, dispensation, or suspension should in fact lead to the conclusion that a suspension or declaration or modification would be appropriate, the holy Council of Basel, after finding that the reasons given in the bull of dissolution or transfer issued by Pope Eugene were not really conclusive, declared the pope's action invalid since it violated the canon *Frequens* of the Council of Constance and because the reasons cited in the bull were inadequate and consequently he could not transfer it [the council].[42] I do not say, however, that if the reasons had been valid he would have been able to do it on his own authority without the consent of the council but that if they had been valid, he could have done so because the council would have consented. And this is proven in the fourth action of the Eighth Universal Council where, in a letter to Photius in answer to his

---

[41] Mansi 16, p. 21.   [42] Mansi 29, pp. 24ff.

objection that in the Second Council Nectarius had been appointed as a layman to the bishopric of Constantinople, Pope Nicholas says that necessity was the reason for the dispensation, and adds that the Second Council neither confirmed the practice nor agreed that it might be done again, because what was clearly done out of necessity in violation of the laws of the fathers and the canon law should not be cited as an authority. And below he says, "You see, Nectarius was appointed to rule the church because of the need for priests, Tarasius for reasons of church dogma and the expulsion of the heretics who dared to destroy the venerable images, and Ambrose because of miraculous signs."[43]

187.   From this we conclude that necessity, utility, and miracles are conclusive reasons for modifying a law or general canon, see D. 55 [c. 1] *Priscis*. But the Old Gloss commenting on [C.] 1 q. 1 [c. 41] *Quod propter necessitatem* says "because of necessity," "because of utility," on [C.] 1 q. 1 [c. 24: *Dahibertum*; "out of mercy," on C. 1 q. 5 [c. 3] the last canon, "because of widespread custom," on D. 4 [c. 6] *Denique*: "by reason of numbers," on [C.] 23 q. 4 [c. 32] *Non potest*. The common law is also often violated when dispensations are given because of necessity or utility contrary to the Council of Nicaea which prohibited changes and transfers of sees. This is proven in [C.] 7 q. 1 [c. 34] *Mutationes* and in the following canon. As to necessity there is no doubt, because necessity is not subject to human legislation, [and] even excuses what is done against such legislation, see *De Consecratione* D. 1 [c. 36] *Sicut* and D. 4 [c. 36] *Sanctum*. However, action on the basis of utility should be taken with caution so that the canons are not suspended for any reason of utility whatever, as Pope Gelasius says in *De Consecratione* D. 1 [c. 6] *Basilicas*. Hence Pope Nicholas in [C.] 35 q. 9 [c. 6] *Sententiam* says that the Roman church can grant dispensations for reasons of age, time, and grave necessity, as did St. Paul. However he says they should be granted if the Roman church has chosen with all due consideration to do so but not because it wishes to repeal well defined laws. And this text is to be noted because as the Gloss on [C.] 22 q. 2 [c. 15] *Faciat* says, power is to be exercised for good purposes, and on that dispensation we should note [what is said in] D. 61, [after c. 8] *Sed sciendum* and the Gloss on the paragraph *Hiis omnibus* in the same place. It cannot be denied that the

---

[43] Mansi 16, pp. 70ff.

pope can dispense from any statute for reasons of necessity or evident utility. The Archdeacon in his lengthy comment on D. 70 [c. 2] *Sanctorum* even says that a bishop can do so. He says among other things that if any canon were to prohibit this, it would be irrational and he gives examples of bishops who have given dispensations from provincial or universal councils for these reasons. But besides this the pope can dispense out of his personal prerogative – which he discusses in the same place.

188.   And from this it follows that the power of supervision of the canons which the pope possesses for the benefit of the church is not, properly speaking, a power over the canons but the authority to declare for reasonable cause that the canons do not apply in a particular case. And thus a dispensation is not actually in its root meaning a suspension of the law but a declaration that the suspension of the law is only apparent [not real]. Therefore if valid reasons are not present to demonstrate that a given case is not under the law, it is not a case of dispensation but of dissolution. Indeed according to what has been said, anyone who is [thus] dispensed since he is subject to the canon and cannot be exempted from observing it except for valid, substantial, and reasonable cause, is still subject to the penalties and command of the law, even if the pope intended to exempt him by dispensation since in the eyes of God he is bound by it like anyone else. However the church militant may not judge this because, in the case of the pope, it is assumed that he did it legitimately and justifiably for valid and reasonable motives. And this is what the gloss on the word *adimplere* of the chapter *Non est* in [the *Decretals* III 34] *De Voto* [c. 5] says, as do all the doctors. On this as well as on what is said above concerning the universal council the excellent text of Pope Pelagius in the [papal] *Register* should be noted, which reads as follows, "Pope Pelagius to the patrician Valerian: If the bishops of those parts have any doubt about the condemnation of the Three Chapters, let them follow the ancient custom and either elect learned men from among them or let any bishop come for himself and, after receiving by God's grace an appropriate explanation from us, let him return to the bosom of our common mother, the holy Catholic church. For as to the proposal of Your Highness that we should meet and form a quasi-synod no canons have permitted or will permit that, after the decision by a universal council which was made as with one voice by nearly four thousand bishops, both through their metropolitans and

individually at Constantinople, a particular council should meet and should return to discord among ourselves. Rather whenever any doubt arises on matters involving the universal council those who desire the salvation of their souls can come spontaneously, or because they desire an explanation of what they do not understand, to their apostolic see to receive an explanation. If perhaps, as Scripture says of such people, 'when the sinner sinks to the depth of evil, he is defiant,' they become obstinate and contumacious and do not wish to learn, they must be led to salvation in some way by those apostolic sees or they must be repressed by the secular powers in accordance with the canons so as not to be a source of perdition for others. Given the 12th of May in the 17th year after the consulate of the great Basil."[44] This decretal of Pelagius is important because it says that a definition by an ecumenical council is final and that the pope should not decide and resolve doubtful cases for petitioners in cases involving matters defined by the ecumenical councils. This decretal is very relevant to our earlier discussion of the authority of the councils, as well as for what is said thereafter, that papal dispensations from the universal canons do not involve a declaration of doctrine.

189. In order for there to be a proper examination of cases cardinals should be appointed by this sacred council as the representatives of the provinces in the way described above, and the cases should be examined with their advice and written authorization as to whether it is fitting to act in a given way. At one time the Roman pontiffs were accustomed to promise publicly in their declarations that they would carry out their office with the counsel and consent of the cardinals, as appears in the declaration of Boniface VIII.

Therefore to conclude, – to prove that except for his power of equity [*epieikeia*] already discussed, the Roman pontiff is normally bound to obey the canons of the ecumenical councils, let it be noted that the first canon of the Eighth Council declares that the canons are given to the universal church by the universal councils, and then states that the Universal Council promises to observe them. And it is evident that the representatives of the Apostolic See and all the others subscribed to this canon and to all the other canons of that council, as appears clearly at the end of the same council where it says, "We

---

[44] Jaffe, p. 1018. The scriptural citation is to Proverbs 18:3. Pope Pelagius ruled from A.D. 555 to 560. The Three Chapters were theological works condemned by the Fifth Ecumenical Council at Constantinople in 553.

[will] observe these apostolic and synodal documents without exception."[45] And a little later, the very reverend representatives of old Rome said, "Because by the providence of God all the concerns of the church have come to a successful conclusion, we should also confirm these things in writing with our own hands according to the procedure of the synod."[46] There is no doubt that the pope is a faithful member of the universal church and that he is obliged by his declaration of faith and signature. The text is as follows: First the title speaks of the canons set forth above and given to the church to be kept and observed everywhere. [Then] the text continues, "If we wish to follow without offense the true way of royal divine justice, we should always maintain what has been defined by the holy fathers as ever-burning lamps to guide our footsteps in the way of God. Therefore like the wise Dionysius we consider them as the second word [of God] and with the divine David we zealously sing of them. 'The command of God is as a light to the eyes' and 'Thy law is a lantern to my feet and a light to my footsteps.' And with the author of Proverbs we say, 'His command is a lantern, and his law a light.' And with the great Isaiah, we cry to the God of all, 'Thy precepts are a light on the earth.'[47] For the exhortations and prohibitions of the divine canons are rightly compared to a light by which the better is distinguished from worse, and the useful and profitable from that which is recognized as useless and harmful. Therefore we declare that we will preserve and guard the norms that have been handed down to the holy, Catholic, and apostolic church by the most holy and glorious apostles and by the universal orthodox councils. We will govern our own life and conduct by them and we decree that the entire priesthood and all who are called Christians are to be punished and condemned or, conversely, absolved and justified in accordance with what is expressed and defined in the canons. Indeed the great Apostle Paul clearly advises us to hold to the traditions that we have received whether by word or by letter from the saints whose brilliance has preceded us."[48]

190.   Note here the very clear declaration that normally the pope is bound by the regulations made by the universal councils. Therefore

---

[45] Mansi 16, pp. 398ff.
[46] Mansi 16, pp. 185, 188.
[47] Proverbs 18:9; Psalms 118 and 105; Isaiah 6:23.
[48] 2 Thessalonians 2:15. Mansi 16, pp. 16off.

an injunction may be placed on him by the universal council to follow them under threat of invalidity and grave penalty except in the case of the exercise of equity powers [*epieikeia*] as discussed above. Today however when – alas! – the universal church is reduced to the Roman patriarchate alone,[49] and what once was only the general patriarchal council subject to the Roman pontiff, is today the universal council representing the whole church of the faithful, in this new situation doubt has arisen on this point. Therefore it is appropriate for this holy council to act without passion and with the greatest gentleness towards the Roman pontiff. Let it not be so proud of its privileged position as a universal council – which, alas, is rather a reason to lament –, that it forgets its subordination in the past to its patriarch when it could not act against an orthodox pope. Rather let due honor be given and all things ordered in peace by unanimous concordance for the increase of faith and divine worship and the universal good of the Catholic church so that they may see our good works and glorify God who is in heaven.

[49] Cusanus' belief that the pope offered the best possibilities for reunion with the Eastern church was a major reason for his abandonment of the Basel Council in 1437.

CHAPTER XXI

THE POPE SHOULD NOT EXERCISE HIS POWER OF
DISPENSATION OR TAKE ANY ACTION WHICH SEEMS
CONTRARY TO THE UNIVERSAL CANONS WITHOUT
CONSULTING THE CARDINALS.

191.   I think that only one thing should be added to what is said above; that this holy council could adopt a law – or more accurately revive the ancient law that provides that the pope cannot take any action on difficult cases – especially a dispensation for urgent reasons from the canons of this or other universal councils – without [the consent of] the lord cardinals in their quality as the clergy represent-ing the universal church in the way described above. If he should act otherwise, that action is to be invalid. The opinions of the Arch-deacon and of Joannes Monachus and of others on this have been

cited already.[1] Their final conclusion on this is to affirm the principle that the pope cannot do anything affecting the universal church without the [consent of the] cardinals. But I believe that to violate or dispense from the canons, even in a particular case, can reasonably be said to concern the universal church, since a canon of the universal church seems to be violated by this kind of dispensation.

Hence because an argument from analogy is a strong one in law, see [C.] 3 q. 5 [c. 15] *Quia suspecti*; D. 20 *In quibus*; D. 10 [c. 7] *Si in adiutorium*, I will add the following argument from analogy here. Legally a bishop has complete administrative control of his diocese with its churches, endowments, and tithes, see [C.] 10 q. 1 [c. 3] *Decretum*, but he does not have the right to transfer, give, or exchange the things over which he has power without the consent and written agreement of his clergy, see C. 12 q. 2 [c. 52] *Sine exceptione*. And the 32nd canon of the African Council says: "The donation, sale, or exchange of ecclesiastical property by the bishops without the approval and written agreement of the clergy shall be invalid."[2] Therefore by analogy, even if the whole church were subject to the disposition of the pope as a single monarch, nevertheless according to the above he could not exchange or transfer church property – especially, I believe, the sacred canons – without the consent and written agreement of his clergy. For the cardinals act in the name of the clergy of the Roman church in so far as the Roman church is monarchical in structure, as is said in a certain place above.[3]

192. Furthermore it is clear that the transfer of church property can only take place for reasons of utility and necessity. Exactly the same thing is true of changes in the canons or dispensation from them. And that is enough for the argument from analogy. This is discussed in the chapter *Non liceat* [c. 20] of [C.] 12 q. 2, a text which seems to compare the pope to the other bishops with respect to the right to transfer property. Furthermore the African synod which Augustine signed says in [C.] 15 q. 7 [c. 6] *Episcopus*: "Let no bishop hear a case except in the presence of his clergy; otherwise the sentence of the bishop will be invalid."[4] And it is clear that the bishop has

[1] Book II, nos. 132, 163, 166.
[2] Fourth Council of Carthage (Hinschius, p. 304).
[3] Book II, no. 132.
[4] See note 2. For Nicholas' source in Beno, *Gesta Romanae Ecclesiae*, see Werner Krämer, "Verzeichnis der Brüsseler Handschriften," *MFCG*, 14 (1980), 182–197.

administrative control of his entire diocese but he cannot hear cases and pass serious sentences except in the presence of his clergy. Therefore it is obvious that the pope is obliged to act in a similar way on matters concerning the universal church.

Furthermore exchanges or transfers by a presiding church authority cannot be made except with the advice of the council or all the priests, see [C.] 12 q. 2 [c. 51] *Placuit* where it says: "Without consulting the council or priests . . ." and the canon [58] *Episcopus* where it says: "In front of the council of the church . . ." Therefore in the same way the pope cannot transfer the property of the church without the consent of the council of the church, i.e. the universal council. Principally included in this property, it is evident, are the sacred canons.

193. Hence although the cardinals can agree in particular cases for reasons of necessity or utility, to actions opposed to the canons and can confirm dispensations with their signatures, this can be done, I believe, only without prejudice to the [continued force of the] canons. But in my view, the pope and cardinals can not repeal the canons of the universal councils without the consent of the universal council. And in a case in which the cardinals have to give their consent, any [of the cardinals] can participate in the decision but a particular individual does not have the right to decide by himself, for that right belongs only to the college as a whole and not to any individual member of the college, according to the note of the doctors following [Pope] Innocent on the chapter *Irrefragabili* [c. 13] *Conquestus* [*Excessus*] in [*Decretals* 1 31] *De officio ordinarii* and this is proven in [C.] 12 q. 2 [after c. 58] *Qui manumittitur*, following the *Digest* [III 4] *Quod cuius*, verse *Sicut* [1. 7] para. 1. For we read the following in the proceedings against Hildebrand who was called Pope Gregory VII: "For it is the privilege of the Roman see that through its cardinals, bishops, and deacons it assists the pontiff or representative of that see who is the one whom that most sacred see makes its spokesman, through whom and by whom it preaches, through whom it administers the sacraments, through whom and by whom it approves what ought to be approved and rejects what should be rejected. However, without the agreement of the see, the opinion of the pontiff is invalid."[5] Note that from ancient times, the opinion of the Roman pontiff was invalid

---

[5] Pope Gregory VII (1073–1085) was a reforming pope who opposed simony and lay investiture.

without the agreement of the cardinals, and that the pope was only the spokesman of the Apostolic See.

CHAPTER XXII

THE PROVINCIAL SYNOD SHOULD BE CALLED BY THE METROPOLITAN WHO IS THE JUDGE OF THE PROVINCE ALTHOUGH HE CAN NOT DECIDE CRIMINAL CASES BY HIMSELF. COUNCILS ARE WISE AND NECESSARY INSTITUTIONS CREATED FOR THE GOOD OF THE CHURCH. THE UNIVERSAL COUNCIL MADE UP OF SEVERAL PROVINCES IS DISCUSSED AND IT IS ARGUED THAT IT IS SUPERIOR TO PARTICULAR PROVINCIAL COUNCILS. LOCAL JUDICIAL AUTHORITIES SHOULD MEET IN THESE COUNCILS AND THEY SHOULD NOT END WITHOUT ESTABLISHING THE PLACE OF THEIR NEXT MEETING AND DECIDING EVERYTHING BROUGHT BEFORE THEM.

194. Let us briefly add a few things regarding provincial councils so as to have a better understanding of the universal councils, the principal matter under consideration. The provincial council of a province consists of the metropolitan and his suffragans and others in the province. It is called by the archbishop to make decisions on matters of concern to the province. Without this it is not a full and perfect council, for he [the archbishop] has the care and responsibility for the whole province. In it he ranks first in honor, and appeals are made to him, see [C.] 9 q. 3 [c. 2] *Per singulos*. Although he is the judge of the province, he should not decide criminal cases or general cases which concern all the bishops of the province without the participation of the suffragan bishops, see [C.] 15 q. 7 [c. 6] *Episcopus nullus* and the canon *Felix* [c. 4] and the observations in [C.] 9 q. 3 [c. 3] *Cum simus* and the final paragraph [*Probatur*]. But as to how he should discuss the common affairs of the province with his suffragans, see [C.] 9 q. 3 *Per singulas* canons 1 and 2, and many other places.
195. This council is very necessary and it has authority given to it by

the ecumenical councils to decide and ordain all things necessary for the province except for those that concern the church as a whole, which require a greater authority. How useful this and other councils would be to the church of God, we read in the third chapter of the Council of Toledo where it says: "Hardly any matter of discipline does more harm to the good work of the church of Christ than the negligence of priests who, in contempt of the canons, fail to hold a synod to improve moral conduct in the church. For this reason, it has been generally defined by us that since time does not permit a council to be convened twice a year in accord with the ancient decrees of the fathers, a council is to be held at least once a year. If there is a case involving doctrine or any other matter of common concern to the church, a general synod of all Spain or Gaul may be called, but if neither doctrine nor matters of common interest of the church are to be discussed, let a particular council be held as the metropolitan of each province decides. But let all who are known to have cases against bishops or judges or authorities or against anyone else come to this council and anything found on examination by the synod to have been criminally usurped by anyone, is to be returned by the king's officer to those to whom it belongs by legal right. Indeed the metropolitan should request a royal executive officer from the prince to compel the judges and laymen to come to the metropolitan synod. A synod should be held in each province on the fifteenth day of June, in the spring when the earth is covered with grass and crops are growing."[1]

Note that this decree was issued in a certain universal council of all Spain and Gaul, and applies to the provinces subject to that council, and that it also says that doctrinal questions and those that affect the whole church should be discussed in this kind of universal council. From this we conclude that a universal synod made up of many provinces is over those provinces and can also treat general cases of doctrine. And these things should be noted on account of what is said below.

196.   In an earlier universal council which was also held at Toledo, it was decided that provincial councils should be held in the autumn at the beginning of November, and that the local judges and tax-collectors should meet by decree of the king so as to learn to act worthily

---

[1] Fourth Council of Toledo – A.D. 633 (Mansi 10, p. 616ff.). The Council was quoted earlier by Gulielmus Durandus in his work, *De modo celebrandi concilium generale* (1311), which is in the library at Kues.

and honestly with the people and not to overburden the individual citizen or vassal with heavy taxes or unnecessary obligations. It was also defined that the bishops should then observe how the judges act with the people and in cases of excess, correct or denounce them to the king. If they were not willing to mend their ways, they would be able to suspend them from communion and they would also decide on the penalty for a judge who did not come to the synod. And it was added: "But the council should not be dissolved until its members have first chosen the place where it will meet in the future. In this way it will not be necessary for the metropolitan to send letters to call the council if the time and place are announced to everyone at the earlier council meeting."[2]

[2] Third Council of Toledo – A.D. 689 (Mansi 9, pp. 997ff.).

CHAPTER XXIII

THE FORM FOR THE CONDUCT OF A COUNCIL IS GIVEN IN THE FOURTH CHAPTER OF THE COUNCIL OF TOLEDO. THIS IS QUOTED WORD FOR WORD AND IS TO BE NOTED IN ITS ENTIRETY, ESPECIALLY THE LAST PART.

197.   But the form in which the council should be held is defined as follows in the fourth chapter of the Council of Toledo which was held at the time of King Sisenandus in A.D. 581:[1] "And so at the first hour before sunrise let the church be emptied. With all the gates closed let the porters sit at one door through which the clergy will enter. Let all the bishops go in together and take their places in accordance with the date of their ordination. After all the bishops have entered and taken their seats, then let the priests be summoned who are needed for discussion of the subject. No deacons are to come in with them. After they come in, let the approved deacons enter whom good order requires to be present, and when the bishops have formed a circle with their seats, let the priests sit behind them, and the deacons stand

[1] The Fourth Council of Toledo from which this quotation is taken was held in A.D. 633.

where they can be seen. Then let the laymen enter who have been invited by the council to participate, and then the notaries who are needed to read out and to record what the council does and then the doors are to be shut. And after the priests have been sitting for a long time in silence with their hearts turned only to God, let the archdeacon say: 'Let us pray.' And at once everyone will prostrate himself on the floor and pray silently for a longer time with weeping and groaning. Let one of the elder bishops arise and pray aloud to God while all the others are still lying on the ground. When the prayer is over and all have answered 'Amen,' let the deacon say again, 'Arise.' And immediately let all arise and let the bishops and priests take their seats in fear of God and good order. And with all sitting in their places in silence, let a deacon clothed in a white robe bring out the text of the canons to the center and read the chapters on the conduct of a council, and when these are finished, let the metropolitan bishop address the council saying: 'Most holy priests, the opinions of the early fathers concerning the conduct of the council have been read from the canons. If any of you wishes us to take any action, let him put it before his brothers. Then if anyone has any complaint of a violation of a canon to bring before this sacerdotal audience, let us not pass on first to another chapter without first taking action on whatever is proposed. For if any priest or deacon or cleric or layman among those who have stood outside believes that he should appeal to the council on any subject, let him bring his case to the archdeacon of the metropolitan church, and he [the archdeacon] should bring it before the council and permission to come in and speak will be granted to him. And no bishop should leave the meeting before the general hour of departure arrives. Also let no one dare to dissolve the council before everything has been decided and whatever is concluded in common is subscribed to by the hands of each of the bishops. For we believe that God is present in the assembly of his priests when church business is concluded with care and in peace without any disturbance.' "[2]

198.   That is the proper order [of a synod], but it is not observed today. At the beginning of his book on the councils, Isidore [of Seville] also discusses the procedure for holding a council.[3] But I have included this canon in this small work because towards the end, it

[2] Mansi 10, pp. 617ff.   [3] PL 130, pp. 11ff.

prohibits its dissolution, and in the last section it says that we should believe that God is present in a council when church matters are concluded with care and in peace. Hence we may make an argument on the basis of the conclusion of a council because even if it has been correctly assembled and everything has been discussed fairly, properly, and at length, if it does not end peacefully it can not always truly be said that Christ was in the midst since he is not the author of discord but of peace.[4] And this should be noted in view of some of the things written above.

[4] The division of the Council of Basel into two contending factions in 1437 was one of the reasons that Cusanus joined the side of the pope.

CHAPTER XXIV

UNIVERSAL COUNCILS OF A WHOLE NATION OR KINGDOM HAVE GREAT POWER AND THE RECORD SHOWS THAT THEY HAVE MADE DECISIONS ON ALL MATTERS, EVEN ON DEFINITIONS OF THE FAITH. THIS COUNCIL DECIDES AMONG CANDIDATES FOR THE OFFICE OF PRIMATE, — INDEED ABOUT EVERYTHING THAT HAS ARISEN IN THE NATION OR KINGDOM. IT IS ASSERTED THAT IT SHOULD ONLY BE CALLED FOR GENERAL AND SERIOUS REASONS, AND THE PROCEDURE FOR DOING SO IS DESCRIBED. FULL CONCILIAR AUTHORITY IS POSSESSED BY THE REPRESENTATIVES OF THE PROVINCES AND THOSE WHO TAKE PART IN THE COUNCIL.

199. There are also other councils of a large kingdom or of a province which are often called universal councils. These are made up of all the particular provinces of that kingdom or nation and they are held in order to settle difficult cases of common interest, as is discussed above. The Second Council of Arles decreed that this kind of council should be convened for [the] Gauls by the bishop of Arles and we also find that it was convened at the request of the provinces

of Gaul.[1] Hence it is said at the beginning of the council: "Since we priests have met in the city of Turin at the request of the provinces of Gaul, and since we are deliberating in the church of that city under the protection and with the assistance of the Lord, let us consider etc."[2] And when Spain and France were under one king as in the reigns of the Gothic Kings Recaredus, Sisenandus, and others, this kind of universal council was often celebrated by royal edict in Toledo on the model, as we read, of the universal councils of the universal church which were convened by the emperors. The kings also were often accustomed to be present along with their nobles and to subscribe to [decisions on] the Catholic faith.

200.   And we find that many solemn decrees were issued providing that the king should be chosen by election as well as others concerning the status of the king especially on the preservation of his life. On this more will be seen below.[3] Many church canons were also adopted in these councils. And in the third chapter of the council held at the time of Sisenandus we read that that universal synod, in accordance with the decrees of the fathers which provided that there should be a uniform usage in a province for prayer and the administration [of the sacraments], commanded that the same rite should be observed in Gaul and Spain because they adhered to the same faith and were parts of the same kingdom.[4]

201.   We find that everything concerning the faith and important church controversies was decided in those councils. And always [a profession of] faith was recited at the beginning. We read in the Council of Toledo held in the time of Chintilanus, that following the custom of the ecumenical council, after the solemn ceremony of prayer was carried out, they were accustomed to give oral expression to the beliefs that they had in their hearts.[5] And in another council held at the time of Sisenandus we read: "And because we are holding a general council, it is proper that the first utterance of our voices should be concerned with God, so that the efforts of ours which follow the profession of our faith may be carried out, as it were, upon a most firm foundation."[6] We read that the candidates for the office of

---

[1] "Second Council of Arles" – a collection of earlier canons assembled in the fifth century (Hinschius, p. 325).
[2] Council of Turin (Mansi 3, p. 859).   [3] See Book III, chs xxxvii, xli.
[4] Fourth Council of Toledo (Mansi 10, p. 616).
[5] Sixth Council of Toledo (Mansi 10, p. 661).
[6] Mansi 10, p. 615.

primate accepted the [council's] decision. Thus it is written in the Council of Turin, "That controversy between the bishops of Arles and Vienne who are contending before us for the honor of primate has been decided by the sacred synod." It took jurisdiction over appeals and sentences passed by provincial councils as appears in the acts of the same council concerning the priest, Exsuperantius, judged by Bishop Triferius, and concerning the layman, Palladius, against the priest, Spanus, whom he charged with a serious crime.[7] The African nation held such universal councils and others appealed to it – as that same council wrote in a letter to Pope Celestine – and it decided everything, even the transfer of bishops, as is contained in the 27th chapter of the same council, and their deposition, and it did not permit appeals to the pope from the sentence of that council, but said that in accordance with the decision of the Nicene council, the cases should end there, as the same council wrote to the Roman pontiffs, Boniface and Zosimus.[8] And in the eighth chapter of the African Council it was commanded that a council should be held in this way every year: "And the council agreed that for church cases which often continue for a long time to the injury of the people a council should be called each year to which all the provinces that have primatial sees should send two members of their councils or more bishops if they choose as representatives so that there may be less rivalry and less expense for the hosts and that once the meeting is assembled it can have full authority. From Tripoli however, because of a lack of bishops let one bishop come."[9] This text is to be noted in two respects: first, because the provincial see is called a primatial see, and second, because the representatives of the provinces confer full authority on the council in the name of the province – which should be noted regarding what was said above about the cardinals. After this that decree was revoked in the Council of Milevis so that the brethren might not be overburdened, and it was decreed that this general council would only be convened for an urgent case which concerned everyone.[10]

202. In addition once the universal council had met, if a number of

[7] Mansi 3, pp. 861ff.
[8] Sixth Council of Carthage (Mansi 4, pp. 511ff.). The letter to Pope Celestine is from the Fourth Council of Carthage (Mansi 3, p. 953).
[9] Third Council of Carthage (Mansi 3, p. 880).
[10] Second Council of Milevis (Mansi 4, p. 329).

cases still remained to be decided and many bishops were present, any province that wished to do so appointed some of them as its representatives and the rest departed. This is what we read in chapter 29 [27] of the Council of Milevis: "Furthermore in order to prevent all the bishops who have met in council from being detained too long, we have agreed that three judges for each province should be elected by the full council. And Vincentius, Fortunatus, and Clarus were elected from the province of Carthage, and Alipius, Augustinus, and Restitutus were elected from the province of Numidia," and so on for the others. The text continues: "And these together with the holy bishop Aurelius shall take jurisdiction over all matters that arise, and they all agreed in writing."[11] From this we should conclude that when a smaller council with general powers is to be created, it should be made up of the representatives of those subject to it or of those who have the right to participate in it. Therefore the same thing should be done in the case of the cardinals who represent the provinces subject to the Roman church in its daily council. That those universal councils are of greater authority than the provincial councils under them is evident from what is written above, and the text of the Council of Laodicea, as well as those of Pope Martin and others that are contained in [C.] 6 q. 4 [c. 1–4] prove this.

[11] Mansi 4, p. 334.

CHAPTER XXV

JUST AS THE ONE WHO CONVENES THESE
UNIVERSAL COUNCILS AS THEIR HEAD IS NO LESS
SUBJECT TO THEM, THE POPE IS SUBJECT TO THE
COUNCIL OF THE UNIVERSAL CHURCH, DESPITE
THE FACT THAT IT IS CALLED AT HIS COMMAND.
JUST AS THE AUTHORITY OF THE EARLY COUNCILS
DOES NOT DEPEND ON THOSE WHO CALLED THEM,
NEITHER DOES THE AUTHORITY OF THE UNIVERSAL
CHURCH COUNCIL DEPEND ON THE POPE. THERE IS
A FINE DISCUSSION OF WHY THOSE COUNCILS
SHOULD BE CONTINUED AND THE REASONS THAT
THEY ARE USEFUL.

203. The Second Council of Arles, in which the legate of Pope Sylvester participated, decreed that the council was to be called by the bishop of Arles, and yet we find that the Council of Turin passed judgment on him in the controversy that he had with the bishop of Vienne concerning the primacy. In the same way the bishop of Carthage was not exempt from the judgment of the Council of Africa despite the fact that he had convened it and previously participated in it, because no one doubted the decision of Nicene Council that every issue which had arisen in Africa should be definitively determined by that council, as appears in [C.] 2 q. 6 [c. 35] *Placuit*.[1] The text there says that appeals should go from the council of the province of Africa to a general council or to the primate, not to anyone across the sea "except for the pope." However the canon *Placuit* of the council itself as well as the same text as it appears in [C.] 11 q. 3 [c. 34] *Placuit* [*Presbiteri*] do not make an exception for the pope because the original text did not make this exception. Therefore the first text, [C.] 2 q. 6 [c. 35], is in error. And many things could be added on these subjects.

Similarly there has never been any doubt that all patriarchal councils even those of the Roman see are subject to the universal council of the universal church. And if a council of the universal church decided that one of the patriarchs had the power to convene

[1] Hinschius, p. 322; Mansi 3, p. 861; Hinschius, p. 319.

such universal councils – Athanasius who attended the Nicene Council while not yet a bishop but worthy to be one, wrote to Pope Felix that the Nicene Council had given the Roman pontiff the power to call the council[2] – this would not mean that he was exempt from the jurisdiction of that synod, any more than it did in the cases of the primates of Arles and Carthage discussed above. The universal councils of a kingdom or nation discussed above were not so dependent on the one who convened them that they would not have had full authority unless they were called by the one whose responsibility it was, for we read that many such councils were celebrated and accepted without such a convocation. Similarly in the case of the council of the universal church we can not say that its authority is so dependent on the one who convenes it that unless it is convened by the pope there is no council, for if this were the case, the first eight universal councils would not be valid, since we read that they were convened by the emperors, and that the Roman pontiffs like the other patriarchs received the sacred imperial commands to participate in the council or to send representatives.

204.   And this is clear from the fact that the authority to convene the council which is given to anyone by a council ceases once the council is already convened, however this may have taken place. But this authority operates only if the council has not been convened, because the one who has the power from the council to convene it may, according to his mandate, call it when he thinks it opportune but when the council has met, his mandate has been carried out. But if a number of churchmen were to meet without the authorization of the one who was responsible for calling the council, and to reject or exclude or not call the one appointed to do so, then it would be an imperfect council – in accordance with what is said above. But if the need to convene the council were made known to the one appointed to do so and he did not care to call it or to meet with the others to take action on the urgent need who would doubt that, provided that the proper procedure is otherwise followed, those present could provide for the difficulties of the church despite that objection? For when the welfare of the church is involved necessity, which has no law, answers all possible arguments to the contrary from positive law.

205.   And such a reform needs to be carried out in the provincial

[2] PL 13, p. 12.

and universal synods of every kingdom or nation. As the canon of the Council of Sardica contained in [C.] 2 q. 6 [c. 36] says, all matters even the deposition of bishops, however they may have originated, should be settled in the councils and when appeals have been made to the Apostolic See that, even then, all cases should be settled in the place where the case arose, according to the form outlined above, with specially appointed papal commissioners participating in the synod. And it is also very useful for provincial synods to be held on a regular basis and for it to be possible to appeal first from a council of a suffragan bishop not to the pope but, if necessary, to the provincial synod, or to the universal national councils of France, Spain, and Germany. And these councils should be reestablished out of zeal for the preservation of the commonwealth and the furtherance of national peace and mutual love.

206.   And the Roman pontiff should not take this command ill since as the fathers of the Council of Africa wrote to Pope Celestine, "The decrees of the Council of Nicaea clearly committed the clergy of lower rank and the bishops to their metropolitans. For in their wisdom and justice they saw that all matters ought to be settled in the areas in which they had arisen where the providence of the Holy Spirit would provide for each case because the priests of Christ would perceive, and adhere to the just course with wisdom and constancy – especially since anyone who objects to the decision of the judges can appeal to the council of his own province or to the universal council – unless perhaps there is someone who believes that God can guarantee justice to any one individual judging a case but deny it to many gathered in council."[3]

207.   Therefore the Roman pontiff ought to be content if matters are discussed by the councils in this way and should not insist that everything be reviewed by himself and set his judgment over that of many priests who have the authority to define and decide from divine law and the Council of Nicaea. The Roman pontiff should be properly satisfied if the [canon of the] Council of Sardica cited above is accepted by all provinces. In the Council of Africa, this was incorrectly alleged by the legates of the Apostolic See, Faustinus and others, to be a statute of the Council of Nicaea and not accepted as such by the Council [of Africa], as is clear in the letter of the same

[3] Sixth Council of Carthage (Mansi 4, p. 516).

Council to Pope Boniface[4] and in the letter to Celestine mentioned above. It is true that the fathers of the Council of Africa, among whom was Saint Augustine, wrote in the aforesaid letter to Celestine that the statute which Gratian ascribes to the Council of Sardica was not adopted by any council of the fathers. Hence there is some doubt as to whether the statute of the Council of Sardica is genuine. Therefore the pope ought to be all the more content if out of respect for the holy Roman church we accept a statute everywhere which the Synod of Africa would not admit, even if there is doubt as to which council, if any, adopted it. And in these and other matters let this holy synod [of Basel] with God's guidance find an intermediate position appropriate to the time and place, so that if any errors have been committed because of an excess of obedience, following the teaching of St. Gregory in [C.] 2 q. 7 [c. 57] *Admonendi*, they will not be encouraged further but will be combatted, as appears in the text of St. Jerome *Sancta quippe* [C. 56] quoted in the same place, and in [C.] 11 q. 3 [c. 99] *Quod Ergo*, [and] D. 86 [c. 4] *Quando*. This should be sufficient on this subject.

[4]Mansi 4, p. 511.

CHAPTER XXVI

THE POWER GIVEN TO THE PRIESTHOOD BY CHRIST IS FREELY ENTRUSTED TO IT FOR THE SALVATION OF SOULS AND THE GLORY OF GOD. FOR THIS REASON THE RIGHT TO DISTRIBUTE THE SACRAMENT OF THE EUCHARIST HAS BEEN GIVEN TO THE PRIESTHOOD WITHOUT ANY LIMITATIONS. THE FAITHFUL CAN NOT BE DECEIVED AS TO THE MANNER OF DISTRIBUTION [OF THE SACRAMENT] WHICH DERIVES FROM POWER FREELY GRANTED TO THE PRIESTHOOD — AND THIS ANSWERS THE FALSE ARGUMENT OF THE BOHEMIANS THAT IT IS NECESSARY TO SALVATION THAT BOTH SPECIES BE DISTRIBUTED.

208. We must still mention a few things on the subject of reform, since departure from the forms handed down to us by the fathers has

caused disorder in the church because not everyone has exercised his power properly. And so we should consider the power of the church – a subject about which many writers have written well – and then the area of competence of each governing power in the church according to its rank so that the true form of each may be determined in this way, and abuses arising from excessive power may be removed by means that are appropriate and suitable to the times. These are profound and broad topics and therefore they cannot easily be summarized. Hence we must first speak at length on the power that is given to the priesthood to distribute the sacraments and preach the gospel. Let it suffice now to say that the ministers and those who distribute the sacraments should know that they are envoys, messengers, and represenatatives of Christ with an obligation to do all things with discretion for the honor of God and the salvation of the people, as is the command of Innocent in D. 90 [c. 11] *Praecepimus.*

209. If a minister acts with discretion and exercises the liberty given him for those aforesaid purposes, even if others act differently and the procedure for administration [of a sacrament] provided by the church is not specified in a definite way, he uses the power given to him properly, as St. Cyprian writes to Antonianus,[1] and as Augustine writes after him to Vincentius Rogatista concerning certain bishops who did not admit adulterers to penitence while others admitted them. These, they write, have not on that account been removed from the body of the bishops or broken the unity of the Catholic church because of the strictness of that punishment or their obstinacy. If others grant forgiveness to adulterers, those who do not are not separated from the church. "For the bond of concord joins us and the one sacrament of the church continues and each bishop performs his duty and conducts himself as one who will justify his actions to his Lord."[2] And this is the opinion of St. Cyprian in various places.

Hence for the aforesaid purposes it was always possible for the priest to vary the manner of administering the sacraments which was strict in ancient times for the sake of discipline and later relaxed. For at one time pardon was not given to relapsed heretics nor hope of communion even on their deathbeds, see *De poenitentia* D. 6, [after c. 4] *Hoc autem,* then later the priesthood met together and writings were brought forward on each side and a salutary modification resulted to

[1] PL 3, pp. 811ff.   [2] PL 33, p. 341.

the effect that pardon would be granted at the point of death. Cyprian writes at length about this to Antonianus. See also *De poenitentia* D. 3 [c. 33] *In Tantum* and many texts in the same place. And Pope Innocent [I] writes, "The earlier custom had it that [the sacrament of] penance was granted but communion denied. Penance was granted and communion was denied because of frequent persecutions so that whoever was admitted to penance might at least be punished this much [by the denial of communion] in the hope that this might prevent those who had returned from relapsing. Today however, since peace has been granted to the church, the earlier stricter observance has been made easier so that they are admitted both the penance and to communion on their deathbeds."[3]

210. It would be superfluous to discuss all these variations here. We know that it was decided at the Council of Sardica – which the whole church has accepted, as appears in the acts of the Eighth Council[4] – that those guilty of corruption [in episcopal elections] should not be admitted to communion even at the final moment of death, although the Council of Nicaea commanded that every sinner should be admitted to communion on his deathbed.[5] Similarly the last chapter of the Council of Carthage, which Augustine signed, commands that communion never be given to those who after taking the vow of chastity and receiving the habit, return to the world and marry.[6]

And from this and other points, we at least can conclude that the priesthood is free to distribute the sacraments in this way or not to do so – for the aforesaid purposes and according to the time and place and the dispositions of their subjects. And from this it follows that just as communion is salutary and healthful, so also excommunication is medicinal, to promote the obedience to which all the faithful are obliged – see especially on this [C.] 11 q. 3 [c. 11] *Si autem* and the chapter *Absit* [c. 14]. For we read that St. Peter said to Clement: "For it is fitting that the one who is in authority should act the part of a doctor." On which [see] the letter of Clement to James, the brother of the Lord.[7]

211. Hence it is clear that the Bohemians are incorrect in thinking that communion under both species is required for laymen for, since laymen can not receive communion by themselves and since the

[3] PL 20, pp. 498ff. [4] Mansi 16, pp. 172ff.
[5] Mansi 3, p. 7 and 2, p. 674. [6] Mansi 3, p. 95.
[7] Hinschius, p. 31. (A forgery – see Cusanus' criticisms in Book III, ch. 2, no. 309.)

power was granted to the priesthood to give and not give it for the aforesaid purposes, as the above examples also indicate, the faithful would then be obliged to do the impossible! And if they say that the priesthood is obliged by the command of Christ to distribute it in this way, let them say how the church observed the commands of Christ before Pope Innocent when it was customary not to distribute communion – also at the time of Cyprian and Pope Cornelius when it was not given to relapsed heretics[8] and at the time of the Council of Sardica when it was denied to the corrupt, and [also] at that time when it was not given to adulterers or to those who had violated the vow of chastity and at the time of the Council of Elvira – as appears in chapter 63 of that Council – when the sacrament was not given even on their deathbeds to adulterers who had killed their baby, nor to those guilty of a serious crime against a priest or bishop as in chapter 75 of the same council, nor to those who corrupted little boys as in chapter 71, nor to a woman who married a man other than the one with whom she had committed fornication, as appears in chapter 72 – to none of these was communion given even at the end of their lives.[9] And now that communion has been distributed for a long time under one species if it were commanded to distribute it under both species, it would not be true that, as Christ promised, the majority of the priests and bishops would always have been in the true faith and law of Christ as St. Cyprian writes and as I have mentioned above.[10] And in a certain little work against this error of the Bohemians, I have made an extensive collection of authorities from the canon of the Bible and the canons of councils and the writings of the doctors, proving that the power to distribute the sacrament of the Eucharist belongs to the priesthood freely and without restriction. Therefore let us conclude this discussion.

212. Let this suffice, for it is not relevant to the present discussion. It is enough to know that the priesthood here assembled has the power to decide freely concerning the responsibility entrusted to it of distributing the sacraments for the glory of God and the salvation of the people, different dispositions and customs notwithstanding.

[8] PL 3, pp. 878ff.   [9] Mansi 2, p. 16.   [10] Book II, no. 79.

CHAPTER XXVII

THE GREATEST DISORDER COMES FROM ABUSES ON THE PART OF THE HEAD, WHEN SUPERIORS USURP THE POWER OF THOSE UNDER THEM.

213.   One should obey one's superiors within the limits of the power of each, – see the Archdeacon's comments on the chapter [c. 27] *Si quis praepostera* of D. 50 and on [C.] 7 q. 1 [c. 18] *Quia frater* and [C.] 11 q. 3 [c. 92] *Non Semper* and the writings of doctors of theology on the text of Matthew: "What they say, do."[1] First we should consider the power of the Roman pontiff, because as Gregory says in [C.] 2 q. 7 [c. 46] *Sicit inquit*, a reforming council should begin with its head. The title attached to the text proves this. Hence if every power governed in accordance with the regulations established by the universal councils, the best possible reform would necessarily result. Thus Pope Leo writes to Constantinus, Audentius, Rusticus etc. "It is a just and reasonable cause for rejoicing when we know that the things that have been done by the priests of the Lord are in harmony with the rules of the canons of the fathers and those established by the apostles. For the whole body of the church must increase in a salutary way if the members who are in authority show vigor in their authority and moderation in their rule."[2]

214.   Hence according to Leo IX, as we have said earlier, all the members of the one church and of the Mystical Body of Christ have their specific functions, the exercise of which cannot be impeded by others without disturbance of order, see D. 89 [c. 1] *Singula*, But a disturbance of order is a disturbance of the entire corporate union of the church. Because of it disorder and weakness spread to the whole body, see [C.] 11 q. 1 [c. 39] *Pervenit*; D. 99 [c. 4] *Nullus* and the canon, *Ecce* [c. 5]. And the text of Gregory, *Singula*, says, "It is harmful and most criminal for one member to usurp the function of another and not to distribute the ministries to individuals. Therefore neither a head nor a member has any right whatsoever to usurp the power of another member, if that member is to be healthy and vigorous and active. If his office is usurped, there will be harmful

---

[1] Matthew 23:3.   [2] PL 54, p. 814.

disturbance to the whole body."[3] Therefore if we know what is proper for each member according to the rules of the ancients, we will see how disorder in the body arises. For it would not be disordered, had not an excess or abuse taken place. And because when the head is ill the other members suffer, it follows that the salvation of the subjects depends on the health of the rulers, see D. 61 [c. 5] *Miramur*, D. 86 [c. 1] *Inferiorum*. Therefore no greater disorder can arise than when someone believes that because of his great power anything is permissible, and he violates the rights of his subjects.

[3] PL 75, 111.

CHAPTER XXVIII

NORMALLY IT IS THE POPE'S RESPONSIBILITY TO DECIDE DIFFICULT CASES, TO CARE FOR THE UNIVERSAL CHURCH, AND TO CONFIRM METROPOLITANS — ACTING IN A WAY SIMILAR TO ANY PATRIARCH IN HIS AREA OF JURISDICTION. HERE WE REFER TO THE OPINION OF [THE COUNCIL OF] CHALCEDON AND TO A CANON OF THE EIGHTH COUNCIL. FROM THESE AND OTHER SOURCES WE CONCLUDE THAT THE ORDINARY POWER OF THE POPE IS TO CARRY OUT THESE FUNCTIONS, AND TO CALL SYNODS, TO SUMMON METROPOLITANS TO ATTEND THEM, AND TO JUDGE CONTROVERSIES AMONG THEM. WE DISCUSS HOW THE PRINCES AND THE EMPEROR USED TO PARTICIPATE ONLY IN THE COUNCILS OF THE UNIVERSAL CHURCH, NOT IN THOSE OF THE POPE OR THE PATRIARCHS. UNLESS EVERYONE MAINTAINS THE LAW AND OBSERVES THE CANONS, THE PEACE OF THE CHURCH WILL BE DESTROYED.

215. Let us see therefore what is the legitimate power of the supreme pontiff. There is no doubt that his power to feed his sheep and to decide doubtful questions is very great, but it has certain specific limits. For although what the pope can do is noted in chapter

1 of [*Decretals* I 7] of *De Translatione Praelati* in the text and the gloss, and in [*Decretals* V 31] *De Excessibus Praelatorum* [c. 8] *Sicut unire*, and in [*Decretals* I 30] *De Officio legati* [c. 4] *Quod translationem*, and in [*Decretals* III 8] *De Concessione Praebendae* [c. 4] *Proposuit*, and in [C.] 25 q. 1 [c. 6] *Sunt quidem*, and in [C.] 1 q. 7 [after c. 5] *Nisi rigor* in the gloss, and in D. 14 [c. 2] *Sicut* in the ancient gloss and in many other glosses, what is within his regular competence is his because he is chief of the bishops of the faith, in matters of faith which are in doubt, as is said elsewhere above,[1] as well as in all matters affecting the general interest of the whole church, and in serious cases. I find this to be the view of his power in the Council of Nicaea, in that of Chalcedon, and in the eighth Council of Constantinople. The sixth canon of the Council of Nicaea says that he has power over those under him on the basis of custom, see D. 66 [D. 63 c. 6] *Mos est*, although I do not find this canon quoted in the same way in the [records of] Council of Chalcedon.[2] The decision of the Council of Chalcedon on the claims of the churches of Rome and of Constantinople speaks of the primacy as follows: "On the basis of the actions and texts quoted by each side, we hold that according to the canons the most reverend bishop of old Rome indeed possesses the primacy and foremost place before all, but the most reverend archbishop of the royal city of Constantinople, the new Rome, should enjoy the same privileges of primacy and should have the power to ordain bishops in the dioceses of Asia, Pontica, and Thrace in the following way: After a decree has been issued by the clerics and the property-holders and most eminent men of each metropolis, all or the majority of the most reverend bishops of the province should elect whomever in the metropolitan church they deem worthy. But the one who is elected should be referred by all the electors to the most holy Archbishop of Constantinople and he should be asked whether he wishes him to come to be ordained there or if he wishes it to be carried out with his permission in the province where he will be bishop. The bishop of each city is to be ordained by all or a majority of the reverend bishops of the province, and the metropolitan [of the province] has the power [of confirmation] which is described in the rule adopted by the fathers, while the most reverend archbishop of Constantinople does not participate in the ordination. These things have

[1] Book II, no. 95.
[2] Mansi 2, p. 670 and 7, pp. 451ff., which also includes the lengthy quotation that follows.

been reviewed by us. But let the holy and universal council deign to teach what we have decided. The most reverend bishops said, – 'This is a just conclusion. We all say it, and we all approve, – etc.' " and at the end "The whole synod has approved what we have discussed."

216. Note that in this decree it is stated that whatever honors the pope enjoys as primate, the patriarch of Constantinople also has. But the patriarch of Constantinople has only the right to confirm the metropolitans, as is evident from the canon, and therefore the Roman pontiff also normally only has this power. And what is said in the whole of D. 100 agrees with this. Nevertheless in [canon] law the confirmation of metropolitans belongs to those under him, see D. 51 [c. 5] *Qui in aliquo* and D. 63 [c. 63] *Quia igitur* in the Gloss, although the Roman pontiff is the only one who hands over the *pallium*,[3] as is said throughout D. 100 and in many other places. And on this see decree 17 of the Eighth Universal Council – the last for which we have the decrees. The heading of that decree says, *On the power of the patriarchs and the coming of the metropolitans to them* etc. . . . . "The holy and universal Council of Nicaea earlier commanded that the ancient custom be observed that the bishop of Alexandria should have power over all the bishops in Egypt and the provinces under it, saying that this was the custom that prevailed in the city of Rome. Therefore this holy and great synod decrees that the ancient custom should be preserved both in the old and the new Romes and in the sees of Alexandria, Antioch, and Jerusalem that the rulers in those sees should have power over all the metropolitans that are appointed by them – whether they receive confirmation of their episcopal rank through the laying-on of hands or by the giving of the pallium – to bring them together in a synodal meeting whenever there is an urgent necessity, and even to coerce and compel them when rumor has perhaps accused them of certain misdeeds. But if there are certain metropolitans who plead that they are detained without reason by secular princes thus preventing them from responding to the call of their apostolic superiors, we decree that such an excuse is altogether invalid. For since princes often have meetings for their own purposes, it is impious that they should prevent the highest church authorities from holding synods on church business or prohibit some of them

---

[3] The pallium is a wool shoulder garment given by the pope to an archbishop. Since the ninth century it has been regarded in the Western church as a prerequisite for the exercise of authority by an archbishop.

from attending their councils – although we have learned that these impediments and specious prohibitions have sometimes been maneuvers suggested by the metropolitans. But the metropolitans have been accustomed to hold synods twice a year, and so they say they can not meet with their patriarchal head."

217. "But this holy and universal synod, while not forbidding the councils held by the metropolitans, considers that those that are held by a patriarchal see are much more important and useful than the councils of the metropolitans. And therefore it ordains that they should be held. Each province is administered by a metropolitan but often a case involving a whole diocese is decided by the patriarch for the common good. And therefore a particular good should be subordinated to the common good as our ancestors have advocated, although among certain metropolitans ancient custom and apostolic tradition seem to have been held in contempt and they do not go to the meetings held for the common benefit. The laws of the church condemn them and oblige them to obey the call of their patriarch, whether this is done in a general summons or by individual sealed letter. And we totally reject what is said by certain ignorant men that a synod can not be held without the presence of the ruler, since the sacred canons have never commanded that the secular princes should meet in the councils, but only the bishops. And we do not find that they were present at those synods except in the universal councils, and it is not right that secular princes should observe some of the things that are done by the priests of God. Therefore except in cases of very serious illness or pagan invasion, any metropolitan who has disregarded his patriarch and disobeyed a summons, whether directed to him alone or to many or to all, and who has not come for two whole months after receiving notice of the summons calling him to come to his patriarch, or if in any way he has tried to hide from, or avoid meeting the messengers sent by him, shall be suspended. But if he has demonstrated the same obstinacy and disobedience for one year, he shall be completely deposed and cease all clerical activity and be removed from office and from the honor due a metropolitan. And he who does not obey this definition, let him be anathema."[4]

218. Notice that according to the canon law regulations the pope only confirms the metropolitans, hands over the pallium, and calls the

---

[4] Mansi 16, pp. 170ff.

council – and on this, see [C.] 3 q. 6 [c. 9] *Dudum*. And note the closing for it says "On the power of the patriarchs." Hence although another text on the right of convocation speaks otherwise, see [C.] 9 q. 3 [c. 21] *Per principalem*, which states that he can summon both monks and all clergymen to himself, according to the ancient gloss this is not proper because he ought to do this [only] after consulting their religious superiors – although, as the [ordinary] gloss says, their consent is not required. Hence if as Pope Nicholas decrees in [C.] 9 q. 3 [c. 8] *Conquestus*, the canons of the Nicene councils are to be observed, it is the intention of the Nicene Council, set down here in the text of the Nicene Council quoted and later repeated above, that his power consists in confirming metropolitans and convening the councils. For if the pope wishes to exercise his power in accordance with the canons of Nicaea, then he will give back their rights to the metropolitans and permit each church to have the freedom to govern its own diocese.

219. And we have already heard enough above about the inviolability and permanence of those canons and the invalidity of anything contrary to them and we have stated that peace is preserved in the church of God when they are observed. Now in order to prove these things let us add a passage from the letter of Pope Boniface to Hilary, the bishop of Narbonne, "We have heard that Patroclus has ordained someone in another province, bypassing the metropolitan contrary to the rules of the fathers. And we cannot bear this in patience for we must be diligent custodians of the laws of the fathers. The law of the Council of Nicaea is known to all – which commands – to quote its words: 'Each metropolitan ought to have jurisdiction over one province and two provinces can not be subject to the same metropolitan.' " And below, "By our authority we prohibit the presumptuousness of those who would unduly extend the limits of their power. And we say this so that Your Grace may note that we are observing the precepts of the canons through this decree of ours which commands that each province should always await the direction of its metropolitan on all questions."[5] And the Council of Nicaea in D. 64 [c. 1] *Episcopi* says that the confirmation of bishops belongs to the metropolitan and the same Council says: "As is generally known, if anyone is made bishop without the knowledge of the metropolitan, this great synod decides

[5] PL 20, pp. 772 and 774.

that he ought not to be bishop," see D. 100 [c. 8] *Illud* and on that subject D. 65 as a whole. And in the chapter [of D. 65] *Non debet* [c. 2] quoted from the Council of [Pope] Martin it is said that an ordination carried out in any other way is invalid. And the Council of Antioch says in the next chapter [c. 3] "If it is done in any other way than as we have commanded, it is invalid." Election and ordination are considered as equivalents, as will be seen below.

And this is a command of God the Father and the law of Mother Church, see [C.] 3 q. 6 [c. 10] *Haec quippe.* Thus Pope Leo says to Anastasius: "According to the canons of the holy fathers established by divine inspiration . . . we decree that those consecrated before the whole world as metropolitan bishops of the individual provinces should maintain their ancient rights undiminished as given to them so that they may not depart from the preestablished rules by either negligence or presumption, etc."[6] And Leo says the same thing to Maximus of Antioch: "Peace and universal tranquillity can not be preserved except by maintaining reverence for the canons."[7]

220.   Note that the law decreed that bishops should be ordained by decision of metropolitans, see D. 24 [c. 4] *Episcopi.* And there are countless laws to this effect. According to Hincmar a bishop should not visit the pope without consulting his metropolitan, and Zosimus writes the same thing to all the bishops in France in the letter beginning *Placuit* in which he discusses commendatory letters.[8] Similarly appeals were to be made through the hierarchical ranks without bypassing the metropolitan unless he was involved in the case, see [C.] 2 q. 7 [c. 54] *Metropolitanum.* As to how the consent of the primate used to be secured when the metropolitan performed the ordination, see D. 65 [c. 4] *De persona.*

[6] PL 54, p. 672.
[7] PL 54, p. 104.
[8] PL 126, pp. 202ff. and 20, pp. 642ff.

CHAPTER XXIX

THE CANONS OF THE EIGHTH COUNCIL, OFTEN
MISQUOTED IN THE DECRETUM, ARE THE BEST
MODEL FOR REFORM. ACCORDING TO THE EIGHTH
CANON OF THAT COUNCIL, METROPOLITANS ARE
NOT TO BE CONCERNED WITH WORLDLY
RESPONSIBILITIES OR TO LET SUFFRAGANS
EXERCISE THEIR SPIRITUAL RESPONSIBILITIES. THE
GREATEST ABUSES RESULT FROM THE FACT THAT
PRELATES ARE SO INVOLVED IN SECULAR
CONCERNS.

221. And because the Eighth Universal Council was, as I have said, the last one whose canons have been written down, we must give proper attention to its legislation. And although its canons are few in the *Decretum*, they are sometimes attributed to Pope Hadrian, as in D. 63 [c. 1] *Nullus* and the chapter *Adrianus* [c. 2] and to the Sixth Council, as in [C.] 12 q. 2 [c. 13] *Apostolicos*. This is why I have taken care to note that they are canons of the Eighth Council. In the first canon concerning metropolitans, canon 24 commanded that metropolitans perform divine offices, litanies, and other sacred functions pertaining to their duties not through suffragan bishops but directly. "As the Holy Scriptures say – 'Cursed be every man who neglects to carry out the work of the Lord.' Certain metropolitans out of negligence and laziness summon bishops subject to them and entrust them with the divine offices of their own church and the litanies and all sacred ministries which are properly theirs, which they [the metropolitans] should carry out joyfully themselves. In this way they make those who have merited the rank of bishop into clerics in their service. And the metropolitans devote themselves to secular concerns and decisions in opposition to the provisions of church law. They neglect to offer prayers and supplications for their own offenses and for the ignorance of the people. Such conduct is hardly ever found among some since it is altogether contrary to the canonical precepts. What is worse, to receive their incomes they [the bishops] are said to be ordered to perform the aforesaid duties at different times in the month which can be demonstrated to be altogether

171

contrary to the apostolic recommendations. But this demonstrates that they should be most strongly condemned, for it is proven that those who do these things are possessed by diabolical arrogance and pride. But after this definition by the holy universal synod, any metropolitan who in a spirit of audacity, pride, and contempt for abuses does not try to perform his duties in his own city in the fear of God zealously and with a good conscience but acts through suffragan bishops, shall be punished by his own patriarch and either corrected or deposed."[1]

222. Observe that if involvement in secular concerns and decisions is completely contrary to the canonical precepts for a metropolitan, how [little] the canonical precepts are observed by anyone from the pope who is the highest metropolitan down to the lowest rank of the metropolitans, as it were! Does not that text truly describe present practice? If therefore there is to be a reform eliminating practices that are contrary to the canonical precepts, according to that canon they must avoid further involvement in secular concerns and decisions, and diligently and readily do what is required by their responsibility to care for souls. If the pope does not think that this is said to him, let him see what St. Clement wrote to James, the brother of the Lord, as to what St. Peter had said to him when he ordained him and gave him the powers of binding and loosing and urged him to act like a doctor for the salvation of those under him. He added that he should not become involved in any worldly occupation, saying, "Christ did not wish you to be ordained today as a judge or administrator of secular affairs lest preoccupied with the present cares of men you might not be able to attend to the word of God."[2] On the same point, see D. 96 [c. 6] *Cum ad verum* and the canon, *Duo quippe* [c. 10]. Observe that it can not be denied that the pope or any other pastor is appointed to give the word and example, as Agatho describes it well in the first action of the Sixth Council, where he says, "Woe to me if I am negligent, etc."[3]

223. Who, I ask, can adequately fulfill this spiritual responsibility? If it is very difficult to satisfy the normal requirements of spiritual care, should it not be conceded that concern for temporals is necessarily a

---

[1] Mansi 16, p. 176.
[2] Hinschius, pp. 31–32. (Nicholas argues correctly in Book III, Ch. 2, no. 309, that this letter is not authentic.)
[3] Mansi 11, p. 242.

serious obstacle to the pastors who govern the church? For if he is
intent on many mutually incompatible concerns, how can a church
ruler perform any one of them properly since one who tries to do two
things completes neither? And circumlocution is not necessary. We
see that on account of the mixing of responsibilities, temporal concerns have overcome and nearly subdued the spiritual. If temporal
resources are so necessary to spiritual activities that they can not exist
for a long time without them, it is not therefore necessary for the care
of temporals to be placed on the shoulders of those concerned with
spirituals, lest one like the pope who as the spiritual leader of the
others is supposed to show the way to heaven, should fall by the
wayside more quickly than the others because of the heavy burden of
temporal concerns.

224.   This was not the way the church was governed after Constantine. In the records of the Eighth Universal Council from which the
preceding canon was taken held 400 years after Constantine and in
the acts of the Sixth Council held at the time of [Pope] Agatho it does
not appear that the Roman pontiff was so involved in temporal concerns. Although we find that Sicily, Calabria, Campania etc. were
parts of the patrimony of St. Peter, there were patricians, and other
rulers responsible for military affairs. On this, see D. 63 [c. 23] *In
synodo* and D. 96 [c. 1] *Bene inquit* and other places discussed below.[4]
Now that with the help of God and in accordance with the canon
quoted above, a solution has thus been found by this holy council for
the problem of temporal involvement, everything else will follow in a
salutary fashion because the formerly overburdened spiritual ruler
will be able to arise, and grow strong and vigorous.

To see how much the ancients were concerned to prohibit the
mixing of the spiritual and temporal concerns among the clergy, see
St. Cyprian's letter to the clergy and people concerning Victor, who
named the priest Faustinus as a guardian etc.,[5] and D. 88 [c. 4]
Perlatum and the entire Distinction. They carried out temporal affairs
through representatives and managers, as in D. 89 [c. 2] *Volumus* and
in the chapter [c. 4] *Quia in quibusdam*, and in [*Decretals* 1 31] *De
Officio Ordinarii*, [c. 4] *Cum vos* and in [C.] 16 q. 7 [c. 22] *In nona
actione*. And on this we should note the opinion of our fellow German,
Hugh of St. Victor, who is most learned in every branch of know-

---

[4] Book III, ch. 39.   [5] PL 4, pp. 409ff.

ledge, when he says in *De Sacramentis*, "Although the church receives
the fruit of earthly possessions for its use, churchmen may not
exercise the power of dispensing justice or carrying out secular judgments. Nevertheless the church can have lay persons as its ministers
to carry out the laws and judgments pertaining to earthly power and
the requirements of earthly law. However let those who exercise this
power recognize that they have it by grant of an earthly prince."[6]
According to this, the patricians and the rulers of the patrimony of the
church are appointed by the prince with the consent of the church.

[6] PL 176, p. 420. Hugh of St. Victor was born in Saxony.

CHAPTER XXX

A GREAT ABUSE IS THE USE OF VISITS FOR
CORRECTIONAL AND PASTORAL PURPOSES AS
SOURCES OF PROFIT. A CANON OF THE EIGHTH
COUNCIL IS QUOTED STATING THAT IT IS A
SACRILEGE TO LAY BURDENS ON THE CHURCHES IN
ONE'S JURISDICTION UNDER THE PRETEXT OF
VISITING THEM. THE AVARICE OF CHURCH
SUPERIORS AND ESPECIALLY OF THE ROMAN CURIA
MUST BE ENDED, AND THE NEEDS OF THE CHURCH
SHOULD BE PROVIDED FOR BY A REGULAR GENERAL
CONTRIBUTION.

225.   Another abuse which must be eliminated henceforth is for
superiors to take advantage of their high position to burden their
subordinates excessively. The Eighth Universal Council in chapter 19
adopted the following canon against archbishops who lay burdens on
their suffragans on the pretext of visiting them: "The great Apostle
Paul decried avarice, comparing it to idolatry, and called on all who
called themselves Christians to abstain from all filthy lucre. Still
worse is it for those who are members of the priesthood to burden
fellow-bishops and suffragans in any way. Therefore this holy and
universal synod decrees that no archbishop or metropolitan may leave
his own church and on the pretext of a [canonical] visitation go to

other churches and abuse his power over his subordinates and consume income which is reserved for the administration of the church and the feeding of the poor, and in this avaricious way burden the consciences of their brothers and fellow-ministers. An exception can be made for the hospitality which may perhaps be required for a necessary trip. But even in this case let him accept with dignity in reverence and fear of God only what can be prepared quickly and easily and continue on his proposed journey speedily, without seeking or demanding anything of what belongs to that church or suffragan bishop. For if the sacred canons decree that each bishop should make sparing use of the goods of his own church and in no way either spend his own resources or consume church income unreasonably, of what impiety do you not think he will be judged guilty who does not fear to burden and solicit the churches entrusted to other bishops and thus incur the crime of sacrilege? Therefore whoever after this definition of ours attempts anything like this, shall be punished by his patriarch at the time in proportion to the degree of his injustice and avarice, and let him be deposed and excommunicated as sacrilegious and a quasi-idolater according to the description of the great Apostle."[1]

226. Observe that those who use some pretext to burden their subordinate churches are guilty of sacrilege. This is why this world cries out at the acquisitiveness of the Roman curia. If simony is in a way a kind of heresy, if it is a sacrilege and according to the great Apostle idolatry to burden subordinate churches, a reform is necessary which will take away all these profits – in particular since the whole church is scandalized by the avarice of its rulers, and by that of the Roman curia more than of the other churches. Therefore this abuse in particular must be abolished by this sacred reform council because it is impious, injurious to souls, and a scandal to the whole church. Let everything done at the Roman curia and in the other metropolitanates be without payment. If a superior lacks money, let a charitable contribution be made without objection when his extortion ceases. If the government of the universal church needs it for the expenses of its legates and of participants in the permanent council and others serving the public welfare, there is no doubt that enough will be provided without difficulty from a collection. If the blind avarice and pompous dissoluteness of the members of the curia

[1] Mansi 16, pp. 172ff.

ceases, the good God will undoubtedly see to it that the church can provide for itself in all proper circumstances, especially when matters which are both Christ's concern and ours are acted upon in a tranquil spirit. Perhaps a permanent rule can not be made now as to how much would suffice for a required annual contribution, for we should always provide for the needs that occur. Hence for the present let this holy synod decree an annual collection which is to continue until the next universal council. But if a difficult situation develops for the Roman pontiff which requires something more to be done, let him convene the universal council to provide for it.

CHAPTER XXXI

A REMEDY FOR EPISCOPAL ABUSES IS PROVIDED IN
THE TWENTY-SIXTH CANON OF THE EIGHTH
COUNCIL WHICH STATES THAT THOSE SUBJECT TO
A BISHOP WHO ARE WRONGED BY HIM MAY CALL
HIM TO TRIAL. APPEALS OUGHT TO BE MADE
THROUGH THE RANKS OF THE HIERARCHY AS FAR
AS THE PATRIARCH.

227. Subordinates are also often unjustly oppressed by a bishop who is suspected of being prejudiced in favor of an adversary or hostile to them. The Eighth Synod decreed a remedy against this in its 26th canon which says: "It has pleased this holy synod that any priest or deacon who has been removed by his own bishop for some crime and says he has suffered an injustice and does not agree with the decision of his bishop, because he suspects that either hostility to him or favoritism to certain others has made him act against him in this way, shall have the power to appeal to the metropolitan of that province and to denounce his removal or any injury which he thinks unjust. And the metropolitan shall receive him freely in this way and call the bishop who removed or in any way wronged the cleric and together with other bishops he shall make an examination of the matter himself in order to confirm the removal of the clergyman as above suspicion or to annul it by decision of a fuller and larger synod. Likewise we decree that bishops may also appeal to their patriarchal

superiors if they believe that they have received similar treatment from their metropolitans and let the case when it is appealed to the patriarch and the metropolitans under him receive a just decision which is above suspicion. In addition let no metropolitan or bishop be judged by the neighboring metropolitans or the bishops of his own province, even if it is publicly known that certain crimes have taken place, but only by his patriarch. We decree that the opinion and judgment of the patriarch is reasonable, just, and above suspicion because he associates a number of most honorable advisers with himself and therefore what is decided by him is considered thoroughly valid and definitive. If anyone does not agree with what we have decreed, let him be excommunicated."[1]

This canon provides a clear remedy for anyone who feels that he has been wronged. He should appeal through the hierarchy to the patriarch over him whose judgment is final because of the fact that he associates a number of most honorable advisers with him in the decision.

[1] Mansi 16, pp. 177ff.

CHAPTER XXXII

MONKS APPOINTED AS BISHOPS SHOULD KEEP
THEIR HABITS AND MONASTIC OBSERVANCE IN
ACCORDANCE WITH CHAPTER 27 [OF THE EIGHTH
COUNCIL]. PRELATES SHOULD BE CHOSEN BY
ELECTION. THESE ELECTIONS SHOULD BE CARRIED
OUT FREELY AND WITHOUT PRESSURE; THOSE
MADE BISHOPS FOR POLITICAL REASONS BY THE
ORDER OF PRINCES SHOULD BE DEPOSED; AND
ONLY THOSE SUITABLE FOR HIGH POSITION WHO
HAVE COME UP THROUGH THE HIERARCHY AND
WHO ARE TONSURED OUT OF LOVE OF GOD, NOT
DESIRE FOR OFFICE, SHOULD BE PROMOTED TO
PRELACIES. [A CANDIDATE] SHOULD FIRST SPEND
FOUR YEARS AS A PRIEST AND PROMOTIONS
SHOULD BE MADE FROM THE RANKS OF THE SAME
CHURCH IF WORTHY CANDIDATES ARE FOUND.
THOSE WHO HAVE HELD SECULAR
RESPONSIBILITIES SHOULD NOT BE APPOINTED,
AND A BISHOP SHOULD NOT BE APPOINTED
AGAINST THE WILL OF HIS SUBJECTS. MANY GOOD
REASONS ARE GIVEN TO PROVE THAT ELECTIONS
ARE BASED ON DIVINE AND HUMAN LAW.

228. The synod also decreed in its 27th chapter that the metropolitan or anyone else for whom it was appropriate should only use the pallium at certain times and that those promoted from the monastic life to the rank of bishop would be obliged to keep the monastic observance and habit.[1] This last particular is very appropriate for our time because we see a number of dissolute men have been made bishops who formerly were monks but who do not maintain the habit or their former observance. The same [Eighth] Council in its 22nd chapter decreed that prelates should be chosen by election saying, "This holy and universal synod in accord with previous councils defines and decrees that promotion and consecration as

[1] Mansi 16, p. 178.

bishop should be carried out by election and decision of the college of bishops. It also promulgates a law that no lay prince or potentate may involve himself in the election or promotion of a patriarch or of a metropolitan or any bishop, lest this cause inordinate confusion and contention, especially since it is not fitting that any secular power or layman should have power in such matters. Rather he should remain silent and wait until the regular election of the future officer is concluded by the church assembly. But if a layman is invited by the church to assist and to cooperate, he may obey with reverence if he perhaps wishes to do so." And further on: "But any secular prince or potentate or layman of another rank who tries to do anything to prevent the commonly agreed canonical election of a member of the church hierarchy will be anathema until he obeys and consents to what the church has shown that it wishes concerning the election and ordination of its rulers."[2] This decree, although with the wrong title, is contained in D. 63 [c. 1] *Nullus* and the chapter [c. 2] *Adrianus*.

229. The 12th chapter also legislates in like manner: "Since the canons of the apostles and the synods absolutely forbid episcopal promotions and consecrations based on the power or orders of princes, we unanimously decree and decide that if any bishop receives consecration to his office in this way through the guile or tyrannous influence of a prince, he shall be deposed immediately as one who desired and consented to possess a gift of God not by the will of God and a proper ecclesiastical decision, but from the will of the flesh and by and through men."[3] We all know how necessary today is this provision, which is expressed in many earlier laws and reiterated in the Eighth Council.

230. Then so that qualified persons could be advanced in order, the fifth chapter decreed as follows: "So that the canons may always be observed in the church through Christ, we renew and confirm the terms and sanctions that were issued by the holy apostles and our holy fathers and set down as the law of the church." And below, "Therefore in accordance with the preceding canons we decree that no one who has renounced senatorial rank or secular responsibilities and become a tonsured cleric or monk in the intention or hope of being made a bishop or patriarch can rise to such a rank in this way, even if it is proven that he has spent considerable time in the various orders

---

[2] Mansi 16, pp. 174ff.   [3] Mansi 16, p. 167.

of the divine priesthood. This kind of person has received tonsure not out of fear and love of God or the desire to adopt a life of virtue but because of love of glory and power. We command this still more strongly, if it is done under pressure from the imperial court. But if in a case in which there is no suspicion of the aforesaid concupiscence and desire but only a humility which is like that of Jesus Christ, someone renounces the world to become a cleric or monk and after going through every ecclesiastical rank for the specified time is found to be blameless and proven, spending a year as a reader, two years as a subdeacon, three years as a deacon, and four years as a priest, it has well pleased the holy and universal synod that he should be elected and admitted [as a bishop]. But in the case of those who after faithfully remaining in the rank of clerics or monks have been judged as also worthy of the dignity and honor of the episcopacy, we shorten the times mentioned above according as their superiors at the time decide. But if anyone advances to the aforesaid divine supreme honor in violation of this decision of ours, he will be condemned and expelled from all sacerdotal positions because he was promoted in violation of the sacred canons."[4] This is a reform canon which is very necessary at this time.

231. And subsequently in canon 13, the council wished to provide that if worthy candidates are found they should be promoted in their own churches. Hence it decreed as follows: "Because Divine Scripture says at one point – 'The laborer is worthy of his hire,' we also decree and proclaim that the clerics of our great church who have remained in minor orders should rise to major orders, and if they appear worthy they should merit greater honors when any of those who presently exercise these offices have been promoted to more important duties or have died. But outsiders should not receive offices and honors which should go to those who have worked [there] for a long time, since this would deprive the clergy of that church of advancement. And those who have taken care of the residences or lands of princes shall have no power to be appointed to the clergy of this great church. For no one who works for God is involved in secular affairs. But if anyone is promoted to any office in this great church in violation of the decree which we have now put forward, let him be removed from every ecclesiastical position as one who has

---

[4] Mansi 16, pp. 162ff.

contravened the great synod."⁵ Observe that after many other ancient laws this reform decree was repeated twice by the Eighth Universal Council and note well that it says: "Let him be removed as one who has contravened the great synod."

232.   From this it is evident that if a bishop is assigned to unwilling subjects he can be rejected, since this is contrary to the great synod which provided that appointments should be carried out by way of election. And the text of D. 61 [c. 13] *Nullis invitis* provides that a bishop is not to be appointed against the will of those over whom he is to rule. The chapter just referred to is explained further there by [Pope] Celestine who says that the priests have the power to refuse a bishop if they see that his appointment would be in violation of the decree. And the chapter [c. 16] *Obitum* of the same Distinction says that they should not be afraid to refuse those whom they consider to have been forced upon them against their wills. And D. 63 [c. 36] *Si forte* speaks on the same point where the text says that in cases where there is disagreement between two people elected [to the same office] the one who is requested by the diocese is to be appointed by the metropolitan. And the reason that no one is to be appointed over unwilling subjects is that a hostile populace would despise a bishop whom they did not wish to have. And C. 31 q. 2 [c. 3] *De neptis* is useful on this for if there is a single spiritual body composed of the bishop and his people, then consent seems to be necessary, as is said there concerning marriage according to the flesh. For there is no doubt that there is a marriage between the bishop and his church, see C. 3 q. 2 [c. 4] *Audivimus* and similar passages. And therefore the text C. 1 q. 1 [c. 113] *Ordinationes* says that "Ordinations not made with the common consent of the clergy and people according to canonical regulations and by those who have the right to perform consecrations we judge to be invalid because those who are ordained in this way do not enter by the gate which is Christ but, as Truth itself [Scripture] bears witness, they are thieves and robbers."⁶

233.   And the reason for this is that consent is essential to a marriage, as is stated above. For a diversity of ranks between rulers and subjects has been commanded for the good of the commonwealth so that when the lower ranks show reverence for their superiors and superiors show love for their subordinates, a true concordance may be

---

⁵ Mansi 16, p. 167. The scriptural quotation is Luke 10:7.
⁶ John 10:7–10.

created out of diversity, and proper administration of office may result, as is said in D. 89 [c. 7] *Ad hoc* and D. 45 [c. 4] *Licet.* Thus the church exists in concord, and it is not right to establish someone as a ruler over subjects who are opposed to him, as D. 83 *Esto* says so well. Anyone who is in authority should be established with the tacit or explicit agreement of all those over whom he exercises authority. If anyone has dared to do otherwise, there is no doubt that he is without power because his action is invalid, as is said in D. 66 [c. 1] *Archiepiscopus* which is a text of Pope Anicetus who says elsewhere, "One who is in authority over all should be elected by all." It is clear that the text *Archiepiscopus* which speaks of ordination, should be understood as also discussing election, both in the original and in the *Panormia* collection of Ivo [of Chartres] which says, "The one who is seen to be over all should be elected and ordained by all."[7] The word, "should," is a word of necessity, see D. 50 [c. 28] *Domino sancto,* that is, it can not be otherwise, see C. 3 a. 6 [c. 9] *Dudum* which is to be noted in favor of the above, along with C. 8 q. 1 [c. 3, 4] *Episcopo.* The canons [c. 19] *Metropolitano* and [c. 3] *Valentinianus* of D. 63 also prove the same point very well.

For ordination is often the same thing as election, see D. 61 [c. 2] *Sacerdotibus.* It is a marriage constituted by consent of electors and elected, as is noted in the chapter [c. 21] *Cum inter canonicos* of [*Liber Sextus* 1 6] *De electione* and D. 63 [c. 10] *Quanto* in the gloss. But election is equivalent to consent as the text in the chapter [c. 13] *Episcopos* of D. 63 says. For according to Innocent the marriage between the electors and the one who is elected, – see C. 7 q. 1 [c. 39] *Sicut* and [*Decretals* 1 7] *De Translatione* chapter 1 etc., – is contracted on behalf of the church by the electors with the one elected. See chapter 1 [2] of *De Translatione,* and the chapter [c. 35] *Obeuntibus* of D. 63. And because every effort for reform requires the establishment of good rulers, authorities, and governors, anyone can easily understand how perilous it is for the subjects, when the one who ought to be living law on earth is not virtuous. Hence in order to establish ecclesiastical authorities without imposing them on unwilling subjects, the divine law commands that an election should take place.

234. Let us content ourselves with a few quotations: St. Cyprian writes along these lines in his letter concerning Martialis and

[7] PL 161, p. 1132.

Basilides, when he says that "the people have the power to elect worthy priests and to refuse unworthy ones." "And it is by divine authority," he says, "that the priest is chosen in the presence of all the people before the eyes of all and that he is approved as worthy and suitable as a result of public judgment and testimony, as the Lord commanded Moses in [the Book of] Numbers; 'Take Aaron, thy brother, and Eleazar, his son, and place them on the mountain before the whole congregation and take Aaron's stole from him and put it on Eleazar, his son, and Aaron shall die there.' God commands that a priest be appointed before the whole synagogue – that is, he shows us that sacerdotal authorities ought to be appointed with the knowledge of the people and in their presence, so that with the people present the crimes of evil men may be revealed and the merits of the virtuous proclaimed and the ordination may be just and legitimate because it results from the participation and the decision of all. And this procedure was followed later, according to the divine teachings contained in the Acts of the Apostles. When Peter spoke to the people of the need to ordain someone in place of Judas the Acts say 'Peter arose in the midst of the disciples, and there was a multitude gathered.' We note that the apostles did this not only for the ordination of bishops and priests, but also for the rank of deacons, and something is written on this as well in the Acts of the Apostles. 'The Twelve called together,' it says, 'the whole multitude of the disciples.' And an election was carried out with care by the whole people gathered together to prevent anyone unworthy from entering the ministry of the altar and the rank of priest."[8]

And the glossators when they comment on that text of Acts, chapter 6, say that the twelve sought to have the consent of the multitude of all the faithful who were called disciples so as to set an example as to the procedure to be observed in ordinations; the people ought to elect and the bishop to ordain. Jerome speaks on the same subject and [what he says] is contained in [C.] 8 q. 1 [c. 15] *Licet* and in the chapter [c. 16], *Si ergo*, on this topic. Also in D. 21 [c. 2] *In novo* Pope Anacletus says that Peter was made head by the will of the apostles and that the apostles elected the 72 disciples.

235. We read in the Epistle of Clement that Peter sent bishops to Gaul and other places and also commanded Clement to send them to

---

[8] Letter to Felix – PL 3, pp. 1061ff.

the places to which he had not sent them,[9] and thus all patriarchs, archbishops, and bishops have gone out from the Apostolic See. This is the way I understand the text of D. 22 c. 1, which quotes Pope Nicholas who lived nearly 800 years after Christ – although it is evident that bishops were not sent out to all parts of the world from Rome, for there were already many bishops in the world before Peter arrived in Rome, as is demonstrated by their presence in Antioch and Jerusalem. Also in Clement's epistle, he writes to James in Jerusalem to send [missionaries] to the Orient. Yet this still does not prove that the pope alone established the patriarchs and primates from the beginning etc., as certain of his adulators say, for the whole church or the apostles who represented the whole church more adequately than did Peter alone, established the primates – cf. D. 99 [c. 2] *Nulli*, which says, "The Apostles and their successors" etc. Nor does it prove that appointments were sometimes made to churches without an election for there were no churches at that time but they were sent to establish churches and therefore an election could not take place because at that time there was no church to carry out an election.

236.   Hence those sent out in this way acting as representatives of Christ, the second Adam, built the Eve whom they had espoused out of the rib which is the Divine Word. And then to the Eve [church] so generated was given only a spouse whom she desired. So today there is no doubt that the pope can send preachers to infidel areas in the same way that Peter and Clement did, as the text *Nulli* quoted above proves. And this is the way Hostiensis understands it in his *Summa* [*Aurea*] commenting on [*Decretals* I 30] *De officio legati* where, when he speaks of the matters reserved to the Apostolic See, he says that the establishment of cathedral sees belongs to him [the pope]. And this is why it is said that all offices originate from the Roman church, see D. 22 [c. 1].

237.   Note therefore that elections exist by divine law – particularly since an unwanted person should not be given to the people and consequently it is against all reason to appoint one who is not desired. Hence Pope Leo in D. 62 says "There is no reason for there to be bishops who have not been elected by the clergy nor desired by the people nor consecrated by their fellow bishops with the approval of the metropolitan." Observe that three things are required for a

[9] Hinschius, p. 39 (apocryphal).

presiding officer in the church to be properly constituted; election by the clergy, the consent of the people, and the approval of the metropolitan. And on this there are an infinite number of legal provisions, as I will indicate. If therefore the church is to be reformed it is necessary that the divine and natural law and the regulations of the canons on the matter of elections be reaffirmed and more fully observed. Hence Pope Siricius writes to the faithful of various provinces on the qualifications of those to be ordained and to be elected: "We may not be silent about complaints that come to us, most beloved brothers, since we fear divine judgment and know that everyone will be rewarded after this life as he has acted. Necessity commands us to speak, as the prophet says, 'Raise up your voice on the trumpet,' and if I, to whom the care for all the churches is entrusted conceal my voice, I shall hear the Lord say, 'You reject the commands of God so that you may keep your traditions.' For what is it but to reject the commands of God when we delight in creating novelties on the basis of private judgment and human counsel. And so it has been brought to the knowledge of the Apostolic See that some have presumed to go against the ecclesiastical canons and the commands of our ancestors that the canons were not to be violated even in the slightest respect, and that a number of new particular usages are being introduced that are built on sand with no foundation. As the Lord says, 'Do not exceed the boundaries which your fathers set.' The Holy Apostle, the preacher of the New and Old Testaments and the spokesman of Christ, also warns: 'Stand firm,' he says, 'and hold to your traditions which you have learned, whether by word or by letter.'" And below, "On which, dearest ones, letters of this kind have gone earlier to you in your sincerity, with the full consent of the brethren and fellow priests, so that the dispositions of the ecclesiastical canons which were stated by the Nicene Council and confirmed by our signature might justifiably remain as a strong foundation."[10]

238. Observe that it is against the commands of God to reject the canons. Hence although the Roman pontiff can sometimes relax inviolable canonical precepts when they are inapplicable, by reason of the necessity and utility of the church, as Innocent and Gelasius say in [C.] 1 q. 7 [c. 23] *Etsi* and the canon [c. 7] *Quod pro remedio*, yet I do not think that the pope can take away all the rights of election alto-

---

[10] PL 13, pp. 1164ff.

gether and reserve ecclesiastical appointments for his own disposal, since election comes from the divine and human law and is a command of God which the pope is obliged to obey because he "may not exceed the boundaries set by the fathers." The provisions of D. 14 [c. 2] *Sicut* and [C.] 1 q. 7 [after c. 5] *Nisi rigor* and [C.] 25 q. 1 [c. 6] *Sunt quoniam* mean that he can not totally abolish laws from which he can grant dispensations for the reasons touched on above.

239.   And because the Roman pontiffs have issued decrees reserving episcopal appointments with the tacit consent of the whole Roman church and the bishops appointed by them have not been repudiated and refused – although in my judgment they could have been refused – silence has become consent, which is sufficient basis for the legitimate title of those who have been appointed. Silence is taken for consent, as stated in the rule, *Qui tacet* – in this case, lack of opposition, as the ancient gloss on the canon [c. 12] *Nosse* of D. 63 notes when it says, "In a public matter whoever does not indicate his opposition when he can is understood to consent. And the [diocesan] chapter in electing its pastor is understood to be contracting the marriage rites of the church. Hence since the church does not protest it is understood to consent, just as when a father contracts a marriage for his daughter, if she is silent she is understood to consent." And the Archdeacon says the same thing on D. 25 [D. 24] [c. 6] *Episcopus sine.* So on our point, if the pope takes the place of a father and provides a spouse and the church is silent and accepts him, its consent is understood. This is what Laurentius says on the canon [c. 6] *Episcopus* of D. 24. When the text says that the bishop may not ordain clerics without a council of his clergy so that he may secure the support and witness of the citizens, Laurentius says, "Support, that is, consent, which he is said to have from the fact that they know and do not oppose, following the *Digest* [XXIV 3] *Soluto matrimonio* law 2, para. *Voluntatem.*"[11] And the text [c. 29] *Cum Adrianus* of D. 63 along with the gloss on the words *ad salutandum* proves this when it argues that they consented to an election in that they were present and saluted him and did not object, because whoever salutes another seems to consent to him, see C. 24 q. 1 [c. 24] *Omnis* etc.

240.   But now because of various abuses this has been carried to excess and opposition has arisen. Therefore I do not think that the

---

[11] Laurentius Hispanus, quoted by the Archdeacon, Guido de Baysio (see Kallen, *DCC*, p. 283).

pope can reserve elective benefices any longer unless he is expressly allowed to do so by this holy council, in view of the opposition which has arisen. For the pope should not appoint a bishop over those who are opposed to him, as the text [c. 2] *In novo* of D. 21 proves when it says that Peter was appointed by the will of the apostles and the gloss argues from this text that the pope should not appoint a bishop unless those over whom he is placed agree, see D. 22 [c. 2] *Sacrosancta* at the verse [5] *inter beatos*; [C.] 8 q. 1 [c. 15] *Licet* and the canons [c. 16] *Si ergo* and [c. 18] *Audacter* which are referred to above.

And the Archdeacon following John of God[12] commenting on the canon *In novo* [of D. 21 c. 2] says that Peter "was chosen for the primacy by Christ before the resurrection but he postponed his confirmation until after the resurrection, so that the disciples over whom he would rule might give their assent as a model for future elections, since no one should be appointed over those who do not wish him, D. 61 [c. 13] *Nullus.*" Hence [an election] is void unless there is consent; see the canon [c. 35] *Obeuntibus* of D. 63 where the text says that an election which is carried out without their consent and support is void, and D. 66 [c. 1] *Archiepiscopus* proves the same point well. On this subject, the gloss on the word, *conniventia*, in the canon, *Obeuntibus* concludes from the text that if anything is to be done with the consent of others, it is invalidated by their lack of consent. See [also] D. 15 [c. 5] *Qui in aliquo*; [C.] 31 q. 2 [c. 1] *Si verum*; D. 62 [c. 1] *Nulla ratio*; [C.] 1 q. 1 [c. 113] *Ordinationes*; [C.] 10 q. 2 [c. 1] *Casellas*; [C. 12] q. 2 [c. 37] *Alienationes* and [c. 52] *Sine*; [C.] 15 q. 7 [c. 6] *Episcopus nullius*; [C.] 23 q. 5 [c. 4] *Quod Deo* and the canon [c. 11] *Manifestum*, and [C.] 20 q. 2 [c. 2] *Puella* etc.

241. And an additional strong reason that consent is necessary could be given. It is evident that knowledge of the law is required of priests, see 2 *Malachy*, and also that the people are not excused by reason of false teaching which has been spread by ignorant or malicious priests. Hence if the consent of the people were not involved in the establishment of their superiors, it would be unjust to punish them for the ignorance or malice of their priest in accordance with the above principle, since their consent never was given to his rule. For in that case nothing can be blamed on that people. Therefore the public good requires that rulers be established by the election and consent of the people.

[12]Joannis de Fantutiis (see Kallen, *DCC*, p. 284).

CHAPTER XXXIII

FOR REFORM IT IS NECESSARY THAT EACH ONE
CARRY OUT THE OBLIGATIONS OF HIS OFFICE.
OTHER NECESSARY CHANGES ARE ENUMERATED IF
AN ORDERLY REFORM IS TO BE INTRODUCED INTO
THE CHURCH AND THE CLERGY.

242. If elections are carried out exactly as described in various places above, and the bishops who are legally obliged to do so, appoint good curates, as in [C.] 10 q. 1 [c. 4] *Regenda* and the chapters [c. 3] *Decretum* and [c. 5] *Quicumque*; [C.] 16 q. 7 [c. 19] *Sicut Domini* and the chapter [c. 10] *Omnes basilicae,* and they visit their churches without becoming a burden to them, as indicated throughout [C.] 10 q. 3, and they make use of the goods of the church as faithful caretakers in accord with the canonical regulations; and if therefore there is harmony in divine worship throughout the whole province, as the text of the Council of Toledo says in D. 12 [c. 13] *De hiis* and the following chapters, and ordinations are made to office on the basis of intelligence and devotion rather than of vocal ability or the wearisome repetition of psalms, as stated in [*Decretum*] *De Consecratione* D. 4 [D. 5] [c. 24] *Non mediocriter,* – for we should sing to God not with our voices but with our hearts, and theatrical modes should not be heard in the church, as Jerome says in D. 92 [c. 1] *Cantantes* – if all these conditions are realized, a sweet concordance which is neither heavy nor wearisome will prevail in the temple of God. Therefore let the council command that each one must carry out the requirements of his office, his vows, his religious duty, and rank. And this command is to be scrupulously obeyed, if we wish to promote the salvation of all. In addition let it command that in the absence of a legal decision superiors who are suspected of any criminal acts are to be freely obeyed – as decreed in the tenth chapter of the [Eighth] Universal Council.[1] As that text also says, let this command be included in the divine services with the penalty for violation being deposition for the clergy and excommunication for monks and laymen.

243. And in addition for the preservation of strict moral standards

---

[1] Mansi 16, p. 166.

in the various church offices, and especially among the bishops, they are not to be subordinated to military authorities, as appears in the fourteenth chapter of the same council which says: "We have decreed that those who by divine grace are called to the office of bishop, since they are the image and figurative representation, as it were, of the celestial hierarchies of the angels, should be considered by all princes and their subjects as worthy of all honor according to their full hierarchical grade and function . . ." Then let the provision of that holy Eighth Council concerning the transfer of church property to others be observed which appears in the chapter [c. 13] *Apostolicos* of C. 12 q. 2.[2] It would also be good to reenact that canon because according to the chapter [c. 20] *Non liceat* in the same section the Roman pontiff would also be forbidden to violate it, and to give his consent [to its violation] in other churches, as has been done up to the present.

244. In addition in the interest of peace among the churches, let the statute be reenacted that provides that goods possessed for thirty years and privileges exercised for the same time continue to be valid, as is contained in chapter 18 of the Eighth Council.[3]

245. And after this let commendations and pensions be taken away since they interfere with proper church administration, as well as dispensations permitting incompatible offices and a plurality of benefices.[4] Let each one carry out his church duties on the basis of one suitable benefice, as is defined by nearly all the universal councils and repeated in the second part of the 23rd chapter of the Eighth Council.[5] At present, the number of petty benefices and consequently of ignorant priests disgraces the church and makes the laity hostile to the clergy when they see so many priests living in a state of idleness and vice. For this reason the holy office of the priesthood is the object of great hatred. The text of D. 59 [c. 2] *Si officia* says that a large number of priests is not desirable because every valuable thing should be scarce. For "it is better to have a few good ones . . ." [*Decretals* I 14] *De aetate et qualitate* [c. 14] *Cum sit ars artium*.

245a. [Basel Manuscript Only.] The object of elections is to express the decision of the majority, and various procedures have been devised for this purpose. Because the decision of all those voting can

---

[2] Mansi 16, p. 168.   [3] Mansi 16, p. 172.

[4] Nicholas was himself a notorious "pluralist." See Erich Meuthen, "Die Pfründen des Cusanus," *MFCG*, 2 (1962), pp. 15–66.

[5] Mansi 16, pp. 172ff.

not be expressed without comparing all the candidates with one another and each one with all the others, and because this is not the case with the procedures now used which make this difficult and uncertain – since voting is not secret and fear and timidity sometimes make the truth keep silent – it seems that a better and truer form of election would be the one described below.[6] It makes it impossible for someone to be elected who is not judged the best by the common judgment of the electors as expressed in a single vote, and at the same time it preserves the secrecy of the vote so that no one can ever know how anyone voted. On the day before the election let the electors meet together and a notary make a list of all who seem to be candidates from that church and from elsewhere, provided that the outsiders are known to the majority of the electors. And after all are registered, let the notary be instructed to make as many ballots as there are candidates, and place one name on each ballot and make them identical. The notary is then to give ballots in the evening to each elector with the names of all of the candidates, except the one who receives the ballot if he is one of the candidates – and he is to do this with all the electors in the evening while everyone is gathered together as a group [*capitulariter*]. When everyone has received his ballots, the superior will say a few words and recall that each is to compare the persons named on the ballots with the others, following his conscience as best he can in accordance with the will of God, and also recall that on the next day each is to swear after receiving communion that he has done this. And then let each one withdraw to a private place in his residence and look at the ballots to decide which one is least fit and place beside his name a single clearly visible mark. Then [he should decide] who is next after him and put down two marks, and after that three marks and so on until he comes to the last one who will have as many marks as there are ballots.

On the next day let them come with their completed ballots and after hearing mass and receiving communion in a public place let them swear that each of them has compared and marked the persons in this way, following the right judgment of his conscience. Each one is to throw his ballots into a sack and when they are all in, let them come together in the chapter hall and read the ballots with the marks.

[6] In the final version of the *Concordantia* the voting procedure described here was moved to Book III, ch. 37, nos. 535–540 (see below).

And the best candidate in the judgment of all will be the one who has the most marks and the worst the one who has the least. And to keep the numbers limited, if there are less than twelve candidates, let him [the notary] note the number of those eligible beside the name on the ballot, and if there are more than 12 let him note only the number 12 and give the names of only 12 of the candidates to the electors. And on the next day after the results are known let the winner be placed on a ballot and run against another group of eleven candidates and follow the same procedure as before. And once the result is computed in the same way, even with many candidates the winner will undoubtedly be the one whom all consider to be best qualified. And for this purpose it is good to place numbers on the side of the ballots so that the electors do not make mistakes in marking and counting points but mark the number on the ballot. And a point will mark the number beneath it, over which it is placed.

Let us suppose that there are three ballots. In my view Nicholas is best, and Conrad worst, and Peter in the middle. Then I will place a mark over the number 12 on the ballot of Nicholas and over number 1 on Conrad's ballot, and 6 on Peter's, and do the same with all the other ballots. But when there are more candidates than twelve the process of voting may be expedited by a single voting procedure. Let the ballots be prepared as above with the 12 numbers and all given at once to the electors – without the name of the one to whom they are given, if he is a candidate. And then let them choose from all the candidates the twelve most qualified and make comparisons and mark them again as before and when the result is computed the one who has the largest number wins. In case of a tie, the older candidate wins – see D. 61 [c. 8] *Statuimus* where this is discussed. And this last method although it is secure and good is not so precise as when comparisons are made among all candidates although it can differ very little from it. To expedite matters more quickly perhaps and also because it is very close to an infallible judgment and the difference is almost imperceptible, the latter method can be used since it is easier to put into practice. It should also be known that the electors should consult the advice of religious men and not exclude them, for it has been decreed in a general synod that if an election is held without their consent and participation it is invalid, see D. 63 [c. 35] *Obeuntibus*. Although custom has led in a contrary direction, it is time for reform. This is how it [the ballot] would read: Nicholas 1, 2, 3, 4, 5, 6, 7, 8, 9, 10, 11, 12; Peter 1, 2, 3, 4, 5, 6, 7, 8, 9, 10, 11, 12; Conrad 1, 2, 3, 4, 5, 6, 7, 8, 9, 10, 11, 12.

246.   And because the holy council has begun to adopt decrees on simony, concubinage, universal and provincial councils, and elections, through the Holy Spirit it will provide for all these things and will reduce to canonical order all pestilential practices inspired by avarice, and make each one carry out his responsibility and ministry. And it will think of the way to apply coercive force to the laws and statutes and how the execution of the sacred canons may be made strong and stable, rigorous and pure. And all power consists in this because [new] canons are not needed but only the application [of existing canons]. And they can only be properly applied by good rulers. If we have them, we would easily and quickly find the ways of our fathers through [one who is] the living law.

CHAPTER XXXIV

A BRIEF EPILOGUE ON WHAT HAS BEEN SAID –
THOSE WHO DENY THAT PETER'S PRIMACY WAS
ESTABLISHED BY CHRIST ARE ANSWERED. IT IS
DEMONSTRATED THAT THE PRIMACY OF THE POPE
COMES FROM CHRIST BY MEANS OF THE CONSENT
OF THE CHURCH, AND THAT HIS POWER COMES
FROM GOD BUT HIS COERCIVE FORCE THROUGH
THE MEDIATION OF THE CHURCH.

247.   The effort of the preceding little work was to begin to analyze the concordance which exists in the church on the basis of fundamental first principles. Its arrangement exhibits our intent in sequence, although not in a way that can be easily studied in a superficial fashion. Nevertheless an attempt will be made to summarize it. There is no doubt that Christ is the way, the life, and the truth, the head and foundation of the church, see Ephesians 4 and 5 and 1 Cor. 10 and the gloss on the verse of Matthew 16: "Thou art Peter" and Augustine in his book, *Retractions,* on the Gospel on John, and in

many of his sermons[1] and many other authors, nearly all Doctors of the Church. The faith will never fail in the church for [the prayer of] Christ was heard and he will remain with the successors of the apostles until the end of the world.[2] Hence there will always be a body of believers in Christ among whom Christ himself will dwell. That Christ-formed body of the faithful in which Christ will dwell is called the Catholic church in which the way and the truth which is Christ will always thus remain. I showed in relatively brief fashion in Book I of this work – which is difficult to summarize – that the one universal church is made up of all rational spirits adhering to Christ and that there is a trinitarian structure in the universal church made up of one part triumphant, and another part militant, and a third sleeping. I also discussed the need to understand the relationship between the church militant where the Truth that is Christ is still understood as a figure and a mystery, and that face-to-face Truth which is in heaven with the church triumphant. In this way as far as possible the admirable order among the various hierarchical ranks in the church militant may be known to some degree for our guidance.

248.   After this in Book II I wished to examine the question of the superiority of the council of the universal church over the particular authority of any individual church ruler and local synod. On the basis of fundamental principles, I directed the reasoning intellect to this conclusion: If the universal Catholic church is infallibly directed by the assistance of Christ, when the assent of all Christians is given to any conclusion as necessary to salvation, it follows that that conclusion is part of the Christian faith and true. And when the universal council comes to such a conclusion with the consent and representation of all the faithful, of necessity it has the assistance of Christ and the inspiration of the Holy Spirit and dictates this truly and infallibly, for no truth that directs one to eternal salvation can exist except through Christ. But the universal council is made up of the bishops and their representatives who come to that meeting to investigate some matter which has not been settled in their own provinces. They meet together in vain, however, if the consent of their subjects to these things has not been given. But if a council is correctly and legitimately called and gathered together and if everyone has received a summons, and it is held in freedom and properly concluded with the common

---

[1] PL 32, p. 616 and 38, pp. 479, 1148, 1238, and 1349.
[2] Luke 22:32; Hebrews 5:7; Matthew 28:20.

consent of all and it issues a decree in any matter concerning the salvation of the faithful, history reveals that it has never erred, since it proximately represents the whole Catholic church and the consent of all the faithful who participate through their representatives and bishops.

249.   But the provincial synods – even those of the Roman pontiffs – do not have this privilege. And because various writings of jurists and theologians, especially those in recent times, exalt the authority of the pope even over that of the synods themselves, it has been necessary to seek to harmonize these writings, while maintaining the aforesaid truth. Therefore I have pointed out the differences between the universal council of the Catholic church and that of a nation, kingdom, or patriarchate on the basis of the acts of the councils which have been approved as authentic – as appears in D. 19 c. 1 – so that anyone who understands the difference may easily see that it is true that the universal council of the Catholic church has supreme power in all things over the Roman pontiff himself. And thus it was necessary to ask what was the authority of the Roman pontiff both as to rulership and as to the power to command and to legislate. And although I have used many arguments, I have emphasized this one – that although according to writings of many of the holy Fathers the power of the Roman pontiff is from God and according to others it comes from man and the universal council, it seems that in fact the intermediate position demonstrable in the Scriptures finally comes to this, that the power of the Roman pontiff as to preeminence, priority, and rulership, is from God by way of man and the councils; namely, by means of elective consent.

250.   I discussed first the freedom of Christ's law to which one adheres voluntarily and without coercion. Hence since Christ himself is the Way of our faith, the only thing necessary for salvation is Christ and free access to him. Therefore in the church which is descended from Christ there should be no coercion but rather grace flowing from the fullness of the source, the Head, down to the Mystical Body of Christ. And this is what [C.] 7 q. 1 [c. 30] *Remoto* says – that the grace of the sacerdotal offices comes from God.

251.   Indeed we say that all the apostles are equal in the grace of the apostolate just as in the grace of the priesthood all priests are equal, but we say that Peter was first among the apostles by virtue of a superabundance of grace. Augustine says in his last sermon on [the

Gospel of] John, that because of abundant grace Peter was both the first apostle and on account of his primacy among the apostles also represented the church as a symbol of the whole.[3] And the sacred writings describe the primacy with which Peter was endowed with a superabundance of grace by Christ, in the first chapter of John where Christ says, "Thou shalt be called Cephas," which is interpreted Peter. Augustine in his seventh sermon comments on this passage as follows: "He made a great change when he changed Simon's name to Peter. But Peter is from rock [*petra*] and the rock is the church. Therefore the name of Peter symbolized the church."[4] Observe that according to the interpretation of the great and learned Augustine, the change in name was important. When Christ said, "Thou art Peter," he used the present tense, where he had said earlier – in the future tense – "Thou shalt be called Cephas." He did not say then, "Thou art named or called Peter" but "Thou art Peter." From this it is evident that the promise of Christ that Simon would in the future be called Cephas was a promise of a real primacy. Hence when Augustine says that Peter had the primacy among the apostles he can not be interpreted as speaking of the time of his conversion or his recognition of the Messiah, as the name Peter is interpreted (according to Bede, incorrectly) to mean "the one who recognizes" by writers such as Alexander of Hales commenting on John.[5] He adds on the same point that his brother, Andrew, who told him earlier that he had found the Messiah had already preceded him in that recognition, as we read in the first chapter of the Gospel of John.[6] Therefore Augustine himself understands the primacy among the others in the church as necessarily referring to the rulership and eminence which Peter received after the college of the apostles had been created when Christ said, "Thou art Peter."

252. From the above it is evident that this is why Simon was called Peter or Cephas. Jerome commenting on the Epistle to the Galatians says that the prince of the apostles is not called both Peter and Cephas with two different meanings because they mean the same thing. Peter in Greek and Latin is derived from *petra* [rock] and is the same thing as Cephas.[7] Bede says that Peter is not Hebrew since the letter "P" does not exist among the Hebrews.[8] Alexander of Hales in his *Postilla*

---

[3] PL 35, p. 1973.   [4] PL 35, p. 1444.   [5] PL 92, p. 22.
[6] John 1:40ff.   [7] PL 26, p. 366.
[8] PL 90, p. 141. The letter P is discussed by St. Jerome (PL 12, p. 892).

super Joannem says that Jerome says the same thing. And some say that Cephas is not Hebrew but Syrian. However this may be, in discussing the text, "Thou art Peter and upon this rock," like Augustine, Ambrose, and other doctors, we should hold that Peter is from *petra*, and thus *Petrus* is a Latin and not a Hebrew name. And this seems to be proven from the text of the first chapter of John because John puts down two Hebrew words directly above in the same chapter – namely, *Rabbi* and *Messiah*, and immediately adds a translation.[9] And so it seems that *Cephas* is either Syrian or Hebrew and *Petrus* its Latin or Greek translation and not the reverse; namely, that *Cephas* is Greek translated into Hebrew as *Petrus*.

253. And while I write this, one thing occurs to me that should be noted. The text of chapter 1 of [the Gospel of] John says that the name, Peter, is the translation of the name, Cephas. Therefore since *kephe* in Greek is translated as *caput* [head] in Latin, the name, Peter, should also have this meaning and not the other translations that St. Jerome gives in his work on Greek names. There is no doubt that John the Evangelist wrote his Gospel in Greek and thus made his own translation of the name, Peter, to show that the name that Christ gave to Simon fits that meaning. Therefore it would perhaps not be absurd to say that the [Latin] name *Petrus* comes from the Hebrew *bet-ros* and so among us is put down as "pet" because the Hebrew "bet" is expressed with a strong hard pronunciation of the first letter, "*b*," in the way that we pronounce "p." In this interpretation Peter would mean in Hebrew, "the head of the house." And this meaning fits the Gospel and the intention of Christ according to that Gospel and the explanation of the saints who say that Peter was constituted as head of the church or house by Christ. This is what is said in the chapter [c. 2] *Sacrosancta* of D. 22 where the term, "Cephas," is interpreted as "head," which would make Cephas a Greek word.[10]

254. But despite what is said in *Sacrosancta*, which is attributed to Anacletus, I think we should rather stay with the first doctors since I believe those letters of Anacletus are apocryphal, as I say below in the third book.[11] However I do not deny that a final point is to be taken into consideration: Peter is named first in the first chapter of the Acts

[9] John 1:38 and 1:41.

[10] As John 1:42 clearly states, *Cephas* is Hebrew for rock (*Petra* in Latin).

[11] Nevertheless, Anacletus' letters are cited in Book II, nos. 118, 140, and 261, as well as in Book III, nos. 307–309.

of the Apostles because he is the head, and as such he proposed that the commands of Christ be carried out which Christ had committed to him in particular as the first of the apostles and their head. Hence although all the apostles were rectors, pastors, and vicars of Christ, as is sung in the Preface of the feastday Mass of any of them, nevertheless in that pastorate, rectorship, and vicariate, the holy doctors affirm that Peter possessed the primacy by more abundant grace because the keys were promised and given to him as the representative of the whole church and his pastorate was commanded in the words, "Feed my sheep."[12]

255.   But since he had been given that pastorate chosen as the first and principal apostle among the others, immediately after the ascension of Christ Peter began to exercise command in every assembly of the faithful in the way that rulers are accustomed to do. Hence Peter first showed that he was the vicar of Christ by teaching and baptizing at Jerusalem as the first among the apostles, as appears in *Acts*, chapters 1, 2, and 3 and in *Luke*, chapter 6. Similarly in the same passages it is clear that Peter was the first bishop of Jerusalem because he did the things that someone in the rank of bishop does. And after that he was bishop of Antioch as appears in the second chapter of Galatians; then in Rome where he wrote his first epistle, as is evident from its conclusion which says, "The church which is in Babylon greets you."[13] And according to Jerome and Bede and all the interpreters whom I have read, that Babylon was Rome because it was the daughter of old Babylon. For Rome acted precisely as the monarchy of Babylon acted, as Paulus Orosius declares at length at the beginning of the seventh book of his *Histories*.[14] And the commentators on the Apocalypse often write that the kingdom of Babylon is that of Rome. But this is not on our subject.

256.   Although a certain Marsilius of Padua whose work I have seen after writing this volume seems to say in a certain place in the second part [of his book] that it can not be proved from the canon of the Bible that Peter was bishop of Rome, or that he even was at Rome,[15] suffice it for us to say that this is false on the basis of the aforesaid epistle of Peter, as the doctors explain. And none of the holy doctors up to this

---

[12] Acts 1:13 and John 21:17.
[13] 1 Peter 5:13.   [14] PL 31, pp. 1062ff.
[15] Marsilius, *The Defender of Peace*, D. 2, c. 16 (trans. Alan Gewirth), New York, II, 1956, pp. 241ff.

time has ever denied this. For instance Alypius, Augustine, Optatus of Milevis, St. Jerome and all the others who have given a list of the Roman pontiffs in their writings, begin with Peter. Optatus says in the second book of *Against Parmenianus* that there is no doubt that the Roman see goes back in unbroken succession to Peter who held the see there first, and that it is joined to Christ through him,[16] and I think that on this point no Catholic can disagree with the holy fathers whose writings are approved by the church. But approved doctors agree with what is said above. For example, in Book 1 of his work, *Against Jovinian*, when Jovinian says in opposition to virginity that the church was founded on Peter, not on John, St. Jerome says, "The church is founded on Peter although in another place it is founded on all the apostles and they all receive the keys of the kingdom of heaven and the strength of the church is confirmed equally in all. One, however, was chosen among the twelve so that by establishing a single head the possibility of schism might be removed. But why was not John chosen who was a virgin? Deference was given to age because Peter was older. Otherwise an adolescent – a mere boy – would have been placed over men who were adults. Also the Good Master who should have eliminated any possibility of contention among the disciples said to them, 'My peace I give unto you, my peace I leave unto you,' and 'whoever wants to be greater among you, let him be the least of all' so as not to provide a reason for envy of the young man whom he loved."[17] Note that this is the opinion of St Jerome whom we can not contradict.

From this we conclude that Peter was established by Christ as head of the apostles with authority over them – notwithstanding the fact that the church was equally founded on all the apostles. And when he [Jerome] writes to Pope Damasus concerning his faith he says that Peter's see was in Rome – "This is the faith" and below "Thou who holdest the faith and see of Peter."[18] To the same effect see Cyprian in [C.] 24 q. 1 [c. 18] *Loquitur*; Gregory in D. 50 [c. 53] *Considerandum*, and Ambrose in the same Distinction [c. 54] *Fidelior*; Clement in D. 80 [c. 2] *In illis*; Augustine in [C.] 2 q. 7 [c. 35] *Puto*. It

---

[16] Optatus of Milevis, *De schismate Donatistarum*, c. 2 (PL 11, p. 947).

[17] St. Jerome, *Contra Jovinianum*, 1, 26 (PL 23, pp. 258ff.).

[18] Gratian's *Decretum* attributed this to St. Jerome, but it comes from another collection (Kallen, *DCC*, p. 299).

is not necessary to quote their writings for the Catholic church has never dissented from this opinion.

257.   But the governing power that belongs to Peter does not consist in superiority in the power of binding and loosing [either] in a matter of penance or in the distribution of sacraments. There is no doubt on the latter point, and the earlier point set forth above is not to be doubted because the power of judging in spiritual matters is the same for all bishops as it was for all the apostles since it comes from Christ through the intermediary of the priest. Thus Jerome says on the passage in Matthew [ch.] 16, "Whatsoever you shall loose." "The other apostles indeed have the same power of judging since he said to them after the Resurrection, 'Receive ye the Holy Spirit.' "[19] And many passages are quoted above on the same point. Nor was Peter greater than the church by reason of his primacy because he was named by and for the church, as Augustine says in the place quoted above as well as Ambrose in D. 50 [c. 54] *Fidelior* and the other doctors referred to above. Therefore that supremacy of Peter was not a supremacy *over*, but *within*, the church. Hence although he was the spokesman and the head of the apostles and of the church and proposed actions in its name, as in the first chapter of the Acts, and spoke for it, as in Acts 2, he was no less subject to it as a member. Therefore he arose in the midst of the faithful and spoke with reverence for the church, and in Acts, chapter 8, allowed it to send him to Samaria. For in their ordination to that true life and truth [who is] Christ, the Lord and our head, all the faithful since they are sons of God by regeneration in Christ are only brothers because there is no master but Christ himself. See Matthew 23, "Do not call one another, Rabbi. For there is one who is your Master," Christ, and "you are all brothers." Hence in this respect, there is a brotherhood of the faithful in Christ, although by divine intention a superiority in grace continues within that brotherhood.

258.   Hence although Peter might have been the first apostle as explained above, that primacy did not contradict that brotherhood of the apostles in the church. For Peter was no more a son of God than any other holy apostle although he might have been given more abundant grace. And we should note the letter of Pope St. Gregory on

[19] St. Jerome, as quoted in the Ordinary Gloss to Matthew's Gospel.

this subject to Patriarch John of Constantinople in the Papal *Register* No. 214 which begins, *Eo tempore*. There he tries to show that no bishop possesses a power to rule in the church by virtue of which all members of the church are subject to him. Rather he says anyone who claims this is like Lucifer because he tries to place his throne or see above the stars of heaven, "For what are your brothers, all the bishops of the universal church, but stars of heaven. When with exaggerated language you desire to make yourself superior to them and to trample their name in the dust in comparison with your own, what are you saying but, 'I shall arise to heaven,' 'I shall exalt my throne over the stars of heaven?' " And below, "Certainly Peter, the first apostle, was a member of the holy and universal church, [and] Paul, Andrew, John, what else were they but the heads of individual communities? And all the members are under one head, Christ." And below, "No Roman Pontiff ever claimed for himself this rash title, universal bishop, lest if they seemed to claim a special honorific title for themselves as pontiffs, they might appear to deny it to their brethren."[20] And the same thing is said in Letter no. 211, written to Anastasius of Antioch, which begins, *Cum praedicator egregius* where he concludes that we are all one in our head, Christ, who is the pastor of all, and there is no man to whom all the members of Christ are subject and consequently there is no universal patriarch because, if it is allowed to say this, the honor of all the patriarchs is denied and no longer is any bishop found to be a true bishop etc.[21]

259.   But as for the members of the church themselves as separate individuals, we see that by more abundant grace the rulership which was necessary to avoid schism was handed over by Christ to Peter for the well-ordered government of the church, as we read in St. Jerome, so that as he was the first among the individual members, he might also be the servant and minister of all; [this is] because if Peter receives his name from *petra* on account of the church, and the church is nothing other than the union of the faithful in the church, rulership exists for the sake of the unity of the faithful in order to avoid schism. Therefore it is for the service and preservation of the unity of the faithful that rulership over individuals exists. From this the union of the faithful which we call the church, or the universal council of the Catholic church representing it, is superior to its minister and

---

[20] *Papal Register*, v, 44, and Krämer, "Die Brüsseler Handschriften" (see II, 21, no. 4).
[21] *Papal Register*, v, 41.

individual ruler. And so I understand the words of the Savior in this way – that he [Peter] should be the greatest of the apostles considered as individuals, but the minister of all of them collectively, as comprising the church. I do not mean by this that the presiding curate is absolved from a special ministerial care of each of those under him, but although he is the minister of each one he remains the superior of everyone in the exercise of his power of pastoral care – although as explained above, he is not superior to all collectively.

260. Also as touched on above: the power to rule is not rooted and established in the church by God in a coercive fashion but for the purpose of ministerial care. This is proved by a quotation from the first chapter of 2nd Corinthians: "For we do not lord it over you in your faith but we are your helpers," on which the Gloss by [St.] Ambrose says, "Faith does not permit domination and coercion since it is voluntary, not forced."[22] And Chrysostom in chapter 3 of the second book of *Dialogues* says, "But in the church, one should be converted to better things by agreement not by force."[23] And Augustine writing on the last chapter of the First Epistle to Timothy, beginning "Whoever are under the yoke" says, "It should be known that some have preached that freedom is common to all in Christ. This is true of spiritual freedom but not of physical freedom."[24] More quotations could be given, [but] it is sufficient to know that only one who comes of his own free will and not under compulsion is acceptable to Christ. Therefore in its basis from Christ all spiritual power is properly founded in freedom and not in coercion.

261. But because that rulership exists from God for the purpose of unity in order to prevent schism, unless an ecclesiastical ruler has some coercive power – although not the domination that princes exercise – unity can not be rightly preserved. For the rotten member and foot should be cut off and the eye that scandalizes torn out of the church if the body of the church is to be kept healthy. Therefore that coercion will not be like that which princes exercise because their way of ruling is by force on the body and over property. It will be a coercion based on the free subjection of all or a majority, and punishment will only be imposed when it works for the salvation of those punished. Therefore Pope Anacletus and others noted above say that

---

[22] 2 Corinthians 1:23.
[23] St. John Chrysostom, *De Sacerdotio*, II, 3 (PG 47, p. 634).
[24] St. Augustine in Gloss on 1 Timothy 6:1.

Christ established Peter as the head with the consent of the apostles.[25] And so the coercive power of a superior over his subjects is based on their election and consent. For those who before were completely free subject themselves to their ruler by election. Hence on this basis it is often said above that the coercive power of a ruler or a law comes from the approval of the subjects and derives its strength from the tacit or express consent of the community. Hence it is said although "all power is from above,"[26] whether coercive, domestic, restraining or commanding, for it to operate externally to restrain or compel free Christian men proper procedure requires their free subjection since they are not constrained by Christian or natural law beyond the limits of freedom.

262. In this way, I attempted above to argue further that every ecclesiastical or spiritual rulership was established by Christ through the mediation of human consent. For legitimate superiors are those established by the consent of their subjects. We are obliged to obey them because of having given them our consent as established in authority by men from among men. But it is quite clear from this that on this basis – which I believe to be true – unless it appeared by some miracle or sign that God wished someone to rule before he had obtained the consent of the faithful (in which case all Christians would be obliged to obey the divine command), the Roman pontiff can still not be proved to be the ruler of the church for all times. For even if Peter definitely had that rulership, we do not read in the sacred writings that therefore the Roman pontiff, his successor – or the [patriarchs] of Antioch or Jerusalem since they are also his successors –, has had or should have it, except with the aforesaid common consent of the church similar to that of the apostles to Peter. Hence although the pontiff in Rome, whether because it was the see of Peter or as the principal city among the other bishoprics in the world, is venerated as the most illustrious and distinguished authority in that great city and the occupant of the great see of Peter, yet unless he had the elective consent to their subordination from the representatives of all the others I would not believe that he was the leader or ruler or judge of all the others. Therefore if, for instance, the Archbishop of Trier were elected as ruler and head by the church gathered together, he would more properly be the successor of Peter as ruler

---

[25] See no. 254, where the letters of Anacletus are declared to be apocryphal.
[26] Romans 13:1.

than the bishop of Rome – although we should believe that the Roman pontiff will never lose the see of Peter and the rulership in this way. But succession in a geographical location does not argue to succession in rule, as is demonstrated by the cases of Antioch and Jerusalem, and that rulership would not cease in the church even if the episcopal see of the city of Rome ceased to exist. I have spoken on this at greater length above.

263. And it is evident that the church has the power freely to choose its head, since it has received from Christ everything it needs for its survival. Prelates have all power of binding and loosing because they have been sent by Christ as Christ was sent by the Father as is evident from the words of Christ in the 20th chapter of John, "As the Father hath sent me," etc. Thus it appears that as Christ was the true Son of God, so the church which is the Mystical body of Christ has a similar mission from Christ. Hence the church has the same missionary power as Christ.

264. And so I adhere to the conclusion that the primacy in the church is established in its reality by Christ through the church for the purpose of church unity and is intended by God as a ministry for its service. And in my judgment the arguments on the one side that coercive rulership in the church comes only from God, and on the other side that it exists only by the election and consent of men and the church, are correctly harmonized in this intermediate position.

265. But I assert none of my ideas so firmly that I would not say that one should accept those of more learned men. For Ambrose says, "One's own writings deceive. They are heard with delight like ill-formed offspring, and thus his shameless words please their author," as he writes in the 33rd letter to Sabinus.[27] Nevertheless I think that this opinion is less offensive to the church and therefore should be considered as more true than those of Marsilius of Padua in his book, *The Defender of Peace* [*Defensor Pacis*], since he can only defend his opinion on the basis of the text of St. Augustine in D. 9 [c. 5] *Ego solis*, and he answers all arguments to the contrary by saying that we are not bound to accept the authority of the doctors except insofar as they are based on the canon of the Bible. This is a pernicious opinion after the church has approved [the writings of] the doctors as acceptable. Hence we should abandon such presumption and follow the texts in

[27] PL 16, p. 1195.

D. 12 [D. 11] [c. 5] *Ecclesiasticarum* and other things said there. As noted above the arguments of Marsilius [on the lack of biblical foundation for papal primacy] are not true, for when the doctors speak of the primacy of Peter they base their discussion on the words of Christ that are contained in the canon of the Bible and not on other historical accounts concerning Peter – although these too should not be denied, for the saints believed that they were true, as letter 76 of Ambrose to Auxentius concerning the handing over of churches, proves.[28]

266. And consequently since all disorder comes from the fact that superiors do not exercise their power for the purpose for which their pastoral rule was established and their subjects do not loyally obey their superiors as their status demands, we have felt obliged to speak of the canonical rules by which the holy fathers maintained the concordance between rulers and their subjects. Therefore we had first to discuss the council of the Catholic church which has supreme authority by consent of all to establish and regulate whatever leads to salvation; then we spoke of other particular councils, and after that of the reforming canons which have now been issued so that this holy Council of Basel may proceed to follow the footsteps of the fathers in what it does, modeling itself on the teaching of the holy fathers and the statutes of the sacred councils.

267. And this is the comprehensive summary of Books I and II, subject to any correction, delivered in writing, however confused and rough, for the sole purpose of providing an incentive for further study by those concerned.

End of Book II

[28] PL 16, p. 1053.

BOOK III

268. If anyone should care to trace out from the beginning the foundations that are both necessary and useful for our purpose, he should look to the principles on which they are based – those of Aristotle, Plato, Cicero, and all the other philosophers who have written about well-ordered political, economic, and monarchic regimes.[1] Natural laws precede all human considerations and provide the principles for them all. First, nature intends every kind of animal to preserve its physical existence and its life, to avoid what would be harmful and to secure what is necessary to it, as Cicero concludes in the first book, third [fourth] chapter of *De officiis*.[2] For the first requirement of essence is that it exist. Therefore for any essence to exist, it possesses inborn faculties designed for this purpose—instinct, appetite, and reason. Hence it happens in different ways in nature that various means are implanted by natural instinct for the purpose of existence and self preservation. On this basis Aristotle concludes in the last chapter of the seventh book of the *Politics* that every art and discipline exists to supply what nature lacks.[3]

269. But from the beginning men have been endowed with reason which distinguishes them from animals. They know because of the exercise of their reason that association and sharing are most useful – indeed necessary for their self-preservation and to achieve the purpose of human existence. Therefore by natural instinct they have joined together and built villages and cities in which to live together. And if men had not established rules to preserve peace, the corrupt

---

[1] The classical authors cited in the preface are taken without acknowledgment from Marsilius of Padua, *Defender of Peace* (1324), a work condemned by the church for its attacks on the pope, but widely read – see Paul E. Sigmund, "The Unacknowledged Influence of Marsilius of Padua on xvth Century Conciliarism," *Journal of the History of Ideas*, 23, 3 (1962), pp. 392–402.

[2] Cf. Marsilius, *Defender*, I, 4, 2.

[3] Marsilius, *Defender*, I, 5, 4; I, 7, 2. Marsilius uses a different order of the books of Aristotle's *Politics* than in modern editions.

desires of many would have prevented this union from improving human life. For this reason cities arose in which the citizens united and adopted laws with the common assent of all to preserve unity and harmony, and they established guardians of all these laws with the power necessary to provide for the public good.[4]

270. It was clear that by a marvelous and beneficent divine law infused in all men, they knew that associating together would be most beneficial to them and that social life would be maintained by laws adopted with the common consent of all – or at least with the consent of the wise and illustrious and the agreement of the others.[5] For just as it is asserted in the preceding Book that according to St. Cyprian Christ has promised that the majority of the priesthood will not depart from the true law,[6] so also when by common consent matters are discussed that concern the preservation of the commonwealth, the majority of the populace, citizens or illustrious men will not depart from the right way appropriate to the time. Otherwise it would happen that a natural appetite would be frustrated in many cases which is considered most unfitting by the philosophers. For we see that man is a political and civic animal naturally inclined to civilized life. Hence the weightier part ought to act for the remainder of the polity, as Aristotle concludes in the first chapter of Book I of the *Politics*.[7]

271. But Almighty God has assigned a certain natural servitude to the ignorant and stupid so that they readily trust the wise to help them to preserve themselves, as appears in the eighth letter of Ambrose after the quotation from Calanus' letter to Alexander, "The unwise man is like a farm; the man who lacks sense is like a vine." "The pruned vine brings forth fruit; cut back, it flourishes; neglected it grows wild."[8]

272. On this subject Ambrose writes most elegantly in his seventh letter, immediately above, "With profound argument philosophers have concluded that the wise man is free and the stupid man a slave. But long before, David said, 'The fool is changeable as the moon.'"[9]

---

[4] The entire paragraph is a summary of Marsilius, *Defender*, I, 3, 3.

[5] Marsilius, *Defender*, I, 9, 10; I, 13, 1ff.

[6] Book II, 4, no. 79. See also Book I, 8, no. 43.

[7] The term "weightier part," is a clear sign of the influence of Marsilius, rather than of Aristotle who simply refers to a "stronger part." See Marsilius, *Defender*, I, 13, 2 and Aristotle's *Politics*, IV, 12, 1.

[8] Marsilius, *Defender*, II, 13, 1; St. Ambrose, *Ad Simplicianum* (PL 16, p. 1141).

[9] Ecclesiasticus 27:11 (not Psalms of David).

The wise man is not overcome by fear; he is not changed by power; not seduced by prosperity nor overwhelmed in adversity. Where there is wisdom, there is courage of spirit, perseverance, and fortitude. For the wise man is constant in spirit; he is not affected by alterations in fortune. He is not changeable as a child nor blown about by every wind of doctrine." And further, "Noah, when he had heard that his son, Ham, had foolishly laughed at his father's nakedness, cursed him saying, 'Cursed be Ham: he shall be a household slave to his brethren.' And he made his brothers masters over him for they had wisely concluded that they should have respect for their father's age. Did not Jacob, a fount of all learning, who was preferred to his older brother because of his wisdom, demonstrate his abundant powers of argument to all? His devoted father was torn between his two sons in fatherly affection but he finally decided between them – since affection acts out of natural necessity but decisions are made on the basis of merit – and gave the one his favor and the other his pity – favoring the wise one and pitying the foolish one because he could not rise up by his own efforts and direct himself to virtue by his own efforts. He blessed him calling on him to serve his brother and be his slave, thus demonstrating that ignorance is worse than slavery, that he was to be a slave as a remedy for his ignorance because the foolish man can not control himself and unless he had someone to direct him he would fail in his efforts. Therefore his loving father deliberately made him a slave of his brother so that he would be guided by his counsel. And so certain wise men act as guides for the unthinking people. They control the ignorance of the people by their own force and rule them through the imposition of their power which they use to compel the unwilling to obey those who are wiser and to submit to the laws. Therefore he put a yoke on the foolish one as if he were a wild animal and since he had said he should live by the sword, he took away his liberty so that he would not perish in his recklessness. He placed his brother over him so that subject to his moderating influence he might be converted. Servitude can be by choice – it is less worthy if by compulsion and better if freely chosen, since good is more meritorious when performed freely rather than out of necessity. Therefore first he placed the yoke of necessity on him, then he also gave him the blessing of a voluntary subjection. For nature does not make a slave, but ignorance, nor does manumission make one free, but learning. Therefore Esau was born free and became a slave and

Joseph who was sold into slavery was chosen to exercise power over those who had bought him."[10]

273. And after Ambrose elegantly describes the freedom of the wise man, how law is only imposed on the ignorant, and how because of sin he is compelled by fear of punishment to obey the law, he adds, "Therefore the sinner is a slave of fear, a slave of desire, a slave of avarice, a slave of lust, a slave of malice, a slave of anger. Though he seems to himself in this way to be free, he is more a slave than if he were subjected to tyrants. For those who live by law are free. But true law is righteousness. True law is not carved on tablets nor cut in bronze but stamped on the mind and imprinted on the senses. Since the wise man is not under the law he is a law unto himself, carrying the work of the law in his heart, inscribed in him with the pen of nature."[11]

274. The most excellent and learned Ambrose writes these and other important words in that letter and the one which follows. From this one thing is to be kept in mind – that although the ignorant could not govern themselves and so became slaves of the wise out of necessity, the subjection based on that necessity which resulted from that need was voluntary.

275. And thus by a certain natural instinct, the rule of the wise and the subjection of the ignorant is harmonized through common laws that have the wise as their special authors, protectors, and executors, and the concurrent agreement of all the others in voluntary subjection. And when a government is so organized, then "it is impossible for an aristocracy, that is a city governed according to virtue" by the wise with the consent of the others for the common good, "not to be well ordered," as Aristotle says in Book IV, chapter 7 [8] of the *Politics*.[12]

276. Legislation ought to be adopted by all those who are to be bound by it or by a majority of their representatives because it should benefit the common good and what touches all should be approved by all and the definition of the common good only comes from the consent of all or of a majority. There can be no excuse for not obeying the law when everyone has imposed the law on himself. "It is not good to adopt good laws and then not obey them," as Aristotle says in Book

[10] PL 16, pp. 1130–1132.   [11] PL 16, p. 1138.

[12] Marsilius, *Defender*, I, 13, 2. Aristotle (in *Politics*, III, 7) said nothing about consent as a prerequisite for aristocracy. That requirement was added by Marsilius.

IV, chapter 7 [8] of the *Politics*. And it is also the duty of those who adopt the laws to interpret them. It is necessary for a kingdom to be governed by laws, since men are subject to the passions of love and hate.[13]

277.   Therefore it is better for a commonwealth to be ruled by laws than by the best of men, as Aristotle concludes when he discusses this in Book III, chapter 9 [15] of the *Politics*, as well as in Book I, chapter 1 of the *Rhetoric*. For where laws do not rule, there is no polity, as is stated in Book IV, chapter 4, of the *Politics*. But laws ought to be adopted with great care and prudence based on long experience, as is said in Book II, chapter 2 [5] of the *Politics*.

278.   Rulers should act to observe the laws and should rule in accordance with those laws as is said in Book III, chapter 6 [11] of the *Politics*, for law is "an eye from many eyes" and "reason free from passion" as is said in Book III, chapter 9 [15] of the *Politics*. Rulers should not change laws made by the majority which have been accepted by everyone.[14]

279.   While the prince should rule according to the laws, yet since he may decide matters about which nothing is said clearly in the laws, as appears in Book III, chapter 6 [11] of the *Politics*, he should be prudent – as is said in Book III, chapter 2 [4] of the *Politics*, and in Book IV [v, ch. 6] of the *Ethics* on justice – and exercise equity [*epikeizare*] correctly in accordance with the spirit of the law where it is not specific about particulars. And then every form of government whether it is a monarchy exercised by one man, or an aristocracy exercised by several wise men, or a polity by all at the same time and each one according to his rank, when it tends to the common good in accordance with the will of the subject is called temperate or just, as is stated by Aristotle in Books III and IV of the *Politics*. But if it tends to the particular good of the ruler and is contrary to the will of the subjects, it is intemperate, as is stated in Book III, chapter 5 [chs. 7–8] of the *Politics*. And thus three types of government arise opposite to the temperate ones mentioned above, tyranny, oligarchy, and democracy. And the history books are filled with these intemperate tyrannical, oligarchic, and democratic governments.[15]

---

[13] Marsilius, *Defender*, I, 12.
[14] Marsilius, *Defender*, I, 11. (The source of all the references to Aristotle in nos. 277 and 278).
[15] Marsilius, *Defender*, I, 15.

280.   For Nimrod began to be a sturdy hunter immediately after the Flood,[16] and it was Ninus, the first king of the Assyrians and the son of Belus, who first took arms because he desired to rule. After him came Semiramis, his wife, who, the historians say, expelled from the kingdom Trebeta, her stepson, the son of Ninus by another Chaldean wife because she was in love with him – which he properly rejected because she was his stepmother. She pursued him and he went to Europe and finally chose a dwelling place in a certain pleasant field with the Moselle flowing by – Ausonius has composed a most admirable poem on the name of this river – and there 42 years after the birth of Abraham he founded our city of Trier which is named after him [*Treberica*] and the ancient histories say it was the first city to be founded in Europe.[17] But this is beside the point.

281.   But it would be superfluous to narrate in this work what is known to all about temperate governments, how Moses and Aaron and Eleazar, and in the Roman commonwealth, first the kings then the senate and consuls and also the emperors, were established by voluntary consent for the common good.[18]

282.   There are many reasons why there should only be one ruler, even if the government is made up of several leading men united in agreement. Otherwise confusion would arise when several compete in ruling and good order would be destroyed when the subjects do not know whom to obey. It is bad to have many rulers, for there should be one to whom a final appeal can be made with certainty. But every monarchical or aristocratic regime, since those regimes must be established over willing subjects, should be established by election, see Book III, chapter 8 [14] of the *Politics*.[19]

283.   Among all the types of tempered regimes monarchy is the best. But among the sub-types of this tempered regime, a monarchy that is established by consent without agreeing on the succession is to be preferred to one that is established by an agreement to a monarch and

[16] Genesis 10:8–9.

[17] In fact Trier (French – Trèves) was named after the Treveri, the tribe that lived between the Moselle river and the Ardennes. Cusanus' sources are the *Gesta Trevirorum*, a medieval history of Trier (printed in *MGSS*, VIII, p. 130), and Otto of Freysing, *Chronica*, I, 6–8 (Engl. trans. Charles C. Mierow, *The Two Cities: A Chronicle of Universal History*, New York, 1928). The poem is Ausonius, *Mosella*, about the river on which both Trier and Kues are located.

[18] Marsilius, *Defender*, I, 9, 2.

[19] Marsilius, *Defender*, I, 17, 2 and I, 9, 4.

his successors. In the latter type, many things occur that are often harmful to the commonwealth. For although illustrious, wise, and noble men, we read, often have been elected as kings together with their posterity to the sometime benefit of the commonwealth, nevertheless, because as in the case of a fertile field the initial offspring of such men are of less quality than their parents' natures and their successors are still less able, the illustrious qualities of the parents finally die out, as Aristotle says in Book II, chapter 24 [15] of the *Rhetoric*. Hence although there are many good reasons for a hereditary monarchy, if the best man is always to rule the commonwealth by the will of all for the public good, the best method is to have a new election, by all or a majority or at least by those nobles who represent everyone with their consent.[20]

284. This seems to be the opinion of Aristotle in the *Politics*, Book I, chapter 9 [12] and Book II, chapter 8 [11], and Book III, chapter 2 [4] and Book VII, chapters 9 [III, 15] and 12 [14]. It is the duty of the ruler to do nothing contrary to the laws. Indeed he ought to be subject to them, and their teaching should give life to the commonwealth as the heart does to the body. He should inflict punishment in accordance with the law in cases of serious crimes which give scandal to the commonwealth, although not for petty offenses or his rule will be the object of contempt. And so the prince, acting as its heart, must watch over the commonwealth continuously and assure the strictest observance of the laws. He should follow the laws, as Aristotle says in Book VII, chapter 6 [8] of the *Politics*, and for his kingdom to be more lasting he should not exercise his sovereign power frequently. Aristotle declares in the fifth book of the *Politics* [ch. 11] that Theopompus because he wished to make his kingdom last longer, rarely used his sovereign power and conformed to the laws and kept the love of the people.[21]

285. Three things are necessary for a ruler: First, devotion to the established constitutional order; second, power to carry out the chief tasks of government; and third, virtue and justice, as is said in Book V, chapter 4 [9] of the *Politics*. And "virtue" means the prudence which is the mistress of the virtues – see the last chapter of Book VI of the *Ethics*. But power is necessary in order to execute judicial [civil] sentences against the rebellious by coercive force. Hence the ruler

---

[20] Marsilius, *Defender*, I, 9, 9; I, 16, 11–17.
[21] Marsilius, *Defender*, I, 16, 13; I, 18, 2–5; I, 15, 6.

should have an instrument appropriate for this – a well-equipped army. For Aristotle says in Book VII, chapter 6 [8] of the *Politics*, "It is necessary for those who are in association to have arms because of those who disobey the government," and that power should be so great "that it is stronger than that of any individuals whether one or several together but weaker than the whole" – this is said in Book III, chapter 9 [15] of the *Politics*. The army should be of intermediate size so that it does not appear to be tempted to dominate the monarch for its own advantage but nevertheless is powerful enough to overcome several or many rebels.[22]

286. The punishment which the prince is obliged to impose should be compared to a medicinal remedy for the commonwealth as Aristotle teaches in Book III [II], chapter 3 [2] of the *Ethics*. The ruler should take special care to avoid great inequality among his subjects. Once balance is lost, the polity is destroyed by the disproportionate increase of some. "The body is composed of many parts which should grow in due proportion for" health and "symmetry to remain – if this is not done the body will be destroyed if it increases disproportionately, not only in quantity but also in quality," as Aristotle declares in Book V, chapter 2 [3] of the *Politics*, and in Book III, chapter 7 [chs. 12–13] of the same work.[23]

287. And so the ruler must exercise his power with great circumspection, prudence, and experience in order usefully to nurse the ailing commonwealth with the medicinal punishments that are appropriate to the time and place as the situation demands. For example Aurelius Augustine tells us in his letter to Volusian that Vindicianus, an expert doctor, cured a young man of a certain illness by using a medicine intended for the young. After a time the young man grew older and fell ill with the same disease. He used the same medicine on his own which had restored him to health earlier but he did not improve. He asked Vindicianus the reason and he answered – "It did not cure you because Vindicianus did not prescribe it." When he was asked afterwards why he gave this reason for the fact that the medicine was ineffective, he said, "I said the right thing. If I had administered it, it would have helped him. But I would not have given an older man the same amount that I gave him earlier when he was young."[24] With this example Augustine teaches us that changes are

---

[22] Marsilius, *Defender*, I, 14, 8–10.   [23] Marsilius, *Defender*, I, 15, 10–11.
[24] Augustine, *Ad Marcellinum*, letter no. 138 (PL 33, p. 526).

made in divine and human laws in accordance with the time for the same purpose.

288. Venerable Sedulius [Scotus] in the tenth chapter of his little work, *De Rectoribus Christianis* [*On Christian Rulers*], describes the principal things that are necessary for a king in these lines –

No structure keeps a fixed form for all time,
If it does not rest on firm foundations,
Neither can temples resplendent with light survive,
Nor the hall of kings remain solid without these.
The commonwealth asks of a gracious God,
That it stand on the true foundations of just rule.
The first supporting column shines with the brilliant gleam of
    truth,
And the second is properly an enduring government.
The third is to give generous rewards to merit,
And the fourth to speak sweet soothing words.
The fifth is to repress and attack evildoers with admirable zeal,
And the sixth one is strong to celebrate the good.
The seventh is to levy taxes with moderation on the people,
But the eighth controls the scales of justice.
The commonwealth endowed with these solid foundations shines
    forth,
As the mount of Zion, and remains strong with these.[25]

289. More fine words by wise men could be quoted here if it were our purpose to discuss government at length. But besides what is said above, the most important requirement is that every ruler who is a faithful Christian should model himself on the figure of Christ whom he represents and succeeds. And so let him look to Christ who is truth itself. And let him consider first that he [Christ] is Lord and master, God and man, and thus every government is composed of human and divine elements. For all power is ordained of God – Romans 13. And Augustine is correct when he writes on the passage in chapter 19 of the Gospel of John, "Thou wouldst not have any power over me, if it were not given from above," that the power of Pilate over Christ also came from God.[26]

290. So also St. Bernard writing to the Archbishop of Sens says, "Christ declares that the power of the Roman ruler over him is

[25] Sedulius Scotus, *On Christian Rulers and the Poems*, tr. Edward G. Doyle, Binghamton, N.Y., 1983, p. 68.
[26] PL 35, pp. 1942ff.

ordained of heaven."[27] Therefore all rulership is sacred and spiritual and comes from God. Rulership also comes from man, just as Christ was the true son of the Virgin Mary. Hence Christ was born, God and man, of the uncorrupted and unstained Virgin by her own free consent when she said, "Be it done unto me according to thy word."[28] On this model true rule over the one uncorrupted church or congregation of men should result from the purest consent, not from violence, or ambition, or criminal simony, but from the purity with which Christ deigned to come into the world out of love for the salvation of the people. And when anyone is chosen and called by Christ the true gate, to be a ruler and accepts the example of Christ in humility and follows as prince in the footsteps of Christ, the commonwealth will necessarily be governed in the best way and the name of the ruler will be remembered forever. For Christ was under the law. He came not to destroy the law but to fulfill it, meek and humble of heart, a most gentle healer. And it is only necessary for the ruler to follow in his footsteps for then he walks in the light of truth and will attain eternal life.[29]

291. These words are sufficient now for this, since our principal intent in this work is directed toward determining the "Catholic Concordance." Keeping to that principal purpose, let us investigate in order the things related to this.

[27] PL 182, p. 832. The references to Augustine and Bernard are taken from Marsilius, *Defender*, II, 4, 12.
[28] Luke 1:38.
[29] Matthew 5:17 and 11:29; John 1:9 and 3:19ff.

INTRODUCTION

Thirdly, by way of a preamble, we should praise the outstanding qualities of our great and most pious Sigismund, here present, who has been crowned Emperor by the will of God. Like Augustus who refused the title of "lord" and like [the Byzantine Emperor] Basil whose virtues will be described later in his humility, he will forgive me if in my uncultivated style (which although it cannot explain trivial things is devoted to great, indeed enormous matters, without offering a true argument for the future where there has already been clarity) I sing the praises of the unconquerable living Caesar who rules over me, his humble servant. To presume to praise or please any prince while he is alive lends little credibility, especially when it comes from someone like myself of humble condition.

And now, turning to our subject, we will direct our attention to the holy empire which is established among the Germans – concerning its power, preservation, and the concordance through which it is united with the holy priesthood in a Catholic way. And so, to begin this difficult subject, we should inquire about the structure of this holy empire, from whom it depends, and how it came to be among the Germans. It is appropriate therefore to investigate first:

CHAPTER I

THE BASIS OF ALL LEGISLATION AND RULERSHIP AND ESPECIALLY THAT OF MONARCHS AND HOW IT IS STRENGTHENED. THE CHAPTER SHOWS THAT THE EMPEROR IS HEAD AND RULER OF ALL IN THE CORPORAL HIERARCHY, LIKE THE POPE IN THE SPIRITUAL HIERARCHY.

292. The preceding collection has resolved many disputed questions; it has demonstrated sufficiently that concord gives the greatest force to the ecclesiastical order; and it has noted this among the things that it has recommended as worth remembering. In particular [it has said] that the church of Christ is made up of sacraments, priesthood, and the faithful. The sacraments correspond to the spirit, the priesthood to the soul, and the rest of the faithful to the body, linked in harmony in the one church as a composite unit to the Mystical Body of the one Christ.[1] Certain things have already been said above about the priesthood. In accordance with our intention, we will now speak of the body [of the faithful] which is organized in a graded hierarchical order up to the one Ruler of all, as anyone can easily understand, from the lowest of the simple laity who are like the

[1] See Book I, no. 47.

feet, through the governors, counts, marquesses, dukes, and kings, up to the emperor as the head.

293. All things that come from God, are necessarily arranged in proper order. And so in this order in the Catholic church, there is one lord over the world who rules over the others in the fullness of power. He is normally said to be the equivalent in the temporal hierarchy of the Roman pontiff in the priestly hierarchy, always keeping in mind the difference between spirituals and temporals. I do not intend to go into detail regarding the similarities and differences in kind between the two powers, but I refer anyone concerned with this question to what is written above, and to this basic principle: he should recognize that His Imperial Majesty has the same legal power over all those subject to the empire that the Roman patriarch has over the bishops subject to the Roman church. And as the Roman patriarch is first among all the patriarchs, so the king of the Romans is first among all the kings. But compare the dukes to the archbishops, the counts to the bishops, and proceed with the rest as does the quotation from Leo IX that is contained at a certain point above.[2]

[2] See Book I, nos. 19–20.

CHAPTER II

THE PROPERLY ORDERED POWER OF THE WESTERN
EMPEROR DOES NOT DEPEND ON THE POPE
BECAUSE OF A GIFT BY CONSTANTINE, AND THAT
FAMOUS DONATION IS APOCRYPHAL AS ARE
CERTAIN OTHER DOCUMENTS AS WELL. THE TRUE
HISTORIES OF PEPIN AND CHARLEMAGNE ARE
BRIEFLY ADDED IN ORDER TO DEMONSTRATE HOW
THE ROMAN CHURCH FIRST ACQUIRED TEMPORAL
POWER.

294. The basic point that should be established first is that the holy empire itself comes from God. Next we ask whether or not it depends directly from him, and after this where it is located today, whether it was actually transferred by the pope from the Greeks to the Germans

as represented by Charlemagne, and what power is exercised by the imperial electors. Since these questions have been treated at length in a variety of ways by many learned men in recent times, I would have preferred to remain silent. But there is one thing that I cannot pass over. Nearly everyone believes that there is no doubt that Emperor Constantine gave the Western Empire to the Roman pontiff Sylvester and his successors in perpetuity, and that therefore even if the argument about the need for a single ruler – namely, that having two heads would be opposed to good order – were not convincing, it is evident that every emperor in the West must in justice recognize that his empire depends on the pope.[1]

295. I have investigated this matter as far as I could, assuming that there was no doubt that Constantine had the power to make such a donation, although this question has not yet been resolved and probably never will be. But in fact I wonder very much if it actually took place in this way since it does not appear in authentic books or approved histories. I have collected all the histories that I could find, the acts of the emperors and Roman pontiffs, the histories by St. Jerome who was very careful to include everything, those of Augustine, Ambrose, and the works of other learned men; I have reviewed the acts of the holy councils which took place after Nicaea and I find no confirmation of what is said about that donation.

296. Pope St. Damasus is supposed to have recorded the acts and actions of his predecessors at the suggestion of blessed Jerome, and in his work the things that are usually said about Pope Sylvester do not appear.[2] In some of the histories we read that Constantine was baptized by Sylvester and that the emperor magnificently decorated the three churches of St. John, St. Peter, and St. Paul and gave them large annual incomes from different pieces of land in various provinces and islands for the support of the lamps, balsam, and incense and candles – all of which you will find specifically mentioned in the *Liber Pontificalis*.[3] But nothing at all appears there concerning a grant of temporal dominion or the donation of the Western Empire. It is true that after Aistulfus, the king of the Lombards, occupied the

---

[1] Nicholas was the first to appeal to historical sources to disprove the authenticity of the Donation. Lorenzo Valla's more famous disproof seven years later was based on style and vocabulary. The reference to the adverse effects of two heads is probably from Pope Boniface VIII's Bull, *Unam sanctam* (1302).

[2] PL 13, p. 1441.

[3] *Liber pontificalis* (ed. L. Duchesne), XXXII, pp. 170ff.

Exarchate of Ravenna and many other places and Pope Stephen II, a Roman by birth whose father's name was Constantine, sent numerous legates to Aistulfus and asked him to return these territories to the empire and Aistulfus was unwilling to do so, Stephen visited Pepin and anointed him and his two sons as kings. Along with Stephen there was a representative of the emperor and they secured Pepin's agreement to persuade Aistulfus to give back the lands to the empire. Pepin sent a request to him but without success. Therefore when he could not obtain the return of the lands from Aistulfus in this way, he promised Stephen that he would take them from him by force and give them to the see of St. Peter. When he had heard this, the representative of the emperor went back [to Constantinople]. Pepin carried out his promise. And the form of this gift is contained in the acts of the aforesaid Stephen, along with the specific names of all the territories.[4]

297. Pope Zacharias transferred the rulership over the kingdom of France to Pepin after King Louis had been deposed, which one can read in [C.] 15 q. 6 [c. 3] *Alius* and in the gloss on the chapter *Venerabilem* [c. 34 of *Decretals* 1 6]. I think that this was why Pepin was favorably disposed to the Apostolic See. After this in the time of [Pope] Hadrian, King Desiderius again took those cities and some others. Pope Hadrian sent numerous legates to him to seek the restoration of the rights of [the see of] St. Peter but he could not obtain it. Then, at Hadrian's request Charlemagne reconquered the lands and gave them back to [the see of] St. Peter in a solemn ceremony which is contained in the Acts of Pope Hadrian.[5] From this it is clear that Constantine did not give the pope the [temporal] rule over the Exarchate of Ravenna, the city of Rome, and the West.

298. Hence we always read that the emperors up to that time and earlier had full legal rights over Rome, Ravenna, and the March along with the other territories in the West. The text, D. 96 [c. 1] *Bene quidem* proves this when it speaks of a patrician appointed in the name of King Odoacer etc.: see also D. 63 [c. 21] *Agatho*; D. 96 [c. 6] *Cum ad verum* and similar passages.

299. And we read that the Roman pontiffs acknowledged the emperors as their overlords. For Pope Agatho writes to the Emperor Constantine who was emperor many years after Constantine I and

---

[4] *Liber pontificalis*, pp. 440, 448, 452ff.
[5] *Liber pontificalis*, pp. 492ff.

called the Sixth Council, that the city of Rome was the "servant city" of that emperor.[6] And Pope Boniface I says to Emperor Honorius that as pope he is to rule the priesthood of the Roman church but the emperor rules over human affairs. And at the end he calls Rome "the city of His Majesty." This text appears in D. 97 [c. 1] *Ecclesiae*. In conclusion, I have never read anything anywhere which contradicts the fact that the emperor remained in possession of the places listed above until the time of Pepin.

300.   And I have not read that any Roman pontiff claimed any legal right for [the see of] St. Peter over those areas up to the time of [Pope] Stephen II. I believe that this is true despite the famous opinion to the contrary which appears in the addition, *Constantinus*, appended to D. 96 [c. 14], because if this section had not been apocryphal, Gratian would undoubtedly have found it in the old manuscripts and collections of the canons. And because he did not find it, he did not include it. Hence whoever added it later inserted that invented story in this way as an additional title [*Palea*], in the same way that many other extracts from apocryphal works appear.

301.   Also I have found this story in full in a certain book which contains much more than the passage in the selection in the *Decretum*, and examining it carefully, I have found clear evidence in the story itself that it was invented and is false, which it would be too long and unnecessary to insert here now.

302.   It is also to be noted that the text [c. 14] *Constantinus* of D. 96 is taken from the legend of St. Sylvester and the one who put it into the *Decretum* bases the authority of that text upon the approval of Pope Gelasius in his synod. I ask, does Gelasius' reference in D. 15 [c. 3] *Sancta Romana* seem to indicate approval? The passage is not persuasive since it says that the author of the text is unknown but that it is read by Catholics and therefore it may be read. Anyone can see what kind of approval that is.

303.   For there are many histories of St. Sylvester: one in which this [the Donation] does not appear which St. Damasus includes, another whose author is unknown which the text does not say is true but only that it may be read, and it does not say that the Donation is contained in it. Also the ancient decrees only have the text up to the passage, *Item decreta Romanorum pontificorum* inclusive, and thus that paragraph

---

[6] Mansi 11, p. 291.

from the history of [St.] Sylvester is not found in those books. Also the Fifth Universal Council which listed the books of all the doctors and the writings which were approved, made no mention of those histories nor did the synod of Pope Martin which was held against Pyrrhus and Sergius who said that there was one will in Christ, when it confirmed the approved writings, as I have seen myself.[7] Neither does anyone else that I have ever seen who is approved or named as true.

304. I have read in the *Histories* of Vincent [of Beauvais], at the end of Book XXIV that, according to St. Jerome, Constantine cruelly killed his wife Fausta and his son Crispus, and, after being baptized at the end of his life by Eusebius, the bishop of Nicomedia, fell into the Arian heresy. And from this time, says Jerome, the pillaging of churches and discord in the whole world have continued down to the present time. These things clearly contradict the book of the Acts of Sylvester which Vincent says was translated from Greek by someone whose name he does not know, as appears in chapter 90 of the same book.[8] Who would not rather believe Jerome who is approved than the writings of an unknown author that are called apocryphal when the author is not known?

305. Also the text that is ascribed to Pope Miltiades which appears in D. 21 q. 1 [c. 15] *Futuram* and seems to be somewhat opposed to this statement is not that of Pope Miltiades according to a certain gloss. The truth of the matter is that Miltiades preceded Sylvester as is clear from the list of Roman pontiffs. And if Constantine was baptized by Sylvester as is usually claimed, then it is evident that the title of that text is wrong when it speaks of the baptism of Constantine. And also if that were a text of Miltiades, there would still be no argument on that basis against what has been said above, since it only says that Constantine departed for Rome, the seat of the Empire, and granted it to Peter and his successors, that is, that the papal see would now be where the imperial seat had been – and no one denies this.

306. And it is true that Constantine was emperor at the time of Pope Miltiades and was a Christian then, as Augustine says in many places and especially in his letter to Glorius, Elusius, Felicius, Grammaticus and others, which begins, *"Dixit quidem apostolus."*[9] And this agrees with Jerome.

---

[7] Mansi 10, pp. 863ff.
[8] Vincent of Beauvais, *Histories*, ch. 13 (p. 102).
[9] PL 33, p. 162.

307.   Also I have seen a decree of Pope Leo [VIII] in the Roman synod signed by the bishops and clergy and citizens of Rome in which Pope Leo gave back to Otto I all the territories given to [the see of] St. Peter by Kings Pepin and Charlemagne and Robert. And all the territories are named in the same decree and it makes no mention of the Donation of Constantine.[10] Those stories about Constantine are apocryphal in my judgment as are also perhaps certain other lengthy writings attributed to St. Clement and Pope Anacletus upon which those who wish to exalt the Roman see more than is fitting or proper for the holy church, base their position almost completely.

308.   If anyone reads carefully through all the writings attributed to those saints and keeps in mind the time when they were written and then uses and remembers the works of all the holy fathers up to Augustine, Jerome, and Ambrose, as well as the acts of the councils where the authentic writings are listed, he will find it to be true that there is no mention in all these writings of those aforementioned letters. Furthermore if those letters are compared with the times when those saints lived they betray themselves as false.

309.   The letters of Clement say that he was pope and successor of Peter, and the writer imagines that he sent them after the death of Peter to St. James who was the brother of the Lord and bishop of Jerusalem. Yet it is established that James died as a martyr eight years before the death of Peter. And this is one of the reasons why the epistles of James come first in the Bible, as Bede writes in the beginning of *Super Canonicis Epistulis*.[11] The letters also say that Clement was the successor of Peter. And the same thing appears in other writings which are ascribed to St. Anacletus.[12] How could St. Jerome, St. Augustine, Optatus of Milevis and others who composed the list of all the Roman pontiffs and did not include Clement not have known this, if they had also seen those same letters then or held them to be authentic?

310.   The distinction between bishops and priests is also mentioned in those letters. Jerome and Damasus say that this distinction arose in the church much later. From what has been quoted in these letters and innumerable other instances these things can be proved and it would be superfluous to put them down here.

311.   It should not be necessary to support the divine, praiseworthy,

[10] Pope Leo VIII's decree is also apocryphal (see Jaffe, p. 3706).
[11] PL 93, p. 9.
[12] Hinschius, pp. 66 and 75. The letters are spurious.

and most excellent first see of Rome with ambiguous arguments of this kind which were taken from those letters and inserted in the *Decretum* of Gratian. The truth would be derived more sufficiently and properly directly from the accepted, certain, and approved Holy Scriptures and writings of the doctors. Likewise, it [the papal see] should not argue that it is greater because of the Donation of Constantine. Even if it were established as certain, everyone knows it would not add any ecclesiastical power to the spiritual teaching function of the church. And there still would be doubt as to its validity since Accursius in his commentary on the *Authentica,* [*Novellae* 6] *Quomodo oportet episcopos* after the beginning holds that it is not valid while Joannes Teutonicus writing on D. 63 [c. 30] *Ego Ludovicus* holds the contrary. See the gloss on the word *Constantinus* in the *Clementinae* in the chapter beginning *Romani* of [II 9] *De Jure Jurando.* I only write what I have been able to find as true by diligent investigation, saving in all things the judgment of the sacred synod.

312. And if all the writings discussed above are to be held as confirmed by the acceptance of the church, I would also agree, for even without those writings every Catholic believes that the holy Roman church is the first see and the highest in power and excellence of all the sees.

CHAPTER III

THE EMPIRE WAS NEVER TRANSFERRED BY THE POPE FROM THE GREEKS TO THE GERMANS OR THE FRANKS, ALTHOUGH THEY [THE GERMANS AND FRANKS] ALSO HAD THE TITLES OF PATRICIAN OF THE ROMANS OR EMPERORS. HENRY IV WAS CALLED PATRICIAN WHEN HE WAS CROWNED AT THE GENERAL COUNCIL OF BASEL. OTTO I WAS THE FIRST TO BE CREATED EMPEROR PROPERLY ALONG WITH HIS SUCCESSORS WITH FULL LEGAL RIGHTS BY THE PEOPLE AND THE CLERGY AND SYNOD OF ROME. HISTORICAL REFERENCES ARE CITED ON THIS SUBJECT.

313. Still certain writers hold – and it is a very common opinion – that the empire was transferred by Hadrian to the person of Charlemagne, as Innocent III says in the chapter [c. 34] *Venerabilem* of [*Decretals* 1 6] *De Electione*. But I confess that I have never read this in the approved ancient books. It is true that [Pope] Stephen II anointed Pepin and his two sons as kings – but this did not involve transfer of the empire. It is also true that Charlemagne is called a Roman patrician in the legislation and the acts of [Pope] Hadrian. For after the cities and territories named in the acts of Stephen II became the legal property of [the see of] St. Peter because of the gift of Pepin, the father of Charlemagne, and more territory was added later because several cities put themselves under the legal jurisdiction of [the see of] St. Peter and their citizens cut their hair in the Roman fashion, there was a need for a patrician to defend all these territories. And Charlemagne was chosen as patrician, as appears in D. 63 [c. 22] *Hadrianus* and in the chapter [c. 23] *In synodo* where he is called the king of France and of the Lombards. And as patrician, a term which was used because he was father [*pater*] of his country [*patria*], he held the office of earthly judge and was in charge of temporals while the pope did not involve himself in these matters. Rather according to the ancient gloss on the chapter [c. 22] *Hadrianus* of D. 63, as patrician he was the father of the pope in temporal matters, just as the pope was his father in spirituals. Isidore in the ninth book of the *Etymologies* says

that patricians were so named because they provided for the commonwealth as fathers provide for their sons.[1]

314.   And after they were crowned the emperors were usually called patricians, as we read concerning Henry IV at his coronation in A.D. 1061. For when [Pope] Nicholas II died, the Romans sent the crown to him and asked him about the election of the pope. After he had called many bishops of Italy together and held a general meeting at Basel and was crowned, he received the title of patrician of the Romans. At Basel with the common consent of all and by election of the representatives of the Romans, Chadelus, the bishop of Parma, was declared pope on the 26th of October, and took the name of Honorius. But Anselm, a certain bishop of Lucca, a city in Tuscany, had been elected 27 days earlier by certain Roman and Norman bishops, and he occupied the see until his death. Hildebrand succeeded him, who was called [Pope] Gregory VII and excommunicated Emperor Henry.

315.   Therefore the present council of Basel is taking place in 1433, 372 years after the earlier council at Basel and now His Most Serene Majesty Sigismund, crowned at Rome by [Pope] Eugene with the imperial diadem, is present at the council as Henry was then and as were other Catholic emperors. It is now precisely 500 years since Henry I, the father of Otto I, built that city of Basel which means the royal city and endowed it with churches, after Augusta Magna which was located not far distant had been totally destroyed by the Hungarians. Let us not speak further on this.

316.   Returning to our main argument – granted what has been said about Charlemagne being called patrician, it does not follow that therefore the empire was transferred to him from the Greeks. Rather it is very clear from the acts of the Eighth Council of Constantinople, and also after that down to the time of Otto I, that the Roman pontiffs Nicholas I and Hadrian II recognized Basil who had convened that council as well as his sons and Leo after that as the Roman emperors. And we do not find in those true histories that Charlemagne is called "emperor," but "king" and "patrician of the Romans," although certain histories would have it that at the end of his life as it were, he received the title of "Augustus" from the Roman people[2] and also

---

[1] Isidore, *Etymologies*, IX, 13 (PL 82, p. 345). For the Latin text with a Spanish translation, see Isidoro de Sevilla, *Etimologías*, Madrid, 1982–1983.

[2] Einhard's biography of Charlemagne (Engl. trans., *The Life of Charlemagne*, London, 1970) says that he was called emperor from the time of his crowning in A.D. 800.

after his death he was sometimes called emperor, as in D. 15 q. 6 [c. 3] *Alius*. For I have seen a large volume in the Cathedral of Cologne containing all the letters of [Pope] Hadrian I to Charlemagne and Charlemagne's answers to him and also copies of all the [papal] bulls and I confess that I have never read of that transfer.[3]

317.   Nevertheless I read that the term, empire, was very common in antiquity. For the one who was chosen by the army was called emperor [*imperator*], as St. Jerome says in D. 93 [c. 24] *Legimus*. Especially in the histories the kings of Italy are called emperors and also I have read that Berengar was called emperor as well as many others. Also Louis the Pious, the king of France, is called emperor in D. 63 [c. 30] *Ego Ludovicus*, and in D. 4 in the chapter [9] *De capitulis* it is proved that Lothar was called emperor and pontiff, and the same is evidently true of Louis in the same place. And if we summarize all these examples, those who exercised rule [*imperare*], particularly in Italy, were customarily called emperors or kings.

318.   We also know that after the death of King Conrad the line of succession of kings from Pepin and Charlemagne was ended, and that at the direction and urging of Conrad himself, already on his death-bed, Henry, the duke of Saxony, was elected king and the royal insignia of Conrad were conferred upon him. And we know further that the kingship went by succession to Otto I, II, and III and that at the time of Henry and Otto I, there were great divisions and wars in Italy and elsewhere, and that now this one, now that one, now Arnulf, then Berengar, and then Hugo, then Alberic waged wars among themselves. For King Hugo had Rome and other neighboring regions under his control for a long time and then when he had been expelled, Alberic occupied the city of Rome.

319.   And whoever reads the history dedicated to Raymond, bishop of Elvira in the province of Spain which was written by Liutprand, deacon of the church of Pavia who was in the chancery of Berengar, can see many similar things, since he wrote clearly and accurately about what took place from the time of the Emperor Basil, Constantine his son, and his [Constantine's] son Leo, and from Charles the Bald [Bold] to Otto I. What he wrote is true since he was present at the time of many of these complex events.[4]

---

[3] The *Codex Carolinus* now in the Vienna Library (Kallen, *DCC*, p. 340).

[4] Liutprand of Cremona, *Antapodosis* (trans. by F. A. Wright, New York, 1930) is Cusanus' source for these and later passages on the German empire in the tenth century.

320. In summary then, from the time of Henry I, and especially through Otto I, the Germans acquired control by force of arms over the kingdom of Italy and the city of Rome, the kingdom of Arles, and that of Germany itself. For this reason their rulers were called emperors, after Berengar, Hugo, Arnulf, and Alberic, and others of the time of Otto I had died. And I have not found that from the time of [Popes] Stephen II or Hadrian that the city [of Rome] ever withdrew from the empire or was taken away from Pepin or Charles, although well after this until [the reign of] Otto many tyrants occupied it until Otto defeated them and freed it from their control. And for this reason, he is called emperor and king in the text [c. 23] *In synodo* of D. 63 and to emphasize the special status of the king the synod declares that no one may use the title, patrician, unless he is the king just as it has made Odoacer a patrician because he was the king, see D. 96 [c. 1] *Bene quidam.* For a patrician is father of the pope in temporal matters, as discussed above.

321. And note that the synodal decree in D. 63 [c. 23] *In synodo* was adopted by the clergy and people of Rome and the Roman people transferred their power to the emperor in such a way that they still retained superiority over him as the Cardinal [Zabarella] notes under the heading *De aere* concerning the chapter *Venerabilem* [of *Decretals* 6]. For, [he says], today there still exists in the church of the Lateran in Rome the bronze tablet on which the senate and people of Rome explicitly set down the power that they gave to Vespasian. What was granted to Vespasian is contained in the Lateran church. This is also proved by the statement of Hostiensis in his *Summa [Aurea]* discussing [*Decretals* 1 2] *De Constitutionibus*, in the paragraph *Quis possit* at the words *Item populus*, where he says that the statement in [Justinian's *Code* 1 17] *De veteri jure enucleando*, law 1, paragraph [7] *Et hoc*, which asserts that the people transferred their power to the emperor means that they granted it with the provision that they retained for themselves the power to revoke it, as law 2, paragraph [16] *Exactis* in [the *Digest* 1 2] *De Origine Iuris* and what follows prove.

322. Therefore since he had been made the victorious king of the Romans and was their liberator and since the Romans were not being protected by the Greek emperor who then lived at Constantinople, they gave their consent that Otto should be emperor. The power to direct the empire comes from the consent of the Romans, as will be shown below. And therefore after Otto was called in to expel the

tyrant and was made king of the Romans and this had been confirmed by the consent of the synod, clergy, and people, at that time he and his successors acquired the imperial power deservedly and legitimately.

323. But it would be too long to describe how the rulership over the city of Rome and Italy was acquired by force of arms by Otto in accordance with the desire of the Romans. And I am very surprised that Gratian when he speaks of the investiture of bishops in D. 63 [c. 23] *In synoda* – a text which proves that Otto was king of Italy and of the Germans – did not mention that he returned the cities to the pope that had once been given to the Roman church by the kings of France. And because he was the ruler of the city of Rome and Italy, Otto was named emperor along with all his successors, although the government of the city of Rome and of the cities once donated by Pepin and Charlemagne and by other kings later, see D. 63 [c. 30] *Ego Ludovicus*, was given back to the Roman pontiff. And there is no doubt that when they (the emperors) returned those territories to the church, they kept some power over them for themselves, and this is why they are described with the title of emperor in addition to that of king, on the model of the ancients, just as Charlemagne was once called patrician and is called the protector in the chapter [c. 34] *Venerabilem* of [*Decretals* 1 6] *De Electione*. For if the emperor did not have power over the men subject to the church how could he constrain them by force to obey the laws of St. Peter? And how could he preserve the rights of St. Peter for the Apostolic See as he swears to do in D. 63 [c. 33] *Tibi domino?*

324. But for now I do not want to continue on these matters for they are not relevant to the present discussion. Suffice it to have touched on the above.

CHAPTER IV

THE ELECTORS DO NOT DEPEND ON THE ROMAN PONTIFF. THEY ARE NOT CREATED BY HIM NOR DO THEY HAVE THEIR POWER FROM HIM BUT FROM THE COMMON CONSENT OF ALL THOSE SUBJECT TO THE EMPIRE WHO HAVE THE POWER TO ESTABLISH AN EMPEROR OVER THEMSELVES, NOT FROM POSITIVE LAW BUT FROM DIVINE AND HUMAN LAW. IT IS RIGHT AND JUST THAT THE EMPIRE SHOULD DERIVE ITS POWER FROM ELECTION BY THEM WITHOUT PAPAL CONFIRMATION, AND THEY [THE EMPERORS] CANNOT BE DEPOSED BY THE POPE ALONE.

325. We must discuss further the electors of the empire mentioned in the chapter [c. 34] *Venerabilem* of [*Decretals* 1 6] *De Electione.* The jurists hold that they act as electors in the name of the Roman people, on which see Joannes Andreae in his *Additiones* to the section [II 1] *De Rescripti Praesentiatione* of the *Speculum Juris* (of Gulielmus Durandus), the last word beginning *Item quod obtentum.*[1] As is said in a certain place above every well-ordered empire or kingdom is based on election, and then the ruler is truly considered to have been appointed by the providence of God. Thus Emperors Valentinian and Marcian when they write to Pope Leo on convening the synod, say, "The victorious and august Valentinian and Marcian in glorious triumph, to Leo, most reverend Archbishop of the glorious city of Rome: We have attained this most high rule by the providence of the true God and the election of the most excellent senate and the whole army."[2]

326. Note that it says, "by the election of the senate and army." Following this procedure, Henry I, the father of Otto, we read, was established by election as king at the command of King Conrad while he was still duke of Saxony and became the first king of the Germans. But his son, Otto, received from the synod and Roman people the power to choose a successor, as the text already mentioned, *In synodo,* of D. 63 [c. 23] says, although according to the gloss [on that pass-

---

[1] The manuscript of Joannes Andreae's *Additiones* is in the library at Kues (no. 269).
[2] PL 54, p. 899.

age], he received this [only] for the kingdom of Italy, and the succession was maintained following that procedure down to Otto III.

327. After his death, Henry II, the son of the brother of Otto III, was chosen and this emperor with the consent of the nobles and leaders of both estates, the clergy, and the people, established permanent electors who would carry out the election, acting for all. This was done at the time of [Pope] Gregory V, who was a German and a relative of an earlier Otto. We should not therefore admit that the electors have their power of election from the Roman pontiff, so that if he does not agree they cannot act, or if he wishes to do so he can take that power away from them.

328. Who, I ask, gave the Roman people the right to elect the emperor, if not divine and natural law? For in every kind of government rulers are chosen for their positions in a harmonious rightful and holy fashion through voluntary subjection and consent. For all violence is opposed to law. There is a general agreement among men to obey kings, see D. 8 [c. 2] *Quae contra mores*, sentence beginning *Generale*, and the final law [1. 7] of the *Code* [of *Justinian*, III 13] *De jurisdictione omnium judicum* and [see also] the *Digest, Quod cuiusque universitatis*, law 1, para. 2.

329. In chapter 75 of the Council of Toledo in the year of Our Lord, 581, at the time of King Sisenandus, it was decided that when the king died the leaders of the people along with the priests were to establish his successor with the common counsel of the kingdom so that retaining the bond of unity no dissension in the country or people would arise because of ambition. A decree is added that a tyrant who has wrongly usurped authority should be excommunicated; and terrible anathemas and maledictions are imposed.[3]

330. Thus kings are in Greek called *"Basilici"* since as bases they support the people in a collective harmony, and this is why bases have crowns. "Tyrants" in Greek are the same as "kings" in Latin; for *"tyro"* means "strong," and a tyrant is a strong king. Subsequently it became customary to call the worst and most dishonorable kings – those who loved luxury and exercised cruel dominion over the people – tyrants, as Isidore says in Book IX of his *Etymologies*.[4] They are called tyrants as usurpers of authority who are neither asked to rule nor elected.

---

[3] Fourth Council of Toledo – A.D. 671 (Mansi 10, pp. 638–639).
[4] Isidore, *Etymologies*, IX, 3 (PL 82, p. 344).

331. Summarizing what has been said above, all legitimate authority arises from elective concordance and free submission. There is in the people a divine seed by virtue of their common equal birth and the equal natural rights of all men so that all authority – which comes from God as does man himself – is recognized as divine when it arises from the common consent of the subjects. One who is established in authority as representative of the will of all may be called a public or common person, the father of all, ruling without haughtiness or pride, in a lawful and legitimately established government. While recognizing himself as the creature, as it were, of all his subjects as a collectivity, let him act as their father as individuals. This is that divinely ordained marital state of spiritual union based on a lasting harmony by which a commonwealth is best guided in the fullness of peace toward the goal of eternal bliss. Since the bases of this divine and human law have been shown above, I will not repeat the discussion here.

332. It is sufficient to know that free election based on natural and divine law does not originate from positive law nor from any man upon whose will the validity of the election depends. This is particularly true of the election of a king or emperor whose existence and power do not depend on any one man. Thus the electors – who were created at the time of Henry II by common agreement of all the Germans and the other subjects of the empire – derive their basic authority fundamentally from the common consent of all those who could by natural law have created the Emperor [and] not from the Roman Pontiff who has no authority to give any region in the world a king or emperor without its consent.

333. Gregory V gave his consent to this arrangement but only by virtue of his position as pontiff of Rome who has the right to participate in accordance with his rank in expressing his consent to the common emperor. So also in universal councils, the pontiff as the one in the first rank rightly participates in consenting, along with all the others attending the same council. The force of the decree depends, however, not on his consent as chief pontiff of all, but on the common consent of all, both the pope and the others. The fact that in setting up a king or emperor the consent of priests as well as of laymen must be obtained is not because the kings have the right to rule the priesthood for we know that the priesthood is like the sun and the empire the moon, as is said in the chapter [c. 16] *Solitae*, of [*Decretals* I 33] *De*

majoritate et Oboedientia, but because the temporal possessions of the church without which the priesthood cannot survive in this perishable life are subject to the empire and its laws, as Augustine says in D. 8 [c. 1] *Quo Jure* and [c] 23 9. 7 [c. 1] *Quicumque*.

334. The one responsible for the protection of the interests of the priesthood ought to participate in consenting to the election of the king. Therefore this is of particular concern to the Roman pontiff who bears the chief responsibility for the priesthood. Thus I believe that in fact at the beginning the Roman pontiff consented to the arrangement whereby these electors were established. The latter carry out the election by virtue of a general delegation of authority from all those who are under imperial authority including the entire priesthood and the Roman pontiff. There is no doubt that the one who is elected receives full power by virtue of that election, as Joannes [Teutonicus] notes in his gloss on D. 93 [c. 24] *Legimus* and [Pope] Innocent [III] says in the chapter [c. 34] *Venerabilem* of [*Decretals, Liber Sextus* 1 6] *De Electione* and this is established, as Hostiensis notes in [*Liber Sextus*, v 40] *De Verborum Significatione*, the chapter [c. 26] *Super Quibusdam*, as does the gloss on the word *reges* and the chapter [c. 1] *Romani* [*De jure jurande*] in the Clementine decretals [II 9 *De jure jurande*]. The reason is that having been elected he has received the submission of all and therefore he has the power to command which is the essence of imperial rule.

335. The emperors originally derived their title from commanding [*imperandi*] the army. The anointing and coronation which, we read, is also accorded to other rulers does not prove that the pope has the power to confirm or annul the emperor's election, nor does it demonstrate his supremacy over the empire in temporal affairs; just as nothing of that sort is involved in the anointing of the king of France at Rheims or in the coronation of the emperor himself by the Archbishop of Cologne at Aachen. This is clear from the fact that Otto I was invested as king of Germany and of the Franks by Hildebert, Archbishop of Mainz, at Aachen by the wish and consent of the rulers and all the people of Germany, Saxony, and France. We also read that at the death of King Conrad, Henry I was anointed and crowned by Herger, the Archbishop of Mainz, with the consent of all, and that when he received the diadem he was unwilling to be anointed since he said he was unworthy.

336. Thus it is clear that anointment and coronation in no way add

to imperial authority; for these insignia are added to the ceremonies as a way of symbolizing to the visible material subjects of the empire the sacred majesty that is inherent in the emperor as signs of the reverence with which his power is to be regarded. We know that similar ceremonies are carried out in the case of the Roman pontiff, and yet immediately after his election and before they take place he becomes pope. The title is changed when the pope crowns the emperor – he is called king beforehand and emperor afterwards – but this is no proof that previously he had less governing power, and this is well known. And so when he had full power to rule, he was really emperor even if he did not carry the title. However this title is reserved for this solemn occasion, so that the ruler may desire to be crowned.

337. On the coronation with the imperial diadem and other ceremonies, see the gloss on the word *vestigiis* in *Romani* in the Clementine *Decretals* [II 9 *De jure jurande*]. As Isidore says in Book IX of the *Etymologies*, at a time when army commanders were using the title, *imperator*, the senate decreed that this should be the name of Augustus Caesar alone and that this name should distinguish him from rulers of other nations. Accordingly, the Caesars have to this day assumed this name for themselves, particularly from the time when they are crowned with a diadem by the bishop of the Romans from whom [i.e. the Romans] the Roman power to rule [*imperium*] is derived.

338. Since this matter has been discussed quite eloquently by many writers, it may be sufficient for us to recognize that our imperial electors, when they elect the emperor by virtue of the united common consent of all who are under the empire, do this because all have agreed to transfer their power to them – and that agreement included the Roman pontiff, Gregory V. It follows that the emperor is created by election without confirmation by anyone – just as in electing a pope, the universal authority of the church is rightly transferred to the cardinals by the common consent, tacit or sometimes express, of all, and therefore the pope is elected without confirmation by anyone.

339. Just as elective authority is given by agreement to certain rulers in the two estates so, since an equivalent authority should have the right to take away this power, I do not believe that the Roman pontiff alone can withdraw this power from those princes but when the consent of both the Roman pontiff and of all the others concurs, there

is no doubt that this power can be taken away from them. It is the common opinion of all the experts on the subject that the Roman people can take the power to make laws away from the emperor because he derives his power from the people.[5] Thus we read that when the Roman people, ruled for a long time by kings, could no longer endure their haughtiness, they created annual rulerships and two consuls, and also dictators and other arrangements that seemed to suit their governmental needs at the time.

[5] There continued to be disagreement among the Roman lawyers as to whether the transfer of power described in Justinian's Code (I, 17 *De veteri jure*) was revocable or not, i.e., whether power had been conceded (*concessio*) or transferred (*translatio*) by the people to the emperor.

CHAPTER V

THE EMPEROR RECEIVES SUPREME EARTHLY POWER
FROM CHRIST AND ACTS AS HIS REPRESENTATIVE.
THEREFORE HE IS CALLED THE MINISTER OF GOD
AND THE VICAR OF CHRIST FOLLOWING THE
EXAMPLE OF CHRIST IN HIS RULE OVER ALL
NATIONS.

340. Following in order we should discuss the concordant arrangement that is proper to the empire. First, we assume something that is generally accepted – that by its nature the imperial majesty is independent, first in rank and supreme, and distinct from the spiritual power of the priesthood, see D. 96 [c. 10] *Duo sunt*, and that it is derived directly from God, see D. 97 [c. 1] *Ecclesiae meae*, and is over everyone, see [C.] 7 q. 1 [c. 41] *In apibus*; [C] 11 q. 1 [after c. 36] para. *Hic* [Haec] *si quis* at the word *volumus*. He [the emperor] is the prince and ruler of this world and all things are in his power, see D. 13 [D. 8] [c. 1] *Quo jure*; [C] 24 [23] q. 8 [c. 21] *Convenior*; [and] D. 63 [c. 30] *Ego Ludovicus*. The pope is not superior to him with respect to those imperial rights, see [C.] 23 q. 1 [c. 7] *In summa*; [C.] 2 q. 7 [c. 41] *Nos si*; and D. 9 [D. 10] [c. 9] *De capitulis*. And what has been written above argues for this as do D. 96 [c. 6] *Cum ad verum*, and many singular passages in which he was honored by the pope and

the council, see [D.] 63 [c. 2] *Hadrianus II* and the chapters *In synodo* [c. 23] and *Reatina* [c. 16]. Also the pope often calls him his lord and honors him as such, see D. 97 [c. 1] *Ecclesiae meae*, as was clear in the case of Pope Agatho when he wrote to Constantine [III] that after God he was the common father of all in the *Authentica* [*Novellae* 98] at the end of collection 8 [c. 2], *Neque virum quod ex dote est.*

341. Many legal provisions as well as other writings could be quoted. But it is his high privilege that he is the minister of God, as Paul says in Romans 13, and he acts as the vicar of Jesus Christ on earth as Pope Anastasius says writing to the emperor, "Your merciful heart is a sanctuary of the public good. Thanks to you whom God has commanded to act as his vicar on earth, unyielding pride does not resist the evangelical and apostolic commands, and the precepts of salvation are obeyed."[1] Note that the Christian emperor by virtue of his rulership is the vicar of Christ, the King of kings and Lord of lords.

342. Hence just as Christ is king of kings so all kings have something of the divine in their governing power and therefore reverence and obedience are due them. But when they order something contrary to a divine commandment it is evident that the command does not share in the divine rulership, and so one should not obey it, see [C.] 11 q. 3 [c. 94] *Julianus* with the other texts located there and D. 10 in its entirety. And so he [the emperor] is first over all other princes because he rules in subordination to Christ, victorious and triumphant, and subjects himself by faith to Christ and his laws. Therefore the Christian empire is higher than all other governments because it is the one closest to God.

[1] Hinschius, p. 654.

CHAPTER VI

THE POWER OF THE EMPIRE EXTENDS TO THE
AREAS THAT ARE SUBJECT TO IT, AND OBEY IT.
ALTHOUGH THE ROMAN EMPIRE NEVER INCLUDED
CERTAIN PROVINCES AND KINGDOMS NAMED IN
THIS CHAPTER, THE EMPEROR IS CALLED THE LORD
OF THE WORLD BECAUSE HE RULES THE LARGER
PART OF IT. IT IS RIGHT FOR HIM TO HAVE THE
HIGHEST POSITION OF ALL RULERS BECAUSE HE
MOST NEARLY RESEMBLES CHRIST WHO REIGNS
THROUGH FAITH.

343. We should note that his power to command does not extend beyond the territorial limits of the empire under him, as is evident in the text [D. 63 c. 30], *Ego Ludovicus*, where although Louis describes himself as emperor, he issues commands only to the inhabitants of the kingdom of France and the Lombards who were his *de facto* subjects. And following this we should say that the emperor is said to be lord of the world as ruler of the empire that the Romans once conquered by their valor, as the text [C.] 28 q. 1 para. *Ex hiis* says, deriving that title from the fact that the Romans had the greater part of the world under their rule. They did not rule all of it for they did not gain control of the Caspian Mountains and the gates of Alexander in northern Scythia, and Norway, and the areas beyond the Caspian Sea and the Himalayan Mountains, and the Kingdom of China, as well as the Persian desert towards India and the East, Arachosia [Pakistan] and the parts of India located beyond the Indus and Ganges Rivers, and Ceylon, the largest island of all, and southern Arabia beyond the Persian Gulf towards the Indian Ocean, and the region of the Troglodytes, and Nubia, a very large area, and others located beyond the great desert of Libya and Mauritania.

344. These regions, it appears to me from the *Cosmography* of Claudius Ptolemy,[1] make up no small part of the world – in fact, almost half of the inhabitable land. India alone is said to contain nine thousand walled villages. Scythia also has a very large population

---

[1] See Elwood Luther Stevenson (trans. and ed.), *The Geography of Claudius Ptolemy*, New York, 1932.

although it does not have cities. Nubia and the regions of the Troglodytes which are beyond the circle of the solstice where shadows are cast in both directions [at different times of the year], and the island of Ceylon are not so heavily populated because of the extreme heat nor are Norway and the outer parts of Scythia because of the cold, but there are great kingdoms there.

345. The Troglodyte region contains the empire of the Negus John whom we call Prester John who is said to be a Christian and a most faithful deacon with seventy kingdoms subject to him.[2] But I think that those kingdoms are not very populous or large.

346. But no part of the world is as heavily populated as Europe in proportion to its size since it is not one fourth as large as Asia nor half as large as Africa. It starts at Constantinople and extends to Cadiz near the Pillars of Hercules [Gibraltar] beyond Spain. The city of Rome is situated in its western part so that it is called the Western Roman Empire and is said to be over the whole world because the nations subject to it include the majority of mankind.

347. But now we see what has become of that famed empire. And so we should say that if the Romans had a legal right to their monarchy in the way described, the emperor to whom their power has been transferred is lord of the world by legal right. However if rulership is only rightly possessed through the elective agreement of the subjects as argued above, then he is only lord over those who are actually subject to him and we should conclude that the emperor is lord of that part of the world over which he exercises effective authority.

---

[2] On the Troglodytes and the mythical Kingdom of Prester John, believed to be located in Ethiopia, see Vesevolod Slessarov, *Prester John, The Letter and the Legend*, Minneapolis, 1959. Nicholas writes on the basis of a spurious letter from Prester John supposedly written to the Byzantine emperor in the twelfth century. For the texts see Edward Ullendorf and C. F. Beckingham (trans. and eds.), *The Hebrew Letters of Prester John*, Oxford, 1982.

CHAPTER VII

THE HIGHEST RESPONSIBILITY ENTRUSTED TO THE EMPEROR – THAT BY VIRTUE OF WHICH HE IS OVER THE OTHERS – IS HIS ROLE AS GUARDIAN OF THE ORTHODOX FAITH. HE IS THE EQUAL IN HIS SPHERE OF THE POPE BECAUSE THE FAITH HAS BEEN ENTRUSTED TO HIM AS ITS GUARDIAN IN THE SAME WAY THAT ITS STUDY AND TEACHING ARE ENTRUSTED TO THE PRIESTHOOD. HE ACQUIRES THIS HIGHEST POWER BY THE ELECTION OF CHRISTIANS.

348.   But as the Imperial Excellence is constituted king of all in a way similar to and approximating the rule of God over all we believe that there are gradations in excellence according to [the ruler's] closeness to, or distance from God, and that the one who in his public rule resembles God least is least worthy while the one who resembles him most is the greatest. Thus a king of the Tartars is the least worthy because he governs through laws least in agreement with those divinely instituted; a king who belongs to the Mohammedan sect is greater since he venerates the laws of the Old Testament and certain of those of the New Testament; and a Christian king is the greatest because he accepts both the laws of nature and those of the Old and New Testaments and the orthodox faith. And according to the standard of holiness of rule, I maintain that the authority of the empire is the greatest. For every king and emperor holds public office for the public good. The public good consists in peace, the goal towards which justice and just wars are directed. But the foundation of peace is to direct subjects to their eternal end, and the means to reach that end are the holy precepts of religion. Hence the first duty of the emperor is to observe them.

349.   Thus we read that the pagan emperors were called supreme pontiffs because of the care which they took for religion. If therefore this is the chief concern of rulership and all others are subservient to this, there is no doubt that our Christian empire outranks the others, just as our most holy and pure Christian religion is highest in holiness and truth. And as every king and prince should care for his kingdom

as noted above, so the emperor should care for the whole Christian people. And just as the Roman pontiff is responsible for the faith and whatever is related to it first in his bishopric, then in his metropolitanate, after that in his patriarchate, and finally in the universal church, so the emperor exercises his responsibility of guardianship first over those immediately subject to the empire, after that over those subject to him through the princes directly under him, and then over those subject through kings and princes not properly under him who claim parallel places for themselves but recognize him as first of all.[1]

350. Hence just as the prince who is the administrator of a province in temporal matters is responsible for carrying out the decisions on worship and religion and the welfare of the commonwealth that are adopted in provincial councils, and the king exercises the same function for the councils of the kingdom – which earlier were usually called universal councils of [several] provinces – so the emperor acts to enforce whatever is decided in the universal council of the whole Catholic church. And every ruler must give an accounting of the responsibility that he has to protect the church of Christ, see [C.] 23 q. 5 [c. 20] *Dicat* and the chapters *Regum* [c. 23] and *Omnes principes* [c. 25].

351. In this way the emperor is called the protector [*advocatus*] of the universal church because of the responsibility which he has as guardian of the orthodox faith for the protection of [church] laws. Thus we read that Marcian was called the guardian of the faith in the Council of Chalcedon. And the Emperor Basil at the beginning of the Eighth Universal Council says that a most beneficent Divine Providence has committed the direction of the whole ship of faith to him.[2] For as the teaching responsibility to define and legislate on what pertains to the orthodox universal Christian faith is entrusted to the priesthood by God, so to govern, to confirm, and preserve what is commanded by God through the priesthood is entrusted to the holy empire.

352. The first Christian emperor was Philip – who ruled for a short

---

[1] The issue of the relation of the European kings to the Holy Roman Emperor was already raised by Pope Innocent III in the thirteenth century when in *Per venerabilem* he observed that the king of France recognizes no superior in temporal matters.

[2] Mansi 7, p. 171 and 16, p. 18.

time with little in the way of positive results.[3] Emperor Constantine gave permission for churches to be built throughout the world and after him all the emperors were baptized, although some departed from the faith – as did Constantine himself according to [St.] Jerome, as well as Julian the Apostate, and Constantius. However I do not base the imperial duty to act as universal guardian of the faith on that succession of believing emperors but upon the basic transfer of power from the Christian Roman people.

353.   I mean by the Roman people, the whole Christian people just as when Emperor Marcian said in the Council of Chalcedon that what had been defined by the Council would be useful to the Roman people,[4] he meant by the Roman people all Christians, since all those who were then subject to the empire were Christians. Hence once the Roman people became Christian, they chose as their rulers emperors of the same faith as the people. Therefore I believe that it is true, as is stated in chapter [34] *Venerabilem* of [*Decretals* I 6] *De electione*, that it is the intention of the people only to transfer power to a ruler if he has the faith, so that a heretic may not receive power over the empire by election, and if the pope who is the chief of the bishops of the faith should find that the one who was elected is in error as to the faith, he could declare that he was not emperor.

354.   Nevertheless I do not deny that the rule of succession also operates in this case so that when we read in many synods that the responsibility for protecting the faith was assigned to the emperors named, it was also given to their successors. For this reason I find the following acclamation in praise of Marcian expressed by the Council of Chalcedon: "Everlasting remembrance to the new Constantine." And the Eighth Synod said to Basil, "Everlasting remembrance to the new Marcian, the new Constantine."[5] And this method may be used to analyze the true bases of the supremacy of the Christian empire over all empires and of the emperor himself over all Christian kings and princes.

355.   Because he is the guardian of the universal faith and the protector of universal [church] statutes which could not be effectively

---

[3] Philip the Arabian, emperor between 244 and 249. Orosius, *History against the Pagans*, claims that he was the first Christian emperor, but modern historians are dubious.
[4] Mansi 7, pp. 107ff.
[5] Mansi 7, p. 134 and 16, p. 143.

executed without [one] ruler over all, and since the universal statutes respecting the Catholic faith bind all faithful Christians to maintain and apply them, all are subject to the emperor's rule insofar as he is established to maintain those directives.

356. And therefore I believe that if the emperor should add some laws to assure the observance of these holy definitions of faith, as did Justinian, Marcian, and the other emperors, they would bind just as universally as the originals, although the other laws would perhaps not bind those who as a matter of fact or of exemption do not recognize the supremacy of the empire.

CHAPTER VIII

LAYMEN SHOULD SPEAK AT COUNCILS WHEN THEY MUST DEFEND THEMSELVES BUT OTHERWISE THEY SHOULD ONLY LISTEN. PRINCES SHOULD CALL COUNCILS IN AREAS UNDER THEIR RULE IN ORDER TO PUNISH CRIMES AND CARRY OUT REFORMS. THE EXAMPLE OF CHARLEMAGNE IS GIVEN.

357. Relative to what has been said above, the following questions should be considered: First, what are the powers of laymen in councils made up of priests? Second, what is found in the records on the role of the emperor in universal councils? After that something will be added on the usefulness of an imperial council to represent all those subject to the emperor. And finally some thoughts will be developed about the reform of the empire. It has already been noted that laymen invited to a universal synod are present to listen and they sign the acts of the council as witnesses.[1]

358. There is no doubt that laymen may be accused [of crimes] in a parish synod and that they ought to be admitted to defend themselves, as the Council of Mainz decrees.[2] But laymen should not be present in synods where ordinary canonical matters are discussed and examined because it is not proper for them to observe what often happens among priests, as the universal council says above – unless,

---

[1] Book II, nos. 138–139.   [2] Mansi 25, p. 308.

as we read in the sixth chapter of the Council of Chalons, and in chapter 119 of the Council of Carthage they are invited to be present. But princes can be present when general matters involving their rule are treated, although not when cases involving the clergy are discussed.[3] Even then they should be auditors as we read in the records of innumerable councils, many of which, we read, were convened at their [the princes'] request.

359. We read of King Charlemagne [that he spoke] as follows: "I Charlemagne, leader and prince of the Franks on the 22nd of April of the year of our Lord 752 with the counsel of the servants of God and my nobles, have convened the bishops and priests of my kingdom, including Boniface, Archbishop of Mainz and Burchard of Worms in council and synod to advise me as to how the law of God and the ecclesiastical religion may be restored. With the advice of my priests and nobles we have ordained bishops in the cities and have established Boniface, the legate of St. Peter, over them." And below, "We have commanded that a synod be convened every year in order that the decrees of the canons and the rights of the church may be restored to us present and the Christian religion may be purified, and we have now returned the money to the churches which was their endowment and cut off church funds from, and degraded and punished false priests, as well as deacons and clerics who are adulterers and fornicators." And below, "Following the canons of the saints we have decreed that every priest must be subject to the bishop in whose diocese he lives and every Lent he must give an accounting for his ministry regarding baptisms and the [preaching of the] Catholic faith and prayers and the order of masses. When the bishop goes about his diocese administering Confirmation to the people, the priest should always be prepared to receive the bishop with the assistance and aid of the people who are to be confirmed. In conformity with the canonical decree we have commanded that bishops and priests from wherever they come are not to be admitted to the ecclesiastical ministry without the approval of the synod. Likewise we have decreed that any of the servants or handmaids of Christ who has fallen into the crime of fornication shall do penance in prison on bread and water. And if he is a priest, let him stay two years in prison and let him be beaten and racked beforehand. But if he is a cleric [in

---

[3] Mansi 10, p. 1191 (Chalons) and 3, p. 959 (Fourth Council of Carthage).

minor orders] or a monk, after three beatings let him stay a year in prison. Likewise also the veiled nuns should suffer the same punishment and all the hair of their heads should be shaved off."[4]

360. Another synod which Charlemagne attended adopted a law against fornicators which provided that they should be punished by being deprived of their benefices and forced to do penance and transferred to a different place and many other provisions.[5] Pope Zacharias writes about this synod to Archbishop Boniface in two letters, one of which begins, *Susceptis* and the other, *Suscipientes sanctissime.*[6]

361. Note that the king convenes the council and along with the others commands that what is just should be done. Would that today princes would make a similar effort to remove the public evils and vices which are a great scandal to religion, such as fornication committed by those who have taken a vow of chastity. In this respect special concern should be given to the protection of nuns. For St. Boniface writes to Ethelbald, King of the Angles, that the Greeks and Romans considered it blasphemy against God if anyone was guilty of sleeping with a nun.[7]

---

[4] Mansi 12, p. 365.   [5] Mansi 12, p. 369.
[6] Jaffe, pp. 2264 and 2271.   [7] *MG Epistolae*, pp. 146ff.

CHAPTER IX

SAINT GREGORY EXHORTED THEODORIC, THE KING
OF THE FRANKS, TO CALL A COUNCIL OF HIS
BISHOPS AND TO ELIMINATE CONCUBINAGE AND
SIMONY FROM HIS KINGDOM. OTHER EXAMPLES
ARE GIVEN FROM THE REIGN OF RECAREDUS, THE
KING OF SPAIN AND GAUL. KINGS SHOULD
ENFORCE WHAT IS DECIDED BY COMMON CONSENT
IN THOSE COUNCILS.

362. And so kings and princes should make an effort to convene synods as St. Gregory advised Theodoric, the King of the Franks, in the [Papal] *Register*, chapter 273: "Again we exhort Your Grace to command that a council be convened and, as we have written before,

to have the bodily vices of priests and the heretical crime of simony condemned by decision of all the bishops and eliminated from the territorial limits of your kingdom."[1]

363. Also the exarch or prince either personally or through a council ought to urge the adoption of what is required to assure the peace of the church, see [C.] 23 q. 4 [c. 48] *Sicut.* And it would be too long and unnecessary to describe the princely councils that have been held by the Frankish kings in the Gauls and Germanies at Aachen, Cologne, Koblenz, Mainz and in other places. Everyone is aware with what zealous concern those holy princes secured the public good and the true and pure religion. Nowhere can the common good of the public be commanded and ordained better than in holy assemblies in which everything is decided in concord.

364. It is the office of princes to enforce and protect what has been decided in the councils. Hence we read that Recaredus, the king of Gaul and Spain issued the following decree: "The most glorious lord Recaredus, king of all subject to the rule of our authority: Divine truth which makes us solicitous of your good has inspired us to command all the bishops of Spain to appear at our throne in order to restore faith and discipline to the church. Proceeding with careful deliberation they have acted with maturity and intelligence concerning what is useful to the faith and the improvement of morals. Therefore we in our authority command all men belonging to our kingdom that no one is to ignore or dare to violate what had been defined by this holy Council of Toledo in the fourth happy year of our reign. The chapters pleasing to us and appropriate as a rule which have been set down by the present synod are to be observed with full authority by the clergy and all men – and let the earlier canons continue to be observed."

365. And below: "We have decreed that all the church laws which we have discussed in brief summary form, and which are contained in full in the canon, are to remain fixed forever. Therefore if any cleric or layman refuses to obey these commands – if he is a bishop, priest, deacon, or cleric, let him be subject to excommunication by the whole council, but if he is a layman and person of honorable estate, let him surrender half of his property to the treasury, and if he is a person of lesser estate let him be exiled, and his goods confiscated."[2] I could quote many similar statements but it is not necessary. And so it is to

[1] PL 77, p. 1179.
[2] The Third Council of Toledo – A.D. 589 (Mansi 9, pp. 999ff).

be noted that kings and princes should preserve, confirm, and execute the acts of the councils as is commanded in these canons.

CHAPTER X

KINGS AND PRINCES INTERVENED AT THOSE
COUNCILS WITH REVERENCE AND DEVOTION AND
ISSUED MOST SWEET EXHORTATIONS. WE NOTE
THE EXAMPLE OF KING RECAREDUS, AND CITE THE
EXAMPLES OF KINGS SISENANDUS AND
CHINTALANUS ON THE SAME POINT.

366. Kings and princes should approach those councils, addressing them mildly, reverently and humbly with sweet exhortations. We read this of the [King]: Recaredus in another Council of Toledo. When that most glorious prince acting out of sincere faith commanded all the bishops of his kingdom to come together, he addressed the council as follows: "I suppose that it is not unknown to you, most reverend priests, that I have called you to our serene presence for the purpose of restoring discipline in the church. And because in times past heresy threatened the whole Catholic church and prevented conciliar business from being carried out, God who has been pleased to use us to remove the obstacle which this heresy posed has commanded us to reestablish the institutions of ecclesiastical practice. Therefore let there be joy and gladness among you that at God's prompting and to our glory, ecclesiastical practice is being returned to the forms of the fathers. I likewise advise and exhort you first to pay attention to fasts, vigils, and prayers so that the canonical order which forgetfulness has long removed from the consciences of priests and which our age claims it does not know, may by divine gift again be evident to you." At this the whole council began to cry out in praise, giving thanks to God and to the most glorious prince.

367. A three-day fast was then proclaimed. And on the eighth day of May when the priests of God were gathered together and after a prayer each priest was sitting in his proper place, the most serene prince who was present among them, after sharing in prayer with the priests of God and filled with divine inspiration, arose and spoke as

follows: "We know that your holinesses are aware how long Spain suffered from the Arian heresy. When not many days after the death of our father your holinesses recognized us as members of the holy Catholic faith, we know that everywhere there was great and lasting rejoicing. This is why, most venerable fathers, we have called you to carry out this council."

368. And below, "Although Almighty God has granted to us to ascend the throne for the benefit of the inhabitants of the kingdom and has committed the government of no few peoples to our royal care, we remember that we are subject to the mortal condition and that we cannot merit the happiness of future beatitude if we do not venerate the true faith and please our Maker through the saving belief which is his due. Therefore as much as we are superior to our subjects in royal glory, so much more should we be solicitous of the things of God so that we may both attain our hope and provide for the people entrusted to us by God. But how are we worthy to give anything in return for the many benefits of Divine Omnipotence, when all things are his and none of our goods would be lacking to him, unless we confess that we believe in him with total devotion as the Holy Scriptures say he should be known and believed."

369. And below, "Therefore most holy fathers, I offer these most noble nations which have been granted to us by the grace of the Lord, to the eternal God as a holy and pleasing sacrifice in our hands. For I will have an everlasting crown and the joy of the reward of the just if the peoples who have returned to the unity of the church by our efforts remain firm in the same faith. For as by divine intention it was our responsibility to draw them back to the unity of the church of Christ, so may it be your teaching responsibility to instill in them Catholic dogmas so that instructed in the knowledge of the truth they may be able wholly to reject pernicious error, to keep to the path of the true faith in charity, and to embrace the communion of the Catholic church with an intense desire. But as I am confident that pardon will easily be granted for the fact that, out of ignorance, this great nation was in error, so I do not doubt that it will be very serious if it doubts the truth which it has recognized and turns its eyes away – which God forbid – from its powerful light. Therefore I have considered it especially necessary for your holinesses to come together since I have faith in the saying of the Lord, 'Where two or three are gathered together in my name, there am I in the midst of them.' For I

believe that the Blessed Trinity is present in this council and therefore I confess my faith before you as one in the presence of God."[1]

370. Let all kings learn from this to venerate the holy councils, to encourage them to meet, and to show humility in exhorting the holy bishops. Let the holy bishops learn to support kings for through a good king the church of Christ increases in proportion to his power.

371. I will add still another example, that of King Sisenandus. When prompted by the zealous love of Christ and devotion of the most devout king of Gaul and Spain, Sisenandus, the priests had met in the city of Toledo in the year 581 and the assembly was gathered in the basilica of the holy martyr Leocadia, the king himself with a magnificent and noble retinue entered to demonstrate his faith. After first prostrating himself on the ground in front of the priests of God, with tears and sighs he begged them to intercede with the Lord for him. Then with religious concern he urged the synod to be mindful of the decrees of the Fathers and to devote its efforts to affirming the rights of the church and correcting abuses which had developed through neglect and had permitted the usurpation of the rights of ecclesiastics. At the end of that council – which [St.] Isidore attended – the bishops said, "Glory and honor to Almighty God in whose name we have been gathered together. After this, peace, salvation, and a long reign to our most pious and devout lord, King Sisenandus, because of whose devotion we have been convened to adopt this salutary decree. May the glory of Christ strengthen his reign and protect him to the end of his old age by the grace of the Most High God. And after the glory of this present kingdom may he pass to the eternal kingdom and reign forever who rules so well on earth with the aid of the one who is King of Kings and Lord of Lords."[2]

372. Similarly we read that King Chintilanus together with the nobles and elders of the palace entered another council at Toledo as a suppliant commending himself to the prayers of the priests and that with holy exhortation he compelled his subjects to do the same. By divine inspiration he published a law which the council decreed at his command that three days of prayer should be observed from the thirteenth of December throughout his whole kingdom.[3]

373. Know this now, o kings! Learn from these examples, you who

---

[1] The Third Council of Toledo – A.D. 589 (Mansi 9, pp. 977ff).
[2] The Fourth Council of Toledo – A.D. 633 (Mansi 10, pp. 614 and 641).
[3] The Fifth Council of Toledo – A.D. 636 (Mansi 10, p. 653).

judge on earth. For God is thus to be served in fear and praised with trembling. Kings have always had the custom of choosing some outstanding famous men of the past to follow. Follow the examples described above on the way to hold councils and you will live happily.

CHAPTER XI

THE KING IS OBLIGED TO INCREASE THE FAITH AND DEVOTION OF HIS SUBJECTS. THE EXAMPLE IS GIVEN OF THE TEACHING OF ST. GREGORY TO HILPERT, THE KING OF THE FRANKS. THE CHURCH IS ENTRUSTED TO KINGS, AND THEY ARE OBLIGED TO GIVE AN ACCOUNTING OF THAT TRUST.

374. And therefore note the words with which Pope St. Gregory exhorts Hilpert [Ethelbert] king of the Franks [English] chapter 264, where he says, "Almighty God appoints good men to govern nations so that through them the gifts of his power may be given to all those in authority. We see that this has been done in the case of the nation of the English over which you rule in your glory so that the graces that have been granted to you may also by the gift of heaven be shared with the nation under you. And therefore, glorious son, preserve carefully the divine grace which you have received; strive to spread the Christian faith among the peoples subject to you; increase your earnest zeal for their conversion; attack the worship of idols and destroy the houses of worship of the pagans; promote the moral conduct of your subjects exhorting them to great purity of life, instilling fear in them, correcting them, and providing examples of good works so that you will find that the One whose name you spread on earth will reward you in heaven. For he whose honor you seek to preserve among the nations will also glorify your name among your successors. Because the most pious Emperor Constantine turned the Roman commonwealth to Almighty God away from the perverse worship of idols and subordinated himself and the commonwealth to Our Lord Jesus Christ and together with the peoples subject to him was converted with all his heart to God, he outdid all the rulers of antiquity in renown, and surpassed his predecessors in reputation and

good works. And now may Your Grace strive to spread the knowledge of the one God, Father, Son, and Holy Spirit, among the kings and people subject to you so that you too may surpass the earlier kings of your nation in merit and praise, and may be saved from your own sins in the terrible judgment of Almighty God in proportion as you have eliminated those of others who are your subjects."[1]

375. This is the duty of a king – to spread the Catholic faith among his subjects and thus to win a glorious name. St. Isidore speaks this way and other words of his are contained in [C.] 23 q. 5 [c. 20]. The conclusion to which he comes is that God is the author of royal power and often permits a king to abuse that power because of the faults of the people. The king in his power receives from the true God the responsibility for the holy church entrusted to him, for which he is obliged to render an account because all are bound by the laws of faith. The king should not think that he is freed from the laws,[2] for if a law is just it is binding and not otherwise, and therefore it also binds the king himself who is obliged to rule justly.

[1] Pope Gregory I to Ethelbert, King of England (PL 77, p. 120).
[2] A reference to the Roman law statement (*Digest*, 1, 3, *De legibus*) that "the prince is freed from the laws."

CHAPTER XII

THE KING OR PRINCE SHOULD ADOPT LAWS AND GENERAL STATUTES WHICH AFFECT THE PROVINCE WITH THE CONSENT OF GENERAL COUNCILS OF BOTH ESTATES OF HIS KINGDOM, AND – EXCEPT FOR HIS POWER OF DISPENSATION – OBSERVE AND DEFEND THEM. WITH THE AGREEMENT OF HIS UNIVERSAL COUNCIL HE SHOULD HAVE A DAILY COUNCIL MADE UP OF THOSE CHOSEN FROM THE WHOLE PROVINCE SUBJECT TO HIM.

376. In summary the main point to be understood is that it should be the aim of the ruler to establish laws by agreement. It is, therefore, fitting that all general laws affecting the commonwealth should be adopted and ordained in a council of primates and rulers of both [the

spiritual and temporal] estates. And the king should execute what is enacted with the agreement of the council, since this constitutional arrangement is the way in which the subjects wish the authority of the king to be limited. No one doubts that a universal council that acts by agreement of the head and members functions as a limit on the power of the executive [*presidentialem*] for the good of the commonwealth. It is true that in accordance with the principle of equity, if there are doubtful cases the king, acting for the public good and for the furtherance of justice, may dispense from, or interpret a law even though it has been established as described above. However this should be understood in the way that we have already described when we discussed the relation of the Roman pontiff to the canons: it does not mean that without action by the council the king can abolish a law which it has enacted, but that he has the right to declare that the spirit of a law does not apply in a particular case. It is sufficient to know that the function of the king in conciliar gatherings is to support, exhort, and confirm, and to obey and enforce ecclesiastical legislation on faith and divine worship.

377.   In matters related to the public welfare he must decide and act in the manner accurately described above when we spoke of the metropolitan as one who, as the head of his council, can only decide matters affecting the whole province with the consent of his suffragans. For the king ought to preside over a council in which matters pertaining to the government of the commonwealth are discussed; and he ought to decide each matter by consent, with the counsel of the nobles and bishops subject to him.

378.   For this purpose the ruler should have the best qualified of his subjects chosen from all parts of the realm to participate in a daily council with him. These counsellors ought to represent all the inhabitants of the realm, in the same way as was described above concerning the cardinals who assist the Roman pontiff. These counsellors ought constantly to defend the good of the public which they represent, giving advice and serving as the appropriate means through which the king can govern and influence his subjects and the subjects on proper occasions can influence him in return. The great strength of the kingdom comes from this daily council. The counsellors should be appointed to this task by agreement in a general meeting of the kingdom, and they should be publicly bound legally by oath to speak out openly for the public good. Since St. Thomas, Aegidius

Romanus, Sedulius Scotus, and before them Plato, and Cicero, (although the books of these last are not available) and also many others have left many volumes to us concerning the government of the commonwealth, everyone may refer to these works for the rest.

379. Next we should consider what the records show about the role of the emperor in the universal council of the Catholic Church.

CHAPTER XIII

THE EMPEROR IN ASSEMBLING, SUPPORTING, AND
OTHERWISE AIDING THE COUNCIL, ACTS IN THE
UNIVERSAL COUNCIL OF THE WHOLE CATHOLIC
CHURCH IN THE SAME WAY AS DOES THE KING
WITHIN HIS KINGDOM. HOW AND WHEN THE
EMPEROR WAS ACCUSTOMED TO CALL THOSE
UNIVERSAL COUNCILS. IMPORTANT EXAMPLES OF
OTHER EMPERORS ARE QUOTED AT LENGTH IN
ORDER TO ANSWER THOSE MODERNS WHO HAVE
SEEN FEW OF THE OLDER RECORDS.

380. From earlier chapters we know that the emperor always convened the holy meetings of the universal councils of the whole church. I have found this to be true after perusing the records of all the universal councils up to and including the Eighth Council held at the time of [the Emperor] Basil. Thus in the Fifth Action of the Eighth Council we read that the most worthy priest, Elias, secretary of the see of Jerusalem, said to all those assembled, "Know that in the past it was the emperors who convened the councils. They brought together representatives from the whole world to settle matters in this way. Following their example our most religious emperor has convened this universal council."[1] And I have read in the commentary on this statement by Anastasius, the librarian of the Holy See who translated the records of that synod from the Greek, that it had been customary for the emperors to convene universal councils from the whole world. We never read however that they convened local synods.[2] And the

---

[1] Mansi 16, p. 78.   [2] See Book II, no. 94.

canonical decree by the same council which was quoted earlier that says that the prince, i.e., the emperor, ought to be present at the universal council and not at others, is in agreement with this.

381.   Hence I repeat briefly what I said above, that the emperor acts in relation to the universal council of the Catholic Church as does the king in relation to the universal council of his kingdom. He should not convene it by force but by persuasion, as the letter of the Synod of Aquileia meeting at the time of St. Ambrose by decree of Emperors Theodosius and Valentinian states: "All are called by the princes, but no one is invited under compulsion."[3] But it was customary for the emperors through imperial decrees to remind the patriarchal sees of the need for a council, to establish the time and place of meeting, and to guarantee freedom and protection against oppression and intimidation, in accordance with the conditions laid down above for a council.

382.   And the decisions and decrees of the council do not derive their strength from being convened in this way but from the agreement of all to come to that meeting and from the participation and presence of those who are called – which is also discussed above. For when there is a general threat to the faith or something disturbs the universal church of Christ, then the emperor as guardian both of the faith and of the peace should take care first of all to suggest the need for a council to the Roman pontiff and to secure his consent to the calling of the council in a particular place, following the example of Emperors Valentinian and Marcian when they wrote as follows to Pope Leo: "For the sake of the holy Catholic religion and the Christian faith which, we believe, guides and strengthens our government, we believe that Your Holiness who possesses the primacy among the bishops of the faith of God should say what is proper in sacred letters at the outset. To strengthen the condition of our empire we invite and urge you to entreat the Eternal God that it may be our purpose and desire through the celebration of a council under your direction to remove all impious error and to maintain the greatest part of all the bishops of the Catholic faith pure and unsullied by sin."[4]

383.   Similarly we read that other emperors always invited the pope and the other patriarchs and all the bishops to hold a universal council. For we read that Emperor Marcian wrote as follows to Pope Leo: "Marcian to Leo, the most reverend bishop of the church of the

---

[3] Mansi 3, p. 615.   [4] Mansi 6, p. 94; PL 54, p. 899.

city of Rome: Your Holiness must be aware from our zealous prayer that we wish the true Christian religion and apostolic faith to remain strong and to be observed with piety by all the people. Further we do not doubt that our concern should be with our true religion and the worship of Our Saviour. Therefore we have received with joy and a properly grateful heart the most reverend men whom Your Holiness has sent to us. It is not necessary to say that if it should please Your Holiness to come to these parts and hold a council, to do this would greatly aid religion. May Your Holiness satisfy your desires and decide what is useful for the holy religion. But if it is too difficult to come to these parts, Your Holiness should tell us this in your letters so that we may send official letters throughout the East and to Thrace itself and Illyria, [decreeing] that all the most holy bishops should meet at a certain specific location as it shall please us in order to make a formal declaration as to what is good for the Christian religion and the Catholic faith, as Your Holiness has determined in accordance with church law."[5]

384. Also Emperor Constantine III [IV] who convened the Sixth Council in the year of Our Lord 686 or thereabouts wrote as follows to Pope Agatho: "The faithful Emperor Flavius Constantine to the most holy and blessed lord archbishop of old Rome: Your Paternal Blessedness and your many churches in old Rome have known that from the moment that God commanded us to rule as prince, certain men have wished to create a disturbance due to a verbal disagreement over religious dogma, involving groups both in your holy church and in this holy church of almighty God. However we have prohibited this as inopportune since we knew that particular disagreements not only cause disunity but lead to greater evils."

385. And below: "The truth of God is precious and according to the word of the Lord, 'He who wishes to be first over all, let him be minister to all.' And again it is said, 'Let all men know that you are my disciples from this, that you love one another.' Therefore when the circumstances indicate that a full council can take place we exhort Your Paternal Blessedness by this holy letter to send worthy and modest men who by God's inspiration have full knowledge of all doctrine and are learned in dogma, to represent your Apostolic See

[5] Mansi 6, p. 98: PL 54, pp. 903–905.

and council. They should bring the books which should be produced and they should possess authorization to meet with the most holy and blessed patriarch of this city, and with Macharios, the most holy patriarch of Theopolis, that is the city of Antioch, and search through them in all mildness and modesty. By the grace of the Holy Spirit they will find and consent to the truth. This present letter will serve as formal notification to those who come here from your see. By almighty God we swear that we do not favor either party but we will maintain absolute impartiality toward both parties and require nothing in the way of a decision from those who are sent by you, but we will honor them and give them a splendid and worthy reception. And if both sides agree, then it will be well. But if they do not, we will send them back to you in all humanity, excusing ourselves from further action before the judgment of God who established us to preserve the holy and spotless faith which we have received, for which we will render a full and proper account before the holy and terrible divine tribunal. For we can invite and urge a settlement and the unification of all Christians but we do not wish to impose compulsion."

386. "But let the persons be decided who will be sent by Your Paternal Blessedness. And so from your holy church, if it seems appropriate to do so, three persons may suffice but if it sends more – let it send as many as it desires. The council may send up to twelve metropolitan bishops. But from the four Byzantine monasteries four monks may come from each one. For if time permitted, we would have striven to establish a plenary council."

387. And below, "But God has advanced our council that we were delaying at this time. For all these reasons we bid Your Paternal Blessedness to place no impediment in the way of the will of God, but to send your representatives. For we hope that God who in his mercy has wished that this matter be discussed, now will grant that through the Holy Spirit the truth may shine forth and all may be enlightened and abandon division or contention."

388. And below: "We have commanded Theodore, the most glorious patrician and exarch of our province of Italy, beloved of Christ, to provide ships and expenses to all those coming and everything useful to them including, if required, armed galleys for their protection so that they may come to us, with God's cooperation,

unharmed and free of danger. May God preserve you for many years, most holy and blessed father."[6]

389. This letter which was translated by the most eloquent Leo of Sicily, Pope of Rome, [Leo II] who was learned in both the Greek and Latin languages, is found at the beginning of the Sixth Council with many important provisions. Note especially that the emperor should propose the appropriate time for a holy council and should call it in all reverence, and guarantee full liberty and complete impartiality to those who come. And we read likewise that other emperors wrote the bishops in the same way in their sacred letters.

390. Thus the aforesaid Emperors Valentinian and Marcian wrote as follows: "We think that what tends to the true faith and orthodox Christianity should be preferred above other things." And below: "Hence let Your Holiness with whatever reverend bishops you have approved who are over the holy churches under you, accompanied by experts in the Holy Scripture and orthodox doctrine and the true faith, and eminent before all, hasten to come to the city of Nicaea on the first day of September next. For anyone who refuses a universal council which will be useful for the whole world, commits a sin and offends against our imperial majesty. And Your Holiness should know that we in our devotion will be present at that council unless some unavoidable public responsibilities require us to be away."[7]

391. The letter speaks of Nicaea because Valentinian directed the council to that city but later it was transferred to Chalcedon. Hence the same emperors wrote to those gathered in Nicaea, "It is our desire that decrees be issued concerning the holy orthodox religion so that all doubt may be ended and genuine peace may return to the holy Catholic churches. We think that this should take precedence over everything else. Because therefore we wish to be present at the holy council but necessary public concerns keep us away, let Your Holinesses [lit. – Religion] not think it serious that our presence is delayed, but pray that with God's help we may settle the things which we have at hand and come there so that decisions may be made in our presence which will end all dissension and questioning and confirm the true and venerable orthodox faith."

392. After this the same emperors wrote that the representatives of Pope Leo strongly wished them to be present at the council. And

---

[6] Mansi 11, pp. 195–202.   [7] Mansi 6, pp. 551ff.

because the requirements of their office made it easier to participate in Chalcedon than in Nicaea, they wrote as follows: "Therefore if Your Holinesses agree, please come to the city of Chalcedon." And because their safety was in doubt because of Eutyches, they sent to the emperors who were in Thrace indicating this to them, and they replied promising them full protection.[8]

393. We may conclude from this that the emperors ought to place matters of faith above everything else and to do whatever is necessary for the success of the councils with due reverence and charity and without compulsion – also that they should be present at the council to confirm its [decisions on] faith, not to exercise compulsion, as the emperor Marcian said, quoting Constantine, D. 96 [c. 2] *Nos ad fidem.*

[8] Mansi 66, pp. 553, pp. 558–559.

CHAPTER XIV

THE EMPEROR SHOULD WORK TO PREVENT ANY DISTURBANCE OF THE COUNCIL. HE SHOULD EXPEL THOSE WHO DESERVE TO BE EXPELLED AND PUNISH THOSE WHO DISTURB THE CHURCH FATHERS, SO THAT THE COUNCIL MAY PROCEED IN TRANQUILLITY AND FREEDOM. MANY GOOD EXAMPLES OF THIS ARE GIVEN.

394. Also the emperor and all kings when councils meet in their domains should strive to prevent any disturbance and expel those who should be expelled. Thus the most devout Empress Pulcheria wrote to the consul who was general in Bithynia that he should concern himself with the good order of the council which had met in Nicaea and had not yet been transferred to Chalcedon, "All the reverend bishops have met at our direction, awaiting our presence, and with God's help we shall participate shortly. However we have learned that certain clerics, monks, and laymen who are in the habit of disturbing the good order which is pleasing to God, have come to Nicaea and are trying to create a disturbance in a way which is displeasing to us. Therefore we have directed these worthy letters to you so that you will speedily expel from the city and its environs those clergymen who

remain there without having been summoned by us or without the permission of their bishops – whether they are included among the clergy or in some cases have been removed by their own bishops – as well as all monks and laymen who have no reason to be at the council. Thus the council may sit in proper order without commotion or dissension and all may approve in common what has been revealed by Christ the Lord. You should know that if anyone is found there still making a disturbance before we come and particularly after our arrival, we will see to it that there will be trouble for you."[1]

395. Observe that laymen, monks, and clergy, especially those who do not have the permission of their bishops, should not be present at universal councils. For no disagreement or tumult should be permitted in the councils. In the First Action at Chalcedon when the reading of the acts of the Council of Ephesus was prevented by the noise, we read that the most glorious judges and the full assembly said, "These outcries of the people do not please the bishops nor do they aid the participants." This was foreseen in the Council of Toledo and a penalty of three days excommunication was provided for those who disturbed the council at the holy meeting place.[2]

396. Thus we read in the acts of the Council of Chalcedon that to protect the Council of Ephesus the following instructions were given by the emperors to Elpidius, a worthy man, and a count of the Sacred Consistory, "Therefore we have chosen you and Eulogius, a worthy man and a tribune and notary, to be responsible for defending the faith since you are proven in many other matters and we consider you most upright and zealous for the worship of God and worthy to carry out our commands faithfully. You should permit no disturbance to take place concerning what may be decided by the holy council in Ephesus. But if you see anyone trying to injure the holy faith through disagreement and disturbance you ought to place him in custody and note this in your report so that the case may be discussed in proper order. But you ought to be present at its decisions and expedite its labor so that the holy synod may know that its actions are being observed and approved. And make known to us whatever is decided."

397. And below, "No other business concerning financial matters should be discussed until the questions concerning the Catholic faith are formally resolved. For we have given you both civil support

---

[1] Mansi 6, p. 555.   [2] Mansi 6, p. 591 and 7, p. 137.

through the letters that we have written to the worthy proconsul as well as auxiliary military aid, so that with your own resources or with this assistance you can do what we have commanded. Questions of faith are much more important than any others since divine matters are superior to those that are human. And hasten to give us a report on what has been done on this matter. A similar letter has been sent to the worthy Eulogius."[3]

398.   Observe that the emperor ought to be especially concerned with the protection of the universal council and should do everything to avoid tumult and disturbance and to ensure that what has been decreed is observed. These are the responsibilities of the emperor at the beginning of a council – to convene it by exhortation and protect its liberty without the necessity of exercising compulsion.

[3] Mansi, 6, pp. 595ff.

CHAPTER XV

THE CONVOCATION OF A COUNCIL BY THE EMPEROR HAS THE CHARACTER OF AN EXHORTATION WHILE THAT OF THE POPE HAS THE FORCE OF A COMMAND FOR THE PRIESTHOOD. CONVOCATION BY THE EMPEROR CAN ACQUIRE THE FORCE OF A COMMAND IF THE CHURCH IS IN URGENT NEED AND THE POPE NEGLECTS TO DO ANYTHING.

399.   Doubt could arise on the question of the convocation of the council since it is stated above that this is the responsibility of the pope. However no one could have any justifiable doubt about the rest of what is said there. On that point let us say that the convening of the council is of interest to both the pope and the emperor – to the pope since by virtue of his rulership of the priesthood he has the power to command all the other bishops concerning a meeting to consider the general state of the church, since this is his primary responsibility. Because he has this power entrusted to him he has the right to command faithful Christians to meet, especially all the priests subject

to him. But the emperor exhorts and persuades bishops and commands the laity.

400. The Roman pontiff does not claim that the right to call the council belongs to him alone but that a council may not meet without his authorization. And so in a case of imminent danger to the church when the emperor first urges the pope and then the others to meet, he follows the ancient practice. In such a case he requests the authorization of the Roman pontiff first and then that of the others. And if he did not act in this way but called the bishops together without calling on the Roman pontiff, it would not be a fully authoritative universal council, according to what is said above. It is essential to a council that no one be excluded, especially none of the bishops who desire and are able to be present.

401. This is all the more true in the case of the Roman pontiff. But if a request was made of the Roman pontiff and he did not send representatives and did not come although others obeyed the urging of the emperor, the council should not proceed quickly unless the necessity of the church – which has no law – should demand quick action.

402. But if the Roman pontiff opposes a meeting called by the emperor, it is customary to obey the Roman pontiff unless the necessity of the church demonstrates persuasively that it is rather the emperor who is to be obeyed. Hence I do not think that it is absurd to say that since the responsibility to keep the faith has also been entrusted to the holy empire, the emperor himself can order a synod to provide for the needs of the church if the pope neglects or refuses to do so in a case involving great imminent danger of disturbance to the church. For despite the fact that proper order and positive law have exempted the clergy from the power of the emperor in the interest of peace, placing the priesthood above the empire and the Roman pontiff over all nevertheless when the reasons for which this holy arrangement was established do not apply – since everything was established for the preservation of the holy church – we resort then to methods appropriate for the times to attain that same end, without being concerned about an arrangement that is of no assistance to us. And this is sufficient.

CHAPTER XVI

ACCORDING TO THE RECORDS THE EMPEROR
PRESIDED OVER THE UNIVERSAL COUNCILS. WITH
HIM HE HAD A FEW — RARELY MORE THAN FIFTEEN
— OF HIS SENATORS WHO WERE PRESENT ONLY BY
HIS COMMAND, AND THERE WERE NO OTHERS.
THEREFORE THE EMPEROR HAS JURISDICTION OVER
ALL THE LAYMEN IN THE COUNCIL AND ASSIGNS
PLACES TO THEM.

403.   Now let us seek to discover from the texts of the holy councils of the church when it was at its best, how the emperor and his patricians and senators should act in the council once it is assembled. First of all, I find in the records of all of them – Chalcedon, Constantinople, Nicaea, and Ephesus – that either the emperor himself was present or representatives present by his command from the sacred senate and judges – along with in all cases a few of the wisest and most important princes. I do not find that their number ever exceeded twenty; indeed rarely were there more than fifteen. And when the emperor was present in person, I find that he always presided.

404.   At the Sixth Council, Constantine III presided in the center along with ten of the more important patricians, and on his left sat the representatives of old Rome and of Jerusalem and on his right the other patriarchs, first the patriarch of Constantinople, then the patriarch of Alexandria, and after him that of Antioch. And the bishops from those sees sat together on one bench. At the Eighth Council, Basil presided and on the right in order sat the representatives of the Apostolic See and the other patriarchs. But at Chalcedon, since Emperor Marcian was not present at the beginning, the senate and the judges sat in the center as Constantine III was described as doing. And when Marcian himself came to the Council, he presided with a few members of his senate, and the representatives of the Apostolic See and the patriarchs sat on each side as they did in the Sixth Council. But out of humility Emperor Basil signed the acts of the Council after the patriarchs and the representatives of the patriarchal sees, although the whole council asked him to sign first,

but he refused out of humility as the final acts of that council indicate.[1]

405. Therefore because the senators and patricians and illustrious princes who are part of the emperor's retinue [lit. – body] were accustomed to be present only at the command of the emperor as all the records indicate, it should be noted that none of the secular princes other than the emperor has the right to participate in a universal council unless he has been ordered to do so by the emperor or the holy council. But those who are parts of the imperial retinue such as the patricians, exconsuls, exarchs, and the holy senate should be directly associated with the emperor himself.

406. And so it is an insult to the emperor to prevent him from assigning the seating of secular princes who do not have any legal right to participate in a universal council and whose right to participate derives from his command. For the ranking of the secular participants depends on the emperor, since everyone, including those otherwise not subject to him, is under him in the council because of his role as protector of the council. Therefore he has jurisdiction over all of them. And it is especially insulting to the electors of the holy empire who represent the sacred senate and people of Rome and who comprise a single body closely linked to the emperor if anyone puts himself ahead of them without a command from His Sacred Majesty, especially if he is not of higher rank. For the honor of the holy empire and the public good this kind of ambition should not be tolerated.

[1] Mansi 11, p. 211; 16, p. 81; 6, p. 579; 16, p. 190.

CHAPTER XVII

LAYMEN MAY NOT SPEAK IN THE COUNCIL WHEN
CHURCH MATTERS ARE DISCUSSED. THIS MAKES IT
EASY TO AGREE ON THE SEATING OF THOSE
SECULAR PRINCES WHOSE PRESENCE WOULD BE
USEFUL TODAY. ITS SPECIFICS ARE SET FORTH.

407. Nevertheless to avoid needless controversy on this subject, it should be known that the lay princes mentioned above, even when

they are present because of the emperor's command, do not have the right to speak in the council but only to listen. Hence we read in the Fourth Action of the Eighth Council that when the representatives of old Rome spoke to the princes who were present by order of Basil, they said, "O magnificent and glorious princes, ask those who have come in to sign this document." The princes said, "We will ask them in obedience to your command not because of our power. For this power is yours." And at the end in the chapter which begins *Multam quidem*, the substance of which is reproduced below, Emperor Basil says ". . . although according to canon law they do not have the right to say anything at all about ecclesiastical cases, for this is the responsibility of bishops and priests . . ." – he was speaking about the laity.[1] Similarly Ambrose in his letter no. 75, *Against Auxentius*, says to Emperor Valentinian, "If we review all holy writings and actions of the ancients, no one would deny that in a matter of faith bishops were accustomed to judge Christian emperors, not emperors bishops." And below, "Your father, by God's grace a man of advanced years, used to say, 'It is not mine to judge bishops.' Now Your Highness says, 'I ought to judge them,' while he, although baptized in Christ, thought that he was incapable of making such a weighty judgment."[2]

408.   Observe that the emperor should not make a judgment involving bishops on matters relating to the faith. But venerable Sedulius writes in chapter 11 of his book, *On Christian Rulers*, that after this Emperor Valentinian when he was asked by the holy bishops to be present for the issuance of corrections in holy dogma, said to the council, "It is not right for me, the least of the people, to look into such matters. But let priests whose responsibility it is, come together among themselves wherever they wish."[3] And in the First Action of the Sixth Council (of Constantinople) it says, "Homage to the great and most pious Emperor Constantine, beloved of Christ, presiding in the council-chamber of his sacred palace, to all those present and listening to us at the command of His Highness under God's guidance, and to Niceta, the most glorious exconsul, patrician and count of the imperial court . . ."[4]

409.   Further evidence is provided above where the patrician, Bahanes, speaking in the name of the others by command of the

[1] Mansi 16, pp. 57ff.   [2] PL 16, p. 1046.
[3] Sedulius Scotus, *On Christian Rulers and the Poems*, Binghamton, N.Y.: 1983, p. 70. (Cf. Bk. III, no. 288.)   [4] Mansi 11, p. 210.

Emperor said that the senate was present to listen. And the acts of the Council of Chalcedon prove this where after the princes who were present by order of Marcian are listed by name at the beginning, there is the addition, "also present at the holy and universal council meeting at the imperial command in the city of Chalcedon, Bishops Paschasinus and Lucentius and the priest, Boniface, representing the most holy reverend Archbishop Leo of the sweet city of Rome, and Anatolius, the most reverend bishop of the famous city of Constantinople . . ."[5]

410. Note that the council is composed exclusively of priests and that laymen do not have a legal right to speak in it, especially when it discusses ecclesiastical matters. Therefore since they do not have a legal right to speak and they have come only to listen, for the freedom of the synod it is right that they are subject to the emperor's decision in all matters relating to the council since they should not be present without his order and permission. Therefore secular princes should send bishops rather than laymen so that they can have a voice through them. And then all questioning would cease since according to canon law anyone who wishes to speak should await his turn by seniority of rank. But if kings and princes have something to contribute to the council they can do this through someone speaking in the usual place publicly assigned for this purpose, since no one should be denied a hearing. But it is the right of priests to deliberate about and decide upon church matters.

411. If what was rightly introduced in antiquity were observed, there would be no question about seating and no disturbance of the council would arise on that account. It is true that the princes were invited to the Council of Constance and they are sufficiently well represented in this Council of ours at Basel to arrive at a single concordant agreement of all, for the power of a conciliar decree comes from concordance. And for the preservation of our faith which has been reduced to a limited area – especially since the power of the emperor today does not constrain and compel all as it once did – things should be discussed with the participation and support of the rulers and kings of other parts of Christendom so that all may see that the definitions of the council are just and holy and irrefutable with the result that peace will be preserved and schism avoided.

---

[5] Mansi 6, p. 566. On Bahanes, see Book II, no. 139 and Book III, nos. 425–426.

412. Great caution therefore should be exercised in assigning seats and places to avoid the great confusion that can result from disturbances which frequently arise from competition over honors on the pretext of the defense of one's dignity. And this situation can easily be helped by separating the seats, setting out one bench for the emperor and those immediately associated with him, one for the king of France and those with him, and the same for the kings of Spain and others, so that each ruler is sitting on the bench reserved for his kingdom without mixing the various kingdoms – and all the seats are allocated according to rank. And the order should be observed in giving [the kiss of] peace that the kiss of peace is given according to rank in the kingdom to the one who is first in rank on the bench of that kingdom and passed on to the others. But in processions let the kings be grouped in order at the emperor's side with all the others walking behind them in order, the nobles and ambassadors of each kingdom walking in line behind their king, just as they sit on the bench one after the other without anyone else between. But if two kings are in disagreement over the rank and priority of their kingdoms let both be situated at an equal distance from the emperor, with the older one on the right and the younger one on the left without prejudice to either one.

413. And let the same thing be done with the seats of two who disagree; let the bench of the older one be put on the right, and that of the younger on the left. And in procession anyone who is subject to a lord will be situated in a single file behind him according to his rank. Lacking a better arrangement, perhaps this can easily avoid the scandals that often arise. It is certainly equitable and promotes peace, and is based on the law of precedence indicated above, according to which everyone of whatever rank who represents another as representative or legate should sit in the place of the one he represents.

414. According to this arrangement the bench of the representative of any kingdom is considered as the throne of the king whom the ambassadors if they are present or the princes nearest to him even without special appointment by the king are to represent in the interest of peace. And who doubts that peace will be preserved in the best possible way when this order is also observed on every bench within that kingdom with the representatives of the king in front and the princes following by rank?

CHAPTER XVIII

THE DUTY OF THE EMPEROR AND OF ALL THE
LAYMEN IN THE COUNCIL IS TO PROMOTE CLEAR
AND IMPARTIAL JUDGMENT ON ALL MATTERS THAT
ARE TREATED THERE. THEY SHOULD ACT AS
NEUTRAL JUDGES IN ALL MATTERS. THE
PROCEDURE FOR A DECISION BY THE SYNOD IS
DESCRIBED.

415. Next we should see what His Imperial Majesty should do once the council is in session. But I find that the emperors sometimes appointed the chairman of the council, as appears in a letter of Theodosius and Valentinian to Dioscorus in the Second – condemned – Council of Ephesus, beginning *Ante hoc quidem,* which says "We have considered it necessary to take the occasion of these imperial letters to Your Reverence to make manifest to Your Holiness and to the whole synod that following the rules of the holy fathers we confer the office of chairman upon Your Holiness, both over Theodoric [Theodoret] and all the others who are involved in the meeting of the sacred council." But I have not read that this was done in any council other than this pseudo-council. As appears in that letter this was done out of fear of the Nestorians. Also it is possible that the representatives of the Apostolic See of Rome had not yet arrived, so that Dioscorus of Alexandria held the chairmanship properly.[1] Hence we should not be too concerned over this.

416. But the emperor himself should first make an effort to see that his judges and senators take great care that everything that is to be discussed is properly treated in accordance with canon law – neither abruptly nor too quickly nor under the influence of fear or pressure, in proper sequence without confusion of subject-matter. Let none of the procedures laid down in the holy canons for finding the truth in judicial decision and discussions be omitted. For instance, neutral judges should be appointed so that what is evident and manifest may be made most clear and a definitive conclusion arrived at, which can

---

[1] Mansi 6, p. 599, from the so-called "Robber" Council of Ephesus (449), later overruled by the Council of Chalcedon. Nestorius held that there were two persons, human and divine, in Christ.

be put into execution by His Imperial Majesty without hesitation.

417. And so I read [in the records of] all the universal councils that when the emperors were present, either judges of the sacred palace or [members of] the senate acted as moderators to direct everything to the clear light of truth, even acting as judges, with the advice of the council, on the question of the observance of time-limits and post-ponements. Sometimes they also made decisions with the assent and manifest approval of the council. For instance on the question of the primacy which arose at the Council of Chalcedon between the patriarchs of Constantinople and Rome, the judges decided on the basis of the canons which had been produced and after their decision they asked the holy council whether it agreed or had another opinion. But the whole council agreed, as appears at the end of the acts of the Council of Chalcedon.[2]

418. But the fixed character of the decision and of whatever is done by anyone in a council depends exclusively on the consent of the council, as has been said above. Hence whenever we read that the judges decided something, the force of their decision depended on the consent and authorization of the synod, not on any instructions of the emperor whose authority is not superior to that of the universal council. However by their own authority the emperors can seek to have matters carried out in canonical form so that they cannot be blamed for the conduct of the discussion, since they append their signatures by way of confirmation at the end as witnesses to a proper judgment.[3]

419. It would be too long to review all the details of the interventions by the emperors and judges aimed at finding out the truth of the matter under investigation. But there is one conclusion – it was done in the way in which canonical decisions ought to be carried out – i.e., the accused should be called three times and led into the synod, the charge should be read, the accused should answer, the council should deliberate, what has been denied should be proven, it should be demonstrated from the acts of the councils and the writings of the proper fathers that what is objected to is heresy, [and] the notary with the book should swear that this is the authentic text in the records. These and similar actions should be taken as appropriate for the case. Another good procedure was followed that the canons in which

[2] Mansi 7, pp. 451–454.   [3] Mansi 6, p. 650.

anyone found a relevant passage were produced in writing and the other side indicated whether it believed or suspected that the text had been altered.[4] And so the decisions of the councils were always very clear and open. So much for this matter.

[4] Mansi 7, p. 8.

CHAPTER XIX

THE EMPEROR OUGHT TO EXHORT THE WHOLE COUNCIL, AS DID THE MOST PIOUS BASIL. HIS NOTABLE SPEECH IS QUOTED AT LENGTH.

420. I have said [that] next [we would discuss] the emperor's customary conduct in the council. Since the emperor often gave gracious speeches of exhortation to the councils, I have made an effort to include the speech made at the Eighth Council by Basil, a most devout Christian emperor,[1] whose footsteps our most invincible Emperor Sigismund, crowned by God, is following in this Council of Basel – so that one might properly say that this holy Council of Basel is being carried out with another Basil presiding. At the opening of the council, the most gentle Emperor Basil spoke [as follows]: "Since divine providence has most kindly committed the government of the world to us, we have made every effort to resolve first the public needs of the church and to establish stable tranquillity by settling the quarrels which have increased over the years because of Satan's hatred of the good. By divine inspiration we have long desired a council and we have now decided to bring together representatives from the other patriarchal sees for the aforesaid reason and the King of Infinite Power, the Prince of Peace, who governs our empire has cooperated with our intention. As you see he has filled our council and brought it together for this very purpose."

421. "From old Rome two bishops have come and one deacon of the seven authorized – all known for their prudence, intellect, and religious life; from the eastern patriarchate of Antioch, we see the

[1] On the character of Emperor Basil, see II, 1, no. 73, n. 3, and D. Stiernon, *Constantinople IV*, Paris, 1967.

most holy and reverend archbishop of Tyre; from the holy church of God in Jerusalem, the holy Zion, out of which, as was prophesied, came the new law and the judge of all nations, the Word of the Lord – [we see] its most holy *secretary*, an apostolic man filled with all divine and human wisdom."

422. "Therefore with the cooperation and grace of Christ, the universal king and God who rules over all things, by our imperial diligence and zeal we have removed what seemed to all of you to be insuperable obstacles. We urge and exhort all of you, brethren, to participate with humility and reverence in this holy universal council as a meeting which is generally useful to all. Eliminate unhealthy remedies, movements, or affections and do not look for contention, knowing that it is better to be defeated than to win in a sinful or unjust way. For thus everyone who suffers internal infection will receive health and attain eternal salvation. We give the support of our empire to you who have received from God the power to decide in councils. For we do not doubt that you love and pursue divine truth and justice as far as you can."

423. "But so that it may become clear that insofar as power has been given us in church matters by God we have omitted none of the things that are necessary and convenient, we especially ask you now to rise above all favoritism and hatred and imitate the dispassionateness of the divine nature in not showing partiality to anyone in your decision, whether to the powerful because of their rank or personal friendship, or the poor out of pity for their condition. Thus a most peaceful church order will follow, in accordance with the intention of the will of God and of our most tranquil empire."[2]

424. It would be [too] lengthy to insert the eloquent speeches of other emperors. Every emperor has striven to adapt his exhortation to the matters under discussion as did this and other most pious emperors.

[2] Mansi 16, pp. 18ff.

CHAPTER XX

THE EMPEROR MAY SEND MESSAGES TO HIS REPRESENTATIVES, PERSUADING AND ADVISING THE COUNCIL, AS HAS BEEN DONE IN THE PAST. THE PROCEDURE IN THE EIGHTH COUNCIL ASSEMBLED BY EMPEROR BASIL IS CITED.

425. It was customary for the emperors if they themselves were absent to give those who were to represent them at the council an address containing suggestions on the matters which were to be considered. Thus we read that in the Seventh Action of the Eighth Council, the patrician and prefect, Bahanes, said to the council while Photius was present in the council with his bishops, "Through me, his unworthy servant, our holy emperor wishes to make a speech to these bishops." The most reverend representatives of old Rome said, "As the emperor commands." Bahanes said to Photius and his bishops, "The emperor addresses you. Tell us, men, where you come from. Do you come from heaven, from hell, or from the earth where we live? Show me now for if there has been a heresy or a schism somewhere and anyone is in disagreement with the four patriarchates, why has he been spared? Answer, I am listening. Today there are four patriarchates, in fact five, that condemn you. What do you say about this? Is there anything in your favor? If so, tell me." Photius' bishops said, "The canons of the holy apostles and the fathers." Bahanes replied, in accordance with the command of the emperor. "Tell me what canon is in your favor. Where did the Lord set up his canons – in his churches or somewhere else? And where are these churches today and where is the gospel preached? Is it anywhere else than where these representatives are? Tell me." The bishops of Photius said, "God save our emperor. We have sought a guarantee that we could speak without being punished in order that we might explain our position in full confidence but this was not granted. How then are we to speak?" Bahanes said, "Our holy emperor addresses this warning to you. God has heard my prayer and brought these holy men from the ends of the earth to act not on the basis of appearances but of equity and justice. You say you would accept a guarantee of protection. On this I wish anyone who has been hurt or injured by me to say

so. Now the representatives of all the bishoprics are here so that you may say whatever you have to say to defend yourselves." The bishops of Photius said, "We know that the holy emperor does not wish to cause harm to anyone. What can we say? If we said what we deserved, it would not be done."

426. Bahanes said, "By our holy emperor's orders, you may say anything. For he commands, desires, and agrees that you should speak. But in view of your insults, the judges do not wish to hear you." The bishops supporting Photius said, "We do not recognize those judges." Bahanes said, "Do they violate the rule of the patriarchs and make judgments contrary to reason?" Amphilochus, a bishop under Photius, said, "Totally contrary to reason." Bahanes said, "And do they make judgments in violation of the rules of their patriarchs?" The bishops of Photius said, "Indeed they do." Bahanes said, "Go to the patriarchates and prove it." The most reverend Christian emperor Basil said, "Whatever you think about all this, since you know that these men [the judges] come from the patriarchates with letters of recommendation, accept them and whatever they decide. Whatever doubts you have – you say that they are not fair and so do not act in accordance with the directions of the patriarchs – go there and discuss it with them and bring us better proof and we will so order." The bishops of Photius said, "We did not witness this decision. Why do we have to obey a decision which we did not witness?" At the bidding of the emperor, Bahanes said, "The holy emperor says, do not say, brethren, that I wish to send you there for any of you to perish. God is my witness, before the whole senate and the sacred council, I say that whomever I send there I will bring back here again."[1]

427. Many similar things which should be noted appear in the acts. I have quoted from them because they contain a particular point which is always valid: the emperor should see to it that the council conducts its sessions in the clearest possible way, avoiding any actions which might be called into question.

428. There is another interesting thing in these acts. It appears there that when the bishops supporting Photius wanted to defend themselves with numerous arguments and actions, the emperor said that the persons cited by them had later been forgiven by the church, "But you remain in a state of sin today and lie like dead men in the

[1] Mansi 16, pp. 99ff.

tomb of your iniquity. Hence all the high patriarchs together condemn you. But our divinely-strengthened empire is peace-loving and kind and concerned with your guidance and is taking measures for you to receive the forgiveness that the holy universal council decides. For we all know that you are laymen (not bishops) and we have not brought you to rant and rave and act out of order. All your words are lying and deceitful." The bishops of Photius said, "The devil himself has not dared to say that we are laymen, even if they [our opponents] say it."

429.   The emperor said that they were laymen because they had been ordained by Photius who was not a bishop, and they wished to defend Photius and themselves. And when a certain Eulampius, one of Photius' bishops, came to speak with the emperor, the representatives of the Apostolic See said that Eulampius had been condemned and excommunicated by the Apostolic See and therefore the emperor should not speak to him:

430.   Then Basil said, "I have prayed repeatedly that they might not be lost and therefore I have called them here. If they do not agree with the church, they will confirm what the patriarchs have decided even without wishing to do so. For no one can reject the power given to the patriarchs by Christ, our God and Saviour."[2] Note the devotion and concern that the emperor should have, especially his faith in, and fidelity to, the things decided by the councils.

[2] Mansi 16, pp. 88–89.

CHAPTER XXI

THE EMPEROR CAN AND SHOULD GIVE THE COUNCIL HIS OPINION AS TO WHAT IS NECESSARY FOR THE CHURCH. THIS SHOULD BE DISCUSSED IN THE SYNOD, AS WAS DONE IN THE CASE OF EMPEROR MARCIAN.

431.   The emperor should also give his advice on the business to be transacted by the council and if anything seems appropriate for legislative action, he should suggest what the council should do and press

for its adoption. For example, Marcian, the emperor at the Council of Chalcedon, said to the council, "There are certain points that we have reserved for action by your holinesses out of respect for your honor, thinking that normally it is better for them to be decided by this council than for us to decree them through our laws." At the command of the most holy and devout emperor, Beronicianus, the most devout secretary of the sacred consistory, read out the points. And the first chapter said that monks who are in individual cities and provinces should be subject to a bishop and should observe silence and devote themselves only to fasting and prayer.[1]

432. And this statute on monks was read by King Henry and King Charles meeting in council with certain bishops at Koblenz in the diocese of Trier.[2]

433. The second chapter [at Chalcedon] said that clerics should not involve themselves in worldly possessions, nor amass property, nor become legal representatives in administering the property of others. The third chapter said that clerics should remain at one post and serve where they were first assigned. These chapters were praised, approved, and decreed by the holy council, although, alas, they are not observed today.

434. We read that Emperors Theodosius and Valentinian wrote to the Council of Ephesus about Bishop Ibas as follows: "The victorious triumphant august and beloved Emperors Theodosius and Valentinian, to the holy Council of Ephesus: Numerous reports have been sent here from the city of Edessa in the province of Osdroena [Mesopotamia] along with records from there referring to the deposition of many reverend clergy, most religious archimandrites [abbots], and holders of church offices. And nearly all the people of that city bring testimony against Ibas, the bishop of the city of Edessa, accusing him of impiety and blasphemy. Since therefore it is appropriate that this type of crime should be corrected by your holy council, for it is not right to disbelieve the testimony of so many, please read the testimony and record, depose him, and appoint another religious man in his place. For if the authorities in major cities are orthodox, the others will necessarily follow their teachings."[3] The holy emperors

---

[1] Mansi 7, pp. 174ff.

[2] Henry I of Germany and Charles III of France at Koblenz, A.D. 922 (Mansi 18, p. 343).

[3] From the Second or "Robber" Council of Ephesus (449). Only a Syriac version, translated into German in 1873 survives, but Cusanus seems to have had a Latin version. See Book I, no. 73.

were accustomed to give this and similar advice as appropriate. It may serve as an example for our most glorious [Emperor] Sigismund and his successors.

CHAPTER XXII

LIKE EMPEROR MARCIAN, THE EMPEROR SHOULD UPHOLD THE PRESCRIPTIONS OF THE COUNCILS AND SEE THAT THEY ARE OBSERVED.

435. Finally on this subject, His Imperial Highness should know that he ought to see that the statutes and definitions of the holy councils are observed by also adopting laws that inflict penalties on those who do not observe them. Hence it is proper that he should inquire of the sacred council whether the matters that are communicated to His Majesty have been decided with the counsel and consent of all. The most pious [Emperor] Marcian when the declaration of faith which had been published as dogma at Chalcedon was read to him, asked if what had been read had been confirmed by the consent of all religious bishops. When he received the answer from the council that this was the case – the council gave high praise to the emperor – he adopted a law in the following words, "The holy Catholic faith in the traditions of the fathers has been made known by the holy synod. We are convinced that it is also just and useful that all future contention on matters of religion be eliminated. Therefore if anyone, whether he is a private citizen or a paid soldier or connected with the clergy, should publicly disagree on the faith or stir up a disturbance among the people, let him know that if he is a private citizen he will be expelled from the most holy city, if a soldier he will be removed from his militia, if a clergyman deposed from his church office [and] other additional punishments will be imposed." The holy synod cried out, "Long live the Christian prince. We wish you a long life, O prince!"[1]

436. I could quote similar passages from many conciliar acts. But I could not avoid including a statement by the most pious Basil because

---

[1] Mansi 7, p. 173.

it is notable and worth recording. Thus we read that at the end of the Eighth Council: Basil, the most pious Christian emperor, said to the council:

CHAPTER XXIII

THE ELOQUENT SPEECH OF EMPEROR BASIL TO THE COUNCIL IS REPRODUCED. IN IT HE INDICATES THAT THE EMPEROR SHOULD SEE TO IT THAT THE COUNCIL ARRIVES AT ITS DECISIONS IN GOOD ORDER AFTER EVERYONE WHO WISHES TO BE HEARD HAS SPOKEN, FOLLOWING WHICH NO ONE WHO IS OPPOSED IS TO BE ADMITTED. THE SPEECH HAS MANY OTHER NOTEWORTHY POINTS.

437. "Your holinesses, gathered here by the will of God, have undergone great vexation and labor in coming to our happy city for the purpose of establishing order in the church. For this it has been necessary to remain here for a long time. Many of you have had no regard for your old age and bodily infirmity. You have bravely tolerated the lack of repose and endured with magnanimity the long separation from your spiritual brothers. But now you see how sweet and beneficial to the church is the conclusion of your painful labors. For the common agreement and consent in the Holy Spirit of this great universal synod have removed every scandal and offense from the church, quieted long-standing disturbances, and restored a state of calm tranquillity.

438. "And so we give thanks to the Lord, worthy fathers, for all the good things which God has given us, and we recognize your zeal for God's will. We ask from the munificence of the great King of the universe that a bounteous reward be given to you in recompense for your trials and labors. For this purpose we have striven to refresh and encourage you and to fulfill your every desire. We have thought it right to say this for the common benefit of all and the continuing peace of the holy church of God before all those listening, because there are those who are opposed to the happiness and some are hurt. [lit. – wounded by the serpent's tongue] when ecclesiastical order is

established. Indeed they are pleased with commotion and anger and delighted if they see the church beset by storms.

439. "But to them we say directly today: Whoever has anything to say against this holy universal synod or its canons and conclusions, let him stand up and say what he thinks – whether he is a bishop or clergyman or layman or civil official – although according to canon law he has no right to say anything on church matters [since] that is the work of bishops and priests. However since we wish every iniquitous opinion to be thoroughly answered, we grant permission to all who have any doubts in mind concerning what has been decreed by this holy synod to reveal it in our midst and receive the saving remedy of satisfaction.

440. "We have made this mighty effort and, as you know, have labored to bring together those who have come from Rome and from the eastern patriarchal sees which many before us have tried and failed to do. Most devout high-ranking clergy have suffered not little travail and sorrow, coming from afar to the discussions of this holy synod. Whoever therefore has anything to say, let him say it while the council is in session. For once this holy universal synod is dissolved anyone who appears to oppose the church of God or not be in communion with it, whether he is a bishop or simple priest whatever his rank˙ or office, will not be pardoned by us. Rather he will be condemned and driven from the city as a source of corruption and pestilence, a rotting and useless member infecting the common body of the church.

441. "But you, O high priests who are endowed with the episcopate and who love virtue and are close to God, do not hesitate to warn, each of you, his own flock and lead it to salvation by indicating how evil it is to disturb the peace of the church of God, to rebel against those who rule over its members, and to separate oneself from the divine mysteries for irrational and base reasons. Direct to divine perfection the flock subject to you each Sunday with the words of doctrine and, as good shepherds, convert those who are involved in any heretical errors. For your holinesses in your virtue know that if a heresy becomes known to you in any of your provinces and is not rooted out and returned to the orthodox faith by your assiduous instruction, you will be condemned in accordance with the canons by your own patriarch. Through sacred doctrine and admonition let your most holy flock be fed by saving food.

442. "But be gentle to one another and conserve the bond of unity of the church for which you have labored, and which you have agreed upon, and confirmed in word and action in this holy universal synod. Let no contention or mutual obstinacy bring about a new disruption of the common body of the church and prevent you from receiving pardon on the day of just retribution. Let your friendship and consent be a most stringent norm bringing order to the whole world. Your subjects look to you as painters do to their models. They are guided by your lives and moral direction.

443. "But you who are members of the clergy of the church of God keep your mutual order and concord and in no way depart in your preaching from what has been decided by the Holy Spirit in this great universal synod. For you have agreed on all questions and you have seen the truth to which you have consented and agreed shine forth more clearly than the sun.

444. "But what else shall I say to you who are members of the laity, whether officeholders or not. I do not have anything to say other than that you are not permitted to discuss ecclesiastical matters nor threaten the integrity of the church nor oppose the universal synod.

445. "To investigate and inquire into these things is the responsibility of patriarchs, of bishops, and of priests who have been assigned the responsibility of rule. They have the power of making holy, of binding and loosing. They have been given the ecclesiastical and heavenly keys. This is not our responsibility. We are to be given pastoral direction and made holy, loosed or freed from bonds. If anyone is a layman, no matter how wise or religious he is, even if he has every virtue within him, as long as he is a layman he does not cease to be a sheep in the flock. And again a bishop, however lacking in holiness and every virtue, as long as he is bishop and preaches the word of truth correctly, will not be deprived of the rank of shepherd.

446. "What reason, therefore, is there for us, the sheep, to judge the shepherds with subtle words and to seek to peruse those things which are above us? We should approach them with fear and sincere faith and stand in awe of their countenances, since they are the ministers of Almighty God and they possess his likeness. We should do nothing more than what is appropriate to our rank. But now as we see, malice has incited many here to the insanity of forgetting their own rank. Not recognizing that they are the feet, they wish to make law for the eyes, not as nature would have it but as they desire. Each

one is always ready to accuse his superiors, but slow to correct criminal actions of which he is accused. I advise and exhort all those who act in this way to cease directing their accursed hatred towards others, to desist from judging the judges, and to attend to themselves and to strive to live in accordance with the divine will. For heaven's judgment will not rest but divine anger will descend on the dissident and bring just retribution upon all for their acts. Above all we pray to the Holy God that all the nobles, that is, the leading rulers, not only will remain in his favor untouched by divine wrath, but also will attain their eternal reward by the prayers and intercession of the Most Holy Mother, Our Lady, and of all the saints and by the prayers and supplications of this holy universal synod. Amen."

447. And after the reading, Basil, the great emperor and friend of Christ, said, "Whoever of those in this holy and universal synod wishes to do so should say in what respect he is hesitant or in doubt about what has now been read." The holy synod cried out: "What has been read is pleasing to all. We all agree with it. We all freely subscribe to it!"[1]

448. This is the formula used by the most pious Basil which our own all-merciful emperor, whom we have called a second Basil, and any Catholic emperor should follow. When he has observed that it is evident that everything has been approved orally and by a show of hands by all in the council, he should add his approval and affix his seal in confirmation, thus attaching penal and coercive sanctions so that the decrees will be observed and respected. And as the common father of all, he should also advise all the priests to carry out their offices and pray to the Most High and make special efforts that the flock and members of Christ may be fed the food of salvation by their own true shepherds and not mercenaries. And he should exhibit paternal care for all and bring back those who wander from the path of piety to the right way by every possible method. For man is a noble animal who would rather be led than compelled and the kindly hand pacifies the wild animal.

449. Now in order to show how skilfully this was done by the most sweet Basil, let us add the public statement [*epanagnosticon*] that he sent in that council to the bishops who supported the schism of Photius who had seized the see of Constantinople – for it is full of

---

[1] Mansi 16, pp. 186–188.

sweet instruction. The public statement in the Sixth Action of the Eighth Universal Council on the divisions caused by the schismatics reads as follows:

CHAPTER XXIV

THE NOTABLE EXAMPLE OF THE PIOUS EMPEROR
BASIL ILLUSTRATES THE DEVOTION WHICH THE
EMPEROR SHOULD EXHIBIT AS COMMON FATHER
AND SHEPHERD IN BRINGING BACK THOSE WHO
HAVE GONE ASTRAY. HE OUGHT TO ENFORCE THE
SENTENCE OF THE COUNCIL AGAINST THOSE WHO
REBEL AND WHO DO NOT AGREE TO THE IMPERIAL
EXHORTATION. OUR EMPEROR, A SECOND BASIL,
SHOULD FOLLOW THAT EXAMPLE IN BRINGING
BACK THE ERRANT BOHEMIANS.

450. "Your many common sufferings have caused us to lament and be saddened as we watched and protected you in the past. But a greater evil, a genuine calamity, is the disturbance of the church, the evil work of the devil plotting against it, the destruction of peace and dissolution of the ancient order, the bold attacks of the subordinate against the superior and of the dishonorable against the honorable, and every kind of subversion of the order of the church. While the council attempts to apply justice to those outside it, within the church injustice triumphs and love of domination and self-love, and because of this laxity is widespread along with insane fury against one's spiritual father.

451. "These are the thoughts that seize and disturb my soul. Like a thick cloud they darken my spirit and bring tears to my eyes. I will call upon the Divinity for help in resolving this sad state of affairs. My labor and intention was, if possible, to bring about the unification of the church. This has in fact taken place as all of you who have come to this holy meeting know. I have left every other governing responsibility which is mine and from the outset I have devoted myself to this alone. As requested by each of the dissident parties and following the ancient tradition of the church I have now brought together the other

patriarchal sees to act as judges of what has taken place in our church. With the cooperation of the Holy Spirit, I have done what many of those who have ruled before me wished to see, but none achieved to the same degree.

452. "And whatever pertains to the unity and order of the church has been carefully carried out by me. I have achieved both small and great results without the exercise of the coercive power that some have used. For not only has my government made efforts that the most holy patriarch [Ignatius] may return to his see but much earlier the most holy and blessed Pope Nicholas when he learned the facts of the case decreed in his synod that his see should be restored to him, and with the whole Roman church he declared anathema those who resisted this decree and decision.

453. "We, once we knew this and fearing the promulgated judgment of anathema, felt it necessary to support the judgment of the synod of the Roman church, and for this reason we restored him to his see. Because of the superior prudence of both the Roman see and the sees in the East, our representatives with our approval did not impede or oppose or favor either party. Because of this I did not wish to appear at any synodal judgement – contrary to the idle chatter of many – so that no one could say that in any synodal judgment the hand and sword, protection and earthly power of the empire had subverted the council. One desire and one request alone was ours to the aforementioned judges when we saw them, that they not permit anyone to be lost or expelled from the church of God, if this was possible.

454. "This alone is our crime if anyone wishes to call it that. But everything else we have left to the canons and to those who are in charge of the synod, supporting it firmly and condemning, that is, requesting condemnation, in keeping with the present judgment, and urging that they decide nothing in favoritism or in hatred, but rather conduct themselves with greater humanity toward those who had fallen into error. In the sight of all we ask them individually and collectively, to extend their hands today to those who offer forgiveness and to join in the celebration of a united church.

455. "Go, O spiritual fathers and defenders of truth who are signed with the chrism of Aaron and with the zeal of Phineas and the judgment of Solomon; seek the sheep that was lost; bring back the sheep that have gone astray. Take the solitary by the shoulder and

constrain him with the bonds of compassion. Dress the wound with kindness. Join in forgiveness to the ninety-nine sheep the one that was cast out of the spiritual flock. In imitation of Christ leave an eternal memorial of your compassion for future generations. You also, our friends and dear ones, who need care and healing, precious members of Christ, although I do not know by what evil demon you were separated from the head, the true vine, which your rude and unjust contention has turned to bitterness. If on the contrary you remain in opposition because of irrational hatred and reject unity, hear my words of warning – even, I am not mistaken in saying, of supplication.

456. "The mercy which we have for you had led us to this. Look into your innermost consciences and you will find that you were wrong to separate yourselves from the church. Brethren, the hour is very late and the verdict is imminent. Let us not remain separated from his church and far from its glory. Let us not consider it base to show our feelings and exhibit our wounds, to seek penitence and healing and to enter the company of the saved – lest by thinking that to obey is to be defeated, we experience eternal defeat.

457. "But what kind of defeat is it, brethren, to prostrate oneself before God and seek pardon? For to prostrate oneself before the church and one's spiritual fathers is to prostrate oneself before God. It is true defeat and the greatest shame, indeed it is opposition to God, not to be willing to confess all of our sins and to humiliate ourselves for Christ and to save ourselves and many others.

458. "But if you think that this is defeat, I who have been given the crown of empire, will become a model of the deepest humility for you. I, inexperienced and foolish as I am, will begin for you who are wise and brilliant. Steeped in sin as I am, I will be the prototype for you who are pure and examples of virtue. First of all, I will prostrate myself upon the pavement, disregarding my purple robes and diadem. Come near to my face and look deep into my eyes and do not think it an offense to tread on the shoulderblades of the emperor. Do not fear to touch with your feet the forehead on which God has placed the crown. I am ready to endure everything which seems to you to signify defeat. For me it seems to be glory and greatness. For I do not care for my own glory in this, if I may see us celebrate a united church together. Thus I will avoid the loss of my soul and prevent the devil, the enemy of all, from rejoicing in making me his captive. What I desire is that the light of my hope may not be suddenly extinguished

which has lighted the way to our common happiness and joy. I do not know what was to be done that I have not done, or what words of admonition and entreaty were to be spoken that I did not speak. The responsibility is yours. I am innocent of your perdition.

459. "But if at the great and fearful judgment on the last day you condemn us to give an account, as it were, for you, be aware that I know that there will not a word of justification for you then nor is there here today except for what has emerged in this controversy. But if you wish before that judgment to inquire of the judgment seat of your conscience, you will find nothing other than what has been said by us, your ruler.

460. "And so leave off contention, brethren, and take up fraternal love once more. Flee dissension and embrace unity. Reject hatred and receive love in your heart. Stand with the upright and join with your head. Receive the grace of divine communion through obedience and you will not be concerned with secular things.

461. "For there are many modes of acceptance, that is, of assistance, in our most patient empire through which we can console you and we will make unceasing efforts to give you worldly opportunities. And again we will strive in many ways, asking and bending every effort to persuade your spiritual fathers and the patriarchs to dispense you from whatever sanctions burden your spirit, only to prevent you from acting rashly against your salvation. There is no time more appropriate for the acceptance of repentance than the present, for those who today can bind and loose the affairs of the church are at hand. Cease seeking postponements and expecting a change of circumstances. Even if this takes place some day, it will not help you.

462. "For even if time should change other things, it can not change this. For if the irrational act of one man among you although it was totally in error has created such a furor that it has been very difficult to reverse it, tell me the action and the person who can reverse the decision of the four patriarchal sees? To whom will you flee in search of release from your obligation? To the Roman bishop? But he has just condemned you. To that of Antioch? But he was in agreement with that of Rome. To that of Jerusalem or Alexandria? Those sees agreed to your condemnation. And if the one who has violated all the canons ever commits the see of Constantinople to you and you wish to hold a meeting, who will follow you and how can you open your eyes

and look at anyone when you are impugned by all the priests and patriarchal sees?

463. "Therefore, brethren, do not deceive yourselves and lose the opportunity for your salvation. You will not find it at some other time. Give up your continual contention and obstinacy. Come to the common healing and accept the remedial medicine. Adhere to our spiritual head and enter into communion with the church of God so that you may be cleansed of your crime; find a generous God; make the church and our empire rejoice; bring about a celebration of the spirit; fill the whole commonwealth with the greatest joy and festiveness. Let us all bless the Lord together, our Glory and the Prince of Peace, and the one who has gathered us here and has enabled us to work well together – through the intercession of Our Most Blessed Lady, the Mother of God, and of the angels and all the saints who see God. Amen."

464. After this reading Theodorus, secretary of the representatives of old Rome, stood up and read: "See how the most sweet Christian ruler of the empire granted to him by God does not wish one sheep entrusted to him by Christ to be lost – transforming exile, tribulation, and anxiety into admonition and prayer."[1]

465. Note the humanity and earnestness of the emperor's concern that not even one of the sheep entrusted to him be lost. O most pious Sigismund, successor to Basil, exercise your inborn clemency and apply what has been read with your customary sweet eloquence. Through your prayers and mercy bring back the inhabitants of the noble kingdom of Bohemia who are cut off from the way of salvation, and may each word of this speech serve you in all your efforts.[2] With what zeal did the former holy emperors give their greatest efforts to the increase of the orthodox faith. May your zeal be no less in saving those who have long been a part of the church. May all things possible be done with piety and mercy. When Christ, the spouse of the church, sees this, he will undoubtedly give wonderful effect to your loving prayer. When what humility requires is properly done, victory in war will be assured. The proud, puffed-up, and diabolical cannot overcome those armed with the charity and humility of Christ who seek his honor alone.

---

[1] Mansi 16, pp. 92–95.

[2] A provisional settlement was reached with the Hussites in early 1434. It was similar to the proposals that Cusanus had made in 1433 in his work, *De usu communionis*.

466.   Take action, O most Christian prince, to moderate their cruel ferocity through this sacred council and your gentle persuasion. Although the spirit of the Lord cannot be infused immediately, each day they will become more responsive because of daily contact with Christ's faithful and they will look into their hearts and finally see that they were wrong to rely on their own wisdom and proudly set themselves up against the common opinion of all Catholics.

467.   This matter should be treated with the greatest care and unceasing use of every means, so that Satan who does not easily leave hearts that he has possessed for a long time may finally be overcome. Like your prototype, Basil, you have, O prince, the admirable gift from on high of being able with effort and prudence to bring back any schismatic to unity. In your royal wisdom you did this at Constance when schism infected the Roman pontiffs, as Basil did it in Eighth Council of Constantinople in the case of the opposing patriarchs of Constantinople, Photius and Ignatius. In addition you have made great efforts in this most sacred Council of Basel to bring the members of the church and its head, our most holy pope Eugene, together in unity, as Basil did with the subject bishops who were opposed to Ignatius in that other council at Constantinople.

468.   Now it remains for you to bring back the others who remain in your glorious and flourishing kingdom of Bohemia as Basil, a few years earlier had so laudably done with those image-breakers who destroyed the images of Christ and the saints and condemned their veneration[3] – and many Bohemians are followers of this belief. In this time of troubles for the church much like the time when Basil ruled the empire, by divine intention you have been established as emperor for the general welfare so that following in his footsteps, you may do what he did under the inspiration of God. But it is vain to urge the one who is already running to run. Your natural wisdom and religious belief urge you to these holy works much more than any extraneous persuasion, however erudite. Therefore I will not tire you further with words, O great emperor, to induce you to go on with your work.

[3] The Iconoclast ("Image-Breakers") controversy in the eastern church had been settled in A.D. 843, well before Basil became emperor.

CHAPTER XXV

THE CHAPTER DISCUSSES THE IMPERIAL COUNCIL
MADE UP OF THE PRINCIPAL MEMBERS OF THE
EMPIRE, WHICH HAS MET IN THE PAST AND IS VERY
USEFUL FOR THE GOVERNMENT OF THE
COMMONWEALTH IF IT IS PROPERLY ORGANIZED
AND MEETS REGULARLY. EXAMPLES AND WARNINGS
ARE GIVEN.

469.   At this point we should discuss the imperial council at length, in accordance with the statement above that all matters relating to the good government of the commonwealth should after mature and ample discussion be adopted as laws with the consent of all. This will be easy for us since the universal council of the priests is properly organized along similar lines, and we have already given a description of all aspects of that council above.[1]

470.   We know that the emperor as the head and first of all commands subordinate kings and princes to assemble. But those who are obligated to meet as members with that head in this universal council of the empire are the princes, the heads of the provinces representing their provinces, and also the rectors of the major universities and professors, and those of the senatorial rank which qualifies them for the imperial assembly [*conventus*]. These are either the *illustres* who are the first at his side and parts of his body, see [C.] 6, q. 1 [c. 22] para. *si quis*, or the *expectabiles* in a second intermediate group, or the *clarissimi*, the senators of the lowest group below which there is no grade in the senatorial class,[2] see [c.] 2 q. 6 [c. 28], *Anteriorum, Illud etiam*. On the ordering of these offices, consult the *Digest*.[3]

471.   In the first rank are the kings and the electors of the empire, the patricians. In the second are the dukes, governors, prefects, and others of this sort. In the third are the marquises, landgraves, and others of equal rank. Those who are over the rest and in more direct contact with the emperor compose the imperial body, the head of which is the emperor himself. When they meet in one representative

[1] Book II, ch. 6, nos. 85–86.
[2] Isidore, *Etymologies*, IX, 4, 12 (PL 82, p. 349).
[3] *Digest*, I, 9–19.

group, the whole empire is assembled, as the *Lex Julia* proves which is reproduced in the *Decretum* at [C.] 6 q. 1 [c. 22] *Si quis cum militibus* where it is referred to as *Ad legem Juliam maiestatis*, C. 1, *Quisquis*. See also the text of the Eighth Council cited above, chapter 17, where it says, "Since princes often hold meetings for their purposes . . ."[4]

472.   And because universal decrees for the good of the empire should be made by consent, and also so that a law applying to the whole empire may not be in opposition to that of any part, and in order to give adequate notice of this, the aforesaid leading princes and other most trustworthy sworn representatives meet to demonstrate to all on the basis of their certain knowledge what actions are appropriate to the time and place. In this way the decisions made after careful consideration will be accepted and strictly observed. I have discovered in ancient books that universal councils of the empire used to be held in which the princes personally signed their names after that of the emperor as a lasting guarantee, in the same way as was customary in church councils.

473.   I have also read that a council was held at Cologne by King Dagobert and twenty-four princes in which many matters essential for the preservation of justice and peace were determined with the consent of all. I have also read the laws of Charlemagne which were issued in consultation with the faithful, as the text [C.] 11 q. 1 [c. 37] *Quicumque*, para. *Volumus*, demonstrates, and I have studied those of Childebert and others.[5] The universal council examined, coordinated, and revised the laws when necessary and made additions, adopting different laws for different parts of our empire, for the Alemanni different laws from the Baiuvarii (whom we now call Bavarians), and for the Riparian Franks different laws from those for the Burgundians and Lombards, and it issued other laws which it called the Salic laws for the Saxons and the people of those regions.

474.   I have seen these laws collected in order and I know many of them well, especially the more important ones the formulas of which are in use among the people because of their ancient origin, especially in rural courts rather than in the towns and cities where municipal ordinances are perhaps superseding them.

[4] Mansi 16, p. 171.
[5] Einhard, *Vita Caroli* (*Life of Charlemagne*), ch. 29, does not mention the Council of King Dagobert. The laws of Childebert are mentioned by the Council of Turin, A.D. 567 (MG *Concilia*, I, p. 130).

475. I have read that the ancient kings used to hold these councils which are called assemblies [*conventus*] once or twice a year for the public good in different cities of the empire.[6] The strictest penalties were imposed in these councils on all who disturbed the peace or violated the public law, especially perjurors and those who broke their word. And out of fear of these meetings, to which those who were called were obliged to come by an oath sworn to the empire, individual violations of fealty, pillage, and arson were not committed.

476. No one could avoid or reject the decision of that assembly and the emperor and the assembly demanded that the sentences imposed there be carried out by force of arms on those who did not obey.

477. The principal members of that council are those who are called the princes of the empire, whether they are bishops, or laymen, or abbots. But unless they were especially summoned, others did not participate in this council. At the end of the *conventus* when everything had been taken care of, the time and place of another future meeting was set. It was of course always in the power of the emperor to change the time and place if there were good reasons to do so. There was no better nor more useful arrangement for the good of the whole church – and not only for those living under the empire.

478. The legates of the Roman pontiff used to come for cases involving the church and those of other kings for difficult matters arising in their kingdoms, and useful counsel was given for all public needs. I think that nothing could be more useful for public order than the reintroduction of this holy practice.

479. I have also read that in order to give it the greatest strength what was decided in this way in common council would be subscribed to and signed with a cross by the hand of everyone present. This custom resulted from the provision of the law that if anyone ever attempted to violate a law which he had subscribed to, and signed with his own hand, he would be disgraced and automatically deprived of every honor as one who was untrue to himself and his own pledge.

480. This was the practice of the ancients, as will be evident to anyone who has tirelessly perused the acts of kings and emperors and the above mentioned statutes adopted at their meetings.

481. I do not insist on speaking at length on the internal organiza- tion of that assembly. It follows the order of seating of the electors

---

[6] Hincmar of Rheims, *De ordine palatii*, c. 29 (PL 125, p. 1003).

established by Charles IV of happy memory in his Golden Bull at the meeting at Metz.[7] The other princes know their places according to rank and age. But when the princes are present, let each one speak out freely and openly when asked, and swear to seek faithfully what will best aid the empire and the commonwealth in a given case in accordance with the dictates of their consciences and free of all base motives. These and other things are clear by analogy with what is written above.

[7] The Golden Bull on the procedure for the election of the emperor was adopted in 1356.

<hr>

CHAPTER XXVI

ON THE FLOURISHING STATE OF THE EMPIRE AT THE TIME WHEN EVERY EFFORT WAS AIMED AT THE INCREASE OF THE FAITH, AND LAWS HAD STRICT BINDING EFFECT.

482. The last section of this part is the most difficult of all since we are investigating things based on actual experience rather than simply in books. First we will examine the state of the empire at its prime so that we can measure against this the excesses of today and the degree of its decline. After this we should use our intelligence to suggest and describe healthful remedies drawn principally from what was done in the past so that at the very least, better solutions can gradually be discovered through the use of logical inference.

483. The first point is known to those who are acquainted with the brilliant accomplishments of the emperors who established the foundations of the government of this noble Germany. In order not to have to go back in the remote past to the first great universal emperors, since our reforming effort cannot reach such a high degree now, let us pass them over and begin with Otto I. We read that he was the first emperor to whom true imperial authority was transferred without limit or condition on him and his successors, both by the Roman senate and the whole people and by the pope and his council. For at that time the Western Empire was so shaken by various invading tyrants that he would not accept the office of emperor when it was offered except on the understanding that he would be able to hold the

empire in perpetuity and could restore everything taken away from the Roman church.[1] When by divine assistance this was done exactly as Otto desired, all the [imperial] domains came one by one into his power – the kingdom of Italy and the Lombards, the kingdom of Burgundy[2] – he already had the kingdom of the Germans of which his father, Henry, is supposed to have been the first king.

484.   Some authorities think that Otto II, son of Otto's second wife who was the daughter of the king of Burgundy, acquired the kingdom of Burgundy by inheritance, but it suffices for our purpose to know that our empire is composed of the kingdoms and dominions listed above and they have maintained fidelity and loyalty to it.

485.   Also we find that after this the Hungarians of the Catholic faith, the Bohemians, the Danes, the Norwegians, the Poles, the Prussians, and other important provinces were subject to our rulers. The greatest concern of all the emperors was the protection and expansion of the faith.

486.   And the emperors exercised genuine governing authority because the voice of the emperor was supported by power and force. Even the most important person could not transgress the law with impunity. Unless a law retains its sanction and its punitive force it becomes blunted and falls into disuse. Man's appetite for evil must be controlled by the bridle of the law and restrained by its limitations. Law without coercion has no sanction and loses its effectiveness. It no more merits to be called a law than a corpse should be called a man. But at that time the laws were strong, the imperial statutes were feared, and large annual meetings of the princes were held so that the severity of the law might be strengthened by constant enforcement so that no transgressor of the law, no matter how powerful, went unpunished.

487.   It was necessary not to allow exceptions to the sentence not only of the emperor but of all the princes, even when imposed on parents or close friends. Because of the oath sworn to the empire, no one in the meeting when asked could do other than approve and praise the existing law and follow it in passing judgment if applicable, even against one's own son. But according to the law a decision to be adopted and put into effect had to be unanimous. Thus a legal sanction had impartial effect on the basis of common agreement. And

---

[1] Liutprand of Cremona, *Historia Ottonis* (*MG Scriptores* III, p. 340).
[2] Burgundy was not part of Otto I's empire.

no one could freely transgress it with impunity. This produced general peace and a happy fatherland.

CHAPTER XXVII

THE COMMAND OF OTTO II ON THE GRANT OF TEMPORAL POSSESSIONS TO THE CHURCH WAS MADE FOR WORTHY REASONS.

488.   Later Otto II, since he had only one son, thought that it would be difficult to keep the peace for long in so many kingdoms without the greatest effort. Since he wished to follow in the footsteps of his grandfather, Henry I, and of his father, Otto, he directed his thoughts to church matters and observed that the many properties given to the church by past kings enjoyed great peace, for it was considered shameful to use force against things dedicated to God. He pondered in his heart the decree of the holy council of the Roman church which is quoted in [D.] 63 [c. 23] *In synodo* by which perpetual authority was granted to the emperors to grant investiture to the Roman pontiff and to all the bishops in the empire, or at least that they [the emperors] should always give their consent to any canonical election, as D. 63 [c. 34] *Nos sanctorum* [*Sacrorum canonum*] says.

489.   Therefore when he considered this he concluded that peace could be guaranteed for all time to the subjects of the emperor if temporal domains were given to the Roman and other churches in return for the performance of certain services. For he thought that divine worship would be increased and religion greatly honored if the most powerful of the holy bishops were associated with the other princes. Then no longer would everyone exercise his will for sinful purposes. He hoped that public crimes such as the ravaging or decimating of rural areas or disturbances of public order or arson or similar crimes would not be committed if the holy power of the church was able and willing to resist. Robbers and oppressors of the poor who ruled over a particular government could be corrected, he thought, and thus the people could live free from tyrannical oppression in an empire at peace.

490.   He did not doubt that this arrangement would be most useful if

the status of the empire were maintained by duties of annual service and appointed aids assigned to each church in accordance with the size of its temporal possessions.[1] Also the power of the empire would grow much greater because only the emperor would make appointments over the areas given to the church, and this would be without a hereditary succession, and if a churchman did not live a holy and canonical life he would be deposed by action of the other bishops after accusation by the emperor or synod.[2] Thus those temporal possessions did not seem to leave the hands of the emperor, since in this way they remained under his control to the great profit of the commonwealth.

---

[1] From Otto II the bishops and abbots began to be incorporated into the feudal hierarchy of the empire as direct vassals of the emperor.
[2] Mansi 18, pp. 320 and 499.

CHAPTER XXVIII

AT FIRST PRINCES AND DUKES WHO GOVERNED THE
SUBJECTS OF THE EMPIRE WERE TEMPORARY
APPOINTEES. LATER THEY WERE CONSTITUTED AS
FEUDAL VASSALS FOR GOOD CAUSE IF THEY GAVE
THE EMPIRE AN ANNUAL TRIBUTE AND MILITARY
SERVICE. CUSTOMS-DUTIES, TAXES, AND TALLAGES
WENT TO THE COMMONWEALTH, AND THE
EMPEROR PROTECTED THAT COMMONWEALTH
WITH A PROFESSIONAL ARMY.

491. It was also decreed at that time that princes, dukes, and counts should be appointed to public office at the command of the emperor and should be removable at his will with an obligation to give an account of their ministry to the public treasury. Later, because the sons of the senators although they first were to be knights finally became members of the senate, the practice was introduced that the sons of parents who had properly carried out the duties of their offices, would inherit those offices. This was done so that the fathers would be less avaricious than if they were not certain who would succeed them in office, and also because subjects would be less likely

to be oppressed by a father whose children were to rule over them. Nevertheless to avoid an unfavorable reduction in the domains of his imperial highness in the future as a result of the increase in the power of those office-holders, feudal statutes were introduced as well as strict oaths of fealty which were to be sworn by every new vassal and strictly observed under pain of losing the fief.

492.   Finally another law was published that no one could succeed to several large fiefs at the same time.[1] This was done to avoid an increase in the power of any subject through the accumulation of many large fiefs to the point that, out of tyrannical fury and forgetful of his oaths, he might seek to achieve the supreme power – the desire for which grows as one acquires more – and weaken the empire through rebellion and disturbance.

493.   In addition it was customary for the emperors to listen readily to accusations of the violation of trust and the breaking of oaths. Thus the fidelity which alone holds an empire together was never neglected. The punishment for the breaking of trust was confiscation. Then to prevent envy from perhaps inciting nobles of the same family against someone to whom the confiscated property was given, the holy emperors often gave the church the properties that had been confiscated in this way.

494.   The emperors wisely established many similar worthy arrangements for the good of the commonwealth and the holy empire. For instance they created courts presided over by justices of the peace who passed sentence on the basis of decisions by popular juries which had duly sworn to decide according to their consciences and the merits of the case – thus it was not in the power of the presiding judge to punish those under him at will on the basis of his personal feelings. This was also true in all other cases involving financial affairs, tallages, and customs.

495.   And everything tended to the public good. At that time the emperor had the public responsibility to maintain the peace, and he had an army paid for by the public for this purpose.[2] Everywhere he was feared by princes and rulers; everywhere he was worshipped, venerated and loved by the people as the defender of the fatherland, the protector of liberty, the relief of the oppressed, and the most

---

[1] Large fiefs included those belonging to dukes, margraves, and counts. The law against accumulation of large fiefs was regularly violated.

[2] The imperial army was based on feudal service, not regular payment.

rigorous prosecutor of those who disturbed the commonwealth. At that time an offense against him was one committed against the highest public power and this was the greatest crime because it was committed against the father of his country and of all its inhabitants. But if I wrote down everything that is worth relating I would be more prolix than needed for our purpose.

CHAPTER XXIX

TODAY THE EMPIRE HAS DISCONTINUED THESE PRACTICES AND GREAT ABUSES HAVE BEEN INTRODUCED. THE ROMAN CURIA IS RESPONSIBLE FOR THE EMPTYING OF THE PUBLIC TREASURY AND THE PRESENT DISORDER IN THE ADMINISTRATION OF THE TEMPORAL POWER OF THE CHURCH ALSO HURTS THE COMMONWEALTH.

496. Observe how far the present state of the government has departed from this, since hardly any of these practices are observed. All concern for the commonwealth has disappeared. The bridle is slackened and anyone violates the law with impunity. Where once there was veneration in fear and trembling, now there is disdain and contempt. The laws are enforced with weapons that are like spiderwebs which can hardly restrain a tiny locust. In the past the laws were like strong nets always tensed for wild boars, ready to limit concupiscence and to restrain troublesome transgressors. Now everyone is concerned with his personal advantage. There is no concern for one's neighbor or with the future because of the lack of interest by the emperors who think that good intentions are enough to restore or reform what has gone awry. All sanctions have ceased to operate. Rebels are not punished. And many tyrannous princes grow powerful while the empire declines.

497. What good are the temporal possessions of the church to the commonwealth? What good are they to the empire? What good to its subjects? Little or none. Otto commanded in D. 63 [c. 23] *In synodo* that bishops should be invested with their bishoprics without charge. We see that the pope has not only taken free investiture away from the

emperor, but so much money is charged that everyone in Germany is crushed with a burden that is not merely heavy but overwhelming. Today ambitious bishops have a fierce appetite for the temporal possessions attached to the domains of the church so that we see them do outright after their appointment, what they did in circuitous ways before. All of their concern is with temporals, none with spirituals. This was not the intention of the emperors. They did not want spiritual concerns to be absorbed in the temporal possessions which they gave to the churches for their betterment.

498.   And, alas, all these things are the result of the violation of order. Because the canons are not observed, there is no coercion, no discipline, and no punishment. Furthermore the temporal power of the ecclesiastics now causes great harm to the commonwealth and its subjects. When there is a vacancy in a church office there is always danger of schism or the people must be taxed more heavily than others under secular rulers because if it is filled by election, rivalry produces a division in the voting and if it goes to the papal curia, the one who offers the most money wins out.[1]

499.   And all these burdens are laid on the poor subjects. The curia attracts whatever wealth there is. And what the empire granted and decreed in a holy fashion for the worship of God and the public good, is entirely perverted by avarice and greed through specious reasoning and novel interpretations, and what was imperial is papal and the spiritual becomes the temporal.

[1] Nicholas is speaking from personal knowledge of the election of the Prince-Bishop of Trier.

CHAPTER XXX

THE EMPEROR WHO HAS SOLE ADMINISTRATION OVER IMPERIAL MATTERS IS OFTEN IMPROPERLY LIMITED BY AGREEMENTS AND OATHS MADE TO THE ELECTORS IN ORDER TO GET THEIR SUPPORT. THESE SHOULD BE INVALID AND WE OBJECT STRONGLY TO THIS PRACTICE.

500.   There is another practice which is destructive of the empire. Although the emperor alone governs for the good of the com-

monwealth, he often acquires his office through agreements with electors who seek their own interest, and because of an oath that he has sworn, he does not dare to try to regain the things belonging to the empire which have been taken in violation of law, nor to remove the customs duties that burden the commonwealth, nor to make other useful laws.[1] He is prevented from revoking the things which were unwisely given or promised by his predecessors without a meeting of all, out of inordinate love or affection or blood relationship. And so it happens that as the electors seek their own interest, they abuse the power entrusted to them and thus convert the power which was given to them for the good of the empire into its destruction.

501. Because the electors should not permit the emperors to surrender imperial rights to the prejudice of the empire, they should always help him to increase his power. But because they have made him promise not to take away what was given or promised to them at some point in a false manner by relatives or parents who ruled over the empire, they keep silent when they see the emperor do the same thing [with others] – so as not to condemn their own actions.

502. O how blind they are! The princes should not think that they can become rich from the goods of the empire and possess them for long. If the empire comes to nothing because all are trying to increase their holdings, what will follow but the destruction of everyone? Without a greater power in the empire to preserve the peace, increasing envy and greed will produce wars and divisions and then like every kingdom divided against itself,[2] what has been brought together unjustly will collapse.

503. And so the princes of the empire are mistaken when they take over imperial possessions everywhere in order to become more powerful and stronger, because once the members have dismembered and weakened the entire power of the empire and its head, the hierarchical order will cease to exist. There will be no head to whom one can appeal. And where there is no order, there is confusion. And where there is confusion, no one is safe. And so when the nobles are fighting among themselves, the people will rise up to seek justice through their own arms. Then, as the princes destroy the empire, the people will destroy the princes.

[1] Nicholas is referring to the "capitulations," agreed to by the emperor before his election.
[2] Matthew 12:25; Luke 11:7.

CHAPTER XXXI

THE EMPIRE IS IN SERIOUS DECLINE BECAUSE
JUSTICE NO LONGER REIGNS. FORCE AND SELF-
WILL, BETRAYAL OF FEUDAL LOYALTY, BURNING
AND RAPINE DEVASTATE THE COMMONWEALTH. WE
PROTEST AGAINST THOSE WHO SAY THAT IT IS
HONORABLE TO TAKE PROPERTY IN VIOLATION OF
JUSTICE.

504.   In addition we see great confusion or a complete lack of justice
in the judicial sphere. Today honor has been separated from legality.
And the nobles say that they can licitly occupy vast domains which
they admit they have not had, and do not have any legal right to
possess. Through the base practice of the breaking of fealty [*diffidatio*]
they think that they can protect their honor. After that so-called
breaking of fealty on the basis of some fabricated reason or none at
all, they think that property seized by force either openly or secretly is
somehow legally in their possession, even when it belongs to the
church or the clergy. What presumptuous audacity against all law and
right! What iniquitous reasoning which separates the honorable from
the just and says that property unjustly seized can be held with honor.
Roman law wisely decreed that every breaking of fealty without the
consent of the highest judge would be both dishonorable and unjust,
and those who seized the goods of their enemies in this way would be
robbers, see [*Digest* XLIX 15] *De captivis et postliminio redemptis* [1.24]
Hostes. On this subject, see [c.] 23 q. 2 c. 1 and many other chapters
mentioned by Hostiensis in his *Summa* [I] *De Treuga et Pace* [C. 3 4]
and by Innocent [IV] in the chapter [c. 12] *Olim* of [*Decretals* II 13] *De
restitutione spoliorum* and the doctors cited there.

505.   Besides it is clear that the goods of the church do not belong to
any prelate or cleric and for that reason a crime by a prelate cannot
result in a loss to the church. How, O nobleman, do you think that it is
honorable to break fealty to a cleric, or a religious convent, or a
prelate? Who is so senseless as to admit that it is honorable to do what
cannot be done without major excommunication and sacrilege? If you,
a layman, are prohibited by divine law from seizing and mistreating a
cleric on your own authority, what virtue do you think there is in a

falsified document of breach of fealty? Do you think that all divine and human laws cease to be operative once you publish a little document? Thus if the goods of the church cannot be seized or taken away by force by a layman without committing sacrilege, do you think that this sacrilege is licit? This great and manifest error has, alas, recently infested parts of Germany. God is offended by it and the public peace and all stability disturbed.

506. Who can describe in detail all the abuses which have been iniquitously introduced in our time and still more iniquitously defended? And all this is because the laws and canons have lost their vigor and there are none to act as guardians and executors and pastors.

CHAPTER XXXII

AID MUST QUICKLY BE GIVEN TO THE EMPIRE WHICH IS MORTALLY ILL. WHAT THE EMPEROR SHOULD DO AND PROPOSE IN ORDER TO BRING ABOUT REFORM.

507. Appropriate measures must be taken soon against the disorders and perils besetting the commonwealth that are discussed above. A mortal disease has invaded the German empire and unless an antidote is found at once, death will surely follow. You will seek the empire in Germany and will not find it. As a result others will take our place and we will be divided and subjected to another nation. And there is no better approach to reform than through the well-worn and proven ways of the ancients to which we must return.

508. The fundamental reform is to establish annual general meetings and to begin here in this holy Council of Basel and make it a rule for the future.[1] And so let the most pious emperor take action, as he has always shown himself most diligent to do, and order all the greater princes of the empire from both estates to come together at his sacred command. Let him earnestly set forth the lamentably diminished state of the empire. Let him indicate what remains in Italy or in Lombardy

---

[1] An annual meeting was called for by the Golden Bull (1356).

of the [once] flourishing laws of the empire. Let him add what survives in the kingdom of Arles and throughout the whole of Germany. And when he has indicated the miserable state of this once flourishing and powerful empire let him predict what will happen next unless a remedy is applied. Let him seek a remedy from those who were and are most faithful and who are bound to this by desire and oath.

509. With the provident assistance of His Imperial Highness a proper arrangement should be made for a successor.

CHAPTER XXXIII

FIRST AN ANNUAL MEETING SHOULD BE ORDERED AND JUDGES SHOULD BE APPOINTED IN THE PROVINCES. IN EACH PROVINCE THREE JUDGES SHOULD MEET FROM THE THREE ESTATES – THE CHURCH, THE NOBILITY, AND THE PEOPLE. THE CHAPTER DESCRIBES HOW THEY SHOULD TRY CASES.

510. And because after so great a decline the empire cannot be restored to its original healthy state, provision should be made for recovery. First annual imperial councils and [a system of] justice should be provided for. Indeed I find that Constantine the Great, as will be indicated in a certain text below, provided for this kind of meeting and [established] judges in Gaul.[1] For it was after the imperial courts and meetings ceased, that nearly all the abuses were introduced.

511. And so it seems that it should be ordained that twelve or more courts are to be established in this way throughout the provinces subject to the empire. Each court is to be composed of three judges corresponding to the three social classes – nobles, clerics, and people. Those judges should be able to judge appeals in all cases arising in their assigned territories between any persons – including ecclesiastics – concerning their temporal possessions subject to the

[1] Book III, nos. 520–526.

empire – by way of appeal from their own superiors or as a court of first instance only if the plaintiff or defendant does not have a superior – because, for example, he is a prince, or if his superior is suspected of being favorable to the other side. And a case which was introduced by way of appeal, would be terminated with the decision of that court. What has come to it as a court of first instance could be appealed to the next meeting [of the Reichstag] if it is a serious matter or between important men. Each judge should pronounce sentence and call upon the disputants according to their status, the noble upon the nobles, the churchman upon the churchmen, and the representative of the people upon the people. However no final decision should be adopted without the deliberation of all three together, and in difficult cases let them get the advice of experts. But if one [of the three] disagrees with the other two, the opinion of the majority should prevail.

512. Also those judges should have the power to put their sentences into execution by the ban,[2] and the secular arm, and the payment of fines and punishments into the public treasury.

513. A salary should be given to those judges and all other public officials from the public treasury so that they may swear to observe the text of *Ad legem Iuliam repetundarum*, which is repeated in canon law in [C.] 1 q. 7 [c. 26] *Sancimus*.

---

[2] The ban was a solemn curse, formally invoked by ecclesiastical authority.

CHAPTER XXXIV

UNDER PAIN OF PUNISHMENT FOR THEFT AND
ROBBERY, NO ONE SHOULD BE ALLOWED TO TAKE
THE PROPERTY OF ANOTHER EXCEPT BY JUDICIAL
PROCESS. A LAW ON THIS SUBJECT SHOULD BE
ISSUED WITH THE CONSENT OF ALL IN THE
IMPERIAL COUNCIL, AND SIGNED AND SEALED IN
THE PROVINCES.

514. And a law should be adopted that under penalty of punishment for theft and robbery no one is to be permitted for any reason to seize on his own authority the property of another by force or to impose

punishment on him or his possessions by means of the breaking of fealty. Rather everything should be done by the authority of judges who can authorize reprisals against anyone who resists their sentence. For he who takes the sword on his own authority is to be killed by the sword, see [C.] 23 q. 1, para. 1. Anyone who wages war without the order of the prince is bound by the provisions of the [*Code*] *Lex Iulia* after [IX 8], *Ad Legem Iuliam maiestatis* 1.3 [1.5] and *Authentica* [*Novellae* 17] *De mandato principis*, coll. 3 and [*Novellae* 85] *De armis*, coll. 6, although in a case of imminent necessity the authorization of the chief officer is sufficient, see *Code De fabricensibus*, the final law [1.7] of Book X.

515. But if anyone dares to violate this law, let him be brought before any court in a village or city and punished for theft and robbery. If perhaps the court where he is apprehended is unwilling or neglects to do this when it could have conveniently done so, let the property of those judges be automatically confiscated.

516. Similarly if anyone receives those criminals [lit. – assassins] he ought to be treated as a public enemy and his possessions can be seized without hesitation, as Hostiensis notes in his *Summa* [I], *De Treuga et Pace*, para. 3, v. *Sed et si.*

517. But this law should be adopted by the common consent of all and signed and sent to the provinces to be received and sealed and a copy kept in the province and the original with the seal of the province should be sent back to the chancery of the empire so as to confirm the agreement of all in this way. That law should also be signed and sealed by all the princes meeting together and with it another law which warns that anyone – whether a prince or anyone else – who acts contrary to his own signature on his own authority without the permission of the judges and the emperor, has passed the judgment of public disgrace upon himself by that act, and is deprived of every honor. If he is a prince, the emperor is to have it in his power to seize all his goods for his treasury, but if he is a layman, they are to be automatically confiscated; if he is a clergyman, he is to be deposed by a council of the clergy and at the same time he is to be automatically deprived of the administration of temporals and the judges are to appoint a temporal administrator who is removable at the ruler's will.

518. This law should be signed by everyone along with the others. And the imperial records should keep these signatures so that any transgressor can be convicted by them. And a rigorous judicial system

cannot be properly introduced unless in this or a similar way acts of violence [*via facti*] and the breaking of fealty are eliminated by common consent.

CHAPTER XXXV

THE ORDER FOR THE ANNUAL MEETING SHOULD
FOLLOW THE EXAMPLE OF THOSE FOR EARLIER
MEETINGS. THE EXAMPLE OF AN ORDER BY AN
EMPEROR IN GAUL, WHOM SOME SAY WAS
CONSTANTINE, IS QUOTED AND SHOULD BE
NOTED. IN THIS MEETING WHAT IS OF PUBLIC AND
GENERAL INTEREST IN ALL THE PROVINCIAL
PRACTICES AND JUDICIAL DECISIONS SHOULD BE
REVIEWED AND REGULATED.

519. The annual meeting should be set for about the feast of Pentecost, in Frankfurt, which seems to be the most suitable place from its situation and from other circumstances. All the judges and electors of the empire should come in person to this meeting without pomp or heavy expense. The lord emperor himself should preside, if he can be present in person; otherwise, the chief of the electors should do so in the emperor's name. The affairs of the empire and even local affairs that have come before the judges should be dealt with; and what needs reforming should be reformed. If a critical matter of business really demands that a plenary meeting of all the princes take place there or elsewhere, whatever is most suitable should be done.

520. However the regular annual council of the lord judges, and electors at which cases involving the princes are decided through a common vote should never be omitted. And since it is useful to introduce reform on the basis of concrete examples, I would submit an imperial letter which is attributed to Constantine, who ordered a similar meeting of judges to be held at Arles. Arles, however, was called the city of Constantine [*Constantiniana*].

521. The imperial order, *Saluberrima*, which was directed to the illustrious Agricola, the prefect of Gaul, begins in the following way: "Following the most useful suggestion of Your Magnificence con-

cerning what is to be done in our seven provinces that will be advantageous to the commonwealth, by our everlasting authority we issue the decree awaited by the inhabitants of those provinces. Both private and public reasons, the interest of property-holders as well as the public purpose, demand a meeting of the magistrates or their representatives from the individual cities – not merely from the various provinces. Therefore we consider it especially opportune and expedient that henceforth the seven provinces, should hold a council, perhaps every year at an appointed time in the metropolitan city, that is, in the city of Arles, in which we will take public counsel on both specific and general questions. If arrangements can be made for this meeting of leaders and for your presence as prefect, their advice on individual matters can be very useful. Therefore, what is discussed and decided along with the reasons for it should be made known to the more important provinces, since it is equally necessary to maintain equitable and just procedures for those who are not present.

522. "Besides responding to the needs of government we believe that holding the council every year in the city of Constantiniana [Arles] makes personal contact easier. For it is so well-located, commerce so flourishes there, and there is so much traffic in foodstuffs that products of other regions are easily brought there. No other province enjoys the fertility that the soil of Arles seems to have. Indeed anything outstanding that the wealth of the Orient and perfumed Arabia, the delicacies of Assyria, the fertility of Africa, the beauty of Spain, or the strength of Gaul can possess seems to abound there, as if everything that is marvelous elsewhere were produced there. The southern flow of the Rhone and the northern flow of the nearby Durance are necessary and bring hither whatever the one or the other flows by or around.

523. Since whatever agricultural products may be useful for that city are brought there by sail, oar, wagon, land, sea, and river, how can anyone not think that much has been given to our Gaul when we command that the council be held in a city which, as if by divine gift, has so many conveniences and so many opportunities for commerce?

524. "Even if the illustrious prefect, Petronius, acting on the basis of wise and proven advice has already commanded that this should be done, we decree that if it has been left undone because of neglect over time or the inaction of tyrants, this should be remedied by our customary authority, O dear and loving relative, Agricola.

525. "Hence following this order of ours and the earlier directions of the prior occupant of your office, Your Illustrious Magnificence is to see to it that the magistrates, property holders, and judges of each of the seven provinces know that a council will take place each year in the city of Arles from the Ides of August without interruption until the Ides of September. If business detains the judges in Narbonne and Outer Aquitaine, which are more distant provinces, they should know that representatives are to be sent as is customary. We know that this provision will be most welcome to the citizens of our provinces, and that it will add no little to the prestige of the city of Arles to whose fidelity we owe much, according to the testimony and judgment of our relative and patrician.

526. "Your Excellency should know that the judges are to be fined five pounds of gold, the magistrates and courtiers [*curiales*] three pounds, if they delay in coming to the appointed place at the established time."[1]

527. This is the suggestion to Agricola – that the council be re-established that had been held in the past each year, because it was very useful for the provinces. Note that it is to be held in the city of Arles which at that time was the capital of Gaul and belongs to our [German] empire, although it does not recognize this. We should also observe that not only the [provincial] judges but also the magistrates or their representatives were to come from the individual cities. Observe too that it lasted a whole month and that they were strictly obligated to come under pain of serious penalty.

528. Following this form, an annual council should be established in Frankfurt (which, by reason of its location and the convergence of commerce there, may properly be likened to Arles), to be held for at least the month of either May or September; and along with those mentioned above, at least one representative should come from each city and metropolis and from the large imperial fortified towns.

529. The prince electors should bring with them anyone whom they wish as counsellors and nobles. And all should be bound by oath to contribute their counsel for the public good, according to the right judgment of reason.

530. Provincial customs should be examined there and harmonized

---

[1] Letter of Honorius and Theodosius to Agricola (printed in G. Haenal, *Corpus legum*, Leipzig, 1845, no. 1171, pp. 238ff.). In an earlier draft, an excerpt from this decree appears in Book I, ch. 7 (see above, no. 96a). See Introduction.

as nearly as possible with the common practice; and in particular captious formulae should be completely abolished; for the simple poor are often most unfairly led astray by the quibbles of lawyers over the use of the wrong legal forms, and so lose their whole case, since "he who omits a syllable loses the case," as I have often seen happen in the diocese of Trier.

531. Finally, evil practices such as permitting sworn statements against anyone and allowing an unlimited number of witnesses should be abolished. Throughout Germany there are innumerable such evil practices that are against true justice and even encourage criminality. Therefore judges of the provinces ought to come together and put the customary practice of their provinces into writing and lay them out before the council, so that they may be examined. And a similar procedure should be employed for other defects of the law.

CHAPTER XXXVI

A STRICT FORM SHOULD BE IMPOSED ON THE ELECTORS OF THE EMPIRE WHO HAVE THE POWER TO ELECT THE EMPEROR, INDICATING HOW THEY ARE TO PROCEED WHEN THERE IS A VACANCY IN THE EMPIRE.

532. Finally, this holy imperial Council of Basel should take the greatest care to see that the electors of the holy empire are given a strict and inviolable electoral procedure. In particular it should bind them under oath to choose the emperor without consideration of personal benefit or special interest, purely and simply for the public good and for the preservation and honor of the holy empire, before God and their consciences. If anyone is found acting otherwise, he should be subjected to perpetual disgrace and to the penalties for the crime of treason.

533. It is urgently necessary that the electors should be threatened with most severe penalties in order to maintain the purity of the elections because of the absurd and dishonest practices which, I have read, have occurred in the past. When the electors look out for their own interests using illicit procedures to bind the one to be elected, the

public interest is entirely neglected. Because, it is said, certain electors control towns and forts in the empire, and, because of customs revenues and other special interests of this sort, shamefully corrupt elections are often carried out involving iniquitous agreements.

534. Above all, any controversy that makes electors fear that they will lose what they have had for some time which motivates them to act in this way ought to be settled in a general meeting through genuine and honest discussion, so that thus each elector may act freely in an honest election. And since he who seems best by common decision of all the electors ought to be placed over the empire, I shall now describe a plan that will be useful in this matter, as well as in any council or assembly in which a common decision is to be made with the votes of all. This plan is as follows:

CHAPTER XXXVII

A SYSTEM OF VOTING IS DESCRIBED WHICH THEY CAN USE. IT IS A PERFECTLY GOOD AND USEFUL, TESTED, AND PRACTICAL WAY TO PROCEED.

535. The electors of the holy empire, when they wish to proceed to the election of the next emperor, should assemble on an appointed day in all humility and with the utmost devotion to the service of God and free of all sin, so that Christ the Lord may be in their midst and they may receive the grace of the Holy Spirit. After the solemn introduction of the order of business, they should consider the many persons who, because of their outward or inner qualifications for rule, may be worthy of such a great office. So that the election may be carried out without fear and in complete freedom and secrecy, after having sworn oaths at the altar of the Lord that they will choose the best man in the just judgment of a free conscience, they should have the names of all whom they are considering put down by a notary on identical ballots, with only one name on each ballot; and after that name a series of numbers should be affixed – 1, 2, 3, as many as there are persons that have been recognized in the discussion as worthy candidates.

536. Suppose ten have been found in Germany who appear worthy

and from among them the one most worthy is to be chosen in common: Let the name of only one [candidate] be placed on each ballot, the numbers one to ten placed under or beside the name, and the ten ballots, each containing one of the ten names, given to each elector. When the ballots have been received by the electors, each one should go aside alone and secretly – or with his secretary if he cannot read and write – and with all ten ballots placed before him he should read the name of each.

537.   Then in the name of God he should ponder, following his own conscience, which number among them all is least qualified and place a simple long mark in ink above the number 1. After this he should decide who is least suitable after him and mark the number 2 with a simple long mark [on his ballot]; and so on until he arrives at the best, in his judgment, and there he will mark number 10, or the number which corresponds to the total number of persons.

538.   And it is a good idea for everyone to use the same ink, identical pens, and the same simple marks – long or short, whichever is agreed upon – so that the mark of one cannot be distinguished from the others to guarantee freedom for the electors and peace among all.

539.   When the marks have been made, each of the electors should carry his ballots in his hand and throw them with his own hand into an empty sack hanging in the midst of the electors. When the ballots have been deposited in the sack, the priest who has celebrated the mass, should be called as well as an accountant with a list of the names in order of the ten, let us say, from whom the choice is to be made. Sitting among the electors, the priest should take the ballots out of the sack in the order in which they come to hand and read the name and the number marked. The accountant should write the number at the side of the name and do the same for all. When this is completed, the accountant should add up the numbers for each name, and the one who has the highest number will be emperor.

540.   By following this procedure countless frauds are avoided. Nothing sinister can happen. It would not be possible to devise a more righteous, just, honest, and free method of election and through it, if the electors vote according to their consciences, it is impossible for the one who is judged best by a collective verdict not to be put in power. It is not possible to discover a method which is more secure. Nay, by this method an infallible decision can be obtained, since every sort of comparison of all persons and of all the estimates and argu-

ments likely to be made by each elector are included in this process – which I was only able to devise with great effort.[1] You may well believe that no more perfect method can be found.

541. Still the following precaution should be taken so that no elector can be perverted by self-interest: If one or more laymen has been listed for general consideration among those to be chosen, the form with his own name should not be given to him, although all the others with that exception, should be given to him. This would avoid an occasion for suspicion that he might adjudge himself the best of all, and place the highest number in front of his own name. With this single exception the prescribed procedure should be followed completely and this will result in an election better than any other that can be found.

[1] The proposed electoral system (originally in Book II, ch. 33, no. 245a) is taken from Ramon Llull, *De arte electionis*, which is in the library at Kues (no. 83).

CHAPTER XXXVIII

THIS IS A VERY USEFUL PROCEDURE FOR THE DISCUSSION OF DIFFICULT MATTERS IN COUNCILS IN ORDER TO OBTAIN THE FREE OPINION OF EVERYONE WITHOUT INTIMIDATION. WE ALSO DISCUSS ANOTHER INGENIOUS VOTING DEVICE USED BY THE VENETIANS.

542. Using this same electoral procedure many questions can be decided in the meetings of the princes which can be of great benefit to the commonwealth. For often a question is proposed in which the advantage of some of the princes is on one side and the good of the commonwealth on the other. Then individuals do not dare to give advice openly on behalf of the common good because they are afraid that the others are of a different opinion and they cannot win, and thus if they lose, they would gain the enmity of the prince whose interest would be adversely affected by the advice. Often even the chairman, the emperor or his representative, seems to be too partial to one side of a question. Then his advisors are prevented from freely giving advice out of fear of displeasing him.

543. Therefore since all deliberation ought to be aimed at the praise of God and the public good, and what is of greater benefit to the public and common good should always be more readily chosen, according to this plan when there is any doubtful point on which a decision is to be made let two of the more learned participants stand up in the center and take each side, defending the affirmative and negative positions and analyzing the consequences for each side.

544. For example if the question is whether a customs-system should exist, the affirmative would say, yes, because no one is especially burdened by it but what is paid by the merchants is contributed both by the seller and the buyers and the merchant himself, and that is the most convenient way to raise money for the public good, and unless this easy way is used to raise the money necessary for the protection of the commonwealth, there would be no peace. Therefore for these and other reasons, the affirmative should be chosen.

545. The one who is defending the other side says: This way to collect money is unfair and illicit, taking money for the commonwealth from those who are not its subjects and have committed no crime, and it is of no utility, for the peace is not preserved by it. Therefore the negative should be chosen.

546. When the subject has been discussed, let the question be written down and an affirmative vote put down below and a negative vote under that. Under that let an intermediate position be written if it is expressed – for example, if one of the two says the following: Besides those who say that the affirmative is to be held that customs duties should remain in force, and others who say they should not, others say that they should exist but be modified as follows, no customs duties should be placed on food and drink unless they are transported for business purposes, and some say [the duty should be] not more than one florin for a cart load of wine or one hundred bushels of wheat, and others that customs should be collected as before but the money should be put into the public treasury for public expenditures, others that the money should be divided – half going to the princes and administrative officials and judges and the rest to the public treasury. These opinions and those that probably can be developed should be expressed publicly by these two and if anyone wants to add others, it should be possible to do so. All of these should be written in order under the appropriate heading and ballots should be

prepared according to the number of counsellors voting and a ballot given to each one.

547.   When he has it, each one in his residence, after taking an oath, should choose one and cross out the others with pen and ink by drawing a large line through them. In the morning they should come together in council and each one put his ballot into a sack. When they have been deposited, a secretary should take them out, one after the other, and an accountant should sit there, and after the counting has taken place, the opinion which has the most votes in that election will be the best of all. All the ballots should be the same size and written in the same handwriting, as indicated above.

548.   The same procedure should be followed in case of a dispute among several magnates on the same matter. All their names should be put on identical ballots. After the case has been explained and is understood, then the counsellors should cross out with their pens the names of all except the one in whose favor the matter ought in their opinion to be decided. In this manner the consultation will remain free and secret and will be the result of careful consideration, which is particularly important.

549.   This year I have drawn up a small tract on the way to improve the discussion of controversial subjects.[1] Therefore I will not speak further on this.

550.   It is true that where a simple affirmative or negative decision is to be made on a question, the method of voting employed in the realm of the Venetians would be useful. They have round balls of wool cloth and two vessels or wooden containers shaped like chalices. The wood should be hollowed out at the bottom of the chalice and the balls should fall into that part through a passage from the upper part. One container is black and stands for "no" and the other white and stands for "yes." After the counselor takes one ball between his thumb and forefinger and shows it in the air to the others to avoid fraud, then he lets it fall into the palm of his hand and closes his hand. Then he puts his hand into the white container and if he favors the affirmative opinion he lets the ball drop through the vessel into the bottom and takes his hand out with his fist closed. He also puts his hand into the other container so that no one can know into which one he has

---

[1] This tract has been lost.

dropped the ball. But if he does not favor the affirmative side, he takes his hand out without opening it and puts it into the other one and drops it there. In this way the vote remains secret. After this the balls are extracted by opening the lower part below the passageway, and they are counted and the conclusion is affirmative or negative depending on the number of balls in one container in comparison with those in the other.

551. By agreeing on these procedures one could always decide on the basis of the merits of the case or the situation because freedom of decision and secrecy are preserved.

CHAPTER XXXIX

IF PEACE IS TO BE PRESERVED AND DESOLATION
AND GENERAL DISCORD AVOIDED THE POWER OF
THE EMPIRE MUST BE RE-ESTABLISHED. THIS CAN
BE DONE BY PUBLIC TAXES, TALLAGES, AND A
PUBLIC TREASURY. THE ESTABLISHMENT OF A
PUBLIC ARMY WOULD BE USEFUL TO THE
PROVINCES AND DOMINIONS [OF THE EMPIRE] AND
WOULD RELIEVE THEM OF EXPENSE.

552. A special effort must be made to re-establish the power of the empire. Otherwise all the laws that are adopted will be without effect. The strength of a law lies in its coercive force, and power maintains and carries with it coercion. If it is taken away – since men are attracted to what is forbidden and from adolescence are prone to evil[1] – legal sanctions are weakened and therefore peace and justice do not long endure. Since this is the case, a way to carry out reform must be provided.

553. At one time bishops, abbots, princes, and counts were accustomed to provide personal and financial services to the empire, both on a daily and annual basis, in proportion to the province and territory under them. On this basis paid soldiers were kept as the standing army of the empire for the defense of the commonwealth,

---

[1] Genesis 8:21.

and the emperor was accustomed to maintain his imperial status most honorably. When the imperial army for the defense of the commonwealth ceased to exist, the commonwealth lost a great deal.

554. Every prince and every corporate group is obliged to take action to resist robbers in their areas. This is a very great expense and the subjects spend their time on this and cannot carry on their work freely. Deep divisions are created in all parts of the empire and hardly anyone trusts anyone else. But if there were one public army to keep the peace and defend justice for all, the commonwealth would not have so many useless and wasteful expenses.

555. And so it would be very useful to give serious attention to an arrangement whereby this kind of army would be established to keep the peace and maintain justice through moderate annual contributions proportionate to [the size of] the domain and territory. And so an agreed portion of the imperial customs and salt taxes that have been granted to the princes for the commonwealth could easily be reserved each year for the expenses of the empire and a moderate amount could be deducted from all customs duties. And thus those taxes and provincial contributions would be placed in the public treasury at Frankfurt for the army mentioned above and for the expenses of the empire. The proper disposition of the amount so collected would be decided at the annual council in the presence of the electors and others, so that everything would be determined in a just and prudent manner.

556. Then the great expenses would cease which today the princes are needlessly required to incur, and the provinces would be enriched and the commonwealth and empire strengthened anew. Then the bishops could carry out their spiritual duties and assign their temporal duties to administrators and a national army would eliminate all tyranny for the empire.

557. O God, if the determined spirit of all those who raise these proposals would only attempt to put them into practice, then the empire would flourish again in our day. But if we are indifferent to them and overcome by our blind cupidity and if we continue for a long time in the old perverse way, there is no doubt that the holy empire and the good estate of the commonwealth and of all of us will shortly be terminated.

558. Neither a churchman nor a layman can be exempt from the law. For the government of all temporal things must first be directed

toward the public good. Hence our most excellent Saxon, Hugh, who is called "of St. Victor," in his book, *De Sacramentis*, when he speaks of the property of the church, writes, "Those properties can never be removed from the power of the king. For if reason and necessity demand it, the [royal] power owes them protection and these properties owe the king a contribution in a case of necessity. For just as the royal power cannot refuse to give the protection that it owes to another, so the churchmen who obtain properties on condition of a contribution to the king in return for his protection cannot legally refuse it."[2]

559. What blessed Ambrose has said in his letter, *De Tradendis Basilicis*[3] and what many others have said on this could be cited, but since it all agrees with the above, I omit it for the sake of brevity.

[2] PL 176, p. 420.
[3] PL 16, p. 036 (*Ad Marcellinum*).

CHAPTER XL

LAWSUITS SHOULD BE REDUCED AND APPEALS OF
UNIMPORTANT CASES BEYOND THE PROVINCIAL
LEVEL TO THE ROMAN CURIA SHOULD BE
PROHIBITED. THOSE THAT ARE OF INTEREST TO
THE COMMONWEALTH SHOULD BE DECIDED IN THE
IMPERIAL COUNCIL, EVEN WHEN THEY INVOLVE
RELIGIOUS MATTERS, IN ACCORDANCE WITH THE
CANONS OF THE HOLY FATHERS WHICH SHOULD BE
RE-ENACTED.

560. No doubt there are many other abuses besides those discussed above, that harm the commonwealth but it would be [too] long to enumerate them. We know that the duration of judicial controversies in both the secular and ecclesiastical judicial systems causes great injury to the commonwealth because of the great confusion which it creates and the interminable length of the litigation, especially because cases do not end in the localities where they arise or in their own provinces. The most trivial case involving benefices is thus repeatedly appealed to the Roman curia where only the most import-

ant cases should be discussed. Thus because they wish a grant of "expectancies"[1] or the bestowal of usurped benefices or on account of litigation, all that is earned by parents is brought by their children to the [papal] curia and nothing is brought back except what they had already possessed in the province; for instance, a little benefice – perhaps already granted to their own parents. And because occasional promotions to a fortune are made in the curia, everyone goes to Rome and stays there from their tender years expecting to be made rich, and they postpone their studies and religious exercises. They bring gold and silver and come back with charters. And because the canons of the holy fathers were opposed to this and experience has taught us how much harm is done to the commonwealth on this account, it must certainly be reformed.

561. Let no one be persuaded by the common saying that the secular power may not interfere with an ecclesiastical order made by the authority of the Roman pontiffs, whether the granting of benefices or of favors or judicial decisions in litigation. While the secular power cannot change any ecclesiastical legislation adopted to aid divine worship or in the interest of the freedom of those who serve God, it must at least provide for the [needs of the] commonwealth, while respecting the above.

562. No one should say that the most sacred emperors who adopted many holy laws for the good of the commonwealth concerning the election of bishops, the granting of benefices, and the observance of religion, were in error and did not have the power to legislate in the way that we read they did in D. 63 [c. 34] *Nos sanctorum* which is a text of Kings Charles and Louis. Indeed we read that the Roman pontiffs asked them to make laws for the public good on divine worship and against sinners among the clergy. And if perhaps it is said that the binding force of all those laws came from the approval of the Apostolic See and synod, I do not want to insist on this. Although I have read and collected 86 chapters of the ecclesiastical regulations of the ancient emperors which it would be superfluous to insert here, as well as many others belong to Charlemagne and his successors among which may also be found provisions prescribing what the Roman pontiff and all the other patriarchs should do in consecrating bishops and other matters, I have never found either that the pope was asked

---

[1] Expectancies were legally binding promises of succession to church offices. They were forbidden by Pope Boniface VIII, but the practice continued.

to give his approval or that the legislation was ever said to be binding because his approbation was given. Rather, as is said above in a certain place, it appears that several Roman pontiffs said that they revered and accepted those ordinances.

563. But accepting the fact that those imperial ordinances on church matters do not have any force except insofar as those ordinances are first found in the canons or are approved and accepted by the synods – as is proved to be the case from the common widely-known saying that laws do not disdain to imitate the sacred canons and the fact that in any opposition or conflict in ecclesiastical matters between a law and a canon the canon undoubtedly takes precedence – nevertheless if the reform that we ask to be carried out were based on the ancient legal holy statutes of the church, there would be no doubt about its power and authority. For no one doubts that those laws agree very well with the canonical statutes, and in no way contradict them.

564. To sum up with one word – if the most devout emperor and the whole council subject to him, considering the needs of the commonwealth and reflecting on the reasons and occasions for the decline in divine worship and the shameful state of morals at all levels, would return to the ancient sacred canons and the most holy practices of the ancients and together with his whole council would decree that whatever went against them – whether privileges, or exemptions, or new practices in the granting of benefices or in disputes – was to be abolished and most strict obedience was to be given to the holy canons, I would like to know what Christian could say that he [the emperor] had attempted to do anything beyond his power and authority when these things were done in the interest of the observance of the ancient canons and of the sacred legal sanctions, for the increase of divine worship and the good of the commonwealth?

565. Let no one persuade you, most wise emperor, to abandon this holy intention of yours. For many, while appearing to obey, invent specious reasons to defend their evil lives and to find excuses for their sins. Christ alone who is the way, the truth, and the life,[2] should be sought by following the ways of our fathers. Evil practices introduced out of cupidity, ambition, and avarice should be eliminated so that

[2] John 14:6.

thus the canons without which the peace of the church cannot be preserved nor religion increased may take on new life.

566.   There are many other things that kings should do. In particular they should repress adultery, theft, parricide, perjury, pillage, and similar sins and drive them out of the country, as St. Cyprian says[3] – which is also contained in [C.] 23 q. 5 [c. 40] *Rex debet* along with similar statements. In addition, they should eradicate the deception involved in usurious and criminal contracts, in games of dice, in monopolies and similar practices and they should see that holy feast days are observed, and prevent the excessive expenditures which are customary for weddings and funerals and for fine clothes and the like. In brief they should direct all things to the public good.

[3] Pseudo-Cyprian, *De duodecim abusivis saeculi*, ch. 9, quoted in the *Decretum*.

CHAPTER XLI

NOTHING IS AS HARMFUL FOR THE CHURCH AS
DISCORD BETWEEN THE CHURCH AND THE EMPIRE.
THERE IS A DISCUSSION AS TO HOW HARMONY
BETWEEN THEM CAN BE PRESERVED. BY WAY OF
EPILOGUE, A BRIEF CONSIDERATION OF BOTH
POWERS IS SET FORTH IN A FIGURATIVE WAY AND
WHAT HAS BEEN EXPRESSED AT LENGTH IS
SUMMARIZED IN A BRIEF AND PREGNANT
COMPARISON.

567.   I have shown above that the true concordant harmony of the Catholic Church consists in rightly ordered rule based on common consent and election and the free submission of all or of a majority, and that the canons and both divine laws and those adopted in a human rational way by the common consent of all show this method as the most equitable way from this transitory life to heaven.

568.   But we know that the efforts of the envious and ever-deceitful devil often create divisions between the church and the empire, because of arguments about superiority in power or fear of the loss of

temporal possessions or something similar. As appears sufficiently clear to all from the Gospel saying that a kingdom divided is threatened with collapse,[1] when that conflict rages, neither right nor law nor the enforcement of the ecclesiastical order can continue. Therefore the first and most important effort of all orthodox men will be to preserve from harm the hierarchy of the two powers in continued harmonious collaboration.

569. And so when the disturber of the peace insinuates these things in our minds to cause discord, the Roman pontiff, first of all, should consider that a minister of Christ is exalted in humiliation, and the one who is supreme is supposed to minister to the others, not dominate them by his rule, and that both powers come from God and in our time of grace are truly distinct, as Nicholas, the greatest of the Roman pontiffs, asserts in D. 96 [c. 6] *Cum ad verum.* This is confirmed in D. 97 [c. 1] *Ecclesiae meae.*

570. Let him consider whether the Roman pontiff receives the same high praise and command that his subjects obey as is the case for the empire in [St. Paul's Epistle to the] Romans 13.[2] I speak of the Roman pontiff, not of the holy priesthood. Also the text [c. 22] *Celebritatem* of D. 4 [D. 3] of *De consecratione* and the first section of the [*Novellae* 63] *Authentica, Quomodo oportet episcopis* at the beginning and many similar passages seem at least to prove that the two powers are independent and distinct and that both came from above. And that was the true opinion of all the ancients, although doubts have arisen because of the sinister desire of many writers to please. Let us return to the old views.

571. Even if the pope had the power of both swords, the argument of those writers who say that the emperor has the use of his sword in dependence upon him would not in fact be proved. For no one denies that there have been many different infidel kings in the world whose royal power came from God without their recognizing a superior. On whom, I ask, did the empire depend when Paul appealed to Caesar, or when Christ gave his approval to it [the empire] when he commanded that the things be rendered to Caesar that were Caesar's.[3] Also even if he has the power of the sword, the pope cannot argue that he is first in this, as if the entire power of the sword depended on him, if he calls to

---

[1] Matthew 12:25; Luke 11:7.
[2] Romans 13:1.
[3] Acts 25:9–10; Matthew 22:2.

mind the things that have been rightly said above and an infinite number of other things which have been left to us by our forebears.)

572. The pope should not be exalted by the spontaneous humble reverence of the emperor for the sake of Christ when he addresses and honors him as father, see the last law [1. 8] of the *Code* [1 1] *De summa trinitate et fide catholica*, or because for a long time he has allowed the pope to address him in the second person singular [familiar form] according to the chapter [c. 6] *Quam gravi*, of [*Decretals* v 20] *De crimine falsi*. Rather let him recall that the humble Catholic emperors venerated the Roman pontiff in their writings and works as their spiritual father and the guardian of souls. Also many more quotations can be found that show that the Roman pontiff was accustomed to give much greater honor to the emperor – for instance, the letter of Pope Agatho and his council to Constantine [III] where he says, "All the lowly rulers of the church, servants of your Christian empire ..."[4] And on this let the chapter *Victor* of D. 97 [c. 2] now suffice.

573. In the chapters [c. 4] *Omnes principes* and [c. 3] *Legebatur* of [*Decretals* 1 33] *De maioritate et obedientia* the emperor does not deny that he should obey the bishops as his fathers. This applies to the pope as to the others. Indeed let him remember the chapter [c. 2] *Omnis anima* of [*Decretals* III 39] *De censibus* which is a text of St. Paul, and also how many honors he has received from the empire. Is it not true that when the patriarch of Constantinople with the support of his synod called himself for many years the universal first patriarch and bishop, and after the death of Emperor Mauritius and his sons, Pope Boniface [III] asked Phocas who had succeeded as emperor to restore him to supremacy, we read that the Apostolic See was re-established as first by imperial decree, according to the true writings of Paulus Warnefridus, the historian of the Lombards, who was alive at the time?[5]

574. Let him remember the magnificent gifts and the protection that the church received from the Roman empire when trouble threatened it. Likewise how more than two hundred years after Constantine I, the acts of the Sixth Council say that Pope Agatho, overcome with physical exhaustion because the earlier support for the

---

[4] Mansi 11, p. 286.
[5] Paulus Warnefridus, *Historia gentis Longobardorum*, IV, 36. Warnefridus lived over a century after the events he recounts.

church was little by little disappearing as a result of various calamities, was relieved of these calamities by the emperor.[6] And let the [symbolic] pre-eminence of the sun over the moon or the soul over the body suffice for him without affirming that the empire does not exist except through him and in dependence upon him.

575. If the deposition of kings and emperors and the transfer of the empire and perhaps other events should move the pope to presume that this is his apostolic right, let him know that, if it were not perhaps against religious humility, a clear answer could be given in all of these cases – that perhaps these cases only argue for that power in the pope as pope because of the consent or acceptance of the contending parties. There were those in the past, including cardinals of the Apostolic See at the time and a certain general council held at Rome, who defended Henry IV when he was crowned at Basel by the representatives of the Romans contrary to the excommunication by Gregory [VII] or Hildebrand.[7] Indeed a general synod held at Basel at that time elected Honorius as pope, for which act Henry was finally excommunicated.[8]

576. Strong arguments are also found in defense of Frederick II,[9] a man who was certainly most active in the church for the defense of the faith – as well as in favor of other emperors. The people often yielded to the pope for the sake of obedience. These things should not be cited as examples of papal power unless, as indicated above, they were done because of a crime or sin, as is stated in the chapter [c. 34] *Venerabilem* of [*Decretals* I 6] *De electione* and the chapter [c. 13] *Novit* of [*Decretals* II 1] *De judiciis*.

577. Let all these questions cease to be discussed further. Let us agree with our holy predecessors in the past, that the temporal possessions given to the church should never be preferred to peace. Rather let us follow the example of Pope Leo [VIII] in his council who, as indicated above, gave everything back in perpetuity to Otto I and his successors because [he thought that] in view of the weakness

---

[6] Mansi 11, p. 190.

[7] On Cusanus' use of Beno, *Gesta Romanae ecclesiae*, here, see Werner Krämer, "Verzeichnis der Brüsseler Handschriften," *MFCG*, 14 (1980), pp. 182–197. Gregory VII (1021–1085), a reforming pope (1073–1085), opposed Emperor Henry IV in the Investiture controversy.

[8] Cf. Book III, ch. 3, no. 314.

[9] Frederick II (1194–1250), a Holy Roman emperor who was in continual conflict with the church, especially with Pope Innocent III.

of the faith at that time and the disturbance which had arisen, it was useful for the emperor to be the strong defender of the faith.[10]

578.   When will it be seen how important it is, especially today, for the empire to be strong? For without a defender, we see where we are tending. Let it suffice for the pope [to know] that the empire supports the church in all things. It [the empire] does whatever is possible for the protection of the church, no matter how its forces suffer. It does not seize by force; it does not seek to take back what it has given; but it defends and supports the priesthood which alone it venerates as most worthy.

579.   On the other hand, the emperor should not raise himself up for any reason against the holy priesthood of God, on the basis of [*Novellae* 7] *Authentica, De non alienandis rebus ecclesiasticis* para. *Sinimus*, collection 2, which says that the empire does not differ from priesthood. Neither on the basis of this nor other texts should he make himself the equal of that high ecclesiastical power. For the empire is illuminated by the priesthood as the moon by the sun. Although the moon was created by God as was the sun, its light comes from the sun. If every imperial order should direct man to his end through a righteous life, and God is the end and Christ the way, the empire should seek light for its footsteps from the priesthood. Those earthly things which have been given incidentally by the empire to the priesthood and which benefit it by providing the means for its subsistence are not in any way to be compared to those that are eternal. The emperor who is not the owner [*dominus*] but the administrator of everything in the empire should not think that he has done anything very great with goods not his own, when for the public good and by divine commission he has directed that they be used for the increase of the honor of God. For "the ends of the earth and the earth itself and the plenitude thereof are the Lord's."[11]

580.   The holy priesthood which is related to the empire as the true life-giving soul to the body is especially to be honored. For God is a spirit who is joined by grace to the body, that is the faithful people by means of the sacraments, administered by the priests of the Lord, as their souls, so that man is in God. And so with spirits at peace, all dispute and commotion should be transformed into a harmony and confirmed forever, because as noted above, the whole church is made up of body and soul together and the Holy Spirit inhabits and inspires

[10] See Book III, no. 483.   [11] Psalm 23:11.

the church with concord so that by the action of the Holy Spirit one church made up of all those who believe in Christ can live in concord, with the priests as the soul and the faithful as the body.

581. But as we know, once the harmony and concordant proportion of nature is broken in any living thing, the soul is separated from the body after a period of mortal fever and incurable illness.

582. The Roman pontiff should not elevate himself above all the priests of the Lord, and think that others can take no action unless he has permitted it. Rather he should remember that the papacy has been vacant for long periods, for instance, for seven years after [Pope] Marcellinus and at other times occasionally for two years,[12] and still the priesthood did not cease to act. But he should consider that his superiority which was intended by God to be used for the proper ordering of all and to keep the peace and tranquility of the church undisturbed, gives him nothing in the way of spiritual power which alone can come from Christ – and for this he should rightly rejoice.

583. He should also consider that if the priesthood is like a single soul which is complete in the whole and in every part, then greater or lesser executive power in a given province, since it depends on some-thing external to itself, does not decrease the spiritual power in itself. Hence just as the soul as it exists in a man's foot is not greater or less as to the life which it gives the foot, and is the same soul that resides in the head or the heart, so the papacy itself is like the soul in the head and the patriarchs the soul in the ears or eyes and the rank of archbishop the soul in the arms and the bishops in the fingers and so on for each rank down to the feet which in the commonwealth are called the peasants where the curate properly represents the soul that gives them life.[13]

584. Therefore there is a single power from God of binding and loosing and of giving life to all, although among the members there seem to be some who are greater and others of lesser importance.

585. Therefore the Roman pontiff should be aware that the vital harmony of the church is preserved by the divine and canonical sanctions, which are all rooted in one source, the Holy Spirit and the natural law. The more immediately accessible seat of the soul is in the

---

[12] See *Liber pontificalis*, I, 6 (ed. L. Duchesne) on Pope Marcellinus. The papacy was also vacant from 1241 to 1243.

[13] On the use of comparisons of social organization to the human body, see Ewart Lewis, *Medieval Political Ideas*, New York, 1954, I, pp. 193–224. See also Vincent of Beauvais, *Speculum doctrinale*, VIII, 8 (PL 212, p. 740).

purest blood contained at the center of the heart. With the blood the vital spirits provide a flow of nourishment through all the arteries of the whole body. As therefore those arteries go everywhere in the whole body branching out from one source so that the life-giving spirit flows through them, so the divine laws circulate with equal power throughout the whole body of the church, holding all its members in a sweet vital constraint.

586.   Therefore there is no member – whether head or foot or in-between – through which they do not flow and which is not included in the circulation. In the same way, the veins that start from the liver and spread through the whole body and connect with arteries, merging with the flesh as it were as an intermediary between the flesh and the fine blood of the arteries, are like the canon laws in the body of the ecclesiastical commonwealth that are adopted in a council, which can be compared to the liver where all the veins meet. Like the veins, the canons act as an intermediary through which carnal man is led to the spiritual life.

587.   Therefore the pope should not be flattered into thinking that someone who is a part of the body of the church is over it and exempt from the salutary precepts of the canonical sanctions. And as the tiny veins that supply the particular members do not have life-giving force nor the nourishment of the soul unless they go back to a common source, so all the statutes of the provinces and local areas should conform to the common canons without any contradiction. And the basic principles on this subject can be developed by analogy with what has been said at greater length above.

588.   After this let His Imperial Highness consider how to apply what has been said about the structure of the body to what has been said about the empire. For the body is made up of bones, nerves, and flesh. But the nerves that are in an intermediate position and share the nature of both are all connected to the brain where the second seat of the reason is located and they go out to link all the joints of the body in different ways with the one body. And these are like the imperial laws which strike a balance between severity and laxity and bring all the members together in harmony. And the head which represents the emperor is not exempted, since all those nerves flow from the operation of reason and nature to which law no one is superior.[14]

---

[14] The library at Kues contains a number of medical works. Cusanus may have developed his interest in medicine from his friend, Paolo Toscanelli, in Padua.

589.   Even the lawgiver himself is not exempted. Thus Ambrose in his 75th letter, to the Emperor Valentinian, says, "You have made laws to prevent anyone from being free to act in any other way. What you have written for others, you have also written for yourself. For the emperor makes laws which he is the first of all to be obliged to observe."[15] And there is a popular saying, "Submit to the law which you have made." For no one is obliged to observe an unjust law, and no living person is exempt from a just one.

590.   And so the highest power itself, the head, must see that those nerves are not too loose or too tight since this could harm the whole body. A law should be stretched like a bowstring – not too much or the bow will break, and not too little or when it is released it cannot shoot the arrow.

591.   He should also note that as nerves adhere strongly to the bones even when the flesh has decayed, so the legislation and laws of the country ought to be kept uncorrupted and in perpetual force. The country is rightly compared to the bones that have a sweet marrow and long duration. The flesh, however, may be compared to transitory men who often fail in human ways because of weakness, ignorance, or illness. With these the prince should act as a father now sparing, now dispensing, now punishing, as is suitable for the well-being of each one, always keeping the law in force. For if a law is corrupted in any part the whole body is damaged, just as [happens] when a nerve is injured in any part of the body.

592.   Also particular laws which we may compare to the small individual veins, ought to be revised so that they do not go against the common law which provides for the public good nor against the original source of all laws, the natural law of reason. Otherwise disease would attack that member easily because it is in opposition to the rest and would infect the whole body to which it is connected. And so the king should be like a zither-player who knows how to respect the harmony in the strings, both the greater and lesser ones, and not stretch them too much nor too little so that a common concord is heard in the harmony of all.

593.   And so like an expert doctor the emperor's concern should be to keep the body well so that the life-giving spirit can dwell in it properly because it is well-proportioned. For when he sees any one of

[15] PL 16, p. 1047.

the four temperaments in excess or deficient from the mean and the body therefore unbalanced, whether because the melancholy which is abundant avarice has produced various diseases in the body – usury, fraud, deceit, theft, pillage and all those ways in which great wealth is acquired without labor through some deceptive artifice – which cannot take place without harming the commonwealth – or if he sees the body grow feverish because of choleric wars, dissension and division, or swell up with sanguine pomposity, luxury, banqueting and the like, or become morose because of a temperament which is phlegmatic concerning virtuous efforts both to gain a livelihood and to protect the fatherland, he should seek a remedy and listen to the books and advice of the most learned doctors of the commonwealth in earlier times.

594. Let him compound a recipe. Let him test it by taste, sight, and smell to determine whether it is suitable for the time and place. If he sees that it is, he should recommend it first to his Privy Council, the teeth, to analyze it and find out whether there is any comfort and healing power in that recipe. When it has been well chewed there, if he finds that there is something useful in it, he should send it for fuller examination to the Great Council, the stomach, to be digested, purified, and the pure elements separated from the impure. After this he should send the purified proposal to the consistory of judges, the liver, so that that healing medicinal law may be distributed as required to each member. Let him show paternal care in all things to all the parts and members, sometimes using a sweet ointment, sometimes a cleansing lotion, or a cauterizer, and any other preservative medicines. And let him never move to cut off a member except with sadness and compassion and only when nothing else avails and there is a danger of infection.

595. This sums up all the above. You, O unconquerable emperor, will apprehend it very quickly since it truly contains an accurate description of Your Highness.

596. And so act, O great Caesar, that although nothing in the way of knowledge can be derived from this inept and uninstructive effort, this collection may at least be read quickly as a stimulus to the most studious and ablest minds gathered around you. It is to be hoped that an occasion to do so may be given to the wise and inquiry will be aroused in those most subtle intellects that have been dormant until now and thus when the material is presented, sparked by this little

coal, from the depths of many minds filled with prudence, wisdom, and all circumspection, a great flame igniting and burning continuously may blaze which will destroy all abuses and bring back the justice of law to the earthly empire and make the splendor of the empire shine forth and increase continually.

597. We wait for you eagerly, father of all, to initiate and carry forth this most happy deed in our time. Act with most eager zeal to do this for your immortal glory, o most kind prince, so that thus the way to peace in the church and eternal fame for you and your subjects may be re-established in our time in praise of Christ who reigns blessed for ever. Amen.

598. This is the end of the collection, *The Catholic Concordance*, made from various approved writings of the ancients in praise of Almighty God, which I, Nicholas of Cusa, dean of the church of St. Florin in Koblenz, and lowly doctor of the decrees, offer in all humility to this holy Council of Basel, judging and asserting nothing in all of it to be true or to be defended as true except what this sacred synod will hold to be Catholic and true – and ready to be corrected in all respects by all orthodox teaching.

Index

CAMBRIDGE TEXTS IN THE
HISTORY OF POLITICAL THOUGHT